DATE DUE

			PRINTED IN U.S.A.

Children's
Literature
Review

Guide to Gale Literary Criticism Series

For criticism on	Consult these Gale series
Authors now living or who died after December 31, 1959	*CONTEMPORARY LITERARY CRITICISM (CLC)*
Authors who died between 1900 and 1959	*TWENTIETH-CENTURY LITERARY CRITICISM (TCLC)*
Authors who died between 1800 and 1899	*NINETEENTH-CENTURY LITERATURE CRITICISM (NCLC)*
Authors who died between 1400 and 1799	*LITERATURE CRITICISM FROM 1400 TO 1800 (LC)* *SHAKESPEAREAN CRITICISM (SC)*
Authors who died before 1400	*CLASSICAL AND MEDIEVAL LITERATURE CRITICISM (CMLC)*
Black writers of the past two hundred years	*BLACK LITERATURE CRITICISM (BLC) AND BLACK LITERATURE CRITICISM SUPPLEMENT (BLCS)*
Authors of books for children and young adults	*CHILDREN'S LITERATURE REVIEW (CLR)*
Dramatists	*DRAMA CRITICISM (DC)*
Hispanic writers of the late nineteenth and twentieth centuries	*HISPANIC LITERATURE CRITICISM (HLC)*
Native North American writers and orators of the eighteenth, nineteenth, and twentieth centuries	*NATIVE NORTH AMERICAN LITERATURE (NNAL)*
Poets	*POETRY CRITICISM (PC)*
Short story writers	*SHORT STORY CRITICISM (SSC)*
Major authors from the Renaissance to the present	*WORLD LITERATURE CRITICISM, 1500 TO THE PRESENT (WLC)*
Major authors and works from the Bible to the present	*WORLD LITERATURE CRITICISM SUPPLEMENT (WLCS)*

ISSN 0362-4145

12

volume 57

Children's Literature Review

Excerpts from Reviews,
Criticism, and Commentary
on Books for Children
and Young People

Deborah J. Morad
Editor

Detroit
San Francisco
London
Boston
Woodbridge, CT

STAFF

Deborah J. Morad, *Editor*

Arlene M. Johnson, *Associate Editor*

Sara Constantakis, Motoko Fujishiro Huthwaite, Erin E. White, *Contributing Editors*

Karen Uchic, *Technical Training Specialist*

Joyce Nakamura, *Managing Editor*

Maria Franklin, *Permissions Manager*
Sarah Chesney, Edna Hedblad, Michele Lonoconus, *Permissions Associates*

Victoria B. Cariappa, *Research Manager*
Corrine A. Stocker, *Project Coordinator*
Gary J. Oudersluys, Cheryl D. Warnock, *Research Specialists*
Patricia Tsune Ballard, Tracie A. Richardson, *Research Associates*
Phyllis J. Blackman, Tim Lehnerer, Patricia A. Love, *Research Assistants*

Mary Beth Trimper, *Production Director*
Cindy Range, *Production Assistant*

Gary Leach, *Graphic Artist*
Randy Bassett, *Image Database Supervisor*
Robert Duncan, Michael Logusz, *Imaging Specialists*
Pamela A. Reed, *Imaging Coordinator*

Library of Congress Catalog Card Number 76-643301
ISBN 0-7876-3222-8
ISSN 0362-4145
Printed in the United States of America

10 9 8 7 6 5 4 3 2 1

Contents

Preface vii
Acknowledgments xi

Preface

L iterature for children and young adults has evolved into both a respected branch of creative writing and a successful industry. Currently, books for young readers are considered among the most popular segments of publishing. Criticism of juvenile literature is instrumental in recording the literary or artistic development of the creators of children's books as well as the trends and controversies that result from changing values or attitudes about young people and their literature. Designed to provide a permanent, accessible record of this ongoing scholarship, *Children's Literature Review (CLR)* presents parents, teachers, and librarians—those responsible for bringing children and books together—with the opportunity to make informed choices when selecting reading materials for the young. In addition, *CLR* provides researchers of children's literature with easy access to a wide variety of critical information from English-language sources in the field. Users will find balanced overviews of the careers of the authors and illustrators of the books that children and young adults are reading; these entries, which contain excerpts from published criticism in books and periodicals, assist users by sparking ideas for papers and assignments and suggesting supplementary and classroom reading. Ann L. Kalkhoff, president and editor of *Children's Book Review Service Inc.*, writes that "*CLR* has filled a gap in the field of children's books, and it is one series that will never lose its validity or importance."

Scope of the Series

Each volume of *CLR* profiles the careers of a selection of authors and illustrators of books for children and young adults from preschool through high school. Author lists in each volume reflect:

- an international scope.

- representation of authors of all eras.

- the variety of genres covered by children's and/or YA literature: picture books, fiction, nonfiction, poetry, folklore, and drama.

Although the focus of the series is on authors new to *CLR*, entries will be updated as the need arises.

Organization of This Book

An entry consists of the following elements: author heading, author portrait, author introduction, excerpts of criticism (each preceded by a bibliographical citation), and illustrations, when available.

- The **Author Heading** consists of the author's name followed by birth and death dates. The portion of the name outside the parentheses denotes the form under which the author is most frequently published. If the majority of the author's works for children were written under a pseudonym, the pseudonym will be listed in the author heading and the real name given on the first line of the author introduction. Also located at the beginning of the introduction are any other pseudonyms used by the author in writing for children and any name variations, including transliterated forms for authors whose languages use nonroman alphabets. Uncertainty as to a birth or death date is indicated by question marks.

- An **Author Portrait** is included when available.

- The **Author Introduction** contains information designed to introduce an author to *CLR* users by presenting an overview of the author's themes and styles, biographical facts that relate to the author's literary career or critical responses to the author's works, and information about major awards and prizes the author has received. The introduction begins by identifying the nationality of the author and by listing the genres in which s/he has written for children and young adults. Introductions also list a group of representative titles for which the author or illustrator being profiled is best known; this section, which begins with the words "major works include," follows the genre line of the introduction. For seminal figures, a listing of major works about the author follows when appropriate, highlighting important biographies about the author or illustrator that are not excerpted in the entry. The centered heading "Introduction" announces the body of the text.

- **Criticism** is located in three sections: **Author's Commentary** (when available), **General Commentary** (when available), and **Title Commentary** (commentary on specific titles).

  - The **Author's Commentary** presents background material written by the author or by an interviewer. This commentary may cover a specific work or several works. Author's commentary on more than one work appears after the author introduction, while commentary on an individual book follows the title entry heading.

  - The **General Commentary** consists of critical excerpts that consider more than one work by the author or illustrator being profiled. General commentary is preceded by the critic's name in boldface type or, in the case of unsigned criticism, by the title of the journal. *CLR* also features entries that emphasize general criticism on the oeuvre of an author or illustrator. When appropriate, a selection of reviews is included to supplement the general commentary.

  - The **Title Commentary** begins with the title entry headings, which precede the criticism on a title and cite publication information on the work being reviewed. Title headings list the title of the work as it appeared in its first English-language edition. The first English-language publication date of each work (unless otherwise noted) is listed in parentheses following the title. Differing U.S. and British titles follow the publication date within the parentheses. When a work is written by an individual other than the one being profiled, as is the case when illustrators are featured, the parenthetical material following the title cites the author of the work before listing its publication date.

    Entries in each title commentary section consist of critical excerpts on the author's individual works, arranged chronologically by publication date. The entries generally contain two to seven reviews per title, depending on the stature of the book and the amount of criticism it has generated. The editors select titles that reflect the entire scope of the author's literary contribution, covering each genre and subject. An effort is made to reprint criticism that represents the full range of each title's reception, from the year of its initial publication to current assessments. Thus, the reader is provided with a record of the author's critical history. Publication information (such as publisher names and book prices) and parenthetical numerical references (such as footnotes or page and line references to specific editions of works) have been deleted at the discretion of the editors to provide smoother reading of the text.

- Centered headings introduce each section, in which criticism is arranged chronologically; beginning with Volume 35, each excerpt is preceded by a boldface source heading for easier access by readers. Within the text, titles by authors being profiled are also highlighted in boldface type.

- Selected excerpts are preceded by **Explanatory Annotations,** which provide information on the critic or work of criticism to enhance the reader's understanding of the excerpt.

- A complete **Bibliographical Citation** designed to facilitate the location of the original book or article precedes each piece of criticism.

- Numerous **Illustrations** are featured in *CLR*. For entries on illustrators, an effort has been made to include illustrations that reflect the characteristics discussed in the criticism. Entries on authors who do not illustrate their own works may also include photographs and other illustrative material pertinent to their careers.

Special Features: Entries on Illustrators

Entries on authors who are also illustrators will occasionally feature commentary on selected works illustrated but not written by the author being profiled. These works are strongly associated with the illustrator and have received critical acclaim for their art. By including critical comment on works of this type, the editors wish to provide a more complete representation of the artist's career. Criticism on these works has been chosen to stress artistic, rather than literary, contributions. Title entry headings for works illustrated by the author being profiled are arranged chronologically within the entry by date of publication and include notes identifying the author of the illustrated work. In order to provide easier access for users, all titles illustrated by the subject of the entry are boldfaced.

CLR also includes entries on prominent illustrators who have contributed to the field of children's literature. These entries are designed to represent the development of the illustrator as an artist rather than as a literary stylist. The illustrator's section is organized like that of an author, with two exceptions: the introduction presents an overview of the illustrator's styles and techniques rather than outlining his or her literary background, and the commentary written by the illustrator on his or her works is called "illustrator's commentary" rather than "author's commentary." All titles of books containing illustrations by the artist being profiled are highlighted in boldface type.

Other Features: Acknowledgments, Indexes

- The **Acknowledgments** section, which immediately follows the preface, lists the sources from which material has been reprinted in the volume. It does not, however, list every book or periodical consulted for the volume.

- The **Cumulative Index to Authors** lists all of the authors who have appeared in *CLR* with cross-references to the biographical, autobiographical, and literary criticism series published by The Gale Group. A full listing of the series titles appears before the first page of the indexes of this volume.

- The **Cumulative Index to Nationalities** lists authors alphabetically under their respective nationalities. Author names are followed by the volume number(s) in which they appear.

- The **Cumulative Index to Titles** lists titles covered in *CLR* followed by the volume and page number where criticism begins.

A Note to the Reader

CLR is one of several critical references sources in the Literature Criticism Series published by The Gale Group. When writing papers, students who quote directly from any volume in the Literature Criticism Series may use the following general forms to footnote reprinted criticism. The first example pertains to material drawn from periodicals, the second to material reprinted from books.

[1]T. S. Eliot, "John Donne," *The Nation and the Athenaeum,* 33 (9 June 1923), 321-32; excerpted and reprinted in *Literature Criticism from 1400 to 1800,* Vol. 10, ed. James E. Person, Jr. (Detroit: Gale Research, 1989), pp. 28-9.

[1]Henry Brooke, *Leslie Brooke and Johnny Crow* (Frederick Warne, 1982); excerpted and reprinted in *Children's Literature Review,* Vol. 20, ed. Gerard J. Senick (Detroit: Gale Research, 1990), p. 47.

Suggestions Are Welcome

In response to various suggestions, several features have been added to *CLR* since the beginning of the series, including author entries on retellers of traditional literature as well as those who have been the first to record oral tales and other folklore; entries on prominent illustrators featuring commentary on their styles and techniques; entries on authors whose works are considered controversial; occasional entries devoted to criticism on a single work or a series of works; sections in author introductions that list major works by and about the author or illustrator being profiled; explanatory notes that provide information on the critic or work of criticism to enhance the usefulness of the excerpt; more extensive illustrative material, such as holographs of manuscript pages and photographs of people and places pertinent to the careers of the authors and artists; a cumulative nationality index for easy access to authors by nationality; and occasional guest essays written specifically for *CLR* by prominent critics on subjects of their choice.

Readers who wish to suggest authors to appear in future volumes, or who have other suggestions, are cordially invited to contact the editor. By mail: Editor, *Children's Literature Review,* The Gale Group, 27500 Drake Road, Farmington Hills, MI 48331-3535; by telephone: (800) 347-GALE, (248) 699-4253; by fax: (248) 699-8065.

Acknowledgments

The editors wish to thank the copyright holders of the excerpted criticism included in this volume and the permissions managers of many book and magazine publishing companies for assisting us in securing reproduction rights. We are also grateful to the staffs of the Detroit Public Library, the Library of Congress, the University of Detroit Mercy Library, Wayne State University Purdy/Kresge Library Complex, and the University of Michigan Libraries for making their resources available to us. Following is a list of the copyright holders who have granted us permission to reproduce material in this volume of *CLR.* Every effort has been made to trace copyright, but if omissions have been made, please let us know.

COPYRIGHTED EXCERPTS IN *CLR,* VOLUME 57, WERE REPRODUCED FROM THE FOLLOWING PERIODICALS:

AB Bookman's Weekly, v. 100, November 3, 1997. © 1997 by AB Bookman Publications, Inc. Reproduced by permission of the publisher.—*The ALAN Review,* v. 10, Winter, 1983; v. 11, Spring, 1984; v. 13, Fall, 1985; v. 13, Winter, 1986. All reproduced by permission.—*Apollo,* v. X, November, 1929. Reproduced by kind permission of Apollo Magazine Ltd.—*Appraisal: Science Books for Young People,* v. 15, Spring-Summer, 1982; v. 28, Winter, 1995. Copyright © 1982, 1995 by the Children's Science Book Review Committee. Both reproduced by permission. —*Best Sellers,* v. 27, April 1, 1967; v. 35, May, 1975; v. 39, June, 1979. Copyright 1967, 1975, 1979 by the University of Scranton. All reproduced by permission.—*The Book Collector,* v. 45, Summer, 1996. Reproduced by permission.—*The Book Report,* v. 13, November-December, 1994. © copyright 1994 by Linworth Publishing, Inc., Worthington, Ohio. Reproduced by permission.—*Booklist,* v. 73, July 15, 1977; v. 75, October 15, 1978; v. 75, December 1, 1978; v. 76, January 1, 1980; v. 76, May 1, 1980; v. 77, November 1, 1980; v. 78, January 1, 1982; v. 78, June 1, 1982; v. 78, August, 1982; v. 79, January 15, 1983; v. 80, February 15, 1984; v. 80, April 1, 1984; v. 81, August, 1985; v. 82, September 15, 1985; v. 82, May 1, 1986; v. 83, November 15, 1986; v. 83, December 15, 1986; v. 83, February 1, 1987; v. 83, February 15, 1987; v. 83, April 1, 1987; v. 84, September 1, 1987; v. 84, December 15, 1987; v. 85, January 1, 1989; v. 85, April 1, 1989; v. 85, April 15, 1989; v. 85, May 1, 1989; v. 85, August, 1989; v. 86, September 15, 1989; v. 86, January 1, 1990; v. 86, January 15, 1990; v. 86, March 15, 1990; v. 86, May 1, 1990; v. 86, July, 1990; v. 87, November 15, 1990; v. 87, May 1, 1991; v. 89, November 15, 1992; v. 89, May 15, 1993; v. 90, September 15, 1993; v. 90, November 1, 1993; v. 91, October 1, 1994; v. 91, November 1, 1994; v. 91, January 1, 1995; v. 91, January 15, 1995; v. 92, December 1, 1995; v. 92, January 1, 1996; v. 92, February 15, 1996; v. 92, April 15, 1996; v. 93, December 1, 1996; v. 93, February 15, 1997; v. 93, March 15, 1997; v. 93, August, 1997; v. 94, September 1, 1997; v. 94, September 15, 1997; v. 94, December 15, 1997; v. 94, January 1 & January 15, 1998; v. 94, March 1, 1998; v. 94, May 15, 1998. Copyright © 1977, 1978, 1980, 1982, 1983, 1984, 1985, 1986, 1987, 1989, 1990, 1991, 1992, 1993, 1994, 1995, 1996, 1997, 1998 by the American Library Association. All reproduced by permission.—*The Booklist,* v. 72, February 15, 1976. Copyright © 1976 by the American Library Association. Reproduced by permission.—*Books for Keeps,* n. 67, March, 1991; n. 85, March, 1994. © School Bookshop Association 1994. Both reproduced by permission.—*Books for Young People,* v. 2, February, 1988 for a review of "Baseball Crazy" by Adele Ashby; v. 3, April, 1989 for a review of "Mystery in the Frozen Lands" by Teresa Cowan./ v. I, April, 1987 for a review of "It Isn't Easy Being Ms. Teeny-Wonderful" by Patty Lawlor. Reproduced by permission of the author.—*Books in Canada,* v. XV, December, 1986 for a review of "Plan B Is Total Panic" by Mary Ainslie Smith; v. XIX, October, 1990 for a review of "Can You Teach Me to Pick My Nose?" by David Jenkinson; v. XIX, December, 1990 for a review of "I Spent My Summer Vacation Kidnapped into Space" by Katherine Govier; v. XXI, May, 1992 for a review of "Is It OK if This Monster Stays for Lunch?" by Phil Hall; v. XXIII, Summer, 1994 for a review of "Just Call Me Boom Boom" by Diana Brebner. All reproduced by permission of the respective authors.—*Bulletin of the Center for Children's Books,* v. 28, July-August, 1975; v. 30, September, 1976; v. 30, October, 1976; v. 32, February, 1979; v. 32, April, 1979; v. 33, February, 1980; v. 33, March, 1980; v. 34, March, 1981; v. 35, September, 1981; v. 35, February, 1982; v. 36, November, 1982; v. 36, January, 1983; v. 36, April, 1983; v. 36, May, 1983; v. 37, April, 1984; v. 38, December, 1984; v. 38, February, 1985; v. 39, February, 1986; v. 40, November, 1986; v. 40, January, 1987; v. 40, February, 1987; v. 41, January, 1988; v. 43, November, 1989; v. 43, December, 1989; v. 43, June, 1990; v. 43, July-August, 1990; v. 44, December, 1990; v. 44, May, 1991; v. 44, June, 1991. Copyright © 1975, 1976, 1979, 1980, 1981, 1982, 1983, 1984, 1985, 1986, 1987, 1988, 1989, 1990, 1991 by The University of Chicago. All reproduced by permission./ v. 46, October, 1992; v. 46, April, 1993; v. 47, November, 1993; v. 48, September, 1994; v. 48, January, 1995; v. 50, September, 1996; v. 50, June, 1997; v. 51, October, 1997; v. 51, November, 1997; v. 51, January, 1998. Copyright © 1992, 1993, 1994, 1995, 1996, 1997, 1998 by The Board of Trustees of the University of Illinois. All reproduced by permission.—*Canadian Children's Literature,* n. 26, 1982; n. 43, 1986; n. 45, 1987; n. 56, 1989; n. 64, 1991; v. 21, Spring, 1995; v. 21, Winter, 1995. Copyright © 1982, 1986, 1987, 1989, 1991, 1995 Canadian Children's Press. All reproduced by permission.—*Canadian Literature,* n. 127, Winter,

COPYRIGHTED EXCERPTS IN *CLR,* VOLUME 57, WERE REPRODUCED FROM THE FOLLOWING BOOKS OR PAMPHLETS:

ILLUSTRATIONS APPEARING IN *CLR,* VOLUME 57, WERE REPRODUCED FROM THE FOLLOWING SOURCES:

for "The Man in the Wilderness," painting by Arthur Rackham.—Williams, Garth, illustrator. From an illustration in *Charlotte's Web,* by E. B. White. Harper Trophy, 1952. Illustrations copyright 1952, renewed 1980 by Garth Williams. Reproduced by permission of HarperCollins Publishers.—Williams, Garth, illustrator. From an illustration in *Little House on the Prairie,* by Laura Ingalls Wilder. Revised edition. Harper & Row, 1953. Pictures copyright 1953, renewed 1981 by Garth Williams. Reproduced by permission of HarperCollins Publishers.—Williams, Garth, illustrator. From an illustration in *The Cricket in Times Square,* by George Selden. Farrar, 1960. Illustrations copyright 1960, renewed 1988 by Garth Williams. Reproduced by permission of Farrar, Straus and Giroux, LLC.

PHOTOGRAPHS APPEARING IN *CLR,* VOLUME 57, WERE REPRODUCED FROM THE FOLLOWING SOURCES:

Draper, Sharon, 1997, photograph. AP/Wide World Photos. Reproduced by permission.—Godfrey, Martyn, photograph. Reproduced by permission of the author.—Gomi, Taro, photograph. Reproduced by permission of the author.—Holland, Isabelle, photograph by George Janoff. Reproduced by permission of Isabelle Holland.—L'Engle, Madeleine, photograph by Thomas Victor. Reproduced by permission of the Estate of Thomas Victor.—Pringle, Laurence, photograph. Reproduced by permission of the author.—St. George, Judith, photograph. Reproduced by permission of the author.—Williams, Garth, 1986, photograph by Laura Acosta. Reproduced by permission of the Literary Estate of Garth Williams.

Children's
Literature
Review

Sharon Mills Draper

1952-

American author of fiction.

Major works include *Tears of a Tiger* (1994), *Ziggy and the Black Dinosaurs* (1994), *Lost in the Tunnel of Time* ("Ziggy and the Black Dinosaurs" series, 1996), *Forged by Fire (1997), Shadows of Caesar's Creek* ("Ziggy and the Black Dinosaurs" series, 1997).

INTRODUCTION

Recognized for her powerful and gripping debut novel, *Tears of a Tiger*, Draper, a life-long teacher, began her career as a writer when a student challenged her to enter a writing contest. Her contact with students has strongly influenced her books ever since, leading her to deal with subject matter relevant to young people and adding to the realism of her characters' lives. Draper once told *Something about the Author (SATA)*, "I have been a public school teacher for twenty-five years. I know what kids like, what they will read, and what they won't. . . . American students might need to know about the world of London in the 1860s, but they would much rather read about their own world first. Not only will they read about recognizable experiences with pleasure, but they will also be encouraged to write as well." Draper is praised for presenting just such contemporary realism to her readers, with a particular focus on African-American experiences. Her young adult novels are filled with the traumas and pressures of modern teenagers, and with authentic teen responses to those problems. She deals with drug use, alcoholism, child abuse, and teen suicide. Her characters respond in realistic and varied ways: by turning to religion, to their families or friends, or by giving in and finding other, negative escapes. Some critics feel that Draper's books are overly didactic, and that occasionally her stories seem contrived. She has been criticized for preaching in her novels, but Candace Smith opined in her review of *Forged by Fire*, "Draper faces some big issues (abuse, death, drugs) and provides concrete options and a positive African-American role model. . . ." Other critics have also commended Draper for her efforts to give African-American males a voice in literature; her central characters have all been young African-American men. Her books, with their quick pace and moving characters, have received favorable attention for encouraging reluctant readers to become involved with literature. Draper has been praised, as well, for combining African-American history and heritage with strong storytelling, particularly in her *Ziggy and the Black Dinosaurs* series for primary and middle graders. Dorothy M. Broderick noted the strength of Draper's fiction in a review of *Tears of a Tiger*: "To fully detail all that Draper has packed into this slight book would take thousands of words. Suffice

to say, not only is Draper an author to watch for, but that this is as compelling a novel as any published in the last two decades. Buy it, read it, share it."

Biographical Information

Draper was born in Cleveland, Ohio, and was the eldest of three children raised in a family that placed the highest value on education. She was constantly encouraged to read and write, and going to college was considered a priority. The hard-working student graduated from Pepperdine University in 1971 and immediately returned home to Ohio to begin teaching in the public school system. She later received a Master of Arts degree from Miami University in Oxford, Ohio. As a teacher, Draper frequently challenges her students to enter writing contests, and when one of her students turned that challenge on her, Draper willingly submitted her short story, "One Small Torch," to *Ebony* magazine. She won first prize in the magazine's 1991 Gertrude Johnson Williams Literary Contest, and her writing career was launched. She wrote her first novel, *Tears of a Tiger*, in her spare moments while teaching and sent it out to twenty-five publishers. Draper received twenty-four rejection notices, but the last letter from Simon & Schuster announced the book's acceptance. Published in 1994, *Tears of a Tiger* was embraced by many critics as an engrossing and sensitive novel for young adults, particularly African Americans. Draper, who chooses subject matter based on what will get her students reading, has also cited her teenage daughter as a source of inspiration and a springboard for the teenage dialogue that fills her novels. While her fiction has proven to be very popular with young readers, Draper has not given up her first love, teaching. In 1997 she was named U.S. Teacher of the Year and spent the year lecturing and touring. Draper continues to teach literature in Cincinnati's Walnut Hills High School, and her career as an educator is constantly informing and shaping her books.

Major Works

Draper's *Ziggy and the Black Dinosaurs* books are directed at younger readers. The three works comprising the series focus on the adventures of the Black Dinosaurs club, consisting of Ziggy, Jerome, Rico, and Rashawn, all African-American boys. In the first book, *Ziggy and the Black Dinosaurs,* the boys set out to solve the mystery of a vandalized basketball court and in the process meet Mr. Greene, an old man who provides them with rich tales rooted in African-American history. Claudia Cooper asserted that the book is "intended to present positive role models and to create African-American pride," as are the other two books in the series. *Lost in the Tunnel of Time* finds the Black Dinosaurs on a field trip to the Ohio River, where Mr. Greene tells them the history of the Underground Railroad. Fascinated by the old man's stories, the boys begin exploring the abandoned tunnels, once a part of the Railroad, that run far under their school. When the tunnel they are exploring collapses, the fearful boys are comforted by thoughts of Mr. Greene's tales about a Shawnee woman and the brave escaped slaves she directed through the tunnels to freedom. The third book in the series, *Shadows of Caesar's Creek*, has the boys exploring a state park once occupied by the Shawnee Indians. The Black Dinosaurs learn some Native American history and, after becoming lost in the woods, are directed to safety by a Shawnee chief. Linda Bindner noted that Draper is successful in "showing that it's plausible for 10-year-olds to respect other cultures and the land," and that the book makes a contribution to the discussion of "what makes it into history books and what doesn't."

Tears of a Tiger, Draper's first novel for young adults, is the story of Andy Jackson, a young basketball star whose life is destroyed after he is involved in a car crash in which his teammate Robert Washington is killed. Andy was driving drunk, and cannot overcome his guilt over his friend's death. The story of Andy's decline emerges through snippets of dialogue, homework assignments, transcripts of Andy's sessions with a psychologist, and newspaper reports. "This quick-cutting, MTV-

like approach allows insights into a number of different viewpoints," noted a *Publishers Weekly* reviewer. "[T]he combination of raw energy and intense emotion should stimulate readers." In the end, Andy commits suicide. The novel successfully illustrates the damage done to a young African-American man by his own questionable choices and the insensitive white society that he turns to for help. Although it is written in a more conventional narrative style than *Tears of a Tiger*, *Forged by Fire* also deals with complex issues faced by young adults. The novel traces the growth of Gerald, a minor character from *Tears of a Tiger*, from child to young man. Gerald's mother, Monique, is a drug addict who neglects her son, to the point of leaving him alone at age three when he is burned in a house fire. Gerald is spared from a life with his abusive mother when she is imprisoned and he is sent to live with his loving Aunt Queen. But Queen abruptly dies when Gerald is nine, and he must again live with his mother, now released, and his young half-sister Angel, who instantly clings to Gerald for the love and protection her mother cannot give her. Young Gerald undertakes to defend Angel from their stepfather Jordan's sexual abuse. The tough and courageous Gerald emerges as a powerful and positive image of a young African-American man. Although other critics found the book melodramatic, Kevin Beach and Beverly B. Youree noted, "With nonstop excitement, this is well-written, easy to read, and possibly an inspiration for anyone trapped in family situations involving child abuse or domestic violence."

Awards

For *Tears of a Tiger*, Draper was awarded the American Library Association (ALA) Coretta Scott King Genesis Award for an outstanding new book in 1995. In 1998, Draper received ALA's Coretta Scott King Award for *Forged by Fire*. Both *Tears of a Tiger* and *Forged by Fire* were recognized as ALA Best Books for Young Adults and as Notable Trade Books in the Field of Social Studies by the National Council for the Social Studies, in 1995 and 1998, respectively. Draper's short story "One Small Torch" won the 1991 Gertrude Johnson Williams Literary Contest sponsored by *Ebony* magazine. An outstanding teacher, Draper was named Ohio State Teacher of the Year and U.S. National Teacher of the Year, both in 1997.

GENERAL COMMENTARY

Julia Pferdehirt

SOURCE: "Sharon M. Draper," in *Contemporary Black Biography,* Vol. 16, edited by Shirelle Phelps, Gale Research, 1997, pp. 42-5.

As an author, poet, and master educator named 1997

U.S. Teacher of the Year, Sharon Draper has introduced thousands of children and young people to the world of words. Draper says teaching is her "calling and vocation," describing herself as a teacher who "teaches because I must. It is in my heart and soul; part of the definition of me. I end up teaching wherever I am." As a teacher who is also a writer she has testified to the value of story and the power of words to generations of students. Her published work, including two young adult novels, a series of juvenile fiction, and two collections of poetry are grounded in the conviction that books can and must speak to the lives and dreams of young readers. Choosing African-American male characters is Draper's way of giving the power of words to African-American young men. . . .

Sharon Draper's vision, in the classroom and as she writes, is to challenge young people to embrace learning without limits and without hesitation. She credits her family and early schooling with giving her the gift of unlimited love of learning. Draper entered Cleveland Public Schools in the 1950s from a home where she had grown up surrounded by books. Her mother read stories, poems, fairytales, and nursery rhymes to Draper and her siblings from the time they were very young. She recalls a teacher who once "gave me Os for outstanding, saying an A wasn't good enough." A fifth grade teacher gave Draper and her fellow students poetry by Langston Hughes and Robert Frost. They read and loved Shakespeare. "We didn't know we weren't supposed to be able to do that in fifth grade. She gave it to us and we loved it," Draper said. "It was part of making me the teacher I am today. . . . "

Draper's first personal venture into writing came when a student handed her a writing contest application and said, "Why don't you write something?" The resulting short story **"One Small Torch"** was chosen from 20,000 entries as winner of the 1991 *Ebony* Magazine Short Story Contest. That first success was impetus for Draper to combine her love of teaching with her love of words and story as an author and poet. Her first novel, *Tears of a Tiger,* grew out of Draper's recognition that powerful, once-timely works by authors like Dickens were missing the mark with her students. She wanted to create a contemporary book of literary quality to reach the cultural, ethnic, and daily realities of students in today's high school classrooms. Her novel's main character is the drunken driver in an accident that kills his best friend. Draper encourages young writers by telling the story of rejection by 24 of 25 publishers to which *Tears of a Tiger* was sent. Once published, this book was affirmed as "strong, vivid and ringing true" in *School Library Journal.* It was embraced by young readers and received the 1995 American Library Association Best Book for Young Adults and Coretta Scott King Genesis awards. A 1997 sequel, *Forged by Fire* is her second novel. . . .

As a classroom teacher and mentor to novice educators, Draper knew that even the best contemporary titles often failed to draw young boys into the world of reading.

Fewer books still were written with young African-American boys in mind. Her next venture, the *Ziggy and the Black Dinosaurs* series was written for those young readers. "I know what interests kids," Draper said. "I know what will catch them and make them readers in spite of themselves." In *Lost in the Tunnel of Time,* Ziggy and his fellow clubmates the Black Dinosaurs discover a tunnel once used as a station on the Underground Railroad. Always the teacher, Draper filled the book with history, knowing students would absorb the information effortlessly because of the strong, interesting story. "I tell my students that if they learn nothing else in my class, I want them to understand that a powerful connection exists between historical and cultural events and the literary creations of the time," Draper told the Ohio Department of Education upon her selection as Ohio Teacher of the Year in January of 1997.

Being named 1997 U.S. Teacher of the Year brought diverse facets of Sharon Draper's life and personal gifts together. As a master-teacher and mentor of other educators, Draper was an able spokesperson for her profession. As creator of fiction of interest to hard-to-reach students, Draper was an able model for high standards and innovative teaching. As a teacher "by calling and vocation" she was a spokesperson for the value of teachers and teaching to every child and every community. . . .

TITLE COMMENTARY

TEARS OF A TIGER (1994)

Publishers Weekly

SOURCE: A review of *Tears of a Tiger,* in *Publishers Weekly,* Vol. 241, No. 44, October 31, 1994, p. 64.

Draper's ambitious first novel tackles teenage drinking, suicidal depression and other front-page topics—and relates the action through dialogue or compositions "by" the characters. Exuberant after a high-school basketball victory, athletic stars Andy and Robert down a few beers with friends and then ride around in Andy's car. When Robert is killed in an expressway accident, Andy assumes what turns out to be an unbearable burden of guilt. Short chapters in the form of newspaper articles, diary entries and school writing assignments telegraph the community's reactions and Andy's own feelings; these latter are amplified through Andy's conversations with his coach, with his girlfriend and—poignantly—with the psychologist his concerned parents send him to. This quick-cutting, MTV-like approach allows insights into a number of different viewpoints, ranging from Andy's wrenching internal monologues to the ghastly perkiness of the school's "grief counselor." Casting most of the protagonists as African American, Draper also makes some telling (though not terribly new) points about race and racism. Though the issue-oriented plot can get a bit preachy, the combination of raw energy and intense emotion should stimulate readers.

Merri Monks

SOURCE: A review of *Tears of a Tiger,* in *Booklist,* Vol. 91, No. 5, November 1, 1994, p. 492.

When star basketball player Robert Washington and his three closest friends mix drinking and driving in a post-game victory celebration, Robert is killed in an auto accident. The driver, Andy Jackson, is unable to resolve his feelings of guilt and remorse. Neither Andy's parents nor his psychologist accurately perceive the depth of Andy's depression, with tragic results—Andy, at the end, commits suicide. The story emerges through newspaper articles, journal entries, homework assignments, letters, and conversations that give the book immediacy; the teenage conversational idiom is contemporary and well written. Andy's perceptions of the racism directed toward young black males—by teachers, guidance counselors, and clerks in shopping malls—will be recognized by African-American YAs. Although some heavy-handed didacticism detracts from the novel's impact, the characters and their experiences will captivate teen readers. The novel is also suitable for use in curricular units dealing with alcohol abuse, suicide, and racism.

Roger Sutton

SOURCE: A review of *Tears of a Tiger,* in *Bulletin of the Center for Children's Books,* Vol. 48, No. 5, January, 1995, p. 164.

After the school basketball star is killed in a drunk-driving crash, his teammate and best friend Andy—who was driving—is left not only to lead the team but to wrestle with the devils of guilt, culpability, and loss. Draper uses a collage of conversations, school lectures and homework, and transcripts of Andy's sessions with a psychologist in a way that at first seems insurmountably didactic, but is increasingly dramatic as it becomes apparent that despite the best intentions of family, friends, teachers, and the psychologist, nothing is working. Andy eventually kills himself, and rather than a tidy summary of suicide symptoms and "ways to help," readers instead get a grave portrait of unceasing despair—and a larger picture of how young African-American men like Andy get lost in a system that will not trust or reach out to them. There's a political message at the heart of this problem novel, and it's refreshing to see a wider perspective brought to a genre that too often relies on cliches of pop psychology. Beginning with some salty locker room conversation among the team after a big win, the changes in format, style and perspective give readers a new point of view every few pages; the conversations (unlabeled and uninflected, à la Avi's *Who Was that Masked Man, Anyway?*) are vivid and effective in their shifts between standard English and hip teen-talk. Sure

to provoke lots of thought and debate among young adults, this is one of the more challenging novels we've seen about teen suicide.

Kathy Fritts

SOURCE: A review of *Tears of a Tiger,* in *School Library Journal,* Vol. 41, No. 2, February, 1995, p. 112.

A hard-hitting story of the unraveling of a young black man who was the drunk driver in an accident that killed his best friend. Andy cannot bear his guilt or reach out for help, and chapter by chapter his disintegration builds to inevitable suicide. Counselors, coaches, friends, and family all fail him. The story is artfully told through English class assignments, including poetry, dialogues, police and newspaper reports, and letters. From time to time, the author veers off into overt lessons on racial issues, but aside from this flaw the characters' voices are strong, vivid, and ring true. This moving novel will leave a deep impression.

Dorothy M. Broderick

SOURCE: A review of *Tears of a Tiger,* in *Voice of Youth Advocates,* Vol. 17, No. 6, March, 1995, p. 338.

In as gut-wrenching a book as I have read since Voigt's *The Runner,* first novelist Draper relates the story of Andy Jackson whose already tenuous self-esteem is shattered when he kills his best friend Robert while driving drunk. As he is burning alive, trapped in the car, Robert cries out "Oh God, please don't let me die like this! Andy! . . ." From that horrendous scene, Draper relates how Tyrone and B. J., the other boys in the car, are able to move on with life, Tyrone through a supportive relationship with Rhonda, and B. J. from finding God. But, they weren't driving, and their guilt is minor compared to Andy's.

As Draper moves us toward the inevitable end—Andy blowing his brains out with his father's shot gun—Andy's relationship with the psychologist, Dr. Carrothers, provides insight into the scars a white society can leave on a black male. He doesn't do as well in school as he could because that wouldn't be cool for a black basketball player; he sees his father as a sell out to the white establishment; he and his friends are hassled when entering stores.

In one vignette, Draper has two teachers talking about how little you can really expect from blacks, and how Andy, being black, surely can't be all that upset by the death of his friend. When parting, one reminds the other that they have a Human Relations (!!!) meeting that afternoon. In another, Tyrone and B. J., recognizing how much Andy needs help, go to a school counselor who brushes off their concerns.

Andy does have all kinds of support: his coach is an understanding man; Keisha, his love, is as kind and gentle with Andy as one could ask for until even she has had enough of his tears and depression which he often hides behind outrageous behavior. But at the crucial moment when he needs them, his psychologist is flying to California, the coach isn't home, and Keisha's mother won't wake her up for an after-midnight phone call.

To fully detail all that Draper has packed into this slight book would take thousands of words. Suffice to say, not only is Draper an author to watch for, but that this is as compelling a novel as any published in the last two decades. Buy it, read it, share it.

ZIGGY AND THE BLACK DINOSAURS (1994)

Claudia Cooper

SOURCE: A review of *Ziggy and the Black Dinosaurs,* in *School Library Journal,* Vol. 41, No. 3, March, 1995, p. 202.

When their basketball court is vandalized, Ziggy and his three friends form the Black Dinosaurs to solve the mystery. Obviously intended to present positive role models and to create African-American pride, the 11 short chapters are packed with black heritage. "Tuskeegee" and "Nigeria" become secret passwords, slave history is revealed by old Mr. Greene (who serves as the red herring), Jerome's grandmother furnishes African musical heritage, and Ziggy provides the Jamaican influence. Unfortunately, such grand designs often degenerate into didacticism resulting in characters who are too good to be true. And Mr. Greene, who is brusque with the boys almost to the point of rudeness at their initial encounter in the library, uncharacteristically becomes their great ally and confidant. And this after they frighten him terribly with a fake police raid! A minor flaw (but one that dinosaur experts will catch)—the Apatosaurus is twice illustrated as a Tyrannosaurus rex. However, the plot moves quickly, Ziggy's character provides humor, and the situations will appeal to children. Simple vocabulary and large-print text are appropriate for reluctant readers.

LOST IN THE TUNNEL OF TIME ("Ziggy and the Black Dinosaurs" series, 1996)

Publishers Weekly

SOURCE: A review of *Lost in the Tunnel of Time,* in *Publishers Weekly,* Vol. 243, No. 13, March 25, 1996, p. 85.

An inaugural release in the Ziggy and the Black Dinosaurs series, this tale focuses on four African-American boys who make up the Black Dinosaurs Club. On a class field trip to the Ohio River, the friends are captivated by two stories. A raconteur describes his grandfather's arrival in Cincinnati via the Underground Railroad and also explains that tunnels used in that operation are located under the school the kids attend. And their teacher relates a local legend about a Shawnee woman who helped slaves escape to freedom and whose ghost allegedly haunts the area. When Ziggy and pals attempt to explore the underground tunnels, the walls collapse. The trapped boys are comforted by a breeze they attribute to the ghost's presence. Draper's well-meaning attempts to combine fiction, folklore and history lead to some significant credibility gaps, among them the unlikely circumstances that middle-class African-American middle-schoolers have never heard of the Underground Railroad; and that Ziggy's dog manages to dig through the collapsed tunnel to rescue them. The result is a contrived, disappointingly meager novel.

Anne Connor

SOURCE: A review of *Lost in the Tunnel of Time,* in *School Library Journal,* Vol. 42, No. 8, August, 1996, p. 142.

Rico, his friend Ziggy, and their classmates have been looking forward to a field trip to the Ohio River. Accompanied by old Mr. Greene, they welcome the break from school, but also find themselves fascinated by the man's stories about the Underground Railroad. Intrigued by the fact that runaway slaves hid in tunnels under their school, the boys (all members of the Black Dinosaurs Club) get a map of the tunnels and plan a search. All goes well until one of the tunnels collapses and they are trapped deep below the deserted school. Inspired by the bravery of the escaped slaves who survived similar ordeals, the boys cope with their fear until rescued. This is the first entry in a projected series about a likable group of African American friends. The characters are realistically portrayed, and the history lessons are interestingly conveyed.

FORGED BY FIRE (1997)

Kirkus Reviews

SOURCE: A review of *Forged by Fire,* in *Kirkus Reviews,* Vol. LXIV, No. 23, December 1, 1996, p. 1735.

An African-American boy grows into a decent man, a loving brother, and a steadfast son despite the cruelties of his childhood in this latest novel by Draper. Although three-year-old Gerald is burned in the fire caused by his drug-addicted mother Monique's recklessness, his life takes a turn for the better: The court sends him to live with his aunt, Queen. Wheelchair-bound and poor, Queen has a loving heart and boundless spirit that nourish and cultivate Gerald for six years, until his mother walks back into his life. When Queen abruptly dies, Gerald moves into Monique's home, where he becomes devoted to his younger half-sister, Angel, and suffers at the hands of his mother's new husband. Jordan is a bully, drunk, and child molester; while Angel and Gerald get him convicted (the police show up as Jordan is about to abuse Angel), he eventually returns to haunt the family after serving his jail term. While Draper's narrative is riveting, it is also rife with simplistic characterizations: Aunt Queen is all-good, Monique is all-stupid, and Jordan is all-evil. In addition, there are enough logical twists in the plot without the seemingly gratuitous death of Gerald's friend, Rob.

Lynn Ploof Davis

SOURCE: A review of *Forged by Fire,* in *Children's Book Review Service, Inc.,* Vol. 25, No. 7, February, 1997, p. 82.

The book opens with a scene that will make even the most jaded reader sit up and take notice. Young Gerald, the victim of abuse and neglect at the hands of his mother, suffers through a horrible event that is only the beginning of a life of emotional and physical pain. After the loss of his beloved aunt, Gerald learns that he must dodge fists and think on his feet to survive. He protects his younger sister with a determination that often seems superhuman and leaves the reader wishing for a friend like Gerald. The book is filled with the stark and gritty realities of child abuse. It is a page-turner, not because it is a joy to read, but because there is an intense urge to see it through the end to make sure that Gerald does indeed survive.

Candace Smith

SOURCE: A review of *Forged by Fire,* in *Booklist,* Vol. 93, No. 12, February 15, 1997, p. 1016.

Gerald Nickelby, a minor character in **Tears of a Tiger** (1994), emerges full-fledged and courageous in this companion story. His stable life with a firm but loving aunt (who is caring for him while his mother serves a prison sentence for child neglect) is shattered when his mother returns to claim him on his ninth birthday. With her is a young daughter, Angel, to whom Gerald is drawn, and her husband, Jordan, whom Gerald instinctively dislikes. When Gerald learns that Jordan is sexually abusing Angel, he risks physical assault and public embarrassment to rescue her. Although written in a more conventional form than the earlier novel, the dialogue is still convincing, and the affection between Angel and Gerald rings true. With so much tragedy here (the car crash and death of Gerald's friend Rob in **Tears** are again recounted, though Draper, thankfully, stops before Andy Jackson's suicide), there is some danger of overloading the reader. Nevertheless, Draper faces some big issues (abuse, death, drugs) and provides concrete options and a positive African-American role model in Gerald.

Deborah Stevenson

SOURCE: A review of *Forged by Fire,* in *Bulletin of the Center for Children's Books,* Vol. 50, No. 10, June, 1997, p. 355.

Gerald's life is haunted early: when he's only three, he accidentally sets fire to the apartment where his drug-addicted mother, Monique, has left him alone. After she's imprisoned for neglect, he lives with his indomitable great-aunt Queen, but when Monique is released from prison (with a new husband and a daughter, Angel, born during her incarceration) he ends up living with her following Aunt Queen's sudden death. Gerald bonds with his little sister but hates and fears his abusive stepfather, who soon also goes to prison for his molestation of Angel; unfortunately he is eventually released, and his hold over the family becomes stronger when Monique is seriously injured in an accident. Then Gerald's friend Rob dies, and then there's another fire which kills the stepfather. It's all too much for the reader as well as Gerald, and the writing isn't capable of turning this sequence of events into something other than relentless melodrama that ultimately numbs rather than engages. There's also a tendency for the point of view to wander, especially at the beginning, which makes it hard to focus as firmly on Gerald as one might wish. The relationships between Gerald and Rob's supportive family and between Gerald and Angel are strong and appealing, but that's not enough to overcome the heavy-handed plotting.

Kevin Beach and Beverly B. Youree

SOURCE: A review of *Forged by Fire,* in *Voice of Youth Advocates,* Vol. 20, No. 2, June, 1997, pp. 108-09.

What started out as an award-winning short story in Ebony magazine was expanded into this sad but inspirational story about a young man trying to escape the horrors of a dysfunctional family. As a toddler, Gerald was left alone at home one day while his mother went out to buy street drugs, only one of several irresponsible acts committed by her in the story. Rescued by a neighbor after fire breaks out in the apartment, Gerald is sent to live with strong-willed but loving Aunt Queen. There he thrives until on his ninth birthday his mother returns from jail with a new husband, Jordan Sparks, in tow. Gerald also discovers he has a kid sister, Angel, who was born in jail and apparently has already suffered a series of abuses in her six years. Angel immediately clutches onto Gerald for love and protection, and he responds.

Life is hard in a new household run by an angry, abusive, demanding stepfather and a compliant mother, but Gerald manages to keep Angel away from the stepdad most of the time and finds time to develop his skills in high school as a basketball player. Angel blossoms into a passionate dancer, but the shadow of their sullen stepfather and deteriorating mother continues to cause difficulties. Other tragedies befall the family and one of Gerald's friends before another fire culminates a final confrontation between Gerald and his stepfather.

This is a companion to the author's **Tears of a Tiger,** a

story about one of Gerald's basketball teammates. Prevalent in today's teenagers is Gerald's attitude that he can take care of himself; he is a determined young black man. With non-stop excitement, this is well-written, easy to read, and possibly an inspiration for anyone trapped in family situations involving child abuse or domestic violence. This tremendous novel by the 1995 winner of the Coretta Scott King Genesis Award is recommended for all YA collections.

SHADOWS OF CAESAR'S CREEK ("Ziggy and the Black Dinosaurs," 1997)

Linda Binder

SOURCE: A review of *Shadows of Caesar's Creek,* in *School Library Journal,* Vol. 44, No. 6, June, 1998, p. 103.

Ziggy, Rico, Rashawn, and Jerome's weekend camping trip at Caesar's Creek State Park is far more exciting than they ever expected. Their counselor turns out to be an expert on the history of the park, which once belonged to the Shawnee Indian tribe. Mysterious tales about coming-of-age rituals and shadows that walk at midnight start the boys off on their own nighttime adventure, and soon they are lost in the surrounding woods. Rescued by an equally mysterious man named Hawk, who turns out to be a Shawnee chief, the boys' adventure ends safely, and they all learn valuable lessons as well. The connection between the Native-American adults and African-American kids is real and believable. The children occasionally come across a little too good and too nice, but Draper makes up for it by showing that it's plausible for 10-year-olds to respect other cultures and the land. The plot is predictable and slim at times, but this addition to the series should generate thoughtful questions about the past in general, as well as swhat information makes it into history books and what doesn't.

Additional coverage of Mills's life and career is contained in the following sources published by The Gale Group: *Something about the Author*, Vol. 98.

Martyn N. Godfrey

1949-

English-born Canadian author of fiction.

Major works include *Here She Is, Ms. Teeny-Wonderful* (1985), *Plan B is Total Panic* (1986), *Mystery in the Frozen Lands* (1988), *Can You Teach Me to Pick My Nose?* (1990), *Just Call Me Boom Boom* ("JAWS Mob" series, 1994).

INTRODUCTION

A highly respected and popular Canadian author of mysteries, historical fiction, science fiction, and adventure stories for middle graders and young adults, Godfrey is best known for his comic novels that blend both subtle and not-so-subtle humor with often serious subjects ranging from peer pressure and teenage suicide to atomic disasters. Godfrey's fast-paced, accessible, and entertaining writing style has garnered him a wide teenage readership, primarily of such playful works as *Can You Teach Me to Pick My Nose?*, *Plan B is Total Panic*, and *Here She Is, Ms. Teeny-Wonderful*. His fiction typically features an adolescent protagonist, an eclectic cast of supporting characters, and bizarre plot twists that draw readers into the action. Often playing with the traditional perceptions of boy/girl relations, Godfrey crafts his protagonists into believable contemporaries of his readers by having them speak in a teen vernacular, as well as by placing them in the kinds of situations young people are apt to face once or twice in their lives. Some of his themes include overcoming self-doubt, successfully navigating puberty, and coming to terms with the remarriage of a parent. While many young-adult novels already cover these universal issues, Godfrey's fiction presents a unique edge. In *Can You Teach Me to Pick My Nose?*, for example, Jordy desperately wants to capture the attention of a pretty girl, but must support the false boast of a friend who claims that Jordy is a champion skateboarder. In *There's a Cow in My Swimming Pool*, Nicole must adjust to her mother's remarriage, as well as the fact that, oddly enough, there is a cow in her swimming pool.

Godfrey's surprises are not mere plot contrivances; indeed, his ability to deliver more than a good story is not lost on reviewers. According to Lyle Weis, "Godfrey's strength as a writer for juveniles lies in his ability to blend serious issues with an action-oriented plot, something he accomplishes by placing ordinary kids in demanding or unusual circumstances." Godfrey explained his simple rule of thumb for his fiction in *Something about the Author* (*SATA*): "Writers have to grab their readers in the first few sentences. . . . You know, the last thing I ever write in a novel is the first paragraph. Hook the reader as fast as possible, and then don't let go."

Biographical Information

Godfrey was born in Birmingham, England, in 1949 and emigrated to Canada in 1957. He was educated in Canada, but his early years of school were a difficult experience, as he commented in *SATA:* "I flunked the third grade and I hated writing because I couldn't spell." Within a couple of years, his schooling improved and Godfrey began writing creatively by the fifth grade. In 1973, he received a Bachelor of Arts degree with double honors, majoring in history and English, and one year later, a Bachelor of Education degree, both from the University of Toronto. He taught elementary and junior high-school classes in Ontario and Alberta until a mock challenge from one of his students launched his writing career. Disgruntled by the lack of science-fiction books in the school library, a twelve-year-old student suggested that Godfrey write one for him. The result was *The Vandarian Incident* (1984), an action-packed sci-fi tale about the attempts of the Vandarian Confederation to stop the signing of a treaty between the Galaxy Union and the Andromuse Empire. The book netted mixed reviews after its publication, but won an "Our Choice" award from the Children's Book Centre. Three science-fiction books followed until Godfrey turned to the world around him with *Here She Is, Ms. Teeny-Wonderful.* The switch from science fiction to contemporary material suited Godfrey. He explained in *SATA,* "Now I only write about what I know. In my books you'll find incidents about a fluoride rinse disaster, a student with a raisin caught in his nose, a bear attack, spiders in a cheeseburger, and so on. They're all true. I just twist reality a little on my computer screen to make them more interesting."

Major Works

The first of Godfrey's novels to explore a modern, realistic setting instead of a fantasy backdrop is *Here She Is, Ms. Teeny-Wonderful,* which features Carol Weatherspoon, a tomboyish adolescent who is unwillingly entered into a beauty pageant, along with the very feminine Campbell twins. Although Carol would rather be riding her BMX bike and practicing complicated maneuvers, she wins first runner-up, relegating the malicious Campbell twins to third place. Her success is partially owed to her tomboy behavior: for the talent portion of the competition, Carol jumps six barrels with her bike. Reviewers noted the gender-identity debate driving the story. Marjorie Gunn wrote, "Godfrey has obviously cashed in on a trendy issue: traditional vs. liberated female roles, but he does this with a light touch . . . ." Gunn added, "Carol is a believable tomboy, not a device for convincing preteen girls to burn their Barbies." *Ms. Teeny-Wonderful* encountered enough success that it spawned two sequels: *It Isn't Easy Being Ms. Teeny-Wonderful* and *Send in Ms. Teeny-Wonderful.*

Nicholas Clark, the protagonist of *Plan B is Total Panic,* is not as secure in his identity as is Carol Weatherspoon. Forced to move because of his divorced father's job as an oil worker, Nicholas, now living in northern Alberta, Canada, feels insecure about himself mainly because of his unstable life. He considers himself unattractive, a weakling, and a coward. A moose-hunting trip with his friend Elvis, a native Dene, helps Nicholas grow into someone who can successfully confront his fears and brave whatever situations life throws at him. As in *Ms. Teeny-Wonderful,* Godfrey weaves an inspirational message into an enjoyable story.

Godfrey's *Mystery in the Frozen Lands* is a departure from both science fiction and comedy. Godfrey incorporates factual historical elements into his fictional account of a rescue mission that set out to determine the fate of Arctic explorer Sir John Franklin, leader of an 1847 Arctic expedition to the North Pole. Franklin was never heard from again. The tale is narrated by Peter Griffin, a fourteen-year-old aboard the rescue ship that attempted to find Franklin twelve years later. The hardships of Arctic life and the budding romance with his cousin Elizabeth are shown in Peter's diary. With greater attention to adventure than some of his more notable novels, *Mystery in the Frozen Lands* is, according to Mary Ellen Binder, "a compelling page-turner from the first paragraph" and, as Teresa Cowan concluded, "an entertaining and enlightening read."

Can You Teach Me to Pick My Nose?—as the attention-grabbing title implies—returns Godfrey to more humorous situations than in *Mystery.* The book's main character, seventh-grader Jordy Shepherd, is like *Plan B*'s Nicholas in that his shortcomings, for a time, dictate his actions in the story. Jordy is upset when his mother decides to move from Montana to California. More trouble arises when Jordy's new friend, Chris, boastfully announces that Jordy is a champion ramp skateboarder. The proclamation—meant to net Jordy the girl he has a crush on—sets him up for a grudge match with the girl's older brother, the local skateboarding champ. Because Jordy knows very little about the sport, he befriends the most unpopular girl in school, who also happens to be a skateboarding hotshot, so that she may teach him, among other things, skateboarding moves such as the "pick your nose," to which the title refers. David Jenkinson wrote, "By working together, the unlikely pair uncovers the real people behind the facades. A predictable, upbeat ending is fitting for this fun-filled story," while Diane Claus-Smith commented that the book "has a simple story line with few surprises, but much humor."

Just Call Me Boom Boom's Bryan Benjamin "Boom Boom" Bortorowski has a problem earlier Godfrey characters might not mind. A bruiser of a boy, Boom Boom must work hard to keep his temper in check. This is not easy for the eighth-grader, who manages to find himself in a series of unfortunate situations as a result of his tempestuous behavior. "Fun" was the word reviewers used most frequently to describe *Just Call Me Boom Boom,* but Diana Brebner, with a mocking, backhanded compliment, jested, "The style is pure macho and the vocabulary current. If it gets male airheads reading, I guess it deserves a few points."

Awards

Godfrey won the Metcalf Award for best children's short story from the Canadian Authors Association in 1985 and an award for best children's book from the University of Lethbridge in 1987, both for *Here She Is, Ms. Teeny-Wonderful.* He was the runner-up for the Geoffrey Bilson Award for *Mystery in the Frozen Lands* in 1989, and won the Manitoba Young Reader's Choice Award for *Can You Teach Me to Pick My Nose?* in 1993.

AUTHOR'S COMMENTARY

Martyn Godfrey

SOURCE: "Portraits: Martyn Godfrey," in *Emergency Librarian,* Vol. 13, No. 1, September-October, 1985, pp. 47-9.

[The following interview was conducted by Dave Jenkinson.]

One of the better known anecdotes of contemporary children's literature concerns how Gordon Korman became an author. Gordon, thirteen, and each of his grade seven classmates, received from their English teacher the assignment of writing a novel. Though the other students became discouraged and abandoned their writings, Gordon persevered and ultimately sold his manuscript. To Gordon's tale can now be added another success story except, for Martyn Godfrey, the creative impetus was totally reversed.

[Godfrey:] "I kind of got into writing through teaching. In 1980, I was in a grade five class in Mississauga, Ontario. There had been three science fiction movies that all came out at the same time: *Close Encounters . . . , Alien,* and *The Empire Strikes Back,* and the kids came to me, saying 'Do we have any science fiction stories in the library?' Our school library was really small, and we didn't have any of Monica Hughes's works at that time. I went back to the class and said, 'I can't find anything for you'. We had creative writing period right after lunch. I had this character—I can still remember him . . . row 5, seat 5 . . . sitting at the back of the room—who put up his hand and started snapping his fingers. He said, 'Well, if there's no books for us, and you're making us write stuff, why don't you write stuff. You write us a book—ha-ha-ha!'

"I thought, 'O.K.!' It was a good chance to make a deal with him because he hadn't been doing that much work for me all year and so I said, 'We'll make kind of a contract. I'll sit at my desk, and I'll write a story for you, and you sit back there and write a story for me.' I wrote a couple of pages of foolscap, and we traded off and read one another's stories. 'Well, let's do it next period,' said he, and we did. When I had about seven pages done of foolscap, he said, 'Why don't you send it away to those Scholastic guys?' 'I'll send it if you'll write the letter for me, telling Scholastic what's gone on.' He did, and Scholastic's reply to the seven pages was, 'We like the opening. Go ahead and write a whole book!'

"It took about another three months to write *The Vandarian Incident.* I didn't have any idea about the rest of the story," Martyn admits. While Scholastic liked his first draft, "they wanted me to do a rewrite and include a girl character." In the final version, Tyler Hobart, a fourteen-year-old human, undergoes a survival mission in the desert of the distant planet of Tilyel. Success would mean that Tyler could graduate into the Transport Corporation Institute and earn his wings, for "to be a fluxdrive pilot was the dream of every kid in the Galaxy." Sand blizzards, crust pits, heat and dehydration were challenges Tyler must overcome, or he could die. Unknown to Tyler, a larger challenge awaited him. The Galaxy Union Government and the Andromuse Empire had planned a secret space meeting near Tilyel to establish a military treaty to stand against the Vandars who

"were ruthless and warlike by nature, and notorious for their harsh treatment of their subject territories." The Vandarians, having somehow learned of the meeting, destroy the only inhabited areas of Tilyel so that the peace mission cannot be warned of the Vandarian presence. Tyler and a fellow cadet, a female from another planet, become the only ones who can stop the Vandarian attack on the peace vessel.

Born in Birmingham, England on April 17, 1949, Martyn came to Canada with his family in 1959. After his public schooling, Martyn went to University College at the University of Toronto in 1969, taking his B.A. with a double honors major in history and English literature. A B.Ed. followed. "Teaching was just starting to change then where you couldn't really pick your places. I had a couple of job offers. One was in Kitchener Waterloo which I took. I lived in Kitchener for three years and then moved down to Burlington and taught in Mississauga for three years. Then I moved to Alberta and taught on an Indian reserve up in the northwest corner of the province in a place called Assumption. This is my third year in Edson. Most of my teaching has been in upper elementary and junior high."

The first book, *The Vandarian Incident,* which received an "Our Choice" award from the Children's Book Centre, was, according to Martyn, the result of "just trying to write a story." But since 1981, Martyn has had four other titles published and has contracts for others which are to be out in the near future. He attributes his continuing publication success to his ability to respond to the question, "What do *they* want," where the antecedent for the "they" is twofold. First, there are the publishers and, as Martyn puts it, it is a matter of "reading the market." Different publishers want different things. "Scholastic has kind of said to me that girls are the major buyers of books and in the book clubs, overwhelmingly so. If you've got a good story with a strong girl character in it, then it has a better chance of selling than a book with just a boy character." On the other hand, "James Lorimer (and Company) has been in touch with me recently and wants to give me a contract for a book in their 'Time of Our Lives' series. They wanted a male, with no female, just a strong boy character, because the rest of the books in the series all have strong females."

Martyn's second "they" are the readers. "I have the advantage of teaching. I know what my students pick up and what they read and that's kind of helped along the way." Not only can Martyn observe his student's reading habits, but through them he can get some consumer reaction to his own work. "What I usually do as the book is being written is to make copies and hand them out to some of the kids who want to read it and ask for their feedback. Kids are very tough critics. Sometimes they're right on. They'll say something, and I won't believe them. I'll send it off to an editor, and she'll say exactly the same thing. I'll come back sheepishly and show them the letter and say, 'Well, you guys were right!'"

At least one school-related incident has provided Martyn with the inspiration for a book. "There was a little hill at the back of the school and a creek which by June is all dried up. The kids were borrowing garbage cans from the back lane and laying them side by side and building a ramp over them. Then they charged down the hill on their BMX's and jumped over them. One day at lunch time, the kids came in to me, and this one said, 'Hey! I'm a four-canner' (meaning that the bike had cleared four garbage cans). The person was a girl, and I figured there had to be a story about a girl, a kind of tomboy, who jumps over garbage cans. And I wondered, 'Could you have a contest about it where she enters and goes against all these guys?' A couple of weeks later, I was watching a beauty contest on TV, and the next day in school the kids were talking about it. I asked the grade sevens how they would feel if they were in such a contest, and they replied, 'There's none for girls 12 or 13!' Then it kind of clicked, and that's how I just started—a girl who jumps bicycles to get her into a beauty contest—a young miss contest. That was all I had."

From these few ideas came *Here She Is, Ms. Teeny-Wonderful*. In a world where "a four-canner is a pro, one of the gifted," Carol Weatherspoon and her friend Wally, another grade seven student in St. Albert, Alberta, "are the only kids in town who have jumped five and lived to tell the tale," and they share the goal of clearing six cans. Unknown to Carol, her mother has entered Carol's name in the Ms. Teeny-Wonderful contest. Selected as one of fifty finalists, Carol must compete in Toronto for the crown. Tempted by the prize money which would allow her to buy a Honda 250 trail bike, Carol reluctantly agrees to participate in the three day event and even gets to take Wally along as her male escort. For tough, bike-jumping Carol, the beauty contest becomes quite an adventure, especially when she meets "one" of the contestants, the fiercely competitive Campbell twins.

"I wrote *Teeny-Wonderful* in three weeks, and Scholastic wanted only five pages of revisions. Writing the book, while not a joy because it's still hard work, was an awful lot of fun. It was no problem. Five pages a night, and three weeks later there's the whole book written!"

A pleasant spin off from writing the book was Martyn's winning the Vicky Metcalf Short Story Award given by the Canadian Authors Association to the best children's short story first published in a Canadian periodical or anthology. "I sold the manuscript of *Teeny-Wonderful* to Scholastic, and then they got back to me and said, 'Hey! We're doing the March *Crackers* magazine and it's going to have a BMX theme. What we would like to do is take the first four chapters of *Teeny-Wonderful* and present them as a short story.' There's a couple of things they edited out just to tighten it up, and they also wrote a concluding paragraph to have it sort of make sense. It's kind of funny because it came out in the magazine, and I forgot all about it. It's a nice surprise

to win an award for a short story when you write juvenile novels."

Martyn does very little advance plotting of his stories. "I just take a basic idea, get a character and just start writing wherever it feels good to start writing and see if it takes off. A lot of the time it doesn't. I've got a lot of chapters lying around in my desk drawer and the first twenty pages of such and such a book. I write very little in terms of hours, perhaps at the most, three hours a week. But I'm fairly prolific in the number of pages I can turn out. I usually do about five pages, or about 1500 words, in an hour, and so even at three to four hours a week, I can get a manuscript done within a couple of months. As I said, they're not all good, and I still have three complete manuscripts that haven't sold, two that have been rejected a number of times."

While *Ms. Teeny-Wonderful* took just three weeks to write, three years elapsed from the time Martyn started *Alien Wargames* until it appeared in print. During that period, the work went through nearly four major rewrites. Martyn read a short story about a human who had enlisted in an alien army and then ended up fighting his own species. "I figured why not see if I could do that for kids, and so it's a borrowed idea." When Scholastic asked for numerous changes to Martyn's first draft, "the quantity of revisions was so overwhelming that I just wrote a complete new book with the same title." Scholastic liked the second book, but still preferred Martyn's initial submission and said, "Go back and do the revisions that we asked for."

In *Alien Wargames,* humans have established colonies on the planet Jancan but view the indigenous race, the Diljug, as inferior and unworthy of consultation as the Terrans exploit Jancan's resources. "I had an awful problem trying not to make the book have too much of a message with Native Canada; I was living up north on a reserve when the book was written and was very conscious of the connection and tried to change it as much as possible to make it more of a broad, imperialistic experience. I've had comments from teachers saying, 'I use *Alien Wargames* in my social studies class because it has such a strong parallel to how we treated Canadian natives.'"

Through the numerous rewrites, *Alien Wargames* underwent many modifications, but Martyn is still not totally satisfied with the final product. "After the third manuscript, I asked Scholastic to forget it because I just wasn't pleased with it." However, at his editor's urging, Martyn did finish the book. "I'm not pleased with the ending. It's quite funny the attitudes you get towards your books. When it was finally released, I was kind of dreading the reviews because I felt there were a lot of weak points in that book. It's not my favorite by any means."

In 1983, seeing a notice in the Canscaip newsletter saying that Collier Macmillan was looking for authors for Series Canada, Martyn sent a letter of inquiry to editor

Sandra Gulland. While she was not receptive to his suggestion for a SF story, she asked if he would be interested in doing "kind of a horror story." The result was *The Beast* in which a grade eleven girl in the Northwest Territories has an encounter with a Sasquatch-type creature.

Again Martyn found himself having to respond to the question of "what do they want," but this time the publisher was quite specific. "It has got to be 10,000 words, and there's got to be ten chapters. Each chapter has to have a cliff hanger ending to make readers turn the page. For *The Beast,* they said, 'We want a girl character because we don't have any girls in the other three books that are coming out this year. But we want a male character at the back.' Series Canada is exactly the opposite of Scholastic. Most of the people who read and buy these books are boys. They are designed for junior high, usually special ed. or reluctant readers, and unfortunately most of the people who fit that are boys. Series Canada sent me a word list which they use. Basically they just say don't use any three syllable words unless they fit the list such as 'yesterday.' It's always noun-verb sentences with very few complex sentences. They do all the readability themselves."

"*The Beast* was originally set in northern Alberta; however, Collier Macmillan said, 'We have a book in Alberta in our series, but we have none in the Northwest Territories, and so we're going to change it.'"

When Series Canada found itself short a title for its 1984 publication schedule, they asked Martyn to do another book. Martyn agreed and wrote *Spin Out* in which sixteen-year-old Marc Boswell finds himself assisting an R.C.M.P. officer recapture an escaped convict. The plot is based on a true story; "somebody actually did escape from the Fort Saskatchewan Institute, stop a police cruiser along the highway, overpower the constable, steal his gun and then take a woman hostage."

"After that, it was kind of a long term contract. They said, 'Will you do two a year for us from now until we stop doing the series?'" For 1985, Martyn has written *Fire! Fire!* in which a boy and girl get caught in a forest fire and *Ice Hawk* which features "a boy in his middle teens who is playing Junior B Hockey and who realizes that the position he has is because he is a brawler. He's achieving success, but he's doing it in a way that doesn't exactly make him feel good. Finally he gets a chance to play Junior A, but he gets called up on the condition that he does the same thing he's been doing—take a few heads off and be the policeman of the team."

Martyn's relationship with Collier Macmillan is being continued in another way. "They're doing a new series coming out in March '86 called 'Series 2000.' Four titles a year again. They've told me to write for Series Canada graduates. Again for people in junior high or early high school, but somebody who can handle a grade 5-6 reading level instead of 3.5-4. Word length is increased to 15,000 from 10,000, but it's pretty well the same format though fewer illustrations.

"They're trying to create a new market because they figure nobody's doing it right now for that reluctant reader in grade 10. I've done a manuscript for them which has sold. It's about kids surviving at the end of a nuclear war."

In characterizing his own writing, Martyn says, "There's not a heck of a lot of description. There's a lot of dialogue, a lot of things happening, and I consciously try to write that way. In fact, the criticism that I get, not only from editors, but also from reviewers, is that it's too bare boned, there's not enough meat on it, and the characters come out very cardboard. I figure I'm competing with going outside and playing or with whatever is on the videos. I enjoy talking to kids, and I think I very much write with the kids in mind."

"If I could be a full time writer, I think I would do it. I don't think there's enough for me in it at the present time to support a wife and two children and so that's the big drawback. The problem I have now is that I don't have enough time to write, and I'm getting frustrated because the things that I do have to write are the things I've got contracts for. With the Series Canada books, I'm writing a formula story that is very definitely controlled. You've got to do it in a certain way and it's very much of a job. I don't think any of the things I've written will be around for a long time. When they go out of print, that's it. Nobody will miss them; they are consumable. I figure if I ever make a name or go anywhere, it'll be in the contemporary humorous field. I would love to say, 'Yeah! Let's quit teaching,' and I could then stay home and do my five hours of writing."

GENERAL COMMENTARY

Christine Dewar

SOURCE: A review of *Spin Out* and *The Beast,* in *Emergency Librarian,* Vol. 13, No. 2, November-December, 1985, p. 44.

Martyn Godfrey, author of *The Vandarian Incident* and *Alien War Games,* . . . scores 50/50 with his debut in this series. *Spin Out* is an exciting cops and robbers adventure set in Alberta. Marc, the narrator, is out for a spin in his rebuilt Chevy, which he hopes will win him a few drag races, when the flashing lights of a Mounted Police car present him with a wounded Mountie rather than the expected speeding ticket. As he is driving the police officer to a hospital, he is stopped by the escaped convict responsible for the assault on the officer and is taken hostage. Marc's knowledge of the roads and his driving skill help him to prevent Eldon Doyle's escape and Marc's probable death. Coincidence powers the plot but Marc's feelings and behavior are reasonable, lending the story credibility.

Credibility can't be ascribed to this author's other title, *The Beast,* which is an outdoor adventure about two teens who escape from a legendary bogeyman. The latter story doesn't stretch belief, but it shatters all links with reason because it doesn't supply the atmosphere that would make the incredible believable. Skip this title if you have any respect for your children's intelligence.

Nancy Black

SOURCE: "New Hi-Lo Titles: Formula Writing at Its Best," in *Quill and Quire,* Vol. 52, No. 2, February, 1986, p. 21.

[*Fire! Fire!* and *Ice Hawk*] are good examples of formula writing at its best; they offer a consistently good blend of action, excitement, and information without being too stiff, dry, or pedantic. Simply written, *Fire! Fire!* [and] *Ice Hawk,* . . . present a variety of settings and situations calculated to appeal to reluctant readers. The titles are similar in that the action is fast-paced, moving quickly from conflict to climax to a satisfying resolution. And while there's little character development, personalities are vividly revealed through the action, dialogue, and first-person narrative.

Fire! Fire!, set in British Columbia, is about a native fire-fighting team, and focuses on a conflict between the crew boss, Good Boy, and a young woman, Deea. It is serious, capturing the tension of people working in a dangerous situation. And it also nicely avoids the usual female stereotypes.

In *Ice Hawk,* a young man must decide how he will play hockey: the dirty way, as a "goon", or the fair way. With the support of his friends and the insight offered by a newspaperman, Kevin is able to make a mature decision. *Ice Hawk* moralizes somewhat, but the tone does not interfere too greatly with the story.

Christine Dewar

SOURCE: A review of *Fire! Fire!* and *Ice Hawk,* in *Emergency Librarian,* Vol. 14, No. 1, September-October, 1986, p. 51.

[*Fire! Fire!* and *Ice Hawk*] are well-written, credible and appropriately illustrated. In *Fire! Fire!,* Deea describes her experiences as a new forest fire fighter. Her willingness to work hard and as long as is necessary has earned her the grudging respect of the older men on her crew but Good Boy, her nineteen year old crew boss, resents her presence. He believes that, "This stuff you see on TV about girls doing what men do is trash. Maybe it'll work for city folk and it may be O.K. in an

office, but it doesn't work in the bush." Good Boy's unwillingness to adhere to safety instruction traps both of them in a raging inferno but their combined brains, effort and luck saves them from a sure death. The fire fighting sequences are vivid and the conflict between Deea and Good Boy believable.

Ice Hawk is more of a character study than a story but the problem and the narrator are credible. Kevin Hawkins is offered a trial with the Cougars, the Junior A team to play in Edmonton if one aspires to a professional hockey career. But when it becomes clear that the Cougars want Ice Hawk only for his size and ability to intimidate opposing players, Hawk has to choose between becoming a goon or playing good hockey.

Brenda M. Schmidt

SOURCE: "Bikes and Barrels, Baseball and Bats," in *Canadian Children's Literature,* No. 56, 1989, pp. 78-80.

Some years ago I worked in a library where the novels were clearly labelled "Girls" or "Boys," according to the gender of the main character. Probably this was a common practice at the time, but fortunately today such sexist designations are discouraged. Faced with books like *It Isn't Easy Being Ms. Teeny-Wonderful* and *Baseball Crazy,* librarians would be hard-pushed to decide whether these books should be marked "Girls" or "Boys," because Martyn Godfrey has so skillfully balanced the role of the protagonist between the male and female characters.

It Isn't Easy Being Ms. Teeny-Wonderful is the sequel to *Here She Is, Ms. Teeny-Wonderful,* in which Carol Weatherspoon won second place in a teen pageant, impressing the judges with her prowess in clearing six barrels on her BMX bike. Now Carol has been asked by the popular magazine, *Canada Woman,* to teach a prospective sponsor's son to jump his BMX bike over an equal number of barrels. Throughout the story, Carol's friend Wally Stutzgummer plays a very supportive role. He comes up with ideas, gives advice, and by his good-natured bantering and joke-making shows a maturity which Carol has yet to achieve.

Carol's commission to teach young E. Z. Putton proves to be a real challenge which culminates in a life-threatening situation for them both. Again, it is Wally who arrives on the scene in time to get help and supports Carol in the spate of publicity that ensues.

There is a similar boy/girl relationship in *Baseball Crazy,* between Brent Hutchins and his friend, Cheryl Robinson. Cheryl's brother has won a contest to become Special Batboy to the Toronto Blue Jays Baseball Team; he is accompanied to the Florida Spring training camp by Cheryl and her father. Although the story is told by Brent, Cheryl's bright personality shares the spotlight and plays an integral role in their adventures. Like Carol and Wally in *It Isn't Easy Being Ms. Teeny-Wonderful,* Brent and Cheryl tease each other, turn to each other for help with their problems and face danger together, but they are not sentimental nor are there any overt romantic overtones.

Both stories, however, go beyond winning contests and superficial fun. They deal with growing up and the mixed emotions of adolescence. Carol discovers the "real" world of business deals and relentless publicity. She learns how people can be used by others to promote their own success, and that having wealth does not necessarily make families happy. Brent, on his part, finds dishonest people even in what appears to be paradise and learns that trust can sometimes be misplaced. He has to learn to take his initiation into the Blue Jays' organization with good grace and humour and to sort out his relationship with Clyde, the ballboy, especially when it is complicated by jealousy and misunderstanding.

Both protagonists are faced with taking responsibility when they find themselves in dangerous situations, Carol in saving the life of the headstrong E. Z. Junior, and Brent in preventing the theft of team members' equipment.

Martyn Godfrey brings to his writing a freshness and authenticity derived from his research at the Blue Jays Spring training camp in Dunedin, Florida. He is able to describe details of the area, the grounds, the facilities and the players which satisfy the curiosity of young readers who want facts combined with their fantasies. The practical jokes played on Brent in the story are typical of the good-natured camaraderie between the players and their batboys. Godfrey's knowledge about BMX bikes stems, in part at least, from his experiences while teaching in Alberta. The children with whom he worked were BMX bikers and both *Here She Is, Ms. Teeny-Wonderful* and this sequel fill a need for stories related to their interests.

These books are highly entertaining for boys and girls, grades 4-7. They will have a special appeal for young people who have difficulty sustaining their interest in novels with more traditional themes. The chapters are short and the stories move along at a good pace with humour and also suspense. If there is a weakness in these books it lies in their preoccupation with the contemporary. Living as we do in a time when fads and fashions are very transitory, stories like these become dated very quickly; but on the other hand, if they fill a present need there is justification for making good use of them and enjoying them now. They are also very detailed in their locale and while this may be an added attraction for the reader in Southern Ontario or Alberta, it should not lessen the enjoyment of a child elsewhere.

There is still a dearth of junior stories with sports themes which satisfy the readers' desire for vicarious fun and excitement. Martyn Godfrey's books should be, therefore, welcome additions to any collection.

Patricia Good

SOURCE: "Superheroes Saved by Humor," in *Canadian Children's Literature,* Vol. 21, No. 4, Winter, 1995, pp. 82-4.

It's bad guys beware as Wally in *Wally Stutzgummer, Super Bad Dude* and Boom Boom in *Just Call Me Boom Boom* surprise even themselves by becoming superheroes similar to the ones that they write or fantasize about. In these two books the plots share the same formulaic outline, with Wally and Boom Boom not really meaning to do wrong, but not always making the right decisions. Wally makes an unfortunate bet, using a dinner with his girlfriend, Carol, as the prize, never dreaming that he will lose, and he steals his brother's valuable comics twice, with the idea that he is only borrowing them. Similarly, Boom Boom breaks into a computer disk and trespasses into the deserted Wilson Mansion more out of curiosity than dishonest intent. Lurking in the background of each of these books are the thieves who switch valuable display items for ones of little value. This latter theme is one of the more obvious similarities between the two books. With a flurry of commotion and with true superhero pizzazz, Wally and Boom Boom help apprehend the crooks.

TITLE COMMENTARY

📖 *THE VANDARIAN INCIDENT* (1981)

Adele Ashby

SOURCE: A review of *The Vandarian Incident,* in *Quill and Quire,* Vol. 47, No. 6, June, 1981, pp. 33-4.

The Vandarian Confederation wants to prevent the signing of a treaty between the Galaxy Union and the Andromuse Empire. The first step is a fuzz ray attack on an academy in the middle of a lonely, desert planet. Two cadets, Tyler and Selbe, and an instructor, Faron, survive. They are all that stands between the Confederation and its goal.

Faron is injured, leaving the cadets on their own. The characters are as one-dimensional as their picture on the front cover, the plot does not bear looking into, but young sci-fi fans are unlikely to notice. *The Vandarian Incident* offers lots of action, strange beings and spectacular intergalactic battles. And for a change, it's the girl who first engineers the sabotage of the Vandarian battle cruiser and then their escape.

Raymond H. Thompson

SOURCE: "Danger in Space," in *Canadian Children's Literature,* No. 26, 1982, pp. 64-7.

According to its publishers Martyn Godfrey's *The Vandarian Incident* is aimed at readers in grades 5-8. It describes how two young space cadets thwart the plans of an aggressive race to wreck intergalactic peace talks. It is space adventure of a type that has remained popular since the early days of science fiction, and the fast-moving action and attention to detail help the reader to remain involved. Moreover, young people will readily identify with the narrative point of view, for the cadets must contend with adult scorn and condescension, not only because of their youth, but also because one of them is a human from Earth, a species new to the galactic scene and consequently of unproven capabilities. The cadets display both courage and initiative, yet one cannot but feel that their ultimate success depends too heavily upon luck. Moreover, the focus upon action results in the neglect of other aspects of the novel: the themes rarely rise above the general assertion that luck, courage, determination, and resourcefulness can defeat an enemy who allows his superiority to lead to overconfidence; and the lessons learned initiate too little in the way of character growth and self-discovery. This is regrettable since the potential for developing both character and theme is strong, thanks largely to the presence of the second cadet, a girl of another humanoid species endowed with clairvoyant talents. Nevertheless, this is an exciting, if rather contrived, adventure story with sufficient hints of greater possibilities to deserve a recommendation to all younger readers and to libraries. . . . This is a promising first novel by a young Canadian currently teaching in Alberta, and if he can manage to explore his subject in greater depth, his next novel will be worth looking for.

HERE SHE IS, MS. TEENY-WONDERFUL (1985)

Joan McGrath

SOURCE: A review of *Here She Is, Ms. Teeny-Wonderful*, in *Emergency Librarian*, Vol. 12, No. 5, May-June, 1985, p. 46.

Carol's ambition is to clear six garbage cans on her BMX bike; Carol's *mother's* ambition is for Carol to win the Ms. Teeny-Wonderful Contest, and has entered her as a contestant. Talk about a generation gap! Kids will find the whole complex situation well worth Carol's trip from Saint Albert to Toronto. Who knows whether she will hear the magic words, *Here She Is, Ms Teeny-Wonderful*?

Jane Yolleck

SOURCE: A review of *Here She Is, Ms. Teeny-Wonderful!*, in *Quill and Quire*, Vol. 51, No. 6, June, 1985, p. 22.

In *Here She Is, Ms. Teeny-Wonderful*, Martyn Godfrey departs from science fiction adventure and successfully turns his talents to humour. Tomboy Carol Weatherspoon's aim is to clear six garbage cans on her BMX bike. With her pal Wally, she's achieved five-barrel status, the best in St. Albert, Alberta. But comical, feather-brained Mrs. Weatherspoon has quite different expectations for her daughter and has entered her in a charm and talent contest sponsored by *Canada Woman* magazine. As one of 50 finalists, Carol flies to Toronto with Mum, escort Wally, and the dream of a new Honda 250 trail bike that the $5,000 prize money will bring. At the opening banquet, Carol runs afoul of the beautiful but treacherous Campbell twins. The ensuing pranks are loaded with humour, and the deadpan Wally is a wonderful straight man to feisty Carol. When Carol jumps six cans in the talent competition, she emerges triumphant as first runner-up, bumping the nasty Campbell twins into third place.

Marjorie Gann

SOURCE: "Amateur Writing in Adolescent Fiction," in *Canadian Children's Literature,* No. 43, 1986, pp. 97-9.

Aimed at preteen, rather than teenage, readers, [*Here She Is, Ms. Teeny-Wonderful*] turns upon a clever premise: Tomboy Carol Weatherspoon, a young bike-jumping enthusiast, is entered by her mother in the Ms. Teeny-Wonderful beauty-talent contest, sponsored by *Canada Woman* magazine. Plagued by the ultra-feminine (and ultra-malicious) Campbell twins, Carol succeeds in proving that her "masculine" talent is as admirable as more traditional ones, and in demonstrating gumption in the process.

Godfrey has obviously cashed in on a trendy issue: traditional vs. liberated female roles, but he does this with a light touch:

> "If they ask you what you want to be when you grow up, say a doctor or a social worker, a job that helps other people."

> "I want to be a cop."

Dialogue is natural, and Carol is a believable tomboy, not a device for convincing preteen girls to burn their Barbies.

Unlike Gunnery and McCloskey, Godfrey generates drama with fresh, precise language:

> It was an incredible feeling, being suspended in midair clinging to a metal bike with emptiness passing below. Only, of course, there wasn't emptiness. There were barrels. Six of them with *Canada Woman* painted on them.

> One.

> The first purple and gold barrel vanished beneath me.

Teeny-Wonderful's full potential for humour is unrealized. It never approaches the uninhibited zaniness of a Gordon Korman novel, or the Korman gift for caricature. Still, Godfrey's lightweight work offers an enjoyable few hours to the young reader.

📖 PLAN B IS TOTAL PANIC (1986)

Mary Ainslie Smith

SOURCE: A review of *Plan B Is Total Panic,* in *Books in Canada,* Vol. 15, No. 9, December, 1986, p. 16.

The main character in *Plan B Is Total Panic,* by Martyn Godfrey [battles] against his own timidity [in a] more critical situation. Nicholas, who lives in northern Alberta, has been invited by a native friend to participate in a moose hunt. Although Nicholas hates and fears the bush, he accepts in order to escape from the school bully who is planning to beat him to a pulp for dancing with his girlfriend.

In the course of the weekend, Nicholas treks through the bush, plunges into icy lakes, confronts a grizzly four times, and rescues the town doctor from the wreckage of his downed plane. No wonder by the end of the story he feels he can scrape up the courage to confront the bully. Godfrey's story is by no means complex—a straightforward adventure yarn if there ever was one—but it is fast-paced, entertaining reading.

Lyle Weis

SOURCE: "A Touching, but Unsentimental Story," in *Canadian Children's Literature,* No. 45, 1987, pp. 72-3.

"I guess I got attacked by a grizzly bear because Sandra Travis is one terrific dancer." With this opening sentence, Martyn Godfrey draws his reader into a world where the narrator, Nicholas Clark, discovers adventure and important insights about himself.

Godfrey's strength as a writer for juveniles lies in his ability to blend serious issues with an action-oriented plot, something he accomplishes by placing ordinary kids in demanding or unusual circumstances. Nicholas and his divorced father, an oil worker, have moved around often, coming at last to live in High Level, Alberta. Nicholas hates the insecurity of his life, and has come to translate this feeling into a dislike of himself. He is a thin weakling, he says, and ugly too:

> My nose covers half my face, which wouldn't be so bad if it wasn't painted with freckles. My hair is the colour of a rotting log, and it sticks out like the fur on those bushy guinea pigs.

Worse than his physical shortcomings, however, is an inner failing: he is, in his own words, "a wimp" who will gladly go out of his way to avoid a fight or any other kind of trouble. He seems to be an unlikely hero.

Nicholas is an outsider, but his need to love and be loved by others soon draws him into the very realm of social conflict he wishes to avoid. In the opening scene of the novel, Nicholas secretly yearns to dance with Sandra Travis, but fears her popular and powerful boyfriend. When she finally invites Nicholas onto the floor, he accepts, only to have his fears realized as the boyfriend punches him in the nose. The message Godfrey subtly works into the dance episode is that caring for others often involves risk and, sometimes, pain.

The role of the outsider is important in this novel, and defines two other central characters. Doctor Raghbir, Nicholas's confidant and surrogate father, came from India to High Level under a typical immigration agreement:

> Part of the deal of moving to Canada was that he had to spend six months working in the boons. When his half year was up, we expected him to head for the city. But he didn't. Just that fact made him one of the most popular people around.

The doctor's commitment to the community extends specifically to Nicholas, perhaps because, as an immigrant, he understands the challenge the boy faces. Another minority figure in the novel is Elvis, a Dene boy who befriends Nicholas with an invitation to visit his native settlement. Godfrey gives a touching but unsentimental rendering to the evolving friendship between these two boys; the author uses humor to advantage, especially in scenes such as the one where Nicholas learns from Elvis's grandmother the delicacies of cleaning a duck for supper.

By the time I had read to the part where Nicholas must fight off a bear in order to rescue his friend the doctor, I did not care that the plot converged on coincidence: I liked Nicholas and cheered him on during his supreme test of character. Godfrey's latest book is, I think, his best yet.

📖 FIRE! FIRE! (1986)

Stephanie Zvirin

SOURCE: A review of *Fire! Fire!* in *Booklist,* Vol. 83, No. 11, February 1, 1987, pp. 839-40.

Though she has proved herself to her fellow firefighters, 17-year-old Deea cannot convince her crew boss, Good Boy, that she is capable and hardworking. In fact, to catch her out and prove her incompetent he takes a dangerous chance, putting them both into a situation that, were it not for Deea's quick thinking, would have meant death for both of them. Godfrey conveys the excitement and danger of being trapped in the center of a raging blaze and the frenzy of Deea and Good Boy's frantic efforts to save themselves from being burned alive. With black-and-white drawings to break up the text and extra leading plus larger-than-standard typeface to increase readability, this should be a popular item among reluctant readers as well as teenagers with reading difficulties.

Thomas G. Gunning

SOURCE: A review of *Fire! Fire!* in *Journal of Reading,* Vol. 31, No. 3, December, 1987, p. 295

When Good Boy, the boss of Deea's fire crew, fails to use good judgment, he and Deea are trapped by a blazing fire. Fighting their way to a nearby creek, the two discover that the creek has dried up. Good Boy panics, but Deea suggests that they bury themselves. The plan works and Good Boy learns to respect the strength and courage of female fire fighters.

Fire! Fire! is smoothly written and packed with action. The book is also self-motivating. The reader just has to keep on turning those pages to find out how the two escape the fire.

ICE HAWK (1986)

Hazel Rochman

SOURCE: A review of *Ice Hawk,* in *Booklist,* Vol. 83, No. 11, February 1, 1987, p. 840.

High school ice hockey star Kevin "Hawk" Hawkins gets a chance to play in the minor leagues and maybe even become a professional, but he worries when league officials want him to act "policeman" and play rough. When the coach tells him to hurt an opponent, he refuses. Several action-packed game sequences are interspersed with sports lingo and Hawk's talk to his friend about turning into a "goon." The bright cover (showing hockey gear), large clear type, and many black-and-white illustrations will attract readers to this series high/low title originally published in Canada.

Thomas G. Gunning

SOURCE: A review of *Ice Hawk,* in *Journal of Reading,* Vol. 31, No. 3, December, 1987, p. 295

Hawk plays a rough brand of ice hockey. Angered when his friend is decked by Sloan, Hawk smashes into Sloan, who ends up in the hospital with a serious head injury. On the basis of his rough-and-tumble style, Ice Hawk, who is still in high school, is offered a position on a minor league professional hockey team. Hawk discovers that what the pro team really wants is an enforcer who will intimidate opposing teams. Upset by the injury to Sloan, Hawk refuses to be a goon even though it means he is giving up a sure ticket to a place in pro hockey.

Ice Hawk has lots of suspense and action. Although hockey fans will bring more to the book, its moral dilemmas and universal themes will also appeal to students who have no knowledge of or interest in hockey.

IT ISN'T EASY BEING MS. TEENY-WONDERFUL (1987)

Patty Lawlor

SOURCE: A review of *It Isn't Easy Being Ms. Teeny-Wonderful,* in *Books for Young People,* Vol. 1, No. 2, April, 1987, p. 8.

[*It Isn't Easy Being Ms. Teeny Wonderful*] builds on the momentum of Carol's first runner-up placing in the Ms. Teeny-Wonderful contest, a competition dedicated to discovering the most charming and talented 10 to 13-year-old girls in Canada.

The focus of the plot is once again on Carol's skill at barrel-jumping on a BMX bike. The premise—that a business tycoon will only sign a cosmetic promotion deal with *Canada Woman* magazine, the sponsor of the Ms. Teeny-Wonderful contest, if 12-year-old Carol comes to St. Catharines to coach his eight-year-old son—requires a six-barrel leap of imagination itself. But the resulting sequence of events leads Carol to new levels of celebrity and self-awareness.

It is unfortunate that Godfrey has persisted in this second work with the portrayal of Carol's mother as a bubblehead (indeed, parents seem to be taking a beating in much of recent children's literature). Carol does a lot of wisecracking, but much of what is intended to pass for clever quipping is uncomfortably self-centred and shallow in inspiration. These weaknesses in Godfrey's writing are offset by his ability to create original plots in general and, in *It Isn't Easy,* the uniqueness of the relationship shared by Carol and Wally.

It Isn't Easy will move quickly on library shelves. The BMX bike scene depicted on the cover will attract readers—particularly those who are already fans of Claire Mackay's *Mini-Bike* series.

Pauline Henaut

SOURCE: A review of *It Isn't Easy Being Ms. Teeny-Wonderful,* in *CM: A Reviewing Journal of Canadian Materials for Young People,* Vol. XVI, No. 1, January, 1988, p. 15.

Readers in upper elementary and junior grades who enjoyed *Here She Is, Ms. Teeny-Wonderful* will like this second book in the series. They will again find a humorous, exciting plot and funny, realistic characters who speak in an idiom they can appreciate.

Carol Weatherspoon, runner-up in the Ms. Teeny-Wonderful contest, is called upon to act as honorary Ms. Teeny-Wonderful. The magazine that sponsored the pageant hopes to secure an advertising account with the top cosmetics company in the world. Their success in closing the deal seems to be dependent on Carol's ability to teach the president's eight-year-old son to jump his BMX over barrels.

Carol's assignment is complicated by the fact that E. Z. Putton, Jr., is a spoiled, stubborn risk-taker. Her best friend Wally, who accompanies her on the trip, adds to her difficulties by beginning to display an interest in other girls. In addition, Carol is bothered by her own changing outlook and feelings. After a suspenseful incident in which E. Z., Jr., attempts a hazardous jump over a canyon, Carol and Wally find themselves heroes and more than friends.

Both boys and girls will enjoy this novel.

BASEBALL CRAZY (1987)

Adele Ashby

SOURCE: A review of *Baseball Crazy,* in *Books for Young People,* Vol. 2, No. 1, February, 1988, p. 5.

Fourteen-year-old Brent Hutchins is a baseball junkie, hooked on his home team, the Toronto Blue Jays. When the club has a contest to choose a special batboy to be taken along to Florida for spring training, Brent is determined to write the winning entry. His friend Cheryl disparages his poetic efforts, but he does win, and the two of them are sent south with Cheryl's dad as chaperon. There, when some valued equipment disappears, Brent, Cheryl, and Clyde the ballboy team up to solve the mystery. Later on, Brent has the dream of a lifetime come true when, in an inter-squad team game, he is asked to pitch for the team and strikes out George Bell.

Baseball Crazy will have wide appeal: it's a sports book, a mystery, and it even has a touch of romance (though not so much as to put off the boys who aren't girl-crazy). It's a snappy read, with up-to-the-minute references to all the current players plus the likes of Madonna. It will date quickly, so buy it now. Even this non-sports-minded adult enjoyed it very much.

Floyd Spracklin

SOURCE: A review of *Baseball Crazy,* in *CM: A Reviewing Journal of Canadian Materials for Young People,* Vol. XVI, No. 4, July, 1988, p. 127.

Remember *Here She Is, Ms. Teeny-Wonderful* and *Plan B Is Total Panic*? Well, here's another great book from Martyn Godfrey! Just imagine a young boy who's crazy about baseball and a girl who's equally crazy about that boy. Put the two together and you have the ingredients of a fast-moving story for young readers. Martyn God-

frey uses the eagerness and shyness of his main character, Brent Hutchins, to present both a mystery and challenge to his readers.

Brent wins a contest to become Special Batboy for the Toronto Blue Jays baseball organization for two weeks during spring training in Dunedin, Florida. Brent nearly panics when he cannot find the necessary chaperon for the trip. However, Cheryl's father agrees to go, to the delight of both Brent and Cheryl since she's included!

Brent begins to wonder if everything is as it's supposed to be when Blue Jay members play some crazy practical jokes on him. And then the trouble commences. Someone is stealing baseball gloves from the players' locker room and then selling them. Brent thinks he has the culprit "dead-to-rights" and then, together with Cheryl, becomes involved in a deep mystery that could spell trouble!

WILD NIGHT (1987)

Maryleah Otto

SOURCE: A review of *Wild Night,* in *CM: A Reviewing Journal of Canadian Materials for Young People,* Vol. XVI, No. 2, March, 1988, p. 44.

There are almost two dozen titles in "Series Canada," a group of high-interest, low-vocabulary melodramas for adolescent non-readers. In this one, Tony, a sixteen-year-old boy who works the night shift in a convenience store, is held up by "a punk" who seems to have a gun under his coat. Tony already has his hands full because a suicidal teenage girl has phoned the store by chance, begging for help from anyone. Then a pregnant young woman in advanced labour comes in, and Tony, with the verbal assistance of an arthritic old crone who was once a nurse, finds himself delivering a baby. Meanwhile, there's a scuffle between the punk and the store owner, who trips and injures his head in a fall. Since the phone has gone dead, Tony persuades the punk to drive the store owner and the new mother to the hospital, but not before the eccentric old nurse has made a valiant attempt to get the punk to seek help for his drug addiction. He makes the trip to the hospital all right, but once that's over, he takes off with the store owner's car.

Too much? Well, that's a lot of yarn to spin into ninety pages of large type and plenty of pictures, but the intended audience will probably love it. Godfrey's style is perfect for the purpose: bare bones plot, violent action, abundant dialogue in contemporary street language without the usual obscenities. Greg Ruhl's black-and-white illustrations are really excellent, easily conveying as much of the story-line as the text does. The full-colour cover is boldly inviting.

Teachers of language arts will find good use for this type of material in motivating reluctant readers in grades 6 and up. I have a reservation, however, about the topics and language used in hi-lo books. Although the readers of these stories will easily identify with them, they are in a way putting down these young people by presenting role models with a low socio-economic background. It's as if the formula for this material were— "Yes, this is literary junk food, but these kids don't want anything else anyway." Well, maybe junk food is better than starvation, but there's still a segregational element that disturbs me.

Sue Tait and Christy Tyson

SOURCE: A review of *Wild Night*, in *Emergency Librarian*, Vol. 15, No. 4, March-April, 1988, p. 55.

Martyn Godfrey strikes again with even greater success in **Wild Night,** an incredible thrill-a-minute yarn about a young convenience store clerk on the graveyard shift. It starts calmly enough. Before he leaves for the night, Mr. Mack, the boss, tells Tony the phone is acting up; calls can come in but you can't dial out. Still, a minor inconvenience until a young girl calls in after having taken a bottle of Seconal, a punk attempts holding the place up at gunpoint, and Mrs. Cole, a regular whose husband is out of town, comes for help in the final stages of labor. Fortunately, Mrs. Edna Horton, a retired nurse, has stopped by for a chat. She may look like she's been around since Rome, but no victim she. Before you know it she's firing orders right and left, pausing only to correct the manners of the potential thief. Soon the punk is coaching the would-be suicide and Tony assisting at his first delivery. Just when all would seem to be under control, Mr. Mack stops by and the punk's change of heart proves to be only temporary. Heart-stopping suspense is counterpointed with running comments on the rotten-fruit overtones of Tony's after-shave and with Tony's wry narration itself. Tony is someone readers will be glad they met, and when he invites them to drop by the 7-Eleven some Friday or Saturday night to hear about the time the girl's volleyball team bus had to stop because of a storm—or when the slush machine leaked— or about the drunk who put the pop can in the microwave—they'll be sure to want to take him up on his offer.

REBEL YELL (1987)

Janice Foster

SOURCE: A review of *Rebel Yell*, in *CM: A Reviewing Journal of Canadian Materials for Young People*, Vol. XVI, No. 2, March, 1988, p. 44.

Martyn Godfrey has written numerous books, several of which are included in "Series Canada." These books are intended to generate high interest for adolescent readers with a lower reading level. . . .

In **Rebel Yell,** Dwayne, better known as SC (short for Space Cadet), starts the new school term plagued by problems. Taking SC out of the Educational Opportunity

Class program proves to be the vice-principal's method of forcing SC to either behave or face expulsion. On top of this his girl-friend rejects him and he is informed that the leader of the Hell Cats gang is looking for him. Unable to cope, he heads for the local hang-out. There he's told that Willy Boy has just entered the school with a sawed-off shotgun. Earlier that morning SC had run into Willy Boy, who had rambled on about paying people back. The story continues with SC's being knifed by the Hell Cats and, despite a bad wound, preventing Willy Boy from carrying out his threat.

The subject matter of this novel would appeal to some adolescent readers. The need for the violence in the book is questionable. It's a fact that gangs, knifings and even shootings are present in the school system. However, these issues are presented in **Rebel Yell** only from the viewpoint of one person. The fact that this person is referred to as a space cadet and has been threatened with expulsion weakens the validity of his account of these major crises. His heroics seem television-based and make the plot too contrived and unrealistic in its presentation. Authority, be it that of the school administration or the police, seems to be undermined. SC is the only character to be developed fully, possibly due to the fast pace and the brevity of the book. The text is in large print and is easy to read, with a great deal of dialogue. It's unfortunate that in order to provide high-interest, low-reading-level material, good literary techniques and language are sacrificed. In conclusion, because of the possible appeal of the subject matter and the easy-to-read format, **Rebel Yell** would be conditionally recommended for a teacher-guided novel study.

Sue Tait and Christy Tyson

SOURCE: A review of *Rebel Yell*, in *Emergency Librarian*, Vol. 15, No. 4, March-April, 1988, p. 55.

Martyn Godfrey's **Rebel Yell** offers even tighter suspense in the story of SC, a ninth grade boy classified as "Space Cadet" by his friends and a troublemaker by the school administration. SC is sure he's doing fine, though, especially compared to Willy Boy whose glazed stare and threats toward the math teacher who flunked him give SC chills. Then he hears that Willy Boy has gone to school with a shotgun and no one seems to see the danger. No one will intervene. No one but SC. Despite the melodrama, SC is as spunky a misunderstood hero as can be found in young adult literature. The fact that he can't seem to speak without using double negatives is only a minor irritation.

MORE THAN WEIRD (1987)

Fran Newman

SOURCE: A review of *More Than Weird*, in *CM: A Reviewing Journal of Canadian Materials for Young People*, Vol. XVI, No. 4, July, 1988, p. 127.

This is another in the "Series 2000" for graduates of the "Series Canada" group of high interest/low vocabulary novels that my students have enjoyed for a long time. Although the older, larger books self-destructed after a few readings, these smaller novels seem to be made of sturdier stuff.

Martyn Godfrey has written for this series before, but I had only read *The Vandarian Incident,* which I liked as much as the children did.

More than Weird opens with Cory Johnson and his buddy Chuck sitting in the high school cafeteria in Dawson Creek. They notice a very beautiful girl, dressed in jeans and a halter top on a frigid day, approaching from outside. She enters, ignores the rest of the kids, including handsome, popular Chuck (in fact she lifts him out of her way) and focuses her attention on Cory, saying she wants him. They go out to Cory's beat-up Datsun, and on a ride to a secluded spot (for purposes of further conversation, but Cory is expecting more) she tells him that he has been chosen, because he is so average, to be taken to the future. The girl, Susie, is from 550 years beyond and is a robot. Gradually Cory becomes convinced of this, and he tries to run away from her. The rest of the very short and easily read story tells of his attempts and final victory.

There isn't time to develop much in the way of the character of the protagonist. Godfrey, however, knows what the students want, and the action is fast paced. I recommend this novel very highly.

SEND IN MS. TEENY-WONDERFUL (1988)

Patricia Fry

SOURCE: A review of *Send in Ms. Teeny-Wonderful,* in *CM: A Reviewing Journal of Canadian Materials for Young People,* Vol. XVII, No. 2, March, 1989, pp. 70-1.

This is the third book in the "Ms. Teeny-Wonderful" series and, as you might expect, all the familiar characters are back having another adventure. This time, the action takes place in Ottawa, where Carol Weatherspoon (Ms. T. W.) and her official "escort" and long-time good friend Wally Stutzgummer are representing *Canada Woman* magazine at a BMX conference. Of course, Carol's rivals for the title—the hated Campbell twins— are back as well and are up to their usual petty pranks designed to annoy the heroine.

Just to liven up the plot, there are two new characters— one very macho and obnoxious BMX champion who dislikes Carol on principle (the "girls cannot ride bikes" type) and a real Middle Eastern prince who instantly falls in love with Carol and presses her for a long-term engagement until she's old enough to become one of his wives (apparently the custom in his country!).

Carol is not your typical beauty contest winner, but then this contest with its "Ms." title isn't too typical, either. This reviewer would have felt more comfortable if the author had found a vehicle for Carol other than the in-fighting world of the beauty contest (witness the stereotyped jealousy of the Campbell twins). That's why I was rather relieved to read that Carol had crowned another thirteen-year-old to take her place as Ms. Teeny-Wonderful. My relief was short-lived, however, as I read that another magazine was thinking of holding a Ms. Teeny-World contest for girls in junior high. Guess who is going to be entered as Ms Teeny-Canada? To quote Carol, "I'm not sure I'm ready for another beauty/talent/charm contest," but this book has enough strengths to warrant a place on your modern-series shelf.

MYSTERY IN THE FROZEN LANDS (1988)

Teresa Cowan

SOURCE: A review of *Mystery in the Frozen Lands,* in *Books for Young People,* Vol. 3, No. 2, April, 1989, p. 12.

Martyn Godfrey's novels have covered a wide range of topics, from sports stories to humour and on to science fiction, so it's none too surprising to see a work of historical fiction with his name on it.

Mystery in the Frozen Lands is based on the 1857 McClintock expedition to discover the fate of John Franklin and his crew in the Arctic. The story opens dramatically with the suicide of one of the 25 crew members; the rumoured cause being that he could no longer endure the bleak, cold Arctic surroundings. The reader's attention is instantly captured.

Although the text is in the form of a journal—written by the 14-year-old narrator, Peter Griffin—Godfrey so skilfully constructs conversations and events that the suffering and adventures of the crew are reborn on the page. There is certainly no sense that one is struggling through a dry, personal account. Images of the cold ("It crawled through the jagged edges of the ice") successfully set the mood.

The atmosphere, combined with the crew's and Peter's experiences, makes for an entertaining and enlightening read. This book would serve not only as a springboard for any study of the Arctic, but as an excellent introduction to journal writing.

Marion Scott

SOURCE: A review of *Mystery in the Frozen Lands,* in *CM: A Reviewing Journal of Canadian Materials for Young People,* Vol. XVII, No. 3, May, 1989, p. 123.

What happened to John Franklin's 1845 arctic expedition? This historical mystery is the subject of Martyn Godfrey's latest novel. Set twelve years after Franklin's disappearance, it relates the adventures of a search group sent out to find any information or trace of Franklin and his crew.

Godfrey is a popular and prolific writer for young people. (Among his better-known works are the "Ms. Teeny-Wonderful" series). Here, he is tackling a new genre, and he does so with assurance and authenticity. The story is told through the device of a diary, that of fourteen-year-old Peter Griffin, the ship's boy. (Peter is fictional but other characters and the mission itself are based in fact.) The style and language are appropriate to a boy of Peter's age and time. And it is accessible to the modern reader.

Particularly convincing is Godfrey's portrayal of the cold, bleakness and hardship endured by arctic explorers. A second theme is that of Peter's friendship with a young Inuit man. Their conversations successfully highlight the different world views of native and Englishman.

Godfrey does take some artistic license: for example, discoveries made by other expeditions are attributed to this one. These are noted in the book's foreword and by no means detract from its integrity. The conclusion is satisfying, with enough answers provided to meet the reader's curiosity. And it remains true to what is actually known and hypothesized about Franklin's fate.

The novel does have flaws. Peter is the only character with much development. There are also lapses where the documentary aspects overshadow character and story-line. Nevertheless, this is a good book for readers who enjoy adventure and survival fiction. It would also be a good choice to supplement class units on the Arctic. The paperback is of good quality, and this is the format most likely to appeal to the intended age group.

Sue Tait and Christy Tyson

SOURCE: A review of *Mystery in the Frozen Lands,* in *Emergency Librarian,* Vol. 16, No. 5, May-June, 1989, p. 53.

Discovering the real story is the theme in Martyn Godfrey's *Mystery in the Frozen Lands.* Here, the truth is veiled not by individual perceptions but by time—and by the cold. Peter is 14 and the nephew of explorer Sir John Franklin. In 1845, 12 years ago, Franklin led an expedition to the North Pole. Since then not a trace of the explorers has been found. All are presumed dead, but a search party is being mounted to discover what happened, and Peter has been chosen to serve as ship's boy. His journals describe the years he spends aboard the HMS Fox in which, despite months of darkness and frozen seas that entrap them, they draw closer to solving the mystery. It must have been starvation that led to the expedition's fate. That, plus scurvy, the ice, the cold, the dark—but none of that explains why so many more officers died than crew, or why starving men chose to leave the ship carrying silverware. The facts are all there

for Peter to interpret, but the time isn't right. An introductory note offers the most likely explanation, one based on scientific discoveries made later. Readers know what happened, but Peter is left with no final explanation. This adventure, based on fact, succeeds as a mystery and as a reminder that we are defined by the times in which we live. We may try to see beyond the frozen horizons of our own cultures but the view will always be limited by the circumstances of our lives.

Mary Ellen Binder

SOURCE: "An Arctic Adventure," in *Canadian Children's Literature,* No. 56, 1989, pp. 91-3.

A common complaint heard among intermediate and junior high-school students is that studying Canadian history is so boring! Contrary to this view, Martyn Godfrey's historical novel for teenagers, *Mystery in the Frozen Lands,* is a compelling page-turner from the first paragraph: "George Brand, our engineer, is dead. Four days ago he placed a musket under his chin and pulled the trigger." Set in the mid-nineteenth century, Godfrey's book provides the young reader with an exciting adventure story. . . .

Mystery in the Frozen Lands deals with Captain Francis McClintock's 1857-59 voyage in search of Sir John Franklin, who had disappeared mysteriously in 1847 while searching for the elusive Northwest Passage. Although Franklin had explored and mapped much of the Arctic coastline on two earlier voyages, it is his disappearance and death on the third voyage—leading to the dispatch of numerous search parties over the next twelve years—which have kept his memory alive. To this day, historians wonder why Franklin and all 128 crewmen perished in spite of their extensive Arctic experience and the presence of Inuit in the area. The recent exhumation of three of Franklin's sailors buried on Beechey Island and the discovery that their bodies had been extremely well-preserved by the Arctic permafrost have caused renewed interest in the subject. In addition the recent photographs of the sailor's bodies in such widely read magazines as *National Geographic* and *Macleans* have brought new publicity to Franklin's voyage and made the publication of Godfrey's novel a timely one.

On one level *Mystery in the Frozen Lands* is a tale of the adventures of a ship's boy Peter Griffin, his Inuit friend Anton, and their fellow crew members who were sent to the Arctic to discover the fate of Sir John Franklin. A second level of the story unfolds as, through entries in Peter's journal, we gradually learn why Franklin went to the Arctic twelve years earlier, when he disappeared, and where his men were last seen. Speculation by McClintock's men, information provided by Inuit hunters, and descriptions of difficulties encountered by McClintock's own crew introduce the reader to some possible explanations of Franklin's fate—treacherous ice conditions, scurvy, food poisoning, starvation, madness and suicide. A third story emerges: the romance between Peter and his cousin Elisabeth. Through this aspect of the book, we get a picture of the lifestyle, values and attitudes of mid-nineteenth century England. While this theme is not as well-developed as the other two, it does provide an interesting contrast to the hardships of the northern expedition. Finally, Godfrey gives us an all-too-brief glimpse of the Inuit lifestyle and philosophy, often in conflict with the European experience.

Because Godfrey's book is written as a journal, from the point of view of a fourteen-year-old boy, the story contains emotion, humanity and realism which might have been missing in a straight-forward factual account. Since the two main characters, Peter and Anton, are teenagers, young readers will find it easy to identify with their feelings of excitement, frustration, fear and relief as the search progresses. In the discussions between the two boys, the reader learns about both the British and the Inuit cultures of the time. Peter's journal vividly describes the harsh winter climate where the sun has vanished: "leaving just a feeble glow in the southern sky" and where the wind is constantly blowing around the frozen ship "trying to put its long, cold tentacles inside." We are provided with graphic descriptions of the sailors' day-to-day lives—their entertainment, their constant battle against lice and rats, and their cramped living quarters below deck where smelly fat lamps cover the walls with black grease and fill the air with a burnt-lard smell. Our sympathy is aroused for Peter, who as ship's boy, must scrub the crew's living quarters, serve the officers, wash clothes, make beds, help the cook, tidy the decks and still find time to spare for hunting, studying navigation and mapping and writing a journal! Small details such as these make history come alive as textbook accounts could never do.

While Godfrey does give some information about Inuit beliefs and lifestyle, he could have provided more details about the native culture. After all, one important factor in the success or failure of the various Arctic expeditions was the extent to which the explorers were willing to take on the ways of the Inuit among whom they travelled. The British in particular often refused to adopt native survival techniques, thus bringing unnecessary hardships upon themselves—this may have been the key factor in the Franklin disaster. Character development of the Europeans is also much more realistic than of the Inuit. While the conversation between the British crewman sounds true to life, the speech of Anton the Greenlandic Inuk does not always ring true. As far as I know, for example, Inuit do not habitually end their sentences with the negative.

Martyn Godfrey's novel offers enough mystery and suspense to keep the reader interested. However the end of the book is not really the end of the story, because I'm sure *Mystery in the Frozen Lands* will leave many young readers with the desire to learn more about Sir John Franklin and those who searched for him. This book would make an excellent introduction to the study of Arctic exploration and the search for a Northwest Pas-sage, which consumed the resources of so many nineteenth-century adventurers.

Carole Gerson

SOURCE: "True Stories," in *Canadian Literature*, No. 127, Winter, 1990, pp. 124-26.

Martyn Godfrey's *Mystery in the Frozen Lands,* . . . takes its subject directly from the real world, in this case the disappearance of Sir John Franklin's Arctic expedition of 1845. The book's documentary quality is enhanced with maps, a prefatory "Author's Note" explaining Godfrey's use of historical materials, and its narrative format. To engage the young reader, Godfrey created the character of fourteen-year-old Peter Griffin, Franklin's fictional nephew who serves as cabin boy to the 1857-59 rescue mission aboard the *Fox* and is ordered to record its progress in his journal. Proof of the success of the diary format is my son's comment that, while reading the book, he pretended he was Peter and did everything Peter did; such utter suspension of disbelief must be the highest compliment an author can receive.

Typical of the way juvenile adventure fiction empowers youngsters is Godfrey's attribution of the *Fox* expedition's key discoveries to Peter. Yet while Peter unearths some evidence explaining the failure of Franklin's mission, the major question—the inexplicable behaviour of a handpicked crew—must rest unanswered. The Franklin expedition remains one of the puzzles in Canadian history, which Godfrey has chosen not to resolve—a wise move from the historian's perspective, but a disappointment to the juvenile reader's expectation that mysteries conclude tidily. As if to compensate for this gap in his plot, Godfrey develops a close friendship between Peter and the other young member of the crew, an Inuit from Greenland, who teaches the young Britisher to survive in the North and questions many of his cultural practices and assumptions regarding such matters as relations between the sexes and exploitation of the environment.

WHY JUST ME? (1989)

Joan McGrath

SOURCE: A review of *Why Just Me?*, in *Quill and Quire*, Vol. 55, No. 11, November, 1989, p. 14.

The idea behind the creation of *Why Just Me?* is somewhat startling. A male author has elected, with considerable success, to write a first-person account of a grade-7 girl who is at first apprehensive of, but later comes to terms with, the rapidly approaching onset of "The Big P": puberty.

Shannon MacKenzie, whose personal notebook we read, as it were, over her shoulder, lives in Edmonton and will be 13 on January 11. Shannon's birdbrained mother is totally engrossed in a silly second marriage in distant Dallas and scarcely bothers even to return phone calls, and her father is quite incapable of discussing the facts of life, or indeed anything of a personal nature, with his lonely daughter; so she unburdens herself in the pages of her USSW (Uninterrupted Sustained Silent Writing) exercise books.

From the beginning of grade 7 in September to the milestone birthday four months later, Shannon records her own developing self-assurance, through her first shyness at self-expression even in a notebook meant to be private, to a growing ease and confidence with herself and with others. Recording the life of the classroom, she brings a crowd of full-steam-ahead grade-7 kids to vivid life. She watches helplessly as a friend launches herself on a dangerous path, and learns the first hard lessons about those areas of a friend's life in which it is not safe to trespass.

It is odd that while Godfrey manages to describe so plausibly what he has not experienced—the inner workings of the adolescent female—he quite fails to create any convincing adult characters, resorting to such stock figures as the swinging, popular teacher and the windbag principal. In spite of this, *Why Just Me?* will be enjoyed by the junior-high crowd.

CAN YOU TEACH ME TO PICK MY NOSE? (1990)

Barbara J. McKee

SOURCE: A review of *Can You Teach Me to Pick My Nose?*, in *Kliatt*, Vol. 24, No. 6, September, 1990, p. 10.

Seventh-grader Jordy Shepherd is upset when his school teacher mom decides to move from Great Falls, Montana to Flower Valley, California. Within a short time, Jordy finds himself the center of a bet made by his new friend Chris. In order to win the bet, Jordy must beat the older brother of a girl he is trying to impress in a skateboarding contest. The only problem is that Jordy has never been on a skateboard before! When Pamela, the "different" girl from Jordy's class, offers to teach him, Jordy finds that some things are not as important as he thought. Humorous—a great read for the middle school crowd.

David Jenkinson

SOURCE: A review of *Can You Teach Me to Pick My Nose?*, in *Books in Canada*, Vol. XIX, No. 17, October, 1990, p. 29.

Can You Teach Me to Pick My Nose? actually refers to the name of a skateboard manoeuvre, but, for Godfrey fans, this "gross-out-grabber" title may evoke images of the raisin-stuck-in-the-nose episode in last year's *Why*

Just Me? Seventh-grader Jordy Shepherd's move from Montana to California runs into difficulties when his classmate, Chris Williamson, attempts to promote Jordy's crush on the gorgeous Marissa by falsely bragging that Jordy had been a Montana champion ramp skateboarder. Steve, Marissa's ninth-grader brother, challenges Jordy to beat him in the upcoming local championship. Jordy, having never skateboarded, must discover a way to avoid being publicly humiliated. Help arrives from an unlikely source—the class pariah, Pamela Loseth of the nerdy laugh and acidic tongue. Pamela, an accomplished skateboarder, believes she can teach Jordy enough skateboarding technique in a week to permit him to fake an injury-producing accident. By working together, the unlikely pair uncovers the real people behind the facades. A predictable, upbeat ending is fitting for this fun-filled story.

Diane Claus-Smith

SOURCE: A review of *Can You Teach Me to Pick My Nose?*, in *Voice of Youth Advocates*, Vol. 13, No. 4, October, 1990, pp. 217-18.

Jordy Shepard's mom has relocated him and his little sister from Montana to Flower Valley, California. Day One of school, he realizes that he will have to get with a different program. Paleontology museum shirts just don't make it here. Chris, a new-found friend with a fashion sense, advises Jordy to change his wardrobe and hair style. Jordy soon discovers that he has to act the part of a cool dude as well. In this school that means skateboarding, about which Jordy knows zilch. In a moment of bravado, he declares that he is a champion skater. The in-crowd demands a demonstration. In desperation, he hires Pamela, the most unpopular kid in seventh grade to teach him enough moves to fake out the other kids.

This book has a simple story line with few surprises, but much humor. It is quick paced and loaded with accurate skater-dude terminology. The title refers to a maneuver on the board which Pamela teaches to Jordy. Jordy is a reluctant hero whose need for acceptance at a new school is credible. Pamela proves to be a cute, quirky character who insists on not succumbing to peer pressure. This should move fast with the younger YAs.

Catherine D. Buckhalt

SOURCE: A review of *Can You Teach Me to Pick My Nose?*, in *English Journal*, Vol. 81, No. 2, February, 1992, p. 89.

This humorous and easily-read novel is sure to attract middle-school readers. The teen characters are all believable. Jordy Shepherd, new to California from Montana and still sporting boots and jeans, is a social misfit at school. To his rescue comes Chris Williamson with a plan to make Jordy instantly popular. Chris tells everyone that Jordy is a skateboard champ and proposes a challenge between Jordy and Steve Powell, the indisputable ramp king. The problem? Jordy has never even stepped on a skateboard. Female readers will cheer Jordy's heroine. A secret skateboard whiz and a social misfit herself, Pamela Loseth teaches Jordy everything about skateboarding, including "how to pick your nose." Along the way she also teaches him about true friendship.

I SPENT MY SUMMER VACATION KIDNAPPED INTO SPACE (1990)

Dave Jenkinson

SOURCE: A review of *I Spent My Summer Vacation Kidnapped into Space,* in *CM: A Reviewing Journal of Canadian Materials for Young People,* Vol. XVIII, No. 6, November, 1990, pp. 275-76.

Tongue-in-cheek action science fiction finds two twelve-year-old friends from the twenty-third century, Jared and Reeann, skipping an end-of-school sixth grade party to take an illegal trip to the asteroid belt, where they are captured by alien bandits.

Sold to the hostile Freetal Empire, the pair are to perform in the Imperial Circus but discover their pig-like Freetal captors' understanding of "circus" to be patterned not on the Ringling Brothers variety but rather on the Roman gladiatorial arena.

When Reeann's and Jared's first "performance" against two fifteen-foot-long meat-eating Andovian slime worms is "successful," they are "recruited" to rescue the kidnapped Princess Vinegold, the Emperor's little daughter, from the evil clutches of Rothgar the Terrible, who has rebelled against the Empire. Disguised as monkeys, the twosome are supposedly "pets" being given by the Emperor to his beloved daughter. An extended action-packed rescue sequence naturally leads to a successful conclusion, and the pair return to Earth ready for teachers' favourite back-to-school essay topic, "How I Spent My Summer Vacation."

Not Godfrey at his humorous best, *I Spent My Summer Vacation Kidnapped into Space* will still provide some good chuckles and offers pleasant, undemanding recreational reading.

Katherine Govier

SOURCE: A review of *I Spent My Summer Vacation Kidnapped into Space,* in *Books in Canada,* Vol. XIX, No. 9, December, 1990, p. 33.

I Spent My Summer Vacation Kidnapped into Space, by Martyn Godfrey, is science fiction set in Texas, where two kids graduating from grade six sign out an Academy shuttle and go off-world. There follows a speedily paced action story where the boys are captured and put in a cage, threatened with shooting, bash a nanny over the head, and so forth, heading home to discover that their parents have held a memorial service for them, thinking they were frozen in orbit.

This book is fun, and allows the reader to easily absorb concepts of space technology through the kids' glib use of space language.

Raymond H. Thompson

SOURCE: "Sci-Fi's Breezy and Serious Side," in *Canadian Children's Literature,* No. 64, 1991, pp. 85-7.

Martyn Godfrey, a former teacher who has won a number of awards for his books, may be best known for his Ms. Teeny-Wonderful stories. His first publications were in the field of science fiction, however, and it is to this that he has returned in *I Spent My Summer Vacation Kidnapped into Space.*

Intended for readers aged eight to twelve, this tale describes the adventures that befall two twelve-year-olds in "the near future." Kidnapped while rock-hunting in the asteroid belt, they are transported to a distant planet where they must first fight two giant slime worms for the entertainment of the aliens, then rescue a princess held hostage by her ambitious cousin, before they manage to escape.

These adventures are all far-fetched. Even with the aid of computers, it is unlikely that twelve-year-olds will be allowed to fly space craft, or be capable of handling them if they were. Their perils, moreover, are too easily overcome. But then none of this should be taken too seriously. It is all a light-hearted romp. Reeann and her best friend Jared are a lively and resourceful pair, with the natural adaptability of their age group, and no problems about sex roles. The alien princess is a wilful but likeable three-year-old with an obstinate sense of justice lacking in the adults of her race.

Children should enjoy this book as a lively and at times humorous account of young people triumphing against unfair and autocratic adults. Since they succeed too easily, however, readers are unlikely to learn anything meaningful from it.

MONSTERS IN THE SCHOOL (1991)

Dave Jenkinson

SOURCE: A review of *Monsters in the School,* in *CM: A Reviewing Journal of Canadian Materials for Young People,* Vol. XIX, No. 6, November, 1991, pp. 350-51.

Suppers at the Bennett home include "Bugging Time," an opportunity for family members to share whatever is bothering them. When eight-year-old Selby Bennett expresses concern that neither her parents nor her grade 7 sister Melissa ever listens to her, she meets disagreement.

To make family members "hear," Selby concocts a plan to amaze everyone by predicting the future. At supper, she tells her father, the principal of Spruce Grove School, details about his next day's activities. Selby claims to have gleaned this information by being transported into the future via friend Eric Mercer's time machine. In actuality, Selby has simply peeked at the next day's entries in her father's date book.

When after two days of "successful" predictions Selby cannot get access to her father's planning diary, she uses his extra school key to "break into" the darkened building after hours with reluctant accomplice Eric in tow. Unfortunately, Selby's classroom story-buddy for the month of November has been Brian Butz, and his creative writing pieces concerning Grats, monsters that dwell in schools' boiler rooms and walk the night-time halls in search of "food," now begin to act on Selby's imagination. When the pair "see" Grats, mayhem ensues as the two fleeing students crash into tables covered with baked goods destined for next day's sale. Disaster, however, becomes success as the duo unwittingly captures a thief.

Godfrey has again demonstrated his capacity to produce a light, fun-filled read peopled with engaging characters. [Susan] Gardos's dozen illustrations introducing each chapter plus a further eight full-page realistic illustrations scattered throughout the text reinforce the storyline in this large-print chapter book designed for newly independent readers.

Kathleen Donohue

SOURCE: "'Genie' Wins Out over 'Monsters'," in *Canadian Children's Literature,* Vol. 21, No. 1, Spring, 1995, pp. 69-70.

Selby is an eight-year-old who . . . copes with the adult world. [S]he is a youngest child who attempts to receive more attention by devising an elaborate scheme to convince her family that she has been to the future.

The fact that this book is aimed at slightly younger readers does not excuse its lack of energy and appeal. Selby is presented as a rather reckless, self-absorbed child whose misbehaviour (including breaking into her school) comes across as heroic. Parents and teachers alike may well question why the adults in the story reward Selby for her dishonesty, overlooking the dangerous situation to which she exposes herself.

Illustrations are this book's best feature, especially the one on the front with a shadowy figure chasing the kids down the hall. . . .

First-time novel readers should be encouraged to resist the tempting cover of *Monsters in the School.*

THERE'S A COW IN MY SWIMMING POOL (with Frank O'Keefe, 1991)

Joanne Findon

SOURCE: "Growing Up Complicated," in *Quill and Quire,* Vol. 57, No. 11, November, 1991, p. 28.

Nicole is trying to cope with her mother's marriage to her fifth-grade teacher, Mr. Manning, and she's not sure if she wants Mr. Manning to take the place of her dead father. Her best friend Robyn is only interested in boys and won't listen to Nicole's concerns. But the new boy Brent catches her eye, and before she knows it Nicole has been talked into hosting a mixed pool party while her mom and Mr. Manning are away on their honeymoon—a party that they have forbidden. But all her friends come and the party seems perfect until a friendly cow decides to get in on the fun. In the ensuing disaster Nicole is forced to come to terms with the difficult changes in her life.

This is a light, fun book that nevertheless attempts to address some of the anxieties teens face when a parent remarries. However, the discussion of Nicole's problems is often too obvious, most of the characters are superficially drawn, and the pace is uneven in places (perhaps the result of two authors collaborating?). Still, young readers will probably enjoy the hilarious farmyard antics, and many will relate to Nicole's dilemma.

Dave Jenkinson

SOURCE: A review of *There's a Cow in My Swimming Pool,* in *CM: A Reviewing Journal of Canadian Materials for Young People,* Vol. XX, No. 1, January, 1992, pp. 17-18.

Despite the humorous-sounding title, this collaborative effort between Godfrey and O'Keefe treats a serious theme—death's aftermath. Four years have passed since seventh grader Nicole Peters's father's fatal accident, and her mother is about to remarry.

Nicole acknowledges mixed feelings about her stepfather-to-be. She likes Barry Manning but fears the marriage will bring changes to the existing mother-daughter relationship. Nicole's concerns are seemingly legitimized when Barry overrules a decision just made by her mother. During the newlyweds' honeymoon, Nicole is to take care of their Alberta farm. At the urging of boy-crazy friend Robyn, Nicole asks permission to have a party during her parents' absence. When her mother's affirmative response is contradicted by her new father, Nicole, though confused by her motivation, determines to hurt Barry by proceeding with the party.

Comprehension arrives via gorgeous new-boy-in-town Brent, who shares his family history. During counselling sessions, Brent discovered that his negative reactions to his stepmother were related to fears of losing her, as he had lost his birth mother. Making Barry angry at her, Nicole recognizes, was an attempt to insulate herself from the pain should he also die. As the title suggests, the party ends in disaster, but all is forgiven when Nicole shares her new self-understanding with her parents.

Because *There's a Cow in My Swimming Pool* is meant to be light reading, the authors can be forgiven for having Nicole's understanding and her parents' forgiveness arrive too easily. With the exception of Nicole, characters are essentially types playing plot-advancing roles. Humour is principally physical and includes Robyn's being sprayed by a skunk and losing her bikini top while "swimming" with the cow. With the preponderance of urban settings in juvenile fiction, middle school readers may welcome this fresh locale, which, in one incident, makes them spectators at a calf's birth.

IS IT OK IF THIS MONSTER STAYS FOR LUNCH? (1992)

Sarah Ellis

SOURCE: A review of *Is It OK If This Monster Stays for Lunch?*, in *Quill and Quire*, Vol. 58, No. 3, March, 1992, p. 65.

Is It OK If This Monster Stays for Lunch? by Martyn Godfrey, illustrated by Susan Wilkinson, starts out as an enjoyable romp of the patterned picture book sort. On Monday the protagonist meets a monster named Monty. The boy invites him home for lunch, asking his mom the title question, but she refuses. On Tuesday another monster appears. The language is promising. "Monty was mauve and moldy and a little mangy." But the pattern turns out to be too restricting, the story loses oomph, and by Thursday I was desperate for the weekend. The resolution of the rejected-monster dilemma is cumbersome. There are some good jokes embedded in the pictures but the whole thing doesn't fly.

Phil Hall

SOURCE: A review of *Is It OK if This Monster Stays for Lunch?*, in *Books in Canada*, Vol. XXI, No. 4, May, 1992, p. 59.

I've . . . taken this one to nursery school and tried it out: the unabashed, wonky alliteration of the text was a big hit. Listen for yourselves:

> Tammy was terribly tiny and wore a torn, tattered, too-tight T-shirt. She had a black boot with a buckle on one foot and a blue boot with a bell on the other. She kept a slimy slug named Sloopy in the pocket of her purple, polka-dot pants.

The young girl in this story brings a wild weirdo home for lunch every day of the week, only to be told by each of the members in her family that trolls, gremlins, dinosaurs, space creatures, and monsters may definitely not stay for lunch. When, on Sunday, she meets Michael, a boy with dark skin, and also invites him home for lunch, her family says sure. Why Michael but not the various weirdos? Read and see.

Because this book deals with racism, it does belong in the "thinking" category, the "medicine" category. But its exuberant word-dance, and its tangential, almost unstated way of getting its point across, is a lot more fun than it is "sweet" or preachy.

WALLY STUTZGUMMER, SUPER BAD DUDE (1992)

Lynn Wytenbroek

SOURCE: "Adventure, Mystery, & Fantasy," in *Canadian Literature*, No. 136, Spring, 1993, pp. 170-72.

Godfrey's *Wally Stutzgummer, Super Bad Dude* is [an] adventure story for pre-teens. . . . The writing is terse, the novel is action-packed, and there is distinct character development in the main character, Wally. His development is both emotional and moral, without being either sentimental or "preachy." He makes some bad mistakes in the course of the novel but learns from them, while engaged in outrageous yet somehow typically boyish adventures. The presence of his strong-minded and independent girlfriend adds another dimension to this well-written novel. Further, Wally's fascination with language is a major benefit, as it will encourage young readers to think more about words and how and why they go together the way they do, stimulating an intellectual engagement with language and concepts that goes far beyond the boundaries of this highly entertaining book.

PLEASE REMOVE YOUR ELBOW FROM MY EAR (1993)

Dave Jenkinson

SOURCE: A review of *Please Remove Your Elbow from My Ear*, in *Quill and Quire*, Vol. 59, No. 8, August, 1993, p. 38.

Although its catchy title might suggest to some that *Please Remove Your Elbow from My Ear* is yet another humour-packed Godfrey comic novel, and while it does contain occasional touches of levity, this book actually treats a serious theme: the adolescent struggle to define one's "true" self while being labelled and categorized by others on the basis of external appearances.

Seventh-grader Stormalong "Stormy" Sprague has but one friend at Taft Junior High, fellow "loser" Jonathan Stewart. Both are constantly razzed by classmates at their Burlington, Vermont school—Stormy for saying and doing "stupid" things, Jonathan for willingly taking dance lessons. Paramount among the pair's tormentors are the

Terminators, a school gang that demands 25 cents daily in protection money. Over the book's four-day plot, Stormy's life, along with that of some of the school's other outcasts, takes a turn for the better as he joins four detention hall "dregs" to form a floor hockey team that will compete in the school's elimination tournament. The book's title is taken from a chapter describing the Dregs' first tournament match, in which they successfully overcome the Screaming Eagles, a team of physical and verbal bullies.

Godfrey does not overlook the plot possibilities of emergent adolescent hormones, describing a number of fumbling, nascent romances—including one between Stormy and Loreeta Stewart, a purple-haired transfer student. Serving as an epilogue, the book's final chapter is set two weeks later in Stormy's life and wraps up loose ends. While *Please Remove Your Elbow from My Ear* is certainly not as funny as some Godfrey offerings, fans will not be disappointed.

Faye H. Gottschall

SOURCE: A review of *Please Remove Your Elbow from My Ear,* in *Voice of Youth Advocates,* Vol. 16, No. 5, December, 1993, p. 290.

Middle-graders will love this one. Godfrey, a former junior-high teacher, writes with humor and immediacy about the foibles and fears of this precarious age. Seventh-grader Stormy Sprague joins the Dregs, a floor hockey team comprised of the habitual inmates of the "DT Dungeon," a.k.a. the detention room. The Dregs are, as Stormy explains, "the crud that's left over after the good stuff is gone." Their mission: to put on a good showing in the annual school trophy game. Their story: how they accomplish this mission by using and blending their unique personalities in a smashing game plan. Wholeheartedly recommended for any preteen who ever thought he or she was "different" while desperately wishing to be "normal." Tell 'em they'll laugh over this one; I did.

📖 *MEET YOU IN THE SEWER* ("JAWS Mob" series, 1993)

Ken Setterington

SOURCE: A review of *Meet You in the Sewer,* in *Quill and Quire,* Vol. 59, No. 10, October, 1993, p. 41.

Martyn Godfrey has just converted another reader to membership in the I Love to Read Club he began in an effort to bring books and young people together. His latest novel, *Meet You in the Sewer,* is sure to attract others.

JB Lunn—"J" only, "B" only—has a phobia and recurring nightmares, but being afraid of the dark isn't his only problem. He also has a girlfriend, Vanessa, who continually writes sappy romantic stories in which they play leading roles. And Erin, his new neighbour, is at best a pest. She continually reminds him that his father and her mother just might make a great couple and that then they would be a family. She also names him Jonly Bonly, a name he hates.

JB belongs to the JAWS Mob, an informal writing group, and he is anxious to join the school's scavenger hunt team. Erin follows him to JAWS and to the team tryouts. She is younger, and he tries to rid himself of her attentions without being mean. The exchanges between JB, Vanessa, and Erin provide some of the fastest and funniest dialogue in recent Canadian children's fiction. JB's phobia and the build-up to his encounter in the dark sewer add excitement.

Meet You in the Sewer is sure to be a mass-market hit. Godfrey deserves credit for creating in JB a realistic young male who cares about the feelings of others and in Erin a gutsy, smart, funny girl with a few problems of her own. He should also be congratulated for trying to get children to join his I Love to Read Club. Are institutional memberships available?

Jennifer Johnson

SOURCE: A review of *Meet You in the Sewer,* in *CM: A Reviewing Journal of Canadian Materials for Young People,* Vol. XXII, No. 3, May-June, 1994, p. 75.

With *Meet You in the Sewer* Martyn Godfrey has created a grab-bag of adolescent *angst,* peer stresses, parental expectations, a personal quest against fear of the dark, and actual physical danger.

Godfrey begins the book with a note from the teacher adviser of the writing club at John Allen Watson School, ever after known as "JAWS," in which she explains that the following text was written by club member JB Lunn. Beginning the book this way provides Godfrey with the perfect vehicle for the subsequent "attitude" and vocabulary of his main character. Godfrey excels at this type of atmosphere/character mélange and proceeds to racket along with a plot full of action and challenge.

JB Lunn, grade 8 student at JAWS, tells us first about his fear of the dark and then plunges into a confrontation with his father. JB is told rather than asked to walk newcomer and lowly grade 6 student, Erin, to school. JB complies, but tells Erin in no uncertain terms that he doesn't want anything to do with her. Events and Erin herself conspire against JB and they are soon very much together on a scavenger hunt try-out, a sewer exploration, and then a building fire. The story is resolved quickly and, in the case of the parent interest, unrealistically, but this does not deter from the appeal of the tale.

Meet You in the Sewer is marketed as a "JAWS Mob" book, presumably one in a series about these Toronto students. Based on this first sampling, these books will appeal to a middle school audience as well as younger adolescents reaching up to an attractive age group.

📖 *JUST CALL ME BOOM BOOM* (1994)

Ken Setterington

SOURCE: A review of *Just Call Me Boom Boom,* in *Quill and Quire,* Vol. 60, No. 3, March, 1994, p. 82.

Martyn Godfrey's many fans will not be disappointed by his latest book. In fact, *Just Call Me Boom Boom* should garner the already-popular writer many new readers. Like the first book in The JAWS Mob series, *Meet You in the Sewer,* this one has all the markings of a mass-market hit. The cover art alone should guarantee hefty sales and frequent library circulations.

The JAWS Mob is a writing club that meets informally at the Toronto school in which the series is set. Each new book is presented as the work of one of the club members, this time Bryan Bortorowski, a.k.a. Boom Boom. It seems that Boom Boom has trouble controlling his temper, for which he is repeatedly reprimanded. His one joy is the JAWS Mob. Difficulties arise when a highly confidential disk is left in the JAWS Mob's meeting room and Boom Boom is caught trying to break its security code. Add to the plot a house rumoured to be haunted; a strong and very interesting girl named Gutsy; an opening at the art gallery; and the introduction of Sonea, an artist from Loranu in the Southern Pacific, and there's more than enough opportunity for adventure. When there is a theft at the art gallery and the possibility of disaster at an amusement park, Boom Boom discovers he has ample material for his story.

Just Call Me Boom Boom is fast paced and fun, but Godfrey deserves credit for more than just a fun story. The dialogue between Boom Boom and Sonea, with her limited English, is tremendously funny. Readers will love Sonea's ultimate response when asked if she feels sick: "I will no hurl my cookies." The response is funny, but Godfrey respects Sonea and is sensitive to cultural differences throughout. Moreover, his characters are more realistic and credible than those in many other series books. The JAWS Mob series is sure to be successful, and the books deserve the attention they will receive.

Diana Brebner

SOURCE: A review of *Just Call Me Boom Boom,* in *Books in Canada,* Vol. XXIII, No. 5, Summer, 1994, p. 58.

Just Call Me Boom Boom, by Martyn Godfrey, is geared toward older boys. Godfrey is described as a reluctant-student-turned-teacher-turned-writer, and he seems to be writing for the reluctant reader. Bryan Benjamin "Boom

Boom" Bortorowski has always been the biggest kid in his class. Everybody knows he is basically a good guy but his powder-keg temper keeps getting him into trouble. Boom Boom antagonizes the principal, his writing-club instructor, and his arm-wrestling dream-girl Gusty. Throw in a haunted house, a stolen art treasure in his pocket, and an out-of-control roller-coaster ride and you've got lots of action and attitude to keep the pages turning. The style is pure macho and the vocabulary current. If it gets the male airheads reading I guess it deserves a few points.

Norma Charles

SOURCE: A review of *Just Call Me Boom Boom,* in *CM: A Reviewing Journal of Canadian Materials for Young People,* Vol. XXII, No. 5, October, 1994, p. 179.

In another sure winner by this popular writer of more than two dozen books for children, Martyn Godfrey has included all the necessary ingredients. There is lots of peppy, authentic-sounding dialogue, attractive, believable characters, and a familiar inner-city setting, as well as a fast-paced, action-packed, quite complex plot.

The main character, Boom Boom Bortorowski, is the biggest and toughest eighth grade student in school, but, if he wants to remain part of the "JAWS Mob" and continue to have access to the school's computer lab, he must keep his fiery temper in check. We follow him from one adventure to another as he loses his cool and dumps juice on his friend's head, discovers the access code for a forbidden computer program which controls the local fun fair, falls from the bridge roof to the feet of a girl he's been secretly admiring, meets another very attractive girl when he attends the opening of an art show at the art gallery, and sneaks into a haunted mansion with two friends where they encounter a couple of thieves who are pursuing them.

By that point the reader is reeling and wondering how the writer will be able to bind all these aspects into a satisfying conclusion. But Godfrey manages to come through and cleverly ties up all the loose ends in a dramatic climax at the fun fair where he has our hero's valiant efforts save the day and win the heart of the pretty maiden (as well as the heart of the reader).

Highly recommended.

J. R. Wytenbroek

SOURCE: "Trouble on Wheels," in *Canadian Literature,* No. 148, Spring, 1996, pp. 198-99.

Just Call Me Boom Boom features Godfrey's unbeatable, oversized hero, Boom Boom Bortorowski, who, in this novel, meets his match in his equally large and violence-prone girlfriend Gusty. However, the violence in these novels is amusing rather than appalling, and both Boom Boom and Gusty prove to have good hearts hidden underneath their tough exteriors. As usual, Godfrey's characters have interesting quirks, such as Boom Boom's love of art and frequent, clandestine visits to the art gallery. Perhaps meant as cleverly disguised encouragements to young people to take more interest in cultural matters, these elements add a delightful side to the characters, which make them unusual and yet do not interfere with their wild adventures and high spirits. . . . *Just Call Me Boom Boom* is a lot of fun. . . .

THE MYSTERY OF HOLE'S CASTLE
("Adventures in Pirate Cove" series, 1996)

Elaine E. Knight

SOURCE: A review of *The Mystery of Hole's Castle,* in *School Library Journal,* Vol. 42, No. 7, July, 1996, pp. 84-5.

Garrett is leery of the new boarder at his grandmother's seaside bed-and-breakfast inn. Mr. Pickering avoids the other guests, is rude to the staff, and shows a decided interest in the local haunted-house legends. Garrett suspects the man is a criminal seeking the treasure that is supposedly hidden in Hole's Castle. Unfortunately, the boy has a history of being suspicious of Gram's customers, so neither his family nor the authorities will listen to him. He resolves to investigate on his own, but is distracted from his detective work by his crush on the newest girl in class, a flaky New Age type with an extremely obnoxious younger brother. The mystery angle actually gets rather short shrift in this lightweight story. Garrett's comical romantic escapades are the basis of the plot. Even the solution of the mystery depends on the boy's efforts to impress Stacey. Garrett's fantasies get monotonous as he has the same day-dream about every girl in the class. The many body jokes and puns skirt the edge of being off-color. This is a quick and easy read but, in the end, doesn't offer much substance.

Additional coverage of Godfrey's life and career is contained in the following sources published by The Gale Group: *Contemporary Authors New Revision Series,* **Vol. 68 and** *Something about the Author,* **Vol. 95.**

Taro Gomi

1945-

Japanese author and illustrator of fiction and picture books.

Major works include *Minna Unchi* (1977; English edition as *Everyone Poops*, 1993), *Hayaku Aitaina* (1979; English edition as *Coco Can't Wait!*, 1983), *Minna go Oshietekuremashita* (1979; English edition as *My Friends*, 1990), *Wanisan Doki Haishasan Doki* (1984; English edition as *The Crocodile and the Dentist*, 1994), *Basu ga Kita* (1985; English edition as *Bus Stops*, 1988).

INTRODUCTION

An internationally recognized author and illustrator with more than two hundred titles published in Japanese, of which more than fifteen have been translated into English, Gomi creates highly-stylized picture books for preschoolers and primary graders that incorporate bold, vibrant colors and graphic simplicity. Two of his earliest works, the companion volumes *Who Ate It?* and *Who Hid It?*, have been printed more than forty times. Gomi is also lauded for his attention to detail, his whimsical story lines, and his unassuming, yet aesthetic display of basic concepts. He approaches each work with an artisan's eye, paying attention to such factors as the color reproduction and paper quality. Often adding cutout eyeholes to his engaging color-ink paintings, Gomi fashions his picture books, board books, and concept books into interactive texts that invite children to look through windows and peek through open doors. Although trained as an industrial designer, Gomi invents warm, playful worlds of precocious children and intriguing sights, and imparts a unique flair to his subjects, relying heavily on his master craftsmanship and sense of play to differentiate each tale. His humor, however, has come under fire in the critical community, primarily with regard to his best-known work, *Everyone Poops*. Offended by the book's subject, reviewers have questioned the book's appropriateness, and have noted that Gomi is not above taking liberties with his more interactive titles, typically adding details to scenes that were not mentioned in previous pages. Many of his books also impart messages as important to children as family love, in *Coco Can't Wait!*, and friendship, as in *My Friends*. Gomi also approaches universal subjects such as sharing, overcoming fears, and the change of seasons.

Gomi, though, is facetious when imparting his wisdom. In *Santa through the Window*, for example, a helicopter-riding Santa Claus delivers presents based on brief glimpses through windows. Readers see what Santa sees through window-shaped holes on the page. When readers turn the page, however, they see that Santa has miscalculated, and has mistaken rabbit ears for crocodile teeth, and

a balloon for a small boy's head. All is well in the end when those who got more than they need share with the others, and misidentified gifts are put to the best use possible. In *The Crocodile and the Dentist*, both the dentist-wary crocodile and crocodile-wary dentist express identical fears when meeting each other. Their confrontation of those fears is cleverly detailed in typically ebullient Gomi fashion. Gomi's precision pays off, as articulated by a *Publishers Weekly* critic in a review of *My Friends:* "Gomi's meticulous sense of design and careful use of brilliantly colored, highly delineated images imbues the story with a sense of the wonder and delight to be derived from life's simplest—but bountiful—moments."

Biographical Information

Gomi was born in 1945 in Tokyo, Japan. Interested in industrial design, he attended Kuwazawa Design School from 1964-66. He married Yumi Morimoto in 1968 and the couple had two daughters. Although Gomi does not recall any special reason why he started drawing, he eventually began creating children's picture books. His first, *Michi*, was published in Japan in 1973. Gomi once noted in *Something about the Author* (*SATA*), "I am interested in undifferentiated, unspecialized forms of expression and illustration and thus in those who are receptive to undifferentiated messages." He further added, "I think a picture *is* words. I am very much interested in pursuing a method of speaking in picture form. Consequently, I have found expression in picture books. . . . How I felt during my childhood has always been the basis for my work. I don't intend to make children's books, but I like to make books that even children can understand." In addition to his efforts as a children's book writer and illustrator, Gomi is an essayist and critic and has been involved in creating children's clothing, videotaped cartoons, and an interactive game book for children that he calls *File Book*. Gomi and his family live in Tokyo.

Major Works

Coco Can't Wait! concerns a child and grandmother desperate to see each other. The only problem is, they keep missing each other. As soon as Coco arrives at Grandma's house, Grandma arrives at Coco's house. This destination seesaw continues until they finally meet on a country road and enjoy a picnic, agreeing that, in the future, they should meet under a familiar tree. Millie Hawk Daniel wrote, "*Coco Can't Wait!* is a wonderful story with rich, engrossing illustrations of warm brown-skinned characters and a landscape of deep purple, blue and orange hills and houses, that heightens the sense of eager anticipation. But it is the simplicity of the story itself that makes it so delightful."

Encouraging observation from its readers, *Bus Stops* chronicles the rounds of a bus as it makes its way through the city, depositing a variety of passengers at a number of locales: baseball players get off at the playing field and sightseers get off at the church. Readers are also encouraged to locate other nearby objects such as a cow, an orange car, and a girl on a bicycle. Praising Gomi's talent for capturing the attention of very young children, a *Kirkus Reviews* critic wrote, "With pleasing design and a multiplicity of details to discover, this variation on the game of 'I Spy' is sure to please the youngest," while a *Publishers Weekly* reviewer commented, "Gomi's pictures are beautifully composed."

In *My Friends*, a young girl tells readers all the things she has learned to do from her various animal friends—the crocodile who taught her how to count, the rooster who taught her how to march, and many other activities, from jumping to climbing to studying. Although Carolyn Vang found some of the activities "unsettling, let alone unrealistic," Denise Wilms regarded *My Friends* as "[a]n elemental story that will reach toddlers and older preschoolers alike." Marita Ott further noted, "The straightforward text is rhythmic, and the graphic collage style is brilliantly colored. Subtle and humorous details, expressions, actions, and objects encourage careful rereading."

Everyone Poops is probably Gomi's best-known work, largely because of its controversial subject matter. True to the promise of the title, the book is about the universal activity of waste removal. A great many creatures—fish, birds, children, camels—and their poop, are covered. Nancy Vasilakis welcomed the book as a method for teaching children about the subject: "Some adults may be squeamish about the facts of life so honestly confronted, but younger children will find their curiosity satisfied, and those in the throes of toilet training will appreciate the book's directness." A *Publishers Weekly* reviewer, however, was not amused: "Okay, so everyone does it—does everyone have to talk about it? . . . Call it what you will, by euphemism or by expletive, poop by any name seems an unsuitable picture book subject—a view not helped by this artless presentation."

The Crocodile and the Dentist focuses on dental hygiene. The crocodile, suffering from a painful cavity, fears his upcoming visit to the dentist. By the same token, the dentist does not really wish to put himself in harm's way as he fills the crocodile's tooth. Both manage to overcome their fears and the crocodile is treated by the dentist, who emphasizes the importance of regular brushing. Dot Minzer found fault with the book's implication that the mere brushing of teeth could excuse the crocodile from future dental visits, and concluded that the book "does young readers a great disservice." Liz Rosenburg reacted more enthusiastically, stating, "Even kids who have never been to the dentist will be able to relate to the idea of being afraid. Gomi's pictures are as simple as a brilliant child's paintings, but with great subtlety and feeling."

Awards

Gomi won the Sankei Award for Children's Books (Japan) in 1978, the Graphic Prize "Fiera di Bologna" for Children (Italy) in 1981, and the Copper Medal for Well-Designed Children's Book (East Germany) in 1987.

TITLE COMMENTARY

📖 *KINGYO GA NIGETA* (1977; English edition as *Where's the Fish?*, 1986)

Kirkus Reviews

SOURCE: A review of *Where's the Fish?*, in *Kirkus Reviews*, Vol. LIV, No. 4, February 15, 1986, p. 302.

A shocking-pink fish plays hide-and-seek with young readers here, who first see it swimming in a bowl. "Where's the fish?," we're asked, as it leaps out of the bowl? On the next page are the words "There's the fish" (the only other line used in the text, until the last page), and perceptive eyes will find it hiding on a dot-covered curtain. The peripatetic fish then appears as a flower on a plant, in a jar filled with candy, in a bowl of strawberries, as a picture on a TV screen, hidden among a tantalizing display of toys, as an image in a three-way mirror and, finally, swimming with many other identical fish in an outdoor pond, where he is "home at last."

Gomi's creation is simple but quite clever, combining brilliant colors and the never-fail thrill of a hiding game.

Susan Hepler

SOURCE: A review of *Where's the Fish?*, in *School Library Journal,* Vol. 32, No. 8, May, 1986, p. 74.

The entire text of this brilliantly colored fish search is "There's the fish. Where's the fish?" repeated until the fish is "Home at last" in its brick-lined pool. A neon-pink fish leaps from its bowl and is seen camouflaged against backdrops such as a pink-spotted curtain, a jar full of candy or a pot of flowers. The words are more or less extraneous, as each spread, whether it's a "where" or a "there" page, features a fish to find. A similar text by Charlotte Pomerantz—*Where's the Bear?*—has more rhythm, and Byron Barton's illustrations for that book make for more of a story. However, Gomi's clear and brightly colored graphics set against the white page make this one clearly visible and a good choice for the read-and-point crowd at story hours.

Publishers Weekly

SOURCE: A review of *Where's the Fish?*, in *Publishers Weekly,* Vol. 229, No. 22, May 30, 1986, p. 61.

A glowing cerise fish swims in the shining turquoise water of a fish bowl, eye-catching and intriguing. "There's the fish," the minimal text declares. On the following pages, when the fish leaps out of its bowl and hides chameleon-like among the dots of a curtain, on one of the stems of a bunch of flowers, and among brightly-covered candies in a jar, readers will be hooked as they are asked, "Where's the fish?" The simple game becomes more complex and challenging, ending when the fish becomes one among many of its kind in the sea, "home at last." The author of *Coco Can't Wait!* and *Hi, Butterfly!* has concocted a playful, entertaining feast for the mind and the eye that stimulates imagination as it sharpens observation.

Eve Gregory

SOURCE: A review of *Where's the Fish?* in *The School Librarian,* Vol. 37, No. 3, August, 1989, p. 99.

This is a book for the very young or for those children just beginning to learn English. The entire text comprises the question and answer: 'Where's the fish? There's the fish.' On each page, the little pink fish flies from

one place to the next around the house, and very young children will need to scan the pictures to search for it. The fish finally finds its friends in the pond and the text changes correspondingly to 'Home at last.' The book is aesthetically appealing. The illustrations are attractive, colorful and excellent for studying pattern and symmetry. The storyline is subtle, and teacher and child may both need time before seeing its significance. It is the tale of a little fish looking for freedom from its fish-bowl and, finally, after overcoming all odds, finding it. This is a theme which will highlight a common plight and will fit well into class work on animals.

Frances Ball

SOURCE: A review of *Where's the Fish?*, in *The Junior Bookshelf,* Vol. 53, No. 5, October, 1989, p. 226.

Taro Gomi uses brightly coloured shapes set against a white background to illustrate two simple repeated sentences: 'Where's the fish?' and 'There's the fish'. Only on the final page does the text change to say 'Home at last'.

The fish in the story leaves its goldfish bowl to search for others of its kind. Along the way it makes many mistakes as it comes across fish-like shapes. Eventually, it finds a whole pool of fish and joins them. The underlying theme of the book is about identity and belonging. The style makes it suitable for very young children who would enjoy anticipating the repeated sentences while looking for the 'fish' hidden amongst the fish-like shapes.

Moira Small

SOURCE: A review of *Where's the Fish?*, in *Books for Keeps,* No. 67, March, 1991, p. 6.

A completely satisfactory book for very young children because it's bright, clear and simple. It makes a game out of looking at every picture to find the same fish. Alternately asking 'Where's the fish?', and answering 'There's the fish', adult and child travel along, noticing much on the way, until a safe and happy conclusion is reached.

MINNA UNCHI **(1977; English translation by Amanda Mayer Stinchecum as** *Everyone Poops,* **1993)**

Publishers Weekly

SOURCE: A review of *Everyone Poops*, in *Publishers Weekly,* Vol. 240, No. 5, February 1, 1993, p. 93.

Okay, so everyone does it—does everyone have to talk about it? True, kids at a certain stage of development may find the subject riveting—but their parents may well not want to read to them about it. Here we learn that birds do it, bees do it, kids with bended knees do it. We are told about big poop and little poop, animals that poop while moving and animals that poop from a stationary position, why and where people poop—in short, we get the scoop on poop. The pictures, far from Gomi's best work, leave nothing to the imagination either. In case the message hasn't sunk in, the final spread presents a chorus line of creatures, backsides forward, each producing poop. Call it what you will, by euphemism or by expletive, poop by any name seems an unsuitable picture book subject—a view not helped by this artless presentation.

Roger Sutton

SOURCE: A review of *Everyone Poops,* in *Bulletin of the Center for Children's Books,* Vol. 46, No. 8, April, 1993, p. 250.

Birds do it, bees do it . . . everyone poops. That's the message of this concept book, which begins with a simple comparison ("An elephant makes a big poop . . . A mouse makes a tiny poop") and goes on to explain the variety of excreta ("Different shapes . . . Different colors . . . Even different smells") as well as excretory techniques ("Some stop to poop . . . Others do it on the move") found in the animal kingdom. The next step is a logical one: "Grown-ups poop . . . Children poop too." Daddy is shown sedately reading on the toilet, while three children in descending age are shown, respectively, on a toilet, astride a potty, and pooping into a diaper. Toilet-training toddlers will enjoy the book's acknowledgment of their current obsession, and the direct tone of both text and pictures is a welcome contrast to Alona Frankel's odiously cute and ubiquitous *Once Upon a Potty.* The watercolor illustrations are flat but friendly, with the expressive, cartoon-like detailing of the animals echoed in the specificity of their poops. For a couple of pages, the book wanders away from its focus, asking "Which end is the snake's behind?" and "What does whale poop look like?", the former irrelevant and the latter a question that is left unanswered. The last two double spreads are a classic pair; the first showing a little boy and six different animals eating, the second, an inevitable—and unforgettable—rear view of the results.

Ilene Cooper

SOURCE: A review of *Everyone Poops,* in *Booklist,* Vol. 89, No. 18, May 15, 1993, p. 1693.

Since this was first published in Japan in 1978, it has apparently taken Americans 15 years to discover *Everyone Poops.* They won't forget it, however, not with pictures like these. Gomi's simple-shape watercolors prove that birds do it, bees do it, and every species inbetween does it. Alongside or underneath the animal is the poop itself—little bitty mouse poop, great big elephant poop. For those more interested in their own

species, there's a picture of a grown-up and an older child on toilets, a toddler on a potty, and a baby with a dirty diaper. If kids are even more curious (and some are), the text informs them that when it comes to poop, there are "different shapes, different colors, even different smells." A short book, but definitely to the point.

Denise L. Moll

SOURCE: A review of *Everyone Poops,* in *School Library Journal,* Vol. 39, No. 6, June, 1993, pp. 75-6.

Well yes, they do, but does anyone really need an entire book on the subject? In this Japanese import, readers are informed on page one that "an elephant makes a big poop, a mouse makes a tiny poop." Later on, they are told that it comes in different shapes, colors, and smells, and that, depending on who is doing it, it is done in different places. The summarizing statement is that "all living things eat, so everyone poops." However, there is never any explanation offered as to why. Overall, the text is merely a series of rather dull pictures of back ends of people on toilets and animals, with captions identifying them and occasionally posing questions such as "What does a whale's poop look like?" (No answer is provided.) There is even a little joke: "A one hump camel makes a one hump poop. And a two hump camel makes a two hump poop. Just kidding." I wish I were.

Sonja Bolle and Susan Salta Reynolds

SOURCE: A review of *Everyone Poops,* in *Los Angeles Times Book Review,* June 20, 1993, p. 7.

At a certain age all kids are bound to embarrass everyone around them by piping up publicly about their body's wonderful functions; the question is how enthusiastically you're going to encourage or suppress them. Taro Gomi's title says it all, and the illustrations show it. Some animals make big poops, some make small, some cover it up carefully, some let it lie. There's no puritanical, lips-pursed, grin-and-bear-it earnestness about the story. Moms, have you put up with years of scatological humor, only now to hear a lot of squeamish "Eeeeewwwws" from the guys about the most natural occurrence of the smelly stuff? Here's a good pay-back.

Nancy Vasilakis

SOURCE: A review of *Everyone Poops,* in *The Horn Book Magazine,* Vol. LXIX, No. 5, September-October, 1993, pp. 620-21.

There's no mincing words here. As the straightforward text explains, "Fish poop. And so do birds. . . . Grown-ups poop. Children poop too." Unabashed illustrations, featuring plainly drawn figures against brightly-colored backgrounds, show a variety of beasts and bugs. Indeed, variety is the key word. As text and art point out, "poop" comes in different shapes, colors, and smells. Some animals do it on the move; some, in a special place. Pictures show a male figure sitting on a toilet and a baby with a soiled diaper. The digestive process is summed up in the simplest terms: since all living things eat, everyone poops. The book was originally published in Japan, and some American adults may be squeamish about the facts of life so candidly confronted, but younger children will find their curiosity satisfied, and those in the throes of toilet training will appreciate the book's directness.

📖 *HAYAKU AITAINA* (1979; English edition as *Coco Can't Wait!*, 1984)

Karen Stang Hanley

SOURCE: A review of *Coco Can't Wait!*, in *Booklist,* Vol. 80, No. 15, April 1, 1984, p. 1115.

This deceptively simple, nearly wordless picture book by a Japanese author/artist will challenge and expand a young child's comprehension of spatial relationships. The full-page, mottled watercolor paintings and pithy text tell the story of Coco and her grandmother, who live across town from each other. One day Coco sets out on a bus to visit her grandmother, but when she arrives, Grandma isn't home; at the same time, Grandma has taken the train to Coco's with a like result. Their paths cross once more as each returns home. Then, both frowning in distress, they take off again to look for each other, Coco on her scooter and Grandma riding a moped. This time, luckily, their route is the same, and they joyfully collide in the middle under a convenient shade tree that they agree will be their meeting place in the future. A first-page bird's-eye view of the thoroughfares between the two houses will help young viewers trace Coco and Grandma's peregrinations, which are pictured simultaneously on facing pages. Highly stylized, two-dimensional artwork is rendered in predominately muted tones, enlivened by splashes of vivid color, while expressive faces and gestures leave no doubt as to the affection shared between child and grandmother.

Susan Sickling Browning

SOURCE: A review of *Coco Can't Wait!*, in *School Library Journal,* Vol. 30, No. 9, May, 1984, pp. 65-6.

Coco wants very much to see her rather unusual grandmother (who harvests apples and drives a motorcycle), and her grandmother is impatient to see Coco. Both of them independently decide to visit the other but repeatedly miss each other in transit. Great confusion ensues until the two finally meet in the middle. The gentle mood is enhanced by the muted colors of the illustrations. There is little enough text so that very young children will sit through the story but enough plot to keep older children interested. Textless, fully illustrated pages enable creative children to add to the story as they read. This is a charming book about family love that will be enjoyed by both pre-readers and beginning readers.

Publishers Weekly

SOURCE: A review of *Coco Can't Wait!*, in *Publishers Weekly,* Vol. 225, No. 18, May 4, 1984, p. 59.

In pictures full of verve and flashing colors, Gomi illustrates a tale of missed connections. Coco and her Grandma leave their homes, far apart, to visit each other at the same time. The two spend a large part of the day trying to get together as they pass each other going in opposite directions. At last, luck smiles on the flurried travelers. Coco and Grandma meet halfway between their two houses and agree to rendezvous "next time right under this tree." The illustrations leap with appealing extras: a curious cat watching the developments, a goat startled by the rushing about, unconcerned dragonflies and bright, summery flowers. The childlike naïveté in the figures makes the book special, a treat for all ages.

Millie Hawk Daniel

SOURCE: A review of *Coco Can't Wait!*, in *The New York Times Book Review,* May 13, 1984, p. 20.

Many adults fondly remember going to spend an afternoon, a weekend, or longer with older relatives. I remember well the chocolate cake and fried chicken my mother prepared for the long car ride from Chicago to Huntsville, Ala., where both my mother's and father's parents lived. But thoughts of those trips had been long buried, until these stories released a stream of reminiscences about going to the house where Mama Bettie, my maternal grandmother, lived.

The excitement of anticipation is what the Japanese author Taro Gomi's *Coco Can't Wait!* is all about. Coco, who "lives on top of the hill" and her grandmother, who "lives on the mountain" are longing to see each other. So, they each set out for a visit. Coco travels by bus, while Grandma opts for the train. As might be expected, they unknowingly cross paths. Coco and Grandma arrive at each other's house only to discover they've just missed each other. So it goes, back and forth, using different modes of transportation each time. Finally, in a series of full-page illustrations, we see Coco and Grandma, each with fierce determination etched into her face, coming closer and closer. At last in one another's view, they shout, "Hello, Grandma!" "Hello, Coco!" And they vow to meet in the middle from now on, right under the tree where they sit together eating apples.

Coco Can't Wait! is a wonderful story with rich, engrossing illustrations of warm brown-skinned characters and a landscape of deep purple, blue and orange hills and houses that heightens the sense of eager anticipation. But it is the simplicity of the story itself that makes it so delightful. I can imagine reading it to a class of preschool children, and hearing them shout excitedly, "Go back, go back!" or "You just passed her!" Anyone who has ever waited anxiously for someone will immediately identify with Coco.

Ronald A. Jobe

SOURCE: A review of *Coco Can't Wait!*, in *Language Arts,* Vol. 61, No. 5, September, 1984, pp. 523-24.

"I can't wait any longer." A little girl and her grandmother set off simultaneously to see each other. Twice they pass enroute, first as their train and bus speed past each other, then as they return by taxi and truck they miss again! After Coco hops on her scooter and her grandmother bursts forth on her smoke-spewing motorcycle they are, finally, joyfully reunited!

The story is a gem of simplicity. The brief text focuses on the action, heightens the intensity of feelings and through brief repetition allows the young reader to predict what will happen. Children will enjoy the humor of the missed connections: the determined grandmother on her polluting motorcycle and the drama of the impending collision of the two bikes.

Muted earth tones in the watercolor illustrations show stylized characters and landscapes. Stunningly offset by splashes of vivid magenta in the grandmother's headscarf, the girl's jumpsuit and the taxi as well as vibrant orange in the motorbike and the blades of grass, a mood of happiness is achieved. A strong element of line appears in the division of the contoured fields, the sloped train tracks, the hard-edged horizon, and the ever-present road. These illustrations literally explode with emotion and action.

Donnarae MacCann and Olga Richard

SOURCE: A review of *Coco Can't Wait*, in *Wilson Library Bulletin,* Vol. 59, No. 5, January, 1985, p. 339.

Coco Can't Wait! by Japanese writer/illustrator Taro Gomi revolves around a single idea: affection between child and grandparent. It takes only a few parallel lines of text (e.g., "One day Coco wanted to see Grandma very much. And Grandma wanted to see Coco very much.") to convey this message. But the book is full of frantic movement because Grandma lives on the opposite side of town from Coco. Several times we see this devoted pair ride in trains, taxis, or trucks that pass one another on the road, until finally Coco (on her scooter) and Grandma (on her motorcycle) meet at the midpoint and enjoy the present in Grandma's basket: some nice juicy apples.

If this plot line sounds somewhat bland in its simplicity, it has nonetheless aroused feelings of great pleasure in

our three-year-old listeners. The art work is both exquisite and accessible. Gomi uses a stunning range of grays, blacks, and browns, combined with accents in purple, magenta, and orange. Uneven paint textures and changing values against a white background make the pages glow with luminosity, and there are many ingenious scale changes and three-dimensional illusions. The first illustration is a panorama of the country-side with crisscrossing roads and rail lines, foreshadowing the travel motif and the aura of speed that Gomi sustains from page to page.

📖 *RAPPA WO NARASE* (1979; English edition as *Toot!*, 1986)

Margo Showstack

SOURCE: A review of *Toot!*, in *Children's Book Review Service Inc.,* Vol. 14, No. 14, August, 1986, p. 149.

Poor Albert! When he had the flu, he had to stay in bed and couldn't play his trumpet. Then, when Albert got better, his trumpet had the flu. Albert put the trumpet to bed, and then it got better too. This is a very simple book with simple, stylized illustrations. It might be useful for first-time parents who feel sick children should stay in bed even if they don't feel like it.

Publishers Weekly

SOURCE: A review of *Toot!*, in *Publishers Weekly,* Vol. 230, No. 8, August 22, 1986, p. 93.

When Albert recovers from his illness, he discovers that his trumpet—"Blat! Blatchoo!"—has caught his flu. "Sleep well," Albert says as he tucks the trumpet in bed. By morning the trumpet is "Good as New!" First published in Japan, Gomi's colorful book contains bright illustrations and a slight text that is sometimes misleading, as when we see Albert jumping just when the text insists "he had to stay in bed." But whimsical humor abounds, as the "Blat!" of the trumpet causes animals to fall senseless out of a purple tree. Particularly charming are the ubiquitous rabbits with whiskers white as icing who tumble through the pages, silently commenting on the action.

Heide Piehler

SOURCE: A review of *Toot!*, in *School Library Journal,* Vol. 33, No. 4, December, 1986, pp. 86-7.

Simple rhyming text tells the tale of Albert and his trumpet. While stricken with the flu, Albert is unable to make music. As soon as he is well, he takes his trumpet out to play, but instead of emitting a cheerful "toot," the trumpet goes "blat," a noise so awful that rabbits' ears twist, birds fall from the trees, and an elephant collapses. The trumpet has caught the flu. Albert knows that with a little bed rest and TLC, his trumpet will soon be as "good as new," and he's right. The bold, vividly colored collage-style illustrations highlight the story's playful nature.Children will be especially delighted with the picture of the horrified rabbits' knotted ears. Unfortunately, the story itself isn't as successful. The rhythm of the text is uneven at times, and a case of trumpet influenza is sure to bother some logically-minded children. Still, the book offers light fun and may be used to soothe the impatience of a bedridden child.

📖 *MINNA GA OSHIETEKUREMASHITA* (1979; English edition as *My Friends,* 1990)

Publishers Weekly

SOURCE: A review of *My Friends,* in *Publishers Weekly,* Vol. 237, No. 23, June 8, 1990, p. 51.

In this ode to everyday activities and things, a free-spirited girl hops, jumps and kicks her way across the countryside, paying homage to her friends along the way. Like a satellite launched into perpetual motion, the constantly moving child praises—among others—the rooster who taught her to march, the ant who taught her to explore the earth and the teachers who taught her to study. In spare, luminous landscapes, the minute world reveals a special beauty to those still and attentive enough to behold it. The activities depicted are alternately lively and quiet, but the prevailing mood is one of continuous celebration. Gomi's meticulous sense of design and careful use of brilliantly colored, highly delineated images imbues the story with a sense of the wonder and delight to be derived from life's simplest—but bountiful—moments.

Denise Wilms

SOURCE: A review of *My Friends,* in *Booklist,* Vol. 86, No. 21, July, 1990, p. 2088.

A little girl recites all the pleasurable things she has learned from her friends: "I learned to jump from my friend the dog. I learned to climb from my friend the monkey. I learned to run from my friend the horse." The litany continues, including such meaningful things as reading and studying and, most importantly, loving. Gomi's simple watercolors, marked by spare, cutout shapes, are set against a clean white background. An elemental story that will reach toddlers and older preschoolers alike.

Carolyn Vang

SOURCE: A review of *My Friends,* in *School Library Journal,* Vol. 36, No. 7, July, 1990, p. 60.

"I learned to . . . from my friend(s) . . ." is the one sentence a young girl repeats on each double-page spread in this simple concept book. The primitive watercolors are, for the most part, bright and attractive against a white backdrop. However, the quality is inconsistent; occasionally dark or poorly defined objects and animals appear, limiting the book's use to the one-on-one situation. The repetitious text quickly becomes tedious, and there is no sign of real movement in any of the characters. Facial expressions are almost nonexistent. Some of the size relationships are inaccurate (rabbit-girl/owl-girl), and a few of the activities the child engages in are unsettling, let alone unrealistic. A good attempt that misses the mark.

Marita Ott

SOURCE: A review of *My Friends,* in *The Five Owls,* Vol. V, No. 1, September-October, 1990, pp. 8-9.

Winner of the Graphic Prize at the 1989 Bologna Children's Book Fair, Taro Gomi has once more created a perfect blend of art and text in this simple picture book in which a little girl's animal friends demonstrate some basic actions learned in life. The little girl gives credit to a variety of living creatures for exemplifying things humans are apt to take for granted, from walking to star-gazing and from singing to smelling the flowers.

The young learner accepts easily the examples provided by her animal friends and then moves smoothly to learning from books, teachers, and human friends the more complicated tasks of reading, studying, and playing together. The straightforward text is rhythmic, and the graphic collage style is brilliantly colored. Subtle and humorous details, expressions, actions, and objects encourage careful rereading.

Although children in the illustrations are Japanese and the style has a distinct Far East flair, the ideas about learning from nature and humans are universally accepted and respected. The youngest child and the oldest grownup would do well to remember this simple and honest approach to friendship and to the environment in which we all live.

Karen D. Wood and Susan G. Avett

SOURCE: A review of *My Friends,* in *Language Arts,* Vol. 70, No. 1, January, 1993, p. 62.

The joy and power of friendship is depicted through the eyes of a little girl. Her friends range from the animate to the inanimate as she remarks, "I learned to read from my friends, the books." Among her many lessons, she learns to nap from her friend, the crocodile; to march from her friend, the rooster; and to study from her friends, the teachers. The warm message that accompanies each striking illustration can help children see that friendship is everywhere.

📖 *KOUSHI NO HARU* (1980; English edition as *Spring Is Here*, 1989)

Publishers Weekly

SOURCE: A review of *Spring Is Here,* in *Publishers Weekly,* Vol. 235, No. 26, June 30, 1989, p. 100.

A winsome calf provides the backdrop—literally—for this charming story. With each turn of the page, the young animal is imaginatively transformed to reflect some activity of the four seasons: snow melting, seedlings springing up, harvest, all the way to the snow melting again and revealing that—the calf has grown. The story line follows the cycle of the seasons from one spring to the next, and its spare, fluid text—wedded to the vigorous graphics—vividly conveys the underlying themes of renewal and growth. Japanese artist Gomi won the Graphic Prize at the Bologna Children's Book Fair for this work, and it's easy to see why. The colors are joyful and fresh, and the artist's playful approach to perspective makes this a perfect picture book.

Ilene Cooper

SOURCE: A review of *Spring Is Here,* in *Booklist,* Vol. 85, No. 22, August, 1989, p. 1976.

A delightful introduction to the seasons for the very youngest. "Spring is here," the book begins; a newborn white calf and a butterfly appear against a hot pink background. The brief text continues ("the snow melts," "the flowers bloom"), and Gomi uses a deceptively simple graphic style to illustrate the words. Only adults may be aware that the change of seasons is taking place on the back of the calf—brown markings turn into muddy patches where flowers eventually bloom, and the whiteness of winter, at the end of the story, melds once more into the body of the now-grown animal. Whether or not children notice the way Gomi toys with reality is unimportant. His pure colors, bold shapes, and whimsical touches are more than enough to engage young minds. The simple wording also makes the book appropriate for those just beginning to read words.

Emily Holchin McCarty

SOURCE: A review of *Spring Is Here,* in *Children's Book Review Service Inc.,* Vol. 17, No. 14, August, 1989, p. 154.

First published in Japan and awarded the Graphic Prize at the Bologna Children's Book Fair, this title reaches across language barriers thanks to its simplistic and effective illustrations. A calf and butterfly go through the four seasons together and when the new spring arrives, they both have grown. The story line coaxes the imagination.

Celia A. Huffman

SOURCE: A review of *Spring Is Here,* in *School Library Journal,* Vol. 35, No. 14, October, 1989, pp. 78-9.

A year from spring to spring is graphically and textually described through the earth's seasonal changes and the maturation of a baby calf. As in *Hi Butterfly!* and *Coco Can't Wait!,* Gomi engages readers and invites them to watch the calf's subtle physical changes plotted against those of the meadow in which he lives. The crisp, clear graphics in bright, distinct colors are sometimes collage-like in appearance, with shapes of the calf and the horizon blending together as the story progresses. These large, uncluttered illustrations and minimal text make this an ideal choice for toddler story time as well as for one-on-one usage with the lap-sitting crowd.

Mary M. Burns

SOURCE: A review of *Spring Is Here,* in *The Horn Book Magazine,* Vol. LXV, No. 6, November-December, 1989, p. 759.

The cycle of seasons is captured for preschoolers in a series of elegant graphic designs in bright colors that emphasize the essence of shape and mass rather than overwhelming detail. The accompanying short, declarative sentences are equally straightforward, allowing plenty of opportunity for looking and thinking about the magic of perspective, beginning with the transformation of a newborn calf into a field of flowers that becomes in succession a field of green grass, a brown wheat field, and a snowy landscape. Corresponding with the passing of the year, these changes continue as the seasons pass until the metamorphosis is complete with the return of another spring and the penultimate observation, "The calf has grown." And so it has, for two small horns crown the calf's head. No months are identified, so that the events described are applicable in any hemisphere. Thoughtfully designed, the book is a consistent entity, an artfully simple, artistically logical execution of a basic concept.

📖 *KIIROINO WA CHOUCHO* (1983; English edition as *Hi, Butterfly!*, 1985)

Darian J. Scott

SOURCE: "Four Stories to Catch a Toddler's Eye," in *The Christian Science Monitor,* May 3, 1985, p. B4.

[*Hi, Butterfly!* is one] of the season's most imaginative and brilliantly conceived children's books. The story revolves around a young boy's attempts to net a bright yellow butterfly. His efforts are very cleverly constructed in almost puzzle-like fashion, so that the action of one page is coupled with that of the next, creating a domino effect of ever-heightening drama.

From The Crocodile and the Dentist, *written and illustrated by Taro Gomi.*

From start to finish the butterfly is cut out of every other page, a device contributing to its "elusiveness," for what at first always seems so catchable inevitably escapes and is transformed into something else. As the boy chases the butterfly through country fields, city streets, construction sites, and even, in the end, into his very own house, he barely escapes one disaster after another.

At one point he prepares to catch what looks like the butterfly near a pile of steel girders in a construction area, but what he actually brings his net down on turns out to be the yellow hard hat of one of the workers!

The illustrations are as engaging as the story. It is author/illustrator's use of the cutout, however, that makes this simple, very visual tale so original.

Amy G. Gavalis

SOURCE: A review of *Hi, Butterfly!* in *School Library Journal,* Vol. 32, No. 1, September, 1985, p. 118.

Despite some inconsistencies, this vividly illustrated story with few words will be great fun for toddlers, older preschoolers and beginning readers. Every other double-page spread holds a surprise when a butterfly eludes a little boy's attempts to capture it. As in *Coco Can't Wait!,* Gomi creates a marvelous sense of anticipation which propels the eye through a wonderfully colorful world. Cutouts reminiscent of Eric Carle's work seem to be the butterfly as it is about to be netted. Then, with a flip of the page, it is gone, and the net has bagged something quite unexpected. Artistically, there is a major flaw here. In most cases, the butterfly becomes an object not previously pictured, like a hard hat on a previ-

ously bareheaded worker, a concept that may confuse rather than amuse. Still, this is an attractive book that will have appeal to children.

Sr. Barbara Anne Kilpatrick

SOURCE: A review of *Hi Butterfly!* in *Catholic Library World,* Vol. 57, No. 3, January-February, 1986, p. 187.

A translation of the Japanese tale **Kiiroino Wa Choucho.** Taro Gomi's bright, summery illustrations tells of the lively lighthearted story of a young boy who chases the elusive butterfly. In an almost wordless tale, one little boy tries to capture a butterfly through country fields, city streets and even into his own house. And there's a special surprise on every page!

📖 *MADO KARA NO OKURIMONO* (1983; English edition as *Santa through the Window,* 1995)

Publishers Weekly

SOURCE: A review of *Santa through the Window,* in *Publishers Weekly,* Vol. 242, No. 38, September 18, 1995, pp. 94, 96.

When he relies on peeking through windows to guess the recipients of his Christmas Eve gifts, Santa makes a few inappropriate deliveries. Japanese artist Gomi successfully incorporates a clever book design into his plot. Cut-out windows on each page initially give readers the same partial view as Santa (several pairs of tiny rabbit ears are easily mistaken for rows of crocodile teeth, for instance). But turning the page gives readers the inside story. Gomi's unique twist on the traditional (this Santa flies a helicopter and wears a hot-pink jumpsuit with white boots) may throw some children, but the result is still great fun.

School Library Journal

SOURCE: A review of *Santa through the Window,* in *School Library Journal,* Vol. 41, No. 10, October, 1995, p. 37.

A silly peek-a-boo book. Santa, dressed in pink, hops off his helicopter to peer through windows, trying to guess who lives in each house. He sees what looks like a zebra's stripes through one window and leaves a black-and-white striped scarf. But a turn of the page reveals that it's really three white swans against a black background. And so on, to each house. When Christmas morning arrives, the recipients learn how to make do with—or swap—their gifts and everyone is happy. "Good work, Santa!" Gomi's illustrations in bright colors that saturate the page and round figures without hard edges, and his clever use of shapes, sizes, and angles, combine to make another light but amusing book for the holidays.

Hanna B. Zeiger

SOURCE: A review of *Santa through the Window,* in *The Horn Book Guide to Children's and Young Adult Books,* Vol. VII, No. 1, Spring, 1996, p. 28.

Looking through windows—openings that frame part of the next page—Santa makes incorrect assumptions about who lives inside, but everyone eventually finds uses for the gifts he delivers. Readers will enjoy turning the pages to uncover Santa's mistakes. The cheerful text has been illustrated with some striking graphic surprises.

Mary Berry

SOURCE: "Select Books Now for December Celebrations!" in *Emergency Librarian,* Vol. 23, No. 5, May-June, 1996, pp. 54-6.

Santa through the Window by Taro Gomi is reminiscent of Tana Hoban's *Take Another Look.* On one page there is a hole in which you see a face, an object or a design. Santa looks through the hole, determines who lives there, and then leaves a present that he thinks is appropriate. When you turn the page, you discover that Santa's assumption is wrong. For example, when Santa looks through the window and says, "A small cat must live in this house," instead of a live cat, you see a pig with the picture of a cat on the front of the pig's shirt. However, when everyone awakes to find his gift, each one seems happy. The pictures on each page contain few objects but all are big, bright and colorful. Younger children will like looking at the pictures and trying to read the

few words on each page. This book was originally published in Japanese in 1983.

📖   *ICHIBAN HAJIMENI* (1984; English edition as *First Comes Harry,* 1987)

Publishers Weekly

SOURCE: A review of *First Comes Harry,* in *Publishers Weekly,* Vol. 231, No. 6, February 13, 1987, p. 91.

Harry is the first to wake up, first to breakfast, first to leap over the garbage can, first to tumble down the slide—and the first to get hurt. In fact, a couple of times being first doesn't pay off—Harry ends up first in the bath, and he's the very first to get sleepy. Gomi's book is both fun and surprising, and readers will add up Harry's firsts as he and the other children scamper around the schoolyard and past a farmer's neatly laid out field. Gomi's characteristically clear colors, blocky figures and crisp design keep this story bouncing along.

Ilene Cooper

SOURCE: A review of *First Comes Harry,* in *Booklist,* Vol. 83, No. 12, February 15, 1987, p. 900.

Littlest listeners will be the audience for this pleasing description of Harry's day. Everyone in the house is sleeping—cat, dog, baby, parents—but not Harry. He's up, the first to get dressed, brush his teeth, and be at the head of the line for all of the day's events. But by bedtime, Harry is also the first to get drowsy and the first to be sound asleep. The simple text ("He was the first to laugh") is illustrated with Gomi's unique pictures. The solid geometric shapes seemingly come alive when illustrated in sea blues, deep purples, and grass greens. The simplicity and purity of the pictures keep in touch with the reality of a child's activities and allow for plenty of whimsical humor. (Harry may be the first to climb the slide, but he's also the first to tumble down.) A nice lap book to share as well as one to read at toddler story hours.

Lois K. Nichols

SOURCE: A review of *First Comes Harry,* in *Children's Book Review Service Inc.,* Vol. 15, No. 9, April, 1987, pp. 94-5.

The author uses the idea of "first" to build a sequence of activities that Harry engages in throughout the day, from first wake-up until last good night. Delightfully illustrated in colorful cut paper, this is a very orderly book which will help children sense the sequence and order in their lives. Young readers will find satisfaction in the one-line text under each picture, and young listeners will undoubtedly test their memory on daily events.

Jean Hammond Zimmerman

SOURCE: A review of *First Comes Harry,* in *School Library Journal,* Vol. 33, No. 8, May, 1987, p. 85.

A book in which the illustrations are much stronger than the text. Gomi shows a day in the life of a small boy through vibrantly colored paintings. The first of his family to get up, Harry dresses himself, gets ready for breakfast, and finishes eating first. He plays with other children and is again first in everything, including laughing at himself when he bumps his head after running up the slide. After a full day he goes home, is first into the bath, to eat dinner and to fall asleep. Gomi's paintings are done in bold colors with orange, green, and blue predominating. They have a spareness and simplicity that appears child-like but that shows great care in details such as the varying sizes of the margins and the use of white accents. However, most children will wonder how such a young child can leave home in the morning all alone, stay away all day, and arrive home at dinnertime without anyone wondering where he was. Like Ezra Jack Keats's *The Snowy Day,* Gomi demonstrates artistically that the ordinary life of a particular child can be extraordinary, but Gomi's story doesn't work as well.

WANISAN DOKI HAISHASAN DOKI (1984; English edition as *The Crocodile and the Dentist,* 1994)

Linda J. Gibbs

SOURCE: A review of *The Crocodile and the Dentist,* in *Children's Book Review Service Inc.,* Vol. 23, No. 4, December, 1994, p. 38.

For those children who forget to brush their teeth, this delightful book provides a humorous reminder. Both the crocodile and a dentist are scared when the crocodile needs to have a cavity filled. Although all turns out well, the crocodile is told that if he doesn't want to come back again, he must never forget to brush. The simple, bright full-page illustrations and brief text will catch the attention of the young.

Kay Weisman

SOURCE: A review of *The Crocodile and the Dentist,* in *Booklist,* Vol. 91, No. 9, January 1, 1995, p. 825.

A young crocodile with a toothache doesn't really want to visit the dentist, but he knows he must. His dentist is equally apprehensive about seeing the reptilian patient. Each approaches the other with a brave front that masks high anxiety. Their uneasy inner dialogues mirror each other as the boldly colored illustrations portray their strained exterior civility. When at last the tooth is successfully repaired, the crocodile promises to brush faithfully and to return next year. Originally published in Japan, Gomi's brief text and understated comic illustrations go right to the heart of children's dental phobias. Readers will be particularly amused when the dentist greets his young patient, smiling politely while armed with drill and pincers. Although very young listeners may be unnerved by the invasive procedures, slightly older children will appreciate Gomi's humorous twist on a universal fear.

Dot Minzer

SOURCE: A review of *The Crocodile and the Dentist,* in *School Library Journal,* Vol. 41, No. 2, February, 1995, p. 73.

A story with a dual point of view. An apprehensive crocodile must visit an equally fearful dentist. "I must be brave . . . I'm so scared" declares the croc. This sentiment is repeated by the dentist. "Ouch!" exclaims the croc as the dentist fills his tooth. "Ouch!" returns the dentist as the croc's flailing arm collides with his. The ordeal ends, and each says, "Thank you so much. See you again next year." And then each thinks, "I really don't want to see him again next year." The croc concludes, "So I must never forget to brush my teeth." Gomi's brightly colored art on white background features appealing cartoon characters on each page. However, the inference that continued brushing will eliminate future dental visits is misleading and does young readers a great disservice.

Philip Morrison and Phylis Morrison

SOURCE: A review of *The Crocodile and the Dentist,* in *Scientific American,* Vol. 273, No. 6, December, 1995, p. 114.

"I *really* don't want to see him . . . but I must." We sympathize with the brown crocodile, his four large, white teeth showing, as he stands in front of his dentist's office. "I *really* don't want to see him, but I must," says the green-robed dentist at his desk, the croc's shadow on the office door. We sympathize with him, too, for the crocodile's toothy mouth is big enough to engulf hand, drill and all. "I must be brave," both say. The croc can't help closing down when the dentist can't help entering that back tooth. Two speak the same words: "OUCH! What an awful thing to do. But getting angry won't help." It all ends happily. After they part with polite bows, each murmurs: "I don't really want to see him again next year." There is a way: the croc must recall just what the dentist says about brushing teeth.

The strong, broad drawings are funny, and the near perfection of this endearing human symmetry elevates this tale by a Japanese artist for young readers straight to mathematical glory.

📖 *BASU GA KITA* (1985; English edition as *Bus Stops*, 1988)

Publishers Weekly

SOURCE: A review of *Bus Stops,* in *Publishers Weekly,* Vol. 234, No. 20, November 11, 1988, p. 54.

As a bus progresses on its route to the garage, where it will park for the night, various travelers—actors, commuters, families—hop off at their stops. When a number of riders is named (for example, 10 baseball players disembark and head for a playing field), readers can count along, but more often, the text suggests different objects to pick out from each spread. Gomi's pictures are beautifully composed, using white space to carve out both the horizon and the shape of the bus. Gomi's illustrations will appeal to children for their simplicity, and to adults for their strong graphics.

Kirkus Reviews

SOURCE: A review of *Bus Stops,* in *Kirkus Reviews,* Vol. LVI, No. 23, December 1, 1988, p. 1738.

From an award-winning Japanese illustrator, a very simple picture book. At a series of varied stops (beach, edge of town, fair, baseball field, junkyard), different people (artist, salesman, mechanic, nurse) get off; each time, the "reader" is also challenged to find another detail (a girl on a bicycle, a jogger, a horse). Using bold, flat areas of color in creative, harmonious combinations, Gomi evokes an attractive, clean-cut world that makes few references to its country of origin. With

pleasing design and a multiplicity of details to discover, this variation on the game of "I Spy" is sure to please the youngest.

Ilene Cooper

SOURCE: A review of *Bus Stops,* in *Booklist,* Vol. 85, No. 9, January 1, 1989, p. 788.

Simply shaped objects executed in bold, bright watercolors are the hallmark of this inviting book that chronicles a bus journey on its route about town. As the white, loaflike vehicle picks up and discharges passengers, the brief text identifies the location and notes who gets on and off. The squat, faceless riders range from construction workers to baseball players, and if it is pointed out to them, children can see the bus' path as it moves from the uncrowded outskirts of town to the city center, back through the suburbs, and to the garage. A question appears on each page: "Can you find an orange car?" or "Can you find a cow?"; while fun, this device would have been more effective if the objects had been directly related to the action. An eye-catching book that has appeal for individuals or groups.

Maria B. Salvadore

SOURCE: A review of *Bus Stops,* in *School Library Journal,* Vol. 35, No. 6, February, 1989, p. 69.

Simple full-color, double-page illustrations couple with a straightforward text to chronicle the daily travel of a bus and its many different riders. Children will easily

From Santa through the Window, *written and illustrated by Taro Gomi.*

recognize the people and places, which range from a stop at an old church where two sightseers get off to a baseball field where ten players jog off. A "subtext" invites readers to find another unrelated person or object in each illustration. Clean shapes, effective use of negative space, and minimal text create an appealing, open format. The book lends itself to sharing with individuals or in small groups to stimulate discussion. It may also serve to introduce a variety of concepts such as travel by bus, counting, and different activities that people enjoy.

KOTOBA ZUKAN 1-10 (1985; English edition as *Seeing, Saying, Doing, Playing: A Big Book of Action Words,* 1985)

Publishers Weekly

SOURCE: A review of *Seeing, Saying, Doing, Playing: A Big Book of Action Words,* in *Publishers Weekly,* Vol. 238, No. 18, April 19, 1991, p. 65.

The round-faced children in this inviting, large-format volume are busy indeed—demonstrating just about every action word known to children. In a style suggestive of Richard Scarry, each word is labeled alongside the figure carrying out the action. Twelve boldly colored spreads display familiar settings, including a classroom, swimming pool, farm, campsite, zoo and park. The gerunds presented range from the simple concepts of the book's title to more sophisticated words—sauntering, fluttering, bellowing, nuzzling. Gomi exhibits his characteristic keen sense of humor: a girl at the end of a diving board is identified as "reconsidering," while a child snickering at another who is losing his swimsuit is "teasing." The book ends with a list of the action words included, which kids are encouraged to find. Readers of this book will be engaging in two simultaneous activities: learning and laughing.

Kimberly Olson Fakih

SOURCE: A review of *Seeing, Saying, Doing, Playing: A Big Book of Action Words,* in *Los Angeles Times Book Review,* May 26, 1991, p. 7.

And now, SPLASH! goes Taro Gomi's *Seeing, Saying, Doing, Playing.* Perhaps no book yet rings out like a three o'clock bell, and no one volume can replicate the rattle of a cookie jar. But this one offers an action-crammed pandemonium created from a tumult of energetic "-ing" participles that convey continuity and on-going hurly-burly. Gomi's oversized book thrusts upon readers a dozen spreads showing—Brueghel-like!—hundreds of people of various ages, indoors and out, "Exiting" or "Viewing" or "Sauntering" or "Yawning" or "Honking" or "Ignoring." A swimming pool, a skating rink or a roller coaster are semi-encyclopedic tidal pools of vitality. Published in Japan in 1985 (where has it been all these years?), this volume and others like it

have a ripe and timely emphasis: on the child's *being* a child rather than *becoming* a grown-up.

Publishers Weekly

SOURCE: A review *of Seeing, Saying, Doing, Playing: A Big Book of Action Words,* in *Kirkus Reviews,* Vol. LIX, No. 11, June 1, 1991, p. 735.

From "accusing" and "adjusting" to "zipping" and "zooming," hundreds of verbs organized, Richard Scarry-style, into scenes—home, school, street, farm, zoo, etc. The flavor is only mildly Japanese in the activities, more so in the faces (ironically, an occasional toothy grin would seem stereotypical if the art had originated in the US). The illustrations are not especially imaginative, but the many stylized figures are expressive. Unusually comprehensive, and likely to intrigue children with a fondness for words.

Jody McCoy

SOURCE: A review of *Seeing, Saying, Doing, Playing: A Big Book of Action Words,* in *School Library Journal,* Vol. 37, No. 8, August, 1991, p. 160.

Each large page in this book is busy (but not cluttered) with vigorous Japanese cartoon figures engaged in over 500 actions. Just about every gerund one might use and a few forgotten ones are represented. Although the subtle differences between yelping, yelling, and whooping may be lost in the simplicity of the art, the perky little poppets could be engaged in the identified activity and they are so entertaining that what other "ing" they are doesn't really matter. Two small lads are, through no fault of their own, a bit bare: one loses his swim trunks and the other his towel. Many of the verbs are as accessible as the title implies; however, ascending, suckling, grimacing, and others seem a bit out of the ordinary for the audience the illustrations seem to suit. Although it is easy to like this book, it's difficult to decide how best to use it. A parent and child could spend years discussing the various verbs, but their broad range of complexity combined with the simplicity of the illustrations limits its usefulness in a group or classroom setting. Children may enjoy just looking at the pictures.

"BOARD BOOKS" (*Guess Who?,* 1991; *Who Ate It?,* 1991; *Who Hid It?,* 1991; *Guess What?,* 1992; *There's a Mouse in the House,* 1992)

Publishers Weekly

SOURCE: A review of *Guess Who?,* in *Publishers Weekly,* Vol. 238, No. 38, August 23, 1991, pp. 60-1.

A bevy of bright faces comprises this small, interactive

board book, the first in the Peek-a-Boo series. Sturdy, highly glossed pages showcase the cheerful visages of various animals, humans or toys that have open holes in place of illustrated eyes. These die-cuts let each spread function as a mask to be looked through, and the openings are just the right size for toddler fingerplay. But readers will find the true guessing game in the book's text. Each left-hand page offers a clue to the identity of the character depicted ("I like to chase mice"), while the right-hand page delivers the answer ("I am a cat"). The appeal here extends beyond toddlerdom—beginning readers will enjoy the simple sentence structure. Gomi's lustrous palette will generate enthusiasm even after repeated viewings, and his lumpy, purple monster—sporting two teeth and a fuchsia tongue—is not to be missed.

Kirkus Reviews

SOURCE: A review of *Who Did It?*, in *Kirkus Reviews*, Vol. LIX, No. 19, October 1, 1991, p. 1286.

One of the first two (1977) books, never before published here, of a Japanese illustrator noted for his bold simplicity and striking designs, this seven-inch square book not only challenges children to find objects cleverly concealed in the pictures but is also a counting book. "Who hid the candles?" They serve as horns on one of five giraffes; "Who hid the fork and spoon?" They dangle from the pigtails of one of 12 children. In the same format, the second book, *Who Ate It?*, is equally attractive, but "ate" is not the mot juste: the different foods are hidden on the *outsides* of the animals. A fine, economical purchase for the youngest.

Lolly Robinson

SOURCE: A review of *Who Hid It?*, in *The Horn Book Magazine*, Vol. LXVIII, No. 1, January-February, 1992, p. 58.

"Who ate the cherries?" "Who hid the glove?" Each double-page spread in these small, square books asks a question about an object pictured on the left page, while the right shows a group of nearly identical animals. The object is humorously hidden on one of the animals, usually replacing a body part in a slyly whimsical way. Though the animals are pictured in simple flat areas of color, they appear to be chuckling at their own trickiness. These are books to grow with, as each combines a simple camouflage book, a name-the-animal book, and a counting book, with each spread showing a sequentially larger number of animals, from two to twelve. Each book ends with the object hidden amongst twelve smiling brown children. The watercolor illustrations use bright complementary colors, with the paper fibers showing clearly through the paints, providing a pleasingly soft texture. These apparently simple books have been crafted with such detail and humor that each reading reveals new delights.

Cathleen Towey

SOURCE: A review of *Who Ate It?* and *Who Hid It?*, in *School Library Journal*, Vol. 38, No. 4, April, 1992, p. 92.

Two Japanese imports illustrated with vibrant, cheerful watercolors that feature a seek-and-find format. The title questions are asked, and readers must look for an item in a picture on the facing page. Unfortunately, the verbs used in the simple texts may cause some confusion. The animals and children don't actually "eat" the foods that then show up somewhere on their bodies in the first book or "hide" items that must be searched for in the second. Even though the questions could be posed in a more accurate fashion, these titles will appeal to young children. Lively color combinations make the illustrations leap from the pages, and the interactive format is intriguing.

Kate Moses

SOURCE: "Roar out the Door," in *Hungry Mind Review*, No. 23, Fall, 1992, pp. 10, 15.

Also full of holes is **There's a Mouse in the House**, one of the latest titles from award-winning author and illustrator Taro Gomi. A wide-eyed, green-shod mouse runs through holes in the walls of various deeply colored rooms inhabited by appropriately startled creatures. The text is deceptively spare: one-line rhymes describe the mouse's action as he moves through the rooms. Yet by listing the varied ways in which the mouse runs—"he jogs by the dog," "he zooms while the alligator vacuums"—Gomi suggests to children that, next time they want to go bye-bye, they might try to "roar out the door" instead. This widening of scope through language can occur only after mastering the "go bye-bye" concept. But once you've mastered go bye-bye, there's no telling where a pair of green shoes might take you.

Lisa S. Murphy

SOURCE: A review of *Guess What?* and *There's a Mouse in the House*, in *School Library Journal*, Vol. 38, No. 11, November, 1992, p. 70.

Strong, bright colors are the most appealing features of these books. Both stories revolve around a small die-cut hole. *Guess What?* is the more creative of the pair. Children in a rich cinnamon color peer through the hole at an object that is only partly revealed. They make a guess about what they are seeing, but the next page shows that they are wrong. Some of the choices seem deliberately far-fetched; sand is mistaken for snow, the smell of a bouquet of flowers for an apple pie. The concept and vocabulary is appropriate for pre-schoolers, but the board-book format suggests that toddlers are the intended audience. In *Mouse*, a tiny mouse zips through the holes in rooms with tri-colored walls. In each room, different animals are busy with everyday tasks. The sentences rhyme internally, which does not always work ("He jogs by the dog"). The house seems institutional in its simplicity; the rooms are without furniture or other signs of habitation, aside from a clock or a TV. Also, the fact that the animals in the house seem to have no connection to each other adds to the impersonal feeling. Most children will breathe a sigh of relief when the mouse simply "roars out the door."

Additional coverage of Gomi's life and career is contained in the following sources published by The Gale Group: *Contemporary Authors,* **Vol. 162 and** *Something about the Author,* **Vols. 64, 103.**

Isabelle Holland

1920-

Swiss-born American author of fiction.

Major works include *Cecily* (1967), *The Man without a Face* (1972), *Of Love and Death and Other Journeys* (1975; British edition as *Ask No Questions,* 1978), *The House in the Woods* (1991), *Behind the Lines* (1994).

INTRODUCTION

The versatile veteran author of more than fifty books for children, young adults, and adults, Holland is noted for her memorable characters, storytelling skills, contagious faith, and love of fun that permeate her writings. She is widely acclaimed for her realistic young adult fiction, including the controversial *Man without a Face* for which she is best known, and for her sensitive portrayals of the complex problems experienced by many modern adolescents. Despite mixed critical reaction to her inclusion of a brief episode of homosexuality in *The Man without a Face*, Holland's treatment of the subject is generally described as tasteful and discretionary. While Holland frequently deals with gripping emotional situations, she tempers the intensity of the topic with a subtle sense of humor and a strong feeling of hope. She also examines the relationships between adults and lonely, often troubled adolescents, focusing on such themes as the need to love and be loved, accepting personal responsibility, and the importance of individual choice. "My books have always dealt with the relationship between the child or adolescent and the adult or adults who live in and dominate the young person's portrait of self," Holland explained in *Literature for Today's Young Adults*. "It is that struggle between the child and the adult in the creating of that self-portrait, that often preoccupies my writing. . . . [I]f my books are about wounds given . . . they are also about the healing that can take place, given the right adult at the right time." In addition to her young adult fiction, Holland has written works for younger children, in which she reveals her love for animals, as well as several highly celebrated Gothic mysteries for adults. Although criticized for being moralistic and, at times, for oversimplifying the problems of her characters, Holland, critics generally agree, excels in portraying believable people in extraordinary situations with insight and compassion.

Biographical Information

Born in Basel, Switzerland, the daughter of the American Consul, Holland spent the first twenty years of her life abroad,chiefly in Guatemala and England. She had a brother who was considerably older and seldom home. Thus growing up as a foreigner and virtually an only

child, isolation and loneliness became prevalent themes in her fiction. When Holland was a child, her mother, a gifted storyteller, regaled her with lively tales that Holland later learned were from history, legend, mythology, and the Bible. After graduating from Tulane University in 1942 and spending two years working for the U.S. War Department, Holland began writing fiction in her spare time while working for various publishing houses in New York. Her first book, *Cecily,* classified as an adult book, was based on time spent in a boarding school in Liverpool, England, where she suffered as the only short, fat, misfit, thirteen-year-old American. Recognizing her gifts, a perceptive editor encouraged Holland to write for young people, thus launching her on a career that led to over thirty books for children and young adults in addition to several works for adults, mainly romantic suspense. In recent years, Holland has become fascinated with the history of New York City, or Manhattan, the setting of her historical fiction, *Behind the Lines*. "New York is like a kaleidoscope," she commented in an interview for *The ALAN Review*. "Everything is there and you're at the center of a lot of conflicting ideas. It influences my writing by energizing me."

Major Works

Cecily, marketed originally for adults, was a forerunner of the young adult novel featuring a chubby teenage protagonist who is disdained by a sophisticated stylish teacher at an exclusive English boarding academy. Critics praised Holland's knowledge of adolescent feelings and her polished writing. Ruth Hill Viguers pronounced the book "a short, almost flawless novel. . . . Several of the mistresses of Langley School, the girls who play even small parts in Cecily's misery or reclamation, and certainly the main characters are so well understood, so alive, that they demand the reader's complete involvement. A beautifully polished gem of a novel . . . that will be a relief from tired stories written especially for teen-agers."

The topic of much debate for its brief inclusion of homosexuality, *The Man without a Face* is about the growing friendship between fourteen-year-old Charles, whose father has died and whose mother has remarried and divorced four times, and Charles's mysterious scar-faced tutor, Justin. Although the title refers to the face of the teacher, badly burned in an accident, it also relates to the boy's late father, whom Charles can no longer remember. Through his mentor, Charles is able to face his own feelings, gain discipline and confidence, and reach out to others around him. "A highly moral book, powerfully and sensitively written; a book that never loses sight of the humor and pain inherent in the human condition," concluded Sheryl B. Andrews.

In *Of Love and Death and Other Journeys,* Holland creates her first positive mother figure, a lovable, flighty, and unforgettable woman who organizes European tours for travelers, mostly in Perugia, Italy, a place Holland knew and loved. Nominated for the National Book Award, *Of Love and Death* won acclaim for its convincing portrayal of teenage angst and its story of fifteen-year-old Meg who learns that her mother is dying of cancer and her father, whom she has never met, is coming to see her. The novel, lightened by the lively dialogue and unconventional cast of characters, captures the roller coaster of adolescent emotions and skillfully juxtaposes comedy with tragedy. Bridget, adopted into a motherless family in *The House in the Woods,* is desperately unhappy when the father hires a new nanny, Ingrid, and brings the family to a lakeside cottage in New Hampshire instead of their usual Maine vacation spot for the summer. When Bridget comes across an empty mansion in the woods, she begins to solve the mystery of its past and discovers its ramifications on her own life. Death, divorce, alcoholism, parental abuse and neglect, sibling rivalry and affection all contribute to a fast-paced, intricate plot that Holland unravels in her masterful storytelling style.

Set during the U.S. Civil War at the time of the New York Draft Riots, *Behind the Lines* tells of the days when poor Irish men and boys were sent down South to fight in place of those draftees who could afford to pay them. Featuring a feisty Irish housemaid, the novel deals with a little known perspective on the War between the States, exploring racial, class, and ethnic discrimination and once again Holland's signature love of animals. Elizabeth Bush noted that "historical fiction buffs will find this topic, which receives little attention in children's literature, to be of interest."

Awards

Of Love and Death and Other Journeys was nominated for the National Book Award in 1976. Both *Abbie's God Book* and *God, Mrs. Muskrat, and Aunt Dot* received the Ott Award from the Church and Synagogue Library Association in 1983.

AUTHOR'S COMMENTARY

Isabelle Holland with Lucy Rollin

SOURCE: An interview in *The ALAN Review,* Vol. 13, No. 1, Fall, 1985, pp. 9-10, 12, 54.

When **The Man without a Face** was published in 1972, Isabelle Holland became famous as a ground-breaker, a crusader for freedom of expression in novels for young people, a writer willing to address the subject of homosexuality in a juvenile novel. Since then, she has written many other books, and while she steadfastly denies the role of crusader in favor of that of storyteller, she remains one of the most competent, sensitive and wise authors of books for young people. In a recent interview following her guest appearance at the Clemson University Children's Literature Symposium, October 1984, she spoke about her books, her interest in Jung and her romanticism.

[Rollin:] *When you wrote* **The Man without a Face,** *how did you decide on your narrator and plot?*

[Holland:] That book just happened in my head. It was the easiest book I ever wrote; it took only three months to complete. And I had no idea that I was doing anything especially unusual or courageous. There was already one book on the market about homosexuality: John Donovan's *I'll Get There. It Better Be Worth The Trip.* It took an American view. I, on the other hand, had a rather English view of homosexuality, as a sort of hero-worship phase. I grew up in England, and English public schools—what we call here private schools—are based on sixth-century b.c. Athens. Things have changed a bit, but for a long time, all English boys in those schools studied were the classics, so they were absolutely soaked in this Athenian concept of romantic love between the pupil and the teacher. Of course, in Athens, they took this to its logical conclusion and it was all right. But the English, being 19th century Christians and with supreme

English illogic, put these boys into the same situation but said, no sex. It was an environment which made them feel guilty.

I've noticed, though, that you rarely have school scenes in your books.

That's because I've never been to an American school. I was in one once in the second grade in St. Louis, and I hated it. My teacher kept trying to make me use the Palmer method, so I usually tried to get croup and stay home. Then I went to England and didn't come back until I was 20, for my last two years of college. So when I put a school into my books, it's usually a private school, because I feel more comfortable with that. *Heads You Win, Tails I Lose* has been my most consistently best-selling book, and that one is set in a public school in America, so it's an exception.

But your first book was set in England, wasn't it?

Yes, *Cecily* was about a fat, miserable, clumsy girl. I made her an outsider because I felt like an outsider. And her teacher in the book is based on a teacher I once had—tall, slim and blond, a very nice product of her upper-class English background. When I wrote it, I believe what I did was to divide myself in two, and both of these people live in me. I think all writers do that, not just me.

I've found your mother characters especially interesting. You seem to make many of them youthful and lively; they often look good in bikinis! But, they are flawed in some way. Are they aspects of you, too?

I was once criticized for having lovable fathers and awful mothers in my books. So I wrote *Of Love and Death and Other Journeys* to create a sympathetic mother, but somehow I couldn't make her your average mother. My editor once said that I gave my fathers all the qualities that I wished my own father had had and my mothers all the qualities that he really did have; that I idealized the fathers and put the responsibility for the family problems on the mothers. There's an element of truth in that.

Less-than-perfect parents like that have been considered a mark of "new realism" in adolescent novels. What do you think is happening to this kind of realism in adolescent books?

I belong to a writers' group in New York, and we do four programs a year. Most of us write for young people. Recently we decided to have a program in which we went to our audience. So we got six children age 12—two from public, two from private and two from parochial schools. We asked them to come with one title that he or she had read and could defend. (Madeleine L'Engle was in this group of writers, too, and she and I disqualified our books from consideration.) When the children talked about what they liked, it was all fantasy, with the exception of one boy who liked animal stories. One

writer in the audience, a writer of realistic books, put up her hand and asked, "Don't any of you like realistic fiction?" One boy replied, "I have trouble enough of my own!" So my impression is that the problem novel, which is what I wrote and which was a big thing for about ten years, has peaked and gone.

*I did notice that your last two books, **Perdita** and **The Island**, are mystery-romances with older characters, rather than problem novels about adolescents. Is that, then, a conscious change for you?*

It's partly the market. *The Empty House,* for example, which is more like my others, has never been bought for paperback. They're not putting things like that in paper now; they very much want the romance, so to some extent I'm governed by economy. I will say, though, that I very much enjoyed writing *Summer of My First Love.* I was bored with the idea of teenage romance, and the contract said that I had to put sex in the book. So I thought about the best teenage love story of all time, Romeo and Juliet, and I based my book on that. I made the girl the daughter of upper-crust academic parents and the boy a Polish Catholic ethnic, and gave them, as an issue, a little strip of land which the boy's group wanted to develop and the girl's group wanted to save. She gets pregnant but loses the baby. I had to get the sex in, but I didn't want to deal with the whole abortion issue, and the book ends unhappily because she comes to feel that he hasn't supported her. I enjoyed writing this enormously. Even though the problem novel faded, I'm sure there will always be issues that people will want to read about. We are a nation of people who talk to each other through the media and we need issues to talk about. I call it the indignation quotient. I sometimes wonder what we'll do when we get to the Kingdom of Heaven and have nothing to be indignant about.

New York City is certainly a place full of indignation. How do you think living there has influenced your writing?

New York is like a kaleidoscope. Everything is there and you're at the center of a lot of conflicting ideas. It influences my writing by energizing me. I liked California when I visited there, but I thought, if I lived here I'd never write another book! There is something about New York hustle that keeps me moving.

How do you relax?

I jog slowly around the reservoir, or go around the track at the 92nd Street Y forty-eight times. I see friends, go to concerts. I'm a member of the Jung Foundation, and I'm slowly working my way through *Memories, Dreams, and Reflections.* Mind you, if I were having a terrible time coping with life I don't think I'd go to a Jungian analyst; I'd need something more practical. But I am fascinated with his theories. I think that Jung is the meeting-place of religion and psychology. I once heard a lecture by a Jungian which had a powerful effect on me. In speaking of Jung's controversial book, *Answer to*

Job, he said, "If you want to know what Jung meant, read the book of *Job.* But instead of the word Job, use the word ego, and instead of the word of God, use the word unconscious." He also said that Jung believed that man is the only creature that can look out and be conscious of what he is looking at and it is that consciousness that produces much of our conflicts. Of course all this is very hard to read. Freud is easy-reading by comparison. I like things to be concrete, and Jung certainly isn't.

Studying Jung sounds like a complicated way to relax!

Well, I don't go to the theater because it's too expensive. And I hate most movies today. I committed a financial indiscretion and bought a VCR and I've been catching up on all the movies I missed. My favorite movies were made in England in the late 40s and 50s. *Brief Encounter* and *Tunes of Glory, The Browning Version,* and movies like that were the last movies made from the point of view and morality of the world as I have understood it.

It's interesting to me that in most critical literature about adolescent writers, you're called a realist. And yet as we talk, you seem much more like a romantic!

Oh, I'm romantic. I'm a late 19th century romantic! I'm optimistic. I like courtship. I was brought up on 19th century novels and all those silly love stories that came after. I had a rather prudish upbringing, I suppose, and somehow to me passion and romance are fueled by frustration. A professor once said that you can read a book in which the main character goes to bed every other page, and it won't evoke the same empathetic passion that you get in *Anna Karenina,* from one kiss.

Speaking of literature, what books do you like to read for enjoyment?

I've long been a fan of Paul Scott's *The Raj Quartet.* I also love Robertson Davies, the Canadian writer; he's devoutly religious, also a Jungian. I also love Herman Wouk. He's not a great stylist, but he tells a good story about interesting people, and he shares my values. I like to read people whose values I share. I'm not a scholarly reader; I prefer people who get me into a story. I love good mystery writers like Agatha Christie; I must say I think the British are better at that than we are. I like the earlier Graham Greene, and I like Josephine Tey. My favorite fantasy is C. S. Lewis's planetary series. He manages to clothe his ideas in believable people and/or creatures—when he isn't doing children or women. His children are too nice, and his women are milksops!

Since 1972's **The Man without a Face,** *you must have communicated with many young readers. What is your chief contact with young people now?*

Mostly they write to me. But I must quote to you something that Malcolm Muggeridge quoted C. S. Lewis as saying: "Most people think that writers who write for children do so because they like children; this is not true. They do so because on some level, they have never stopped being children." So I don't write for people out there; I tell myself a story.

You seem unusual in your field in that you have several publishers instead of just one. What are the advantages and disadvantages of that?

One of the disadvantages of having one publisher is that they can take you for granted. And also if they don't like what you do, you're dependent on them. On the other hand, I write for a living, so if somebody comes to me and says, "Will you do a book for us," if there's a contract, I'll do it. This has happened with all the genres that I've done. The disadvantages of having several publishers, though, is that you're nobody's prize baby. They won't send you on trips as much as they would if they have all your books.

And reviewers? What is your impression of them?

Because I worked in publishing for so long, I saw many of the journals; now I only get the reviews of my own books. I remember that **The Man without a Face** was raked over the coals by *School Library Journal* because I had Justin, the homosexual, die and because I did not portray a homosexual's life as happy. It was the beginning of the gay movement and people were sensitive. Of course, I must say that nobody has been savaged by reviewers the way Judy Blume has. Nowadays she is taken more seriously and is treated better, but shortly after I saw her in 1976, they published her least successful book, *Starring Sally J. Friedman as Herself.* This wasn't really a children's book; it was more a personal memoir. But one trade review was so awful that I called her long distance to tell her I liked the book. She said she had been warned about the reviews, but when they came out she cried for a week. I think I have a typical writer's deep resentment of the fact that a lot of reviewers overlook how much blood, sweat and tears go into a book while they trample over it bouncing their own theories. It gets to be a showcase for them.

It's fashionable, perhaps, to think that our tolerance for certain moral latitude in books has increased. But you once defined a truly moral book as one which shows that what one does about things matters. What would you call a truly moral book for a teenager now?

I think **The Man without a Face** is truly moral. My problem with a lot of teenage novels now is that the parents are all bad guys and the kids are all good guys. The kids are the Noble Savage, so that many books become purveyors of institutionalized self-pity. I can think of at least two fine writers of young adult books who do this. And another highly thought of novel, this time a fantasy, distressed me because it seemed to say that the moral dilemma that had been set up didn't matter. And to me, that matters more than anything else. I have a profound view that we all come from God and that all life is a journey back, but every choice we make is either toward or away, and what we're here for is to learn to go toward. This is not just Christianity; it's universal religion.

Should we think of that theory as we read your books?

I'm a great anti-theorist. In good books, the philosophy is carried by the characters, the people. It has to work in practical terms or it's no good. My father once advised me, "Isabelle, don't read for the story; read for the philosophy." I thought that was lousy advice at the time and I still think it's lousy advice. I say, read for the story. The rest, if it's going to go in, will sink in.

GENERAL COMMENTARY

Corinne Hirsch

SOURCE: "Isabelle Holland: Realism and Its Evasions in *The Man without a Face*," in *Children's literature in education,* Vol. 10, No. 1, Spring, 1979, pp. 25-34.

Deeply troubled youths struggle through the pages of Isabelle Holland's young adult novels. The divorced mother of fifteen-year-old Margaret, in *Of Love and Death and Other Journeys,* dies of cancer and Margaret faces life with a presumably uncaring father whom she has never met. The overweight Melissa, of *Heads You Win, Tails I Lose,* is constantly harangued about her weight and personality defects by parents who detest each other and her; in desperation, she surreptitiously resorts to diet pills and nearly becomes addicted to them. An emotionally disturbed, motherless young girl is all but abandoned to the self-defeating ministrations of a totally inept governess in *Amanda's Choice.* Eleven-year-old Alan, in *Alan and the Animal Kingdom,* attempts to hide the death of the latest in a series of guardians in order to protect his beloved pets from the incursions of unknown adults.

Holland uses this material successfully to explore her characters' loneliness and need for love, but she seems to mistrust her adolescent reader's ability to face the disturbing consequences of the situations she creates. To prevent her novels from becoming terribly distressing, she resorts both to shallow psychologizing and plot manipulation to ameliorate her characters' problems. In *Amanda's Choice,* for example, twelve-year-old Amanda has been rejected by her wealthy parents throughout her life; she is a deeply disturbed child as the novel begins. Filled with hate, she responds to the least frustration with violent tantrums. Her attraction to a ghetto youth, met with a highly ambivalent response, leads her to realize that she can choose between self-control and violence. Despite the boy's reluctance to fulfill Amanda's emotional needs, we are led to believe that she will be all right because her father, totally neglectful until

now, suddenly realizes what a poor parent he has been. Brought to his senses by the family's old-fashioned country doctor, he talks it all out with Amanda, introduces his new, understanding wife, and Amanda, surrounded by concern, discipline, and love, thinks "Things were looking up." There is simply not enough here to convince us that the prospects for so deeply disturbed a child could change to the extent that they have in the course of the novel. Furthermore, her father's change of heart and the promise of a new relationship are unconvincing. Cold and uncaring fathers do not become warm, understanding parents overnight.

Another such parent is pulled out of the hat for Margaret in *Of Love and Death.* The father who has known of her existence since she was two without attempting to see her turns out to be a sensitive, loving parent, complete with kind and understanding wife. Less drastic, but nevertheless difficult to believe, is the change of heart that occurs in *Heads You Win.* Melissa's father, cuttingly cruel to her throughout her childhood, takes out on his daughter his antagonism toward his wife. He denigrates Melissa's first scholastic prize, won at an experimental school chosen by his wife, as a "consolation gift . . . for making the poorest showing"; regarding his overweight daughter with distaste and contempt, he makes her feel repulsive. Nevertheless the story ends with father and daughter in friendship and understanding.

A further problem in Holland's fiction lies in her attempt to impose her moral values on her adolescent readers. Her eagerness to condemn what she sees as the loss of traditional authority in child rearing, education, and religion often leads her to oversimplification and distortion of character and situation. We can be sure that in a novel of Holland's, a permissive adult will be weak and foolish, while a stern, generally conservative disciplinarian will be presented sympathetically. For example, while Melissa feels warmth and understanding for her father, who is about to leave home to live with his mistress, she feels nothing for her pathetic mother, now a lonely alcoholic. In this and other instances, Holland's preference for conservative ideology, to the detriment of believable characterization, tilts the balance.

Nowhere are Holland's strengths and weaknesses more apparent than in *The Man without a Face,* her most interesting novel to date. Resting on two conflicting sets of inner logic, it is a deeply affecting but nonetheless flawed novel. On the one hand, we have the cautionary tale of Charles, the fourteen-year-old product of a ludicrously permissive upbringing, who must experience the influence of traditional authority in order to develop a sense of responsibility and self-discipline. Character and plot are manipulated in order to illustrate the dangers of permissiveness and the value of discipline. Concurrently, we have the compelling development of a deep relationship between the lonely, fatherless Charles and his isolated, guilt-ridden, homosexual tutor. Holland movingly depicts their tentative groping toward one another and Charles's consequent emotional enrichment. It is only at the conclusion of their relationship, where the imposition of Holland's ideology is substituted for convincing human interaction, that belief falters.

The Man without a Face makes a two-pronged attack on what Holland views as the obtuseness of those embracing liberal ideas either in child rearing or in politics. The chic inhabitants of the resort island where Charles spends his summers and the progressive New York private schools he has had the misfortune to attend are Holland's targets. Charles's mother is the prime example of those taken in by liberal doctrine. An exaggerated shallowness is the chief characteristic of her ideas, which change depending upon the latest fad or the identity of her latest husband. Her marriage to an editor in a New York publishing house, replete with fashionable literary parties, ends when her husband discovers that she has neglected to read a controversial book he has published. The parties end and protest marches begin with her next husband, a leftist college professor:

> This prof must have been on a dozen committees, because his name kept turning up in those full-page *Times* ads opposing everything and showing up the Establishment. It's the one period in her life when Mother got exercise, carrying pickets of one kind or another. Twice I saw her on television, but one time didn't really count, because there was a counter demonstration going on across the street, and when she was discovered on camera she had somehow wandered into the opposition.

The contempt accorded Charles's mother is carried over to liberal protests in general.

Charles's mother's ideas about child rearing are similarly half-digested liberal theories. With the uncharacteristic articulateness that Holland reserves for Charles's promulgation of her ideas, he explains why he need not fear his mother's curiosity regarding his whereabouts: "the older generation [is] thoroughly housebroken. If they get too nosy you can drag in words like "authoritarian" and "over-compensatory" and they're so well trained by TV and all those articles in magazines about adolescents and Dr. Spock that they immediately begin to feel inadequate." Charles's mother is not alone in the ease with which she is manipulated. Neighbors with whom Charles boards for a time can also be counted on not to interfere with his activities, "since they had been successfully brought up by their children never to ask where I'd been or intended to go." The foolhardiness of permissive parents is brought to the point of absurdity in Charles's story of a boy who, angry at being asked to bring out the garbage, empties it on the living room rug. His parents, shocked at their insensitivity to his needs, apologize, blame themselves, and buy him the bicycle he has been asking for.

Holland's permissive adults are not merely foolish and shallow; they are insensitive as well. Mother's last husband, the leftist professor, supports Charles's use of obscenity as a way for the boy to express his feelings fully. Nevertheless, he stifles one of his wife's few positive qualities, a gift for storytelling, on the grounds that "it retards the development of social consciousness to feed a neurotic need for entirely mythical heroes." Walking uninvited into Charles's room one day, he sees a photograph of Charles's father and asks contemptuously who "the lifeguard type" is, wounding Charles in his most sensitive area, the memory of his dead father.

The progressive schools Charles attends are filled with teachers who lack any understanding of their students' individuality. Although they pay lip service to the goal of individual development, the teachers approve only of ideas that follow a liberal line. The one essay Charles writes that has some personal meaning, a paper about flying, is treated with contempt because it conflicts with his teacher's ideology. His teacher, a crudely caricatured environmentalist who hates technology, mockingly reads the paper to the class, gives them a lecture on nature and ecology, and then tears the paper up and throws it away. Charles has better luck with a paper entitled "Why the System Must Be Changed," plagiarized from a friend's older brother. Although it is clearly not the sort of paper anyone knowing Charles could believe he would write, he hands it in several times, always receiving high praise from his teachers.

Holland's distortions of character and idea in the service of her conservative bias leave us unprepared for the delicacy of the Charles-McLeod relationship. But they certainly facilitate her positive characterization of McLeod, a traditional disciplinarian. She need only contrast his reactions to Charles's behavior with those of the other adults depicted. Predictably, McLeod sees right through Charles's plagiarized paper and appreciates his interest in airplanes. He is not taken in by the crass manipulation Charles successfully practices on permissive adults. When Charles defends his poor grammar by calling grammar "a racist device for repressing the language of the people" and his use of obscenity as "a legitimate expression of authentic feeling," McLeod appears a model of intelligent discipline by merely responding sensibly to these parroted responses and insisting on hard work.

It is not so much in the fullness of characterization of Charles and McLeod that the novel's strength lies, but rather in the development of their intense emotional relationship and the corresponding enrichment of Charles's sensibilities. Both are intensely isolated individuals at the outset. Withdrawal is Charles's answer to his familial and scholastic difficulties. It is a habitual defense, as Charles explains when he describes his reaction to McLeod's initial refusal to tutor him. He is miserable at first, "And then, inside of me, I just quit. Turned everything off. Nothing mattered. Periodically this happens to me. Sooner or later I snap out of it, or something snaps me back, but for a while I'm not there." What does matter to Charles is avoiding the emotional demands of his mother and the jealous taunts of his older sister Gloria. His immediate desire is to be accepted at a boarding school in order to be away from his mother and Gloria. His dream is to join the Air Force, partly because of his interest in flying, but also in order to escape his family.

McLeod's isolation, if no more intense, is more romantic. He lives in a picturesquely lonely house overlooking a cliff, his only companion a huge, frightening dog. Although he has lived on the island for twelve years, he has made no acquaintances, and rumors about his past are rife. He is physically flawed, and his disfigurement is emblematic of some past tragedy or guilt. Half his face is horribly burned, and he has chosen not to undergo plastic surgery to repair it. Otherwise, his appearance is rugged and masculine. His almost Promethean power is emphasized by the control he exerts over his dog and skittish horse, as well as by his masterful authority as a teacher.

Initially Charles and McLeod feel less than positive about one another. Charles is intimidated by and antagonistic toward McLeod's sternness and reserve, but it is, ironically, just those ostensibly negative qualities in McLeod that permit the withdrawn boy, fearful of suffocating relationships, to move toward him. His aloofness gives Charles the freedom to think about and become interested in him without threat to his emotional integrity. As the barriers between the two begin to break down, McLeod's evident capabilities, coupled with his masculine qualities and keen understanding, draw him into the center of Charles's fatherless universe. The undercurrent of physical attraction Charles feels for McLeod is realized through the romance and mystery of McLeod's characterization, the emphasis on his masculinity, and the constant tension of attraction and repulsion in the development of their emotional intimacy.

Charles's emergence from self-absorption to sensitivity and love for McLeod is movingly delineated. His interest in others' feelings has previously been nonexistent, except where his own selfish interests were immediately concerned. As he states early in the novel, "I'm usually more interested in what I think of people than what they think about me, barring, of course, crucial types like Mother and Gloria where the answer has great bearing on how comfortable I am." Since he is not generally given to self-analysis, the early changes in Charles's feelings are appropriately divulged as a series of surprises to himself; then, as he becomes closer to McLeod, he develops a more conscious sensitivity to his tutor's feelings.

Charles's burgeoning trust in McLeod several weeks into his tutoring becomes apparent to him through a conversation he has with his young sister, Meg, who asks how things are going. His overt feelings are negative, and he characterizes McLeod as "gruesome," but when Meg asks if he will pass his exams, he finds, to his own surprise, that he has no doubts that his tutor will get him through. Still early in their relationship, Charles walks toward McLeod's house, calling him "Monster McLeod" because of his authoritarian approach to education, and is nearly attacked by his tutor's nervous horse. Having assumed the horse's skittishness to be caused by Mc-

Leod's poor handling, Charles learns that the horse had been abused by others and rescued by McLeod. Again, Charles is taken aback by the development of his own trust in McLeod: "I thought it would be hard to imagine him gentling a frightened animal, but to my surprise, it wasn't." Charles's altered vision of McLeod comes as a further revelation to himself when McLeod becomes self-conscious in the mistaken belief that Charles is staring at his disfigurement: "'Your face doesn't bother me,' I blurted out, and realized as I said it that it was true. . . . 'I don't think about it that way any more.'" These changes in Charles's feelings, creeping up on him unaware, prepare him for a more conscious change. He begins to see McLeod as a separate person whose emotions matter.

As Charles's interest in his work and in McLeod increases, he becomes consciously concerned not to injure McLeod's sensibilities. After McLeod saves Charles from his nervous horse, there is a moment of warmth and humor between them, until Charles looks away from the burned side of McLeod's face. He immediately senses a change in the older man: "His voice this time was different—so cold I wondered if he had seen me look away from him. I glanced back at him and for a second, just before he turned his face and walked off, I knew he had seen how I felt." On another occasion McLeod mistakenly believes that Charles is staring at his disfigurement and responds with angry sarcasm. Charles's initial reaction is stunned embarrassment. Previously, this response would have been followed by withdrawal; now, Charles cares enough to move beyond his own embarrassment to reach toward McLeod and, with difficulty, to tell him that his scarred face no longer bothers him.

Charles shows a further increase in sensitivity to McLeod by attempting to predict his emotional responses. Overcome by curiosity, he asks whether there is truth to the rumor that McLeod writes pornography under a pseudonym. He immediately becomes furious with himself, fearing that he has overstepped his bounds: "If McLeod had made one thing clear above all others it was that he had a highly developed sense of privacy. It spread out like a moat around him. Every so often, like this afternoon, I would find myself inside it and then, instead of leaving well enough alone, I'd shove my whole leg in my mouth and start asking pointy little questions." His concern is so great that when McLeod responds with a laugh, he feels "weak." Charles takes a further step toward emotional maturity by actually moving beyond himself and putting himself into McLeod's place. As he finds himself asking McLeod whether he was injured in World War II, he becomes uncomfortable wondering, for the first time, "what it could be like for him." During his summer with McLeod Charles moves from egocentrism and emotional repression to tactfulness and richness of emotional response.

Holland uses Charles's dreams to express depths of feeling beyond the boy's ability to articulate or even to understand consciously. Immediately before his first dream, Charles arrives at McLeod's, and, finding his tutor out riding, goes into the stable and romps in the hay. His frolicking has a distinctly sensual quality:

> I poked around the barn . . . breathing in the smells of hay and horse and leather. There was a ladder going up to the upper part so I went up and waded around in the hay. It was really cool. I lay down and rolled like a puppy. The hay tickled my nose and my mouth and my midriff where my shirt rolled up . . . I put my hands under my chin and closed my eyes to see if I could smell both salt and hay at the same time. . . .

He falls asleep and dreams of attempting to saddle McLeod's horse, which has grown to four times its actual size. The horse gets larger and larger and is about to kill him when the actual arrival of McLeod's frightened, rearing horse merges into the dream and wakes Charles.

The episode presages the undercurrent of physical desire and repulsion that runs through the novel. The coupling of the dream with Charles's sensual feelings as he plays in the barn underlines his desire, expressed in his wish to ride McLeod's frightened horse, to be both like McLeod and one with him. The disproportionate size of the horse and its terrifying attack emphasize Charles's sense that there is something fearfully wrong with his desire for identification and intimacy with McLeod.

Charles's need for McLeod as a substitute for the father he can barely remember is the ostensible subject of another dream, which occurs immediately after an upsetting incident. McLeod has divulged the guilty secret behind his burned face, and Charles puts his hand on the arm of his guilt-ridden friend as a comforting gesture; McLeod pulls away and walks off. Hurt and angry at the rejection, Charles storms off to his friends, smokes marijuana, and betrays McLeod's confidence. He reacts badly to the drug, faints, and dreams of flying over the sea, landing, and swimming to shore toward the open arms of his father, whose face is McLeod's. Suddenly McLeod becomes angry, and Charles feels himself drowning: ". . . the sky was almost black. McLeod's face was as white as the stones and he was terribly angry. He was so angry I knew I would never be forgiven and that, anyway, I was going to die because I had forgotten about the undertow which was pulling me out and down, down into the water where I couldn't breathe. . . ."

Although the dream certainly depicts both Charles's desire for McLeod as a father and his remorse for betrayal of a confidence, the horrifyingly nightmarish quality of his guilt and fear points to a further disturbance. His sense of being out of his element and lacking control is similar to the feeling he has in his dream of McLeod's horse. Like the earlier dream, this one seems to deal with Charles's unacknowledged and uncontrollable sexual desires. His subconscious knowledge of the ambiguous nature of his feelings toward McLeod would explain both his apprehension that McLeod cannot satisfy his need for a father and his guilty horror at this realization.

Holland further develops the theme of sexual desire in scenes of physical activity between Charles and McLeod. In Charles's description of a swim they take together, his feeling of physical well-being is reminiscent of his mood in the barn preceding the dream of the horse:

> Then I started to play. I rolled over and duckdived, then came up and rolled over some more and lay on my back, thrashing my feet, and then tried a backward dive. Coming up, I saw McLeod above me in the water and butted him gently in the stomach then shot away laughing as I came up. I felt marvelous. He turned, shaking the water out of his hair, and started after me. I knew I couldn't outswim him, so I went down again and swam underwater and looked around and there he was, so I surfaced and changed course and then went down and butted him again on the side. . . . I forgot everything but the water and being in it and chasing and being chased, far from the shore with nothing around or moving except us.

Charles's previous attempts to touch McLeod affectionately have been rebuffed; but after this swim they do finally have physical contact. McLeod takes Charles's arm to comfort him as he confesses to having betrayed McLeod's past to his friends, and they end up lying on a rock holding hands: "There was something beating in his [McLeod's] hand or mine, I couldn't tell which. I wanted to touch him. Moving the arm that had been across my eyes I reached over and touched his side. The hot skin was tight over his ribs. I knew then that I'd never been close to anyone in my life, not like that. And I wanted to get closer." McLeod averts any further physical intimacy, but Charles is clearly disturbed and asks whether McLeod thinks he is a "queer." His tutor reassures him, attributing his feelings to a need for affection and for a father. Such assurances are hardly enough to deal with the intensity of desire and guilt Charles evinces through his dreams, and later events bear out their inadequacy.

During the last weeks of Charles and McLeod's relationship, the two have become open, warm, and affectionate. Physical desire may be present, but it is expressed as companionable affection. Charles's mother and sisters have gone away for a while, so Charles has given the run of his cottage to a smelly stray cat he has befriended, whose presence in the house is forbidden. One evening, Charles returns home to find the cat kicked to death by Gloria's boyfriend for having soiled her bed. Gloria is having intercourse on Charles's bed. Distraught, he returns to McLeod for comfort, spends the night in his bed, and has a vaguely described sexual experience there.

This sudden onrush of melodramatic events is used to create a startling denouement which Holland proceeds to wrap up neatly and simply. We are led to believe that Charles deserves much of the blame for the cat's death because of his irresponsibility in allowing it into the house. Charles accepts the boyfriend's assertion to that effect: "Percy was telling the truth. It was his boot. But it was as much my fault as his." Similarly, Charles is responsible for the sexual encounter, since, as he realizes, "[McLeod] hadn't done anything. I'd done it all." Evidently these disastrous incidents are further lessons in the responsibility and self-discipline that had been so lacking in Charles's permissive upbringing. Life is not all bad, however. McLeod conveniently dies of a heart attack, leaving a note forgiving Charles for rejecting him after their night together, and willing him all his belongings. Charles's mother marries her fifth husband, a good man who will make a good father (why he would want to marry her remains a mystery). Charles continues his education at boarding school, presumably a more responsible, self-disciplined person for his experiences.

The cautionary tale has taken over. It is unfortunate that Holland reverts to unconvincing plotting and rather questionable moralism to end her novel. Is a boy who allows an animal he loves into the house equally at fault with a young man who kicks it to death? Can a fourteen-year-old boy be held morally responsible for a sexual act with a grown man who knows himself to be a homosexual, no matter who actually initiated and most actively carried it through? Furthermore, as realistic fiction, *The Man without a Face* owes its readers fidelity to human experience; it cannot sweep under the rug the problems it has been dealing with throughout. Having introduced themes rich with ambiguity, the exigencies of the novel demand that they be worked out more fully. How might Charles deal with the complicated emotional and sexual feelings he has developed? What would be a realistic outcome of his relationship with McLeod?

Adolescents, no less than adults, deserve a fully developed fictional experience. If Holland wishes to consider the difficult problems she does, she has a responsibility to explore their implications. Neither the desire to teach nor the wish to provide her readers with a positive ending is adequate reason for oversimplification. In *The Man without a Face* more than anywhere else in her adolescent fiction, Holland perceptively raises and partially explores complex questions; but in the end she evades them by lapsing into didacticism and melodrama.

TITLE COMMENTARY

📖 *CECILY* (1967)

Edith C. Howley

SOURCE: A review of *Cecily*, in *Best Sellers*, Vol. 27, No. 1, April 1, 1967, p. 7.

The time is now, the setting an upper-middle-class English boarding school for girls. Elizabeth Marks, a more than competent young woman, is completing her last year of teaching before marrying Tim, an American teacher in a nearby boys' school. Although their backgrounds and temperaments are different, they are happily anticipating their approaching marriage and have never had any serious differences of opinion. Until Cecily, that is. Elizabeth is a good teacher and a good disciplinarian, enjoying both her work and her students who like her, respect her and learn from her. Cecily Matthews is the exception. Cecily who "sat like an island that would not be absorbed, emanating . . . gusts of emotion: injury, outrage, wild spates of giggles, or spasms of embarrassing, uncontrolled affection". Elizabeth considers her hopeless and the situation becomes acute when Elizabeth is assigned as house mistress to the dormitory which includes Cecily.

This is Cecily's first year in boarding school. Spoiled by her mother and held too strictly to account by her father, she is at 13 awkward, overweight, graceless, muddled. She is mocked and harassed by the more sophisticated girls among her classmates; she is lonely and unhappy and an outsider. Elizabeth's antipathy to Cecily is obvious not only to the other members of the staff and to Miss Geoffreys, the headmistress, but to Cecily and to Tim as well. Tim, who has met Cecily a couple of rare times, rather likes the youngster and is sorry for her; Cecily is filled with adolescent daydreams of the time when she can replace Elizabeth in Tim's affections. The other girls in the house are affected too by this emotional malaise and Cecily is more pecked at by the barnyard animals than ever. Worst for Elizabeth is the way in which the whole affair is disturbing her relationship with Tim and even more her teeth are set on edge by Cecily. Tim is outspokenly appalled by Elizabeth's hardness and total lack of sympathy; Elizabeth is shocked at her lack of control and frightened by Tim's open disapproval. Events come to a high boil when Cecily disappears at half term after saying that she plans to meet her parents. Tim finds her in fairly short order at a local fair and Cecily is restored to her family, but the holiday of many people has been disrupted and the relationship between Tim and Elizabeth has suffered possibly irreparable damage. They are forced into new evaluations and Cecily, too, is forced to make an adult decision about the school.

At 189 pages, this is too slight to be a novel. The time span is short, the three-dimensional characters few, the action limited, and little is finally resolved. What there is, however, is tightly knit and plausible, the characters of Tim, Elizabeth and Cecily clearly enough drawn so that Cecily's catalytic effect on an otherwise emotionally well-balanced Elizabeth is quite believable. It is well done, but slight.

Ruth Hill Viguers

SOURCE: A review of *Cecily*, in *The Horn Book Magazine*, Vol. XLIII, No. 3, June, 1967, p. 353.

In a short, almost flawless novel is told the story of the love between Elizabeth, a teacher in an English boarding school, and Tim, an American Rhodes scholar. So well suited to each other were the young people, so deeply in love and so ready to try to understand the complexities of each other's personalities, that it seemed unlikely that any outside influence could affect their happiness. But there was Cecily, unhappy, untidy, inept, a thirteen-year-old island in a sea of reasonably secure, uncomplicated schoolgirls. Try as she would, Elizabeth could not like Cecily: her sense of fairness, usually so strong, failed her in dealing with a child who made no effort to surmount her own difficulties. And Tim could not reconcile this lack of compassion in the Elizabeth he loved so deeply. Several of the mistresses of Langley School, the girls who play even small parts in Cecily's misery or reclamation, and certainly the main characters are so well understood, so alive, that they demand the reader's complete involvement. A beautifully polished gem of a novel, published for adults, that will be a relief from tired stories written especially for teen-agers.

📖 *AMANDA'S CHOICE* (1970)

Alice Low

SOURCE: A review of *Amanda's Choice*, in *The New York Times Book Review*, May 3, 1970, p. 23.

Twelve-year-old Amanda, "a poor little rich girl," is an emotionally deprived child, rejected first by her mother (now dead) and then by her father (mostly absent). Bored and lonely on the summer island estate with her governess and housekeeper, she uses her anger to tyrannize them and other adults around her.

The story is fragmented, veering between Amanda, the baffled adults who analyze and explain her strong language and delinquent behavior, and Manuel, a resentful Cuban teen-age musician from the New York slums (installed in the guest house to write an opera). The two angry kids slap each other around, shout each other down, and in between meet as human beings with something in common. Manuel disappears after police questioning, Amanda runs away in search of him, and in a soap opera ending, Amanda, her father and his new wife relate with honesty, warmth and reason.

The author understands child-rearing, psychological nuances and social problems, but she uses her characters to carry messages rather than to tell their flesh and blood stories. She makes important points: among them that emotional deprivation scars more deeply than material deprivation, and that Spanish Harlem has a richer, more genuine life than Amanda's insulated island.

📖 *THE MAN WITHOUT A FACE* (1972)

Isabelle Holland

SOURCE: "Tilting at Taboos," in *The Horn Book Magazine*, Vol. XLIX, No. 3, June, 1973, pp. 299-305.

The Man without a Face is about the relationship of a fourteen-year-old boy with a man who tutors him through a summer to pass a prep-school exam. The man is a disfigured recluse, something of a mystery in the New England village where the boy, Charles, is spending the summer with his family. The man, Justin McLeod, is known only for his abrupt manners and generally misanthropic approach. The boy, Charles, starting from dislike, progresses through respect for Justin to affection and finally love. Ultimately, he discovers that Justin is indeed a homosexual and that what has happened to Justin in the past has gone into what he is at the present. There is one incident that is overtly—although by accident—homosexual. The boy turns from this in revulsion, leaves Justin, passes the exam, and goes to school—putting, he thinks, Justin out of his mind. But two months later he faces what has happened and goes back to see Justin, only to find that it is too late.

Now, I didn't set out to write about homosexuality. I started this book with only the idea of a fatherless boy who experiences with a man some of the forms of companionship and love that have been nonexistent in his life. Because the other side of Charles's dilemma or emotional history arises from his feeling of being both suffocated and rejected by the predominant female influence in his home—his four-times married mother and his older sister. His stepfathers have come and gone too fast for him to do anything but dislike them. Emotionally, Charles has lived his life as an armed camp, hanging onto a shadowy memory of his own father. Hence the revolutionary impact that Justin has on him.

I think I might diverge here and say something that has always interested me about the eternally fascinating subject of love: Into one person's love for another goes much of the love, either present or in default, that has gone, or should have gone, into other relationships. The title, *The Man without a Face,* really has two meanings: It refers to the nickname by which Justin is called because of his facial disfigurement; but, on a deeper level, the man without a face is also Charles's father, whom he can barely remember. But Charles has wrapped his memory of his father around himself as a shield against a world that he finds, on the whole, hostile. Behind that shield, Charles is emotionally starved. When Justin steps into his life, he brings three qualities that mythologically as well as psychologically have always been the archetypes of fatherhood: Justin is masculine, he is authoritative, and he is undemonstratively kind. He steps into the vacuum of Charles's emotional life, and the result is cataclysmic.

Now, all of this interested me far more than the almost incidental fact that the book is about love between two people of the same sex. The story could have been about a boy whose deprivations and needs were the exact opposite from Charles's. Given another kind of boy, with another kind of emotional background, the instigator of his youthful love could have been female—as in *Summer of Forty-two*. And if that had been the case, how much of the love could have been that of the male child for the missing or inadequate female parent, and how much that of the male adolescent in his first sexual encounter with a female? As with Charles, I don't think it's either-or. I think it's both.

An English psychologist (whose name I have forgotten, in a book whose title I can't remember) said that it was his personal observation and belief that the child of either sex took its identity from its father. Margaret Mead—this time I can remember—said back in the sixties that when the campus protesters and anti-war demonstrators were chanting "Ho, Ho, Ho Chi Minh," what they were really doing was asking for strong fathers with strong convictions. And that was what Justin was, a strong father with strong convictions who believed that discipline was a necessary element of affection, not its opposite.

Now, about taboos per se. Speaking solely from a storyteller's point of view, I think the sexual revolution has been a somewhat mixed blessing. And I say this even though I realize that without the dropping of taboos, *The Man without a Face* could never have been published as a juvenile. But, in a way, it's also an example of what I mean. Because *The Man without a Face* is a love story—an unusual love story, but nevertheless, a love story.

Art forms come and go. Every few decades there's a great brouhaha over what's happened to the novel—it's dying, it's dead, it's just been resurrected. Poetry changes radically. The one form that has remained constant since the days of the troubadours before reading and writing is the story—and by that, I mean the love story. Prince meets princess, boy meets girl, man meets woman, he (or she) travels over obstacles, either external or internal—and at the end the lovers meet. They may meet only to part or die (as do Romeo and Juliet, Tristan and Isolde, Lancelot and Guinevere) or meet to live happily ever after. But between the beginning and the end, there have to be obstacles, or there's no story.

If you look over any paperback rack, you will see, burgeoning into popularity over the last decade, the romance and the Gothic novel. Why? Because the oldest story of all, the love story, has virtually vanished from hard-core, hardcover literature. For one thing, major review media will rarely review it. It's considered middlebrow and old hat. And anyone who breaks that taboo—and it is a very real one—gets his knuckles rapped. Erich Segal may be crying all the way to the bank, but he is no longer teaching at Yale. The students who used to flock to his Latin class before his book was published, booed him when his sales soared. The intellectual establishment tore his skin off in strips. And all he'd done was to take one of the oldest stories of all, put it into modern jargon, and have it achieve tremendous success. If it had been a homosexual love story, or an interracial love story, or a lesbian love story, or an Oedipal love story, it would, if it were halfway decently written, have had serious consideration. But not a straight love story.

But to go back to my mixed feelings about the sexual revolution: It has destroyed—temporarily, I trust—the old-fashioned love story. A modern story might well have the hero and heroine exchanging smoldering glances across a crowded cocktail party, but they would be in bed by page ten, and what are you going to do with the next two hundred pages? You could still produce a set of obstacles so that hero or heroine would climb out of bed and stay out for a while before getting back in again, but it's not the same. The essence of the true love story, its real mystique, lies in the unattainability to each other, for at least two hundred pages, of the hero and heroine. When physical encounter is easy and casual, even though obstacles remain, the mystique is gone. That moment that used to occur a few pages before the end when the lovers have their first kiss was electric, not only for the participants, but for the reader, and it had all the more impact for being filled with all the yearnings of the preceding pages. Again, speaking entirely from the literary point of view, I think the multiple orgasm is a poor substitute. That is why I am not a tilter of taboos per se and on principle. As a storyteller, I need them.

While I was thinking about this subject, I remembered some of the books I read when I was at school. I grew up in England, and the books I got out of the school library or read in Welsh hotel rooms when we were on holiday would be incomprehensible to the children of today. This, of course, was before World War II. These books, many of them, were even a generation older and were pre-World War I. But I found them less antediluvian and grotesque than I think a child of today would find those written when I was growing up. However, I do remember one that—unsophisticated as I was, growing up in a small town in the north of England—gave me a case of the giggles, although I found it quite touching. It was, at least in one way, a sort of ground-breaking book for its time, because it was about a young lady—capital *L* lady—who went into training as a nurse at a time when it was considered socially very unacceptable. Anyway, after numerous mishaps, she finally had her big moment at the end with the young house surgeon, at which they reached an "understanding." The next line went something like, "[h]e did not kiss me, of course, because we were not yet engaged." We're a long way away from that. And yet—I don't regret those books even though they gave me an indelibly romantic streak.

I realize that in many ways, I had a longer childhood than most young people today who are reading of problems at thirteen that I never heard of until I was eighteen or older. And this, of course, both affects, and is affected by, their reading habits. There are times when it seems to me they go straight from *Peter Rabbit* to *Portnoy's Complaint*. On the other hand, the child of today seems to live the last of her childhood at the same time that she is living the first of her adulthood, so that she can and does switch from D. H. Lawrence to Louisa May Alcott and back again with a versatility that is, to me, dizzying.

To be truthful, I don't write books specifically for children. I just write the books as they come out, and they turn out to be for elderly children. Now that may well be the influence of my long childhood. At some inner depth I remain perpetually twelve. My first book, **Cecily**—about a child in an English boarding school, one of her teachers, and the young man her teacher is engaged to—was actually published by the adult department, although the reason it's still in print is because it did quite well in the Young Adult category. The next book, **Amanda's Choice,** started out as an adult book but became a juvenile; and I have stayed with children's books ever since. As adult novels become more and more adult, I become firmer and firmer in my convictions that I am not yet old enough to write one.

And yet, **The Man without a Face** has received very gratifying reviews outside New York where it was reviewed as an adult book. If I had written it six years ago, it would unquestionably have been published on the adult list. The line between adult and juvenile has moved. But it's a very wavering line even now, depending on geographical area. I am not as acquainted as I should be with other children's books, but I do know that the taboo against any mention or recognition of homosexuality was broken by my friend and neighbor John Donovan in his book, *I'll Get There. It Better Be Worth the Trip.* Vera and Bill Cleaver have pushed the quality and the line higher so that some of the better children's books of today are in every way comparable in viewpoint and sophistication to the bulk of adult books of, say, twenty years ago. And there is no question but that the children of today—hearing nightly on television and daily in the classroom of the problems of war, race, and poverty—require of their books a social depth that the young people of my generation never dreamed of.

Personally, I think the line between adult and children's books is largely artificial, anyway. *Alice in Wonderland*—one of my old favorites—is a children's classic. Yet, it was written by an eccentric professor of mathematics with a humor that is extremely adult. Someone once said erroneously that the charm of Alice lay in the fact that she was an imaginative child caught in a fantastic world. But Alice's charm is that she is a totally unimaginative, very literal-minded child caught in a fantasy; and her statements are funny because she responds to the fantastic, not with whimsy or imagination, but with irritable common sense. The humor is adult in concept because it is based on irony, the subtlest of all forms of humor.

I sometimes amuse myself by wondering what would happen if some of the great favorites of adolescent years, *Jane Eyre,* for instance, were submitted to a publisher now for the first time. The first thing it would do would be to cause a battle between the juvenile and adult departments as to where the real area of interest lay, though I think the juvenile would win. But dividing books in this way is a relatively recent innovation—at least I think it is—except, of course, for the very young books.

My father once told me that when he was twelve years old he got his first library card and took out his first book, *The Vicar of Wakefield*—certainly one of the dullest adult books ever written—and he swallowed it whole. But in his small Southern town's library there were only adult classics. In his whole life he never read what could be called a children's book. So what, strictly speaking, is an adult book? What is a juvenile?

As far as taboos are concerned, I have played devil's advocate on their behalf. To be honest I would be just as outraged as the greatest libertarian if I ran into a taboo standing in the way of something I wanted to do or say—that is, if there are any left. Has anyone written a moving story yet about incest? Other than Sophocles, that is? But unless they obstruct my way, I am forced to admit that taboos frequently help to make interesting stories. The prince still has to climb through the hedge of thorns to find his lady.

Now today's prince may be born in a ghetto or be Puerto Rican, a Chicano, an Indian (American or Eastern), be a mental or physical cripple, an alcoholic or a drug addict. His hedge of thorns may be his environment, justice or the lack of it, his parents, drugs, no job, or some other handicap. But in the sense that a love story is a journey of the heart and the mind as well as of the body, he has to make his journey from here to there, over or through or around his obstacles. And obstacles are frequently the result of, or contingent on, taboos.

What are taboos? Well, one used to be that you cannot portray homosexual love, certainly not sympathetically, certainly not in a children's book. But if there were no taboos, there would be no urgency. Let me say again that I am not speaking for or against a tabooless society. That is a social or moral or even theological question. I am merely talking of what is good for storytelling.

If you have any doubt about it, please consider: If Romeo Montague and Juliet Capulet had been members of the Now generation with no worn-out ideas about obedience to parents or the sanctification of marriage, they would simply have announced to their parents what they were going to do and then left together after the ball. There would have been no tragedy. There would also have been no play. And if Anna Karenina had lived in a society of easy divorce and remarriage, Tolstoy's masterpiece would have ended up being the essay pure and simple on land reform that I thought it was when I first began reading it.

I realize at this point that I could easily be heading for trouble. Because there is no doubt that if we had a tabooless society, many people would think that Utopia had arrived. If prejudice, poverty, greed, and individual and collective ill will had also vanished, then indeed the Kingdom of Heaven would be at hand. But what would have happened to storytelling? Well, perhaps we would all be on a such perpetual alpha wave that we wouldn't need it—a dreary outlook for an author. Not having the hedge of thorns (our taboos, our inequities, our unfulfilled yearnings for our heroes and heroines to overcome and/or fulfill so that each may grasp his or her particular Grail), we'd have to invent taboos. Or we would depend upon the troubadours of the future who, to entertain the travelers as they sped from planet to planet, would begin . . .

"Once upon a time long, long ago, way back in the twentieth century, before people were able to see freely into each others' minds and hearts, there lived a fourteen-year-old boy named Charles Norstadt who had great trouble with his womenfolk and who yearned for the love of a man who could, among other ways of loving him, take the place of a father. Now, to understand the meaning of Charles's and Justin's story, you must realize they had something in those days they called a taboo against any expression of love between members of the same sex. Yes, I know it's hard to believe, but without that there wouldn't even be a story to tell. . . ."

You see the conceit of the author: In interplanetary travel they will be explaining taboos so they can read my book.

So, back to our hero and his hedge of thorns, the taboos in his life. As I said at the beginning, my feelings about them and about abandoning them altogether are very mixed.

Kirkus Reviews

SOURCE: A review of *The Man without a Face,* in *Kirkus Reviews,* Vol. XL, No. 2, January 15, 1972, pp. 73-4.

A teenage misogynist and compulsive underachiever, [Charles] strains to pass his boarding school entrance exams the second time around and thereby escape the constraints of his much-married mother (castrating even in her desire to alter the cat which [Charles] sees as "just part of (her) wholesale plan for the taming and domesticating of the male species") and nymphet sister. Inevitably he finds a mentor in the horribly scarred and romantic recluse Justin McLeod who proves a demanding tutor (smashing some straw-man defenses of "progressive education"). And inevitably again, this relationship between two emotional cripples leads to a once-only homosexual encounter (though the unsophisticated will have a tough time figuring out from the text just "what happened"). [Charles's] bitterness is painfully real and the recognition of his sexual feelings commendably frank, but in return for this measure of honesty, the whole story is slanted to justify the "daring" subject matter—the psychological underpinnings are intrusive (talk of Oedipus complexes and sibling rivalry), the twin mysteries in the pasts of [Charles's] dead father and Justin unlikely, the decadence and nastiness of [Charles's] family over stressed (even Gloria's obnoxious boyfriend probably wouldn't kick the cat to death). For a hero *with* a face and a fully realized individuality, the bulkily packaged moral ("You can be free from everything but the consequences of what you do") just might not be too high a price to pay.

Sheryl B. Andrews

SOURCE: A review of *The Man without a Face,* in *The Horn Book Magazine,* Vol. XLVIII, No. 4, August, 1972, pp. 375-76.

Without being mawkish or false, the author has delved into the joy and sorrow concomitant with love and growth. Charles Norstadt, the Island's answer to Holden Caulfield, is a fourteen-year-old who isolates himself from the female excesses of emotion perpetrated on him by his attractive, four-times-married mother and fairly nasty older sister, Gloria. "People who said I was incapable of applying myself to anything didn't know what they were talking about. I had applied myself to not crying—no matter what." Until the summer he meets The Man Without a Face, Charles has allowed himself to care deeply only for a summer stray, the very musty tomcat Moxie, and to appreciate—only at times—his younger sister Meg, a highly intelligent little girl who uses the refrigerator as an escape from all of her problems. Desperate to get into boarding school at St. Matthew's when he learns that his sister Gloria intends to leave finishing school and come home in the fall, Charles grasps at the only straw he sees that will enable him to pass the entrance exams—being tutored by "The Grouch, alias The Man Without a Face, alias Justin McLeod." As the summer progresses, Charles discovers that sternness and discipline can coexist with humor and tenderness, and he grows to revere the man with the badly scarred face as father and friend. His respect for Justin McLeod gives way to deep love as he learns to like himself. The summer comes to a shattering end for Charles with the brutal death of Moxie, the sudden knowledge that his war-hero father had died as an alcoholic on skid row, and an encounter with his own sexuality when the boy expresses his love for Justin physically as well as emotionally. The author handles the homosexual experience with taste and discretion; the act of love between Justin and Charles is a necessary emotional catharsis for the boy within the context of his story, and is developed with perception and restraint. Justin McLeod is presented as neither a damned soul nor a fallen angel, but as a human being with the talent "'for salvaging flawed and fallen creatures. Himself included.'" Over and over again, the reader is made aware of what maturity entails: *"You can be free from everything but the consequences of what you do."* And by the end of the story, Charles is able to accept the truth of that premise and in so doing accept himself. A highly moral book, powerfully and sensitively written; a book that never loses sight of the humor and pain inherent in the human condition.

Binnie Tate Wilkin

SOURCE: "The Individual: *The Man without a Face,*" in *Survival Themes in Fiction for Children and Young People,* The Scarecrow Press, Inc., 1978, p. 59.

Fourteen-year-old Charles Norstadt has problems with

his family and with school. At a summer island home, he meets Justin McLeod, badly scarred on one side of his face from an accident. Charles asks Justin to tutor him, so that he can pass tests for entering boarding school in the fall.

The relationship between the two develops from near hostility to one of closeness, culminating in a homosexual incident. Again, this author presents sexuality as interwoven with social and psychological needs. The subject is handled well. There is no preaching and emotions are described sensitively. At the end Justin encourages Charles to consider the affair from the point of view of mutual need and not as a physical handicap.

Val Randall

SOURCE: A review of *The Man without a Face,* in *Books for Keeps,* No. 85, March, 1994, p. 13.

Justin McLeod is the man without a face, since he was badly burned in a drunken car crash in which he killed a child. Charles is fourteen and miserable at home, determined to pass the boarding school entrance exam and get away. McLeod is an ex-teacher and Charles penetrates his physical and emotional isolation, forming a working partnership which turns to friendship and then to love.

Isabelle Holland successfully depicts a fraught household, tense with sibling rivalry and she's equally adept at the much trickier task of exploring a homosexual relationship between Charles and McLeod. Charles's rejection of these emotional ties is also credible, but the book's ending, where he returns to repair the damage and finds McLeod has died a month earlier, has a manufactured and awkward feel.

This is a brave attempt at a contentious subject and should be made available for young people to read, explore and make of it what they will.

HEADS YOU WIN, TAILS I LOSE (1973)

Ethel L. Heins

SOURCE: A review of *Heads You Win, Tails I Lose,* in *The Horn Book Magazine,* Vol. L, No. 1, February, 1974, pp. 56-7.

In a *Horn Book* article (June 1973), the author spoke of a "hedge of thorns" to be penetrated, or obstacles or taboos to be overcome in order to achieve the urgency that produces good storytelling. Melissa Hammond's hedge of thorns consisted of tightly intertwining branches: An inordinate eater, she was unattractively overweight at fifteen; she was nursing a long-burning love for the boy next door who plainly despised her; and worst of all, she was at the center of the fighting arena of her parents' miserable marriage. Melissa's handsome

father—who was often in pain because of an old leg injury received in an Air Force crash—seemed to be increasingly stuffy and disapproving. Her mother—weak, ambivalent, and infatuated with the latest fads and theories—ran "a constant, never-ending campaign for the improvement and making over of Melissa." When a teacher whom Melissa respected urged her to take a part in the school play, she undertook a dangerous course of diet pills and later sleeping pills, all of which she stole from her mother's room. Meanwhile, after a particularly ugly quarrel, Melissa's father packed up and left, while her mother took refuge in alcohol. The story is capably written, full of clever, often bitter dialogue. But the author has not produced an important or powerful book—as she did with *The Man without a Face.* Her new book lacks both the unity of theme and passionate focus of its predecessor. Perhaps she has pulled out too many stops and has diffused her creative energies in an attempt to cope with too many problems; for the life of almost every character has been touched by the wretchedness of drug addiction or alcoholism, divorce or estrangement, loneliness or isolation.

OF LOVE AND DEATH AND OTHER JOURNEYS (1975; British edition as *Ask No Questions,* 1978)

Kirkus Reviews

SOURCE: A review of *Of Love and Death and Other Journeys,* in *Kirkus Reviews,* Vol. XLIII, No. 7, April 1, 1975, pp. 383-84.

This begins on a deceptively supercilious note with an odd family assortment of emigres, calling themselves Flopsy, Mopsy, Peter and Cotton, who are eking out their living in Florence by shepherding groups of tacky American tourists they call Goody Packs. Then Mopsy discovers that her Mother (hitherto Flopsy) is dying of cancer and she (and we) begin to understand and admire this vulnerable eccentric. Much of what Mopsy learns is revealed by her father whom she now meets for the first time and who turns out to be an Anglican priest (to her a more shocking occupation than porn writer—which is what stepfather Peter is). Holland is an aggressive writer and some of this—father's button-down sincerity as well as Mopsy's flip sophistication—seems manipulated. But Mother's character and Mopsy/Meg's sorrow at seeing her waste away in silence are genuinely moving, and though later Mopsy's grief is sublimated in a crush on Cotton and worked out through his rejection, one can respect the fact that a mother's death is not treated here as just another YA problem. Awkwardly developed at times, but there's some real emotion here that can't be ignored.

Anne Marie Stamford

SOURCE: A review of *Of Love and Death and Other Journeys,* in *Best Sellers,* Vol. 35, No. 2, May, 1975, p. 33.

The title of this brief novel gives an inkling of its contents but it is not quite so somber as it sounds. It is narrated by Meg Grant, better known as "Mopsy," a fifteen-year-old girl whose life changes dramatically one summer.

Meg has spent her childhood flitting around Europe with her mother and stepfather, being educated here and there along the way. The story is set in Italy where Meg and her mother, and a young painter whom Meg secretly adores, are supporting their rather flighty existence by guiding tourists around Perugia.

The plot thickens when the mother becomes seriously ill. Meg's real father, whom she has never met (her parents were divorced before she was born), is summoned to Italy. Meg knows nothing about her father except through sardonic glimpses that her mother has given her on rare occasions when she spoke of him. Meg is intensely curious about him, but, since she feels that he abandoned her, she also harbors a distrust and dislike for him. The meeting and the events that follow are the turning point in Meg's life where she leaves her childhood behind.

The plot itself is interesting enough, but what makes the book really entertaining is Isabelle Holland's ability to capture all the precarious qualities of teenhood. Difficult as it must be to write through the eyes of a fifteen-year-old when one has passed that transient age, the author manages it with style and wit. The desperate throes of first love, the longing to be twenty-one, can be relived vicariously in these pages. The author's straightforward sense of humor when describing people and situations made me laugh out loud, a response rare indeed to novels these days. I think that adults and older adolescents alike will enjoy this novel as much as I did.

Mary M. Burns

SOURCE: A review of *Of Love and Death and Other Journeys,* in *The Horn Book Magazine,* Vol. LI, No. 3, June, 1975, pp. 274-76.

With sympathetic understanding of adolescent emotions, the author has written a moving study of a young girl's sudden confrontation with life's paradoxes. The setting is Perugia, singularly appropriate to the dramatic subtleties of the plot evidenced in the skillful interplay of joy and grief, love and anger, tragedy and comedy. For Meg Grant, the summer of her fifteenth year was an ending and a beginning. Until then, she had considered hers a nearly perfect existence—traveling throughout Europe with her charming, unconventional mother, her latest stepfather, and the young painter Cotton. Cultural and literal vagabonds, they supported themselves in a variety of ways: Meg and her mother ran a tourist guide operation; stepfather Peter, at heart a scholar of twelfth-century manuscripts, wrote borderline pornography; Cotton spent his winters teaching English in order to purchase artist's materials. Then Meg, whose parents had

been divorced before she was born, learned of her father's projected visit and of her mother's hastily scheduled surgery for cancer—two events which were to act as catalytic agents in determining her future. Artistically balanced, the plot never degenerates into bathos because of the substantial theme, fully realized setting, incisive characterization, and elegant style. There are not only witty conversational exchanges but also brilliant comments on life in general, such as Meg's observation: "If you tell English or French people, even those young and liberated, that they are behaving according to national type . . . the chances are they'll be pleased. If you say that to an American, you'll have a fight on your hands."

Zena Sutherland

SOURCE: A review of *Of Love and Death and Other Journeys,* in *Bulletin of the Center for Children's Books,* Vol. 28, No. 11, July-August, 1975, p. 178.

Meg's parents had been divorced before she was born, and she had lived happily with her mother in Europe, helping guide sightseers, becoming familiar with the languages and the culture of half a dozen countries. She liked her stepfather, she doted on the young artist, Cotton, who was part of their household—but she was curious about her father. She knew that her mother had had an affair and left her father; she learned that he had not known there was a child. Meg is appalled when she learns that her mother has cancer, doubly appalled after the operation, when the doctor gives no hope. And then her father comes to Perugia. It is hard enough, at fifteen, to accept a stranger as father; it is even harder, when her mother dies, for Meg to go to New York with him and start a new life in a strange place. This is a sophisticated book; Holland does not talk down to her readers by explaining references made by the cosmopolitan characters. They are superbly drawn, and the relationships are equally strong. The book ends on a hopeful note, as Meg is helped by her stepmother to face her grief, and it is lightened by the humor of the dialogue throughout all but the ending of the story.

ALAN AND THE ANIMAL KINGDOM (1977)

Kirkus Reviews

SOURCE: A review of *Alan and the Animal Kingdom,* in *Kirkus Reviews,* Vol. XLV, No. 6, March 15, 1977, p. 285.

Alan is an orphan, and when the uncle he once lived with died, the "authorities" had all his animals gassed while Alan waited in a shelter for great-Aunt Jessie to pick him up. That's why, when Jessie dies, Alan decides to keep her absence a secret. A loner anyway, Alan goes on living in his aunt's apartment with his "kingdom" (a dog, a cat, a white rat, a hamster, and some gerbils), and we see him rapidly running out of money and lying more and more desperately to neighbors, the super, his principal, etc. Then the cat's illness drives Alan to an alcoholic vet who guesses the truth and more or less takes him over. But Dr. Harris lets Alan down when he falls off the wagon; Alan, concerned about him, lets down an old neighbor he'd been helping to protect from a gang of teen-age toughs; and before the sympathetic principal takes Alan in, and Harris (whom he prefers) joins AA and promises to try again, Alan has stolen church/school money to pay for his dog's operation by another vet. Sentimental as the basic situation is, Alan's urban milieu and its population are drawn with reasonable verity, and his devotion to his kingdom is understandable, even to those who don't list keeping animals alive as a high priority value. For most kids, of course, Alan's is an eminently sympathetic cause, and the added interest of coping alone enhances his likely appeal.

G. Bott

SOURCE: A review of *Alan and the Animal Kingdom,* in *The Junior Bookshelf,* Vol. 44, No. 3, June, 1980, pp. 143-44.

Twelve-year-old Alan McGowan conceals the death of his guardian aunt by maintaining the pretense that she is helping a sick friend. This unlikely deception is to save his beloved animals—a dog, a cat, a white rat, a hamster and a pair of gerbils—from the Authorities who, he is convinced, will destroy them. He lies valiantly and copes inadequately with the problems of feeding himself and his pets and paying bills. When Muff, the cat, is sick, Alan meets Dr. Harris, an alcoholic vet who befriends the boy and makes a determined effort to conquer his excessive drinking. Alan steals some money, explodes into an orgy of destruction and is forced to tell his story to his headmaster; the animals are dispersed to friendly homes and Alan finds himself with a prospective foster parent.

Granted the initial subterfuge, the plot hangs together firmly, cemented by Alan's passionate concern for his animals. He commands our sympathy, however much we may disapprove of his actions; the clash of values for an orphan who has been badly let down by adults and scorns their trust is sharpened as practical demands overwhelm idealistic devotion. The final resolution is neither sentimental nor engineered; it is an acceptable solution to the differing predicaments of Alan and Dr. Harris.

HITCHHIKE (1977)

Shirley Wilton

SOURCE: A review of *Hitchhike,* in *School Library Journal,* Vol. 24, No. 1, September, 1977, p. 145.

Angry with her father, 16-year-old Pud decides to hitchhike home from boarding school with her dog Ruff instead of taking a plane. She gets two rides: one from a

prosperous middle-aged father-figure who is trying to understand his own daughter's rebellion, and one from four teenage boys in a truck who look like college kids but turn out to be hoods. Pud feels uncomfortable with the man who reminds her of her father, and right at home with the boys her age—until they threaten her with rape and kidnapping. As a result of her frightening experience, she has to rethink her values and her judgments. The messages about the caring side of parental discipline and about learning responsibility come through, and Holland avoids the familiar teen novel trap of damning the older generation, but the relentlessly topical story is didactic and heavy-handed.

Steve Roxborough

SOURCE: "The Novel of Crisis: Contemporary Adolescent Fiction," in *Children's Literature: Annual of the Modern Language Association Seminar on Children's Literature and the Children's Literature Association,* Vol. 7, 1978, pp. 248-54.

Isabelle Holland's *Hitchhike* departs from the model of the novel of crisis presented above by harking back to a much different and older form, the exemplum or cautionary tale, yet its concerns are those common to the contemporary fiction already discussed. A sixteen-year-old who is miffed at her father for allowing a business deal to interfere with a long-anticipated camping trip decides to buy a coat with the money sent for her plane fare and to hitchhike home instead. She picks up a stray dog along the way and so complicates things. (Not since Toto got Dorothy caught in a tornado has a dog caused a heroine so much trouble.) Forcibly detained by a man seeking answers from her about why his daughter ran away and never contacted him, Pud escapes only to be kidnapped and very nearly raped by a group of teenage hoodlums. She manages to escape (with the dog) and so survives the crisis relatively unscathed. Her escapades may have left her a little less certain that she has life figured out, but for the most part they are just an adventurous interlude. At the end of the story she is awaiting the inevitable quarrel with her father with something akin to eagerness. The incident is realistically and convincingly portrayed. Its only apparent significance is to verify the warning, "don't hitchhike."

DINAH AND THE GREEN FAT KINGDOM (1978)

Nancy Bilbie

SOURCE: A review of *Dinah and the Green Fat Kingdom,* in *Children's Book Review Service, Inc.,* Vol. 7, No. 4, December, 1978, p. 39.

Twelve-year-old Dinah is overweight and miserable; she has few friends, and her family nags and teases her constantly about being fat. A fantasy kingdom where "fat is beautiful" provides refuge from the often cruel real world. A new friend, a puppy, and a nutrition counselor help Dinah begin to understand herself and her problems. Dinah is a believable character, but she is supported by a cardboard cast. Her brothers rarely come alive, and her parents spout platitudes at every turn. The last chapter particularly mars an otherwise acceptable story, for there adults give sermons so that it reads like a section from a self-help book rather than a novel. Holland is a fine writer and would have benefitted from more careful editing.

Zena Sutherland

SOURCE: A review of *Dinah and the Green Fat Kingdom,* in *Bulletin of the Center for Children's Books,* Vol. 32, No. 8, April, 1979, p. 138.

There have been other books about fat children, but few have explored causes and reactions with as much depth and perception as this. Dinah's twelve, the only girl in a family of four; her father is understanding but her mother (well-organized, determined, and "task-oriented") nags and nags about Dinah's weight and diet. Having a puppy helps a bit, but not enough to compensate for sharing her bedroom with an irritatingly perfectionist cousin, Brenda, recently orphaned, or for the teasing of her brothers and classmates. While getting counseling with Sister Elizabeth, a nutritionist, who works at a school for special children, Dinah becomes friendly with a handicapped boy and finds some consolation in that friendship; her real consolation, however, is in the dreaming (some of it vengeful, some optimistic) and writing she does: her "Green Fat Kingdom." When a combination of circumstances makes her plight seem unbearable, Dinah erupts; she pours out her bitterness at the dinner table, including her anger at her brothers, her dislike of Brenda, her resentment against her parents, and her belief that her mother doesn't love her, certainly cares more for Brenda—and then she runs out of the house. Hours later, her father brings her home and she has long, candid talks with each parent in turn. There's a clearing of the air that promises better future relations, but Holland never promises Dinah a rose garden; she's lost only five pounds, there's been no change in the behavior of her peers, and the new parental rapport is a hopeful sign but not an unrealistic capitulation. The writing style is smooth, with good dialogue and excellent characterization; it is, however, in insight into motivations and relationships that the author excels.

Eugenia E. Schmitz

SOURCE: A review of *Dinah and the Green Fat Kingdom,* in *Best Sellers,* Vol. 39, No. 3, June, 1979, pp. 111-12.

This early-teenage novel is a thoroughly wholesome story of a twelve-year-old girl with a weight problem. Dinah Randall is the third in a middle-class family of four children. She is short and dumpy with red hair and green eyes, while all the others including Brenda, her ten-year-old half-orphan cousin who lives with the Randalls, are slim with brown or blond hair and brown or gray eyes.

To compensate for her family's overt disapproval of her size, she escapes periodically to a huge, old oak tree on the edge of town where she pulls herself into a fork with a rope. There she communes with the tree spirit and fantasizes about an imaginary Green Fat Kingdom where there are beautiful, fat Green People. Over a period of a year she has been filling three notebooks with stories she has created about them.

A fat, funny looking pug puppy, which she buys for twenty-three cents at an auction, and enforced visits to the nutritionist at St. Monica's School for Special Children complicate Dinah's life. The conflict explodes one night at dinner when Dinah, burning under her family's kidding, upsets a gravy bowl, loses complete control of her emotions, and runs away with Francis, the pup, to her refuge in the Green Fat Kingdom.

The book explores modern society's cruel treatment of people who are slightly different—the obese and the physically or mentally handicapped. It involves a perfectly normal family. Dinah learns that her parents really do love her, and that neither the pup nor the Green Fat Kingdom can compensate for her resentment of her rejection by society. She must decide to diet, not to please people or buy their good will but to please herself, or choose to stay fat and accept and respect herself that way.

A more artistic effect might have been created if the moral had been implied rather than completely defined by several characters. With the fiction market glutted with psychoanalyses of moral deviates, drug and alcohol addicts, children of divorced parents, and victims of persecution complexes, it is refreshing to find a well-written, humorous juvenile about normal people. The characters are three-dimensional, the plot simple, credible and fast moving. It recalls Paula Danziger's *The Cat Ate My Gymsuit* and Sheila Schwartz's *Growing Up Guilty,* both of which involve fat teenage girls. Recommended to girls ten to fourteen, and school and public libraries.

NOW IS NOT TOO LATE (1980)

Marilyn Kaye

SOURCE: A review of *Now Is Not Too Late,* in *Booklist,* Vol. 76, No. 9, January 1, 1980, p. 667.

Eleven-year-old Cathy is spending the summer at her grandmother's island home while her father and stepmother are on a holiday. Cathy has been told that her real mother died when she was four, and she has no memories of her; but she is troubled by a recurring nightmare in which she is chased by a woman. When

Cathy meets Elizabeth O'Byrnne, a summer resident and artist, she feels a peculiar attraction and agrees to model for her. A mildly defiant but basically likable child, Cathy works her way through various relationships: with her grandmother, her stepbrother, and most of all, with Elizabeth, who is ultimately revealed as being Cathy's real mother, a reformed alcoholic whom her father had divorced. While this is a complex novel that revolves around an assortment of personalities and situations, it is to the author's credit that the complexity does not overwhelm the essential story or bury the main character in a sea of faces. Cathy comes across as a very real and substantial figure whose hopes and fears are as vivid to the reader as they are to herself. As usual, Holland writes with compassion and a sensitive understanding of human nature and its idiosyncrasies.

Zena Sutherland

SOURCE: A review of *Now Is Not Too Late*, in *Bulletin of the Center for Children's Books*, Vol. 33, No. 7, March, 1980, p. 135.

Cathy, eleven, is the first of her family to come to the island where Granny lives; her father and stepmother are in Europe, her stepbrother at camp, and she misses them all. She's especially looking forward to Andy's arrival, her stepbrother being her favorite person. But by the time Andy arrives, there have been changes; he's thirteen, he brings a friend with him, and both boys ignore Cathy. The other change is that Cathy has been posing for an artist who's visiting the island, an odd but likable woman whose friendship she has kept secret. A trip to the mainland brings disaster, for Andy's friend insists on crashing an AA meeting, and one of the members is Cathy's friend, the artist. Holland builds clues into the story, structuring it deftly so that Cathy's discovery that the artist is her mother (her embittered father had told Cathy her mother was dead) will come as no surprise to the reader. Because Holland writes with polish and perception, the crux of the story is not that the discovery is made but how Cathy will react, for her emotions and especially her feelings about those she loves have been explored deeply. Running throughout the book are some wonderfully intelligent conversations with Granny (a fine character) who helps Cathy see that it is possible to compromise with life and still maintain principles and dignity, that "Now is never too late for good things to happen."

Mary M. Burns

SOURCE: A review of *Now Is Not Too Late*, in *The Horn Book Magazine*, Vol. LVI, No. 3, June, 1980, pp. 296-97.

In contrast to eleven-year-old Cathy Barrett, who narrates the story, Marianne Proudy, her best friend, was "inclined to be obedient." Consequently, when Marianne turns down her suggestion that they visit "the Wicked Witch," a newly arrived reclusive resident of the small community, Cathy is determined to pursue an investigation on her own. The Wicked Witch proves to be Elizabeth O'Byrnne, a fortyish, attractive illustrator of children's books with a strong attachment to animals; unfortunately, Cathy has always had an aversion to pets. But when Elizabeth asks her to model for her, Cathy seizes the opportunity to earn money for a bicycle. Perhaps because of a somewhat nagging ambivalence toward Elizabeth, Cathy keeps their arrangement a secret from all except the discerning grandmother with whom she is staying while her father and stepmother are vacationing in Europe. Then Andy, her stepmother's son by a former marriage, arrives unexpectedly from summer camp bringing a friend with him. A tense emotional climax forces Cathy to confront her subconscious fears and to reexamine her relationship with Elizabeth. The author has once again created a feisty character, bright and articulate, so that the narrative retains its conversational tone while remaining free of clichés. The elegantly crafted story offers palpable descriptions of setting and characters as well as wonderfully pungent and wise observations on the human condition.

📖 *ABBIE'S GOD BOOK* (1982)

Ethel L. Heins

SOURCE: A review of *Abbie's God Book*, in *The Horn Book Magazine*, Vol. LVIII, No. 5, October, 1982, p. 530.

The author set herself an interesting but difficult job and has done it extremely well. When Abigail, almost twelve, asks her father—rather casually—to tell her about God, his initial suggestion is that she first write down her own thoughts on the matter. Thus, beginning with the question, Who is God? Abbie then takes on a variety of traditionally enigmatic concepts in a series of brief, convincingly childlike, conversational chapters. Such subjects as prayer, faith, suffering and evil, envy, forgiveness, responsibility, and free will are dealt with in a modest, relaxed way. And as Abbie expresses her feelings and ruminates on those of her teachers, family, and friends, the well-modulated voice of the author comes through clearly, discussing profound ideas without a trace of patronizing, tenseness, sentimentality, or dogmaticism. Although the theological basis is essentially Christian, the book is nonsectarian; non-Christian ideas are mentioned as well as Abbie's relationships with children of other beliefs.

📖 *A HORSE NAMED PEACEABLE* (1982)

Gerry McBroom

SOURCE: A review of *A Horse Named Peaceable*, in *The ALAN Review*, Vol. 10, No. 2, Winter, 1983, p. 21.

She's running away from her Episcopal bishop father who she thinks is responsible for harming her horse;

he's running away from his Baptist minister father and the law because someone tried to harm his dog. With the exception of their ages and races, Jessamy and Rudd are nearly identical. Both are well-drawn in the usual Holland fashion, with clear backgrounds, motives, and emotions; but, together, these characters are too parallel to be credible.

Twelve-year-old Jessamy is in a boarding school after her mother's death while her father travels around the world, working for his church. When she learns of a fire at Peaceable's stable, Jessamy returns to her empty house to get money to search for her horse. There she discovers Rudd and his dog Weaver who are hiding from the police. Rudd, like Jessamy, is angry with his alcoholic father and is lonely for his deceased mother. Rudd, Jessamy, and Weaver search for her horse, having adventures on the road, eventually finding Peaceable. This unbelievable parallelism continues to the end. The bishop realizes his error and reunites with Jessamy. Rudd's father, not drinking now, wants to make up with his son. Everyone, including Peaceable and Weaver, I suppose, lives happily ever after.

GOD, MRS. MUSKRAT AND AUNT DOT (1983)

Mary M. Burns

SOURCE: A review of *God, Mrs. Muskrat and Aunt Dot,* in *The Horn Book Magazine,* Vol. LIX, No. 5, October, 1983, p. 574.

Rebecca Smith is eleven years old, orphaned and lonely. She has a vivid imagination and a remarkably flexible vocabulary, partly because she has spent most of her life with adults. And like many lonely children she has an imaginary friend, Mrs. Muskrat—soft, furry, and round—who lives in the forest, dispensing comfort and chocolate-chip cookies. But her schoolmates tease Rebecca for talking to herself and thus cause problems, for she is not averse to fighting or speaking her mind. Her inability to make friends is the despair of Uncle Matthew and of Aunt Dot in particular because she had refused to grant refuge to Rebecca's beloved dog. Bewildered and hurt, Rebecca decides to write a letter to God—God I, that is, not God II, the minister's God, who seems remote and unsympathetic. The story is the record of the correspondence chronicling Rebecca's attempts to understand circumstances she cannot control, ideas of good and evil, the nature of God, and the mysteries of human behavior. Reconciling the real and the imaginary worlds is the central conflict, happily resolved through conversations with Mrs. Mushroom, an elderly eccentric, and with Uncle Matthew who reveals that as a boy he, too, had a special friend. The element of fantasy is extended through [Beth and Joe Krush's] characteristic drawings. And in showing the gap between traditional theology and a child's pantheistic view, the story suggests that the gap must be bridged if religion is to become other than an external force.

Faith McNulty

SOURCE: A review of *God, Mrs. Muskrat and Aunt Dot,* in *The New Yorker,* Vol. LIX, No. 42, December 5, 1983, p. 206

After Aunt Dot, her guardian, sends her beloved dog to the pound, eleven-year-old Rebecca is angry at everyone—God included. She turns to fantasy friends, a motherly muskrat, and an eccentric cat lady for comfort and advice. Isabelle Holland tackles large and fascinating questions—for example, Do dogs have souls?—and handles them beautifully in an unusual, quite wonderful story.

PERDITA (1983)

Paul Heins

SOURCE: A review of *Perdita,* in *The Horn Book Magazine,* Vol. LIX, No. 5, October, 1983, pp. 582-83.

In a first-person narrative Perdita Smith tells why she was given her name, meaning lost, because she had been found battered and unconscious in a dry well; and after seven months in a convent sanatorium she still suffered from loss of memory. She did not know her real name, her age, nor what had happened to her; but gradually she recovered some facts about herself. For example, she knew how to drive a car, and she knew about horses and riding. Encouraged by the nuns to seek a job outside the convent, Perdita was hired as a stable hand at the Stanton farm. She was thrown into constant contact with the Stanton family: Penelope, the original owner's intriguing widow, who was browbeating Nancy—her twelve-year-old daughter by another marriage—to participate in riding competitions; and Penelope's stepson John, honest but brusque in manner, struggling against his stepmother's machinations. The young woman loved and understood horses and became Nancy's riding teacher, encouraging the girl, who finally achieved a degree of success. And despite Perdita's overshadowing fear of facing the reason for her loss of memory, her courage and independence helped in coming to grips with the truth. A mystery and a horse story, the narrative also contains an element of wry romance; for Perdita and John Stanton, finally triumphing over their difficulties, found themselves compatible. Except for the epilogue, which serves essentially to tie together the loose threads of the mystery, the book is noteworthy for the realistic interplay of its carefully portrayed characters and for the wholesomely unromantic presentation of events on a horse farm.

Judith Bugniazet

SOURCE: A review of *Perdita,* in *The ALAN Review,* Vol. 11, No. 3, Spring, 1984, p. 31.

The nuns named her Perdita, meaning lost. Perdita had been in an accident and had received a concussion and subsequent loss of memory. She knew she could read

French, play the piano, ride a bike, and had a love and knowledge of horses. She could not remember her name, where she came from, how old she was or where she had lived prior to the accident seven months ago. Perdita realizes she cannot stay at the convent forever, and will only get well by facing the world again. She knows that she wants to know who she is, but at the same time, fears that knowledge.

With a constant feeling of suspense, Isabelle Holland weaves a mystery around every memory. The story, told by Perdita, gives the reader a sense of the frustration, anger, and fear felt by a victim of amnesia. *Perdita* is a sensitive story probing the problems and fears of a psychological problem, but it is not simply a problem novel. It is also an excellent mystery and love story. The ending is dramatic, surprising, and happy. A good escapist story for girls, 12 and up.

THE EMPTY HOUSE (1983)

D. A. Young

SOURCE: A review of *The Empty House,* in *The Junior Bookshelf,* Vol. 50, No. 1, February, 1986, p. 35.

This American teenage romance is set on the Jersey Shore. Betsy, who tells the story, and her brother Rodney are staying with Aunt Marian because their father is in prison and their mother engaged in high-powered journalism in Europe. The complications include Rodney's epilepsy, a house inhabited by an elderly recluse and her fey-acting daughter and a boy called Ted who works in the local malt-and-burger shop. Things are going well between Betsy and Ted until Betsy learns that Ted's journalist father has devoted his newspaper column to a vicious indictment of her father and his trumped-up crime. The plot thickens nicely. Its tangled threads are brought together to a somewhat improbable happy ending with Ted's Dad initiating the campaign to put the course of justice straight.

If the plot is complicated the characterisation is sketchy. Betsy, even though she tells the story, never comes over as more than the stock figure of teenage fiction. She thinks Ted manages to look both highly intelligent and sexy. He wears glasses but the gray eyes behind them are level and very mature. She feels the blood rushing to her cheeks and curses her blush ability. Minor characters are shadowy but play their part in developing the story line. It makes a pleasant relaxation for an unsophisticated and undemanding reader.

GREEN ANDREW GREEN (1984)

Zena Sutherland

SOURCE: A review of *Green Andrew Green,* in *Bulletin of the Center for Children's Books,* Vol. 38, No. 4, December, 1984, p. 67.

After he turned green, Andrew became a pariah, and he began to hate everybody. By walking into a television set, he entered a world where everything was green, but a girl he met there changed the color of his clothes by magic. Back in real life, he found a cat but felt ambivalent about keeping it. Also, he turned purple. Also, he met a man who called himself the Fisher of Men whose dog shared his miraculous powers. In the end, Andrew has to choose between a selfish goal and keeping the cat, and he chooses the cat. Naturally, he loses his green color. This is an awkward juxtaposition of fantasy, realism, and theology, not badly written but weakly conceived so that it is ineffective either as a literary entity or as an object lesson in piety.

Sister Barbara Anne Kilpatrick

SOURCE: A review of *Green Andrew Green,* in *Catholic Library World,* Vol. 56, No. 5, December, 1984, p. 235.

A tale of a ten-year-old boy whose skin turns green. Outside the sun makes him very, very green—and he hates green. Andrew retreats to his room and then into a TV screen where everything is green. In this world Andrew meets a wise fisherman and a feisty tomcat. Realizing that life is unpleasant here as well as at home, he learns a great lesson in faith, and the beauty and importance of love. A poignant novel for the young reader that inspires one about the "recuperative powers of human heart and spirit."

THE ISLAND (1984)

School Library Journal

SOURCE: A review of *The Island,* in *School Library Journal,* Vol. 31, No. 4, December, 1984, p. 101.

Sixteen-year-old Hilda Tashoff is sent to a small isolated Caribbean island to vacation with her mother's distant cousin and finds out that the island is under the complete control of her ruthless wealthy uncle. Aunt Louisa turns out to be a drug addict; the other young person in the big house, cousin Paul, is abrasive and unlikable. Only the enigmatic house guest, Mr. Gomez, appears sympathetic to Hilda's feelings. Hilda's snooping slowly begins to reveal an unlikely and bizarre connection between herself and Mr. Gomez. There are many unanswered questions here. Why did her parents pack her off to this island without first checking it out? Why was her father behaving so uptight towards her prior to her departure? What is the relationship between Gomez and Uncle Brace? Between herself and Gomez? Holland does a fine job conveying Hilda's feelings of claustrophobia as she begins to realize she is trapped. As her plot unfolds, however, it begins to unravel. Her explanation for all that has happened to Hilda is unconvincing. Especially unbelievable is the behavior of Hilda's father. Would a loving man treat his daughter so callously?

Publishers Weekly

SOURCE: A review of *The Island*, in *Publishers Weekly,* Vol. 227, No. 1, January 4, 1985, p. 69.

The author of **The Man without a Face** and other milestone novels, Holland handles with flair a thriller in an exotic setting and an appealing heroine, Hilda Tashoff, 16. Hilda expects to relax and enjoy a vacation with relatives on a southern island, Maenad. But she's uneasy in the palatial house where her mother's cousin, Louisa Kingsmark, seems mentally ill and dominated by her husband Brace. Also staying with the Kingsmarks is John Gomez, an older man who shows an extraordinary interest in Hilda. Although Gomez puzzles the girl, he wins her confidence, for he is the only person she can talk to on Maenad. When she realizes that Brace is a criminal and that he intends to keep her a prisoner on the island, Hilda turns to Gomez for help, but the disclosure of his identity ends her hopes and nearly causes her nerves to break. Although the story is farfetched, Holland's skill makes it plausible and entertaining.

Zena Sutherland

SOURCE: A review of *The Island*, in *Bulletin of the Center for Children's Books,* Vol. 38, No. 6, February, 1985, p. 108.

Since seventeen-year-old Hilda tells the story, there's a communication of her growing uneasiness and suspicion at the situation she's found on a Caribbean island where she's visiting Aunt Louisa (her mother's cousin) and Uncle Brace. It is clear that Louisa is being kept drugged by her husband—but why? It is clear that the tyrannical Brace is subservient to a middle-aged visitor, Mr. Gomez—but why? When Hilda tells Brace she wants to leave the island and go back to New York, he categorically refuses. Why? Hilda's doubts become fears, and the one friend she's made tries and fails to help her escape. All becomes clear, if a bit intricate, when she learns that Gomez is really a German, an ex-Nazi (one who didn't know about the concentration camps until the war was over) and that he's her biological father who is leaving her a fortune. He dies, Louisa shoots Brace, the boy friend shows up with Hilda's Daddy (seems she was the illegitimate daughter of Gomez/von Rucker and a Jewish woman, and that the parents Hilda's loved so deeply are adoptive) and the police from a neighboring island. All's well that ends a bit patly, but this would probably seem lurid rather than far-fetched if it were not capably written. It has enough action and suspense to satisfy any mystery/adventure fan.

📖 *JENNY KISS'D ME* (1985)

Stephanie Zvirin

SOURCE: A review of *Jennie Kiss'd Me,* in *Booklist,* Vol. 81, No. 22, August, 1985, p. 1656.

Bright and pretty but overweight and very short on self-esteem (thanks in part to an alcoholic father who hasn't much self-esteem either), Jill Hamilton is not looking forward to tutoring handsome, private school student Nathan Vandermark. Unfortunately, she needs the money. More unfortunate still, she falls in love with him, letting down the carefully constructed defenses she's adopted to protect herself from snubs by the opposite sex and from being hurt in general. Vandermark takes advantage of Jill's "just love me and I'll do anything attitude" by introducing her to sex, then dumping her when their relationship is no longer advantageous to him. Counsel from a wise adult and a friendship with a paraplegic whose self-esteem is even shakier than her own help Jill turn her experiences with Nathan into a catalyst for her own betterment. If accomplished with a somewhat heavy hand, Holland's portrait of Jill's struggle toward self-worth is both sensitive and perceptive, and its contrivances are wound together by an obviously practiced writer.

Judy M. Butler

SOURCE: A review of *Jenny Kiss'd Me,* in *School Library Journal,* Vol. 32, No. 5, January, 1986, p. 74.

Jill Hamilton is 17, bright, very sensitive about being overweight and motherless. Her father, the doctor in their small New Hampshire town, is an alcoholic, filled with self-pity and resentment toward something in his past. When Nathan Vandermark, a handsome and sophisticated student from the local prep school, pays attention to Jill, she falls in love with him and eventually has her first sexual experience. With Nathan's encouragement, Jill loses weight and gradually develops a new image, both physically and emotionally. After a while, she realizes that Nathan does not love her and she breaks off the relationship. Skillfully interwoven with this primary plot are two subplots: Jill's relationship with an understanding retired teacher and her friendship with Mark Davis, a paraplegic. Holland's phrasing, portrayal of characters and understanding of a contemporary teen's emotional needs are commendable. However, the surprise ending seems somewhat contrived, a little too good to believe. The slang and sexual action are written in frank language. Even so, this novel of contemporary realism is a cut above the ordinary.

Judy Beckman

SOURCE: A review of *Jenny Kiss'd Me,* in *The ALAN Review,* Vol. 13, No. 2, Winter, 1986, p. 39.

Jill Hamilton is lonely after the death of her mother. She finds no company in her father who crawls into the safety of a scotch bottle each night. Even though Jill manages to be the school's top student and does tutoring to earn the college money lost through her father's drunken investments, Dr. Hamilton neither compliments nor supports her efforts. Instead, most mornings find him stark raving sober, hurling verbal daggers that remind Jill that she is overweight and unlikely to win any attention. Against such stabs, Jill emotionally anchors herself with plans for a single life as a veterinarian. But when handsome Nathan, wealthy St. Dunstan's student majoring in wine, women and revelry needs emergency tutoring for the Yale admittance tests, Jill becomes a pushover for his sexual advances.

Readers 13 and up will easily recognize Jill's isolation and follow with interest her efforts to detach with love from her alcoholic father, and take charge of her own life. The reluctant reader will find this book immediately engaging with its swift beginning told in the first person, blocks of easily readable dialogue and cast of fully developed characters.

📖 TOBY THE SPLENDID (1987)

Denise M. Wilms

SOURCE: A review of *Toby the Splendid,* in *Booklist,* Vol. 83, No. 15, April 1, 1987, p. 1206.

An intense mother-daughter conflict fuels this story, which otherwise follows many conventions of the horse-story genre. Janet West is a 13-year-old girl who is so determined to ride that she's bought her own horse and is paying for his upkeep out of her own pocket. Mrs. West is adamantly—and somewhat unreasonably—against her daughter's riding, and Janet is constantly fearful that her mother will force her to give up her beloved Toby. When Janet is injured in a fall from the horse, her mother does indeed insist she give up riding. A bitter Janet withdraws from family, friends, and school and vows to leave home as soon as she is of age, if not before. Then Toby is seriously injured. Janet desperately bargains to care for him, promising her mother that if she is allowed to nurse Toby to health, she will consent to selling him to a good home. The intensity of emotions between Janet and her mother has taken its toll on Mrs. West, and in the end, she agrees to allow Janet to keep her horse. The story has some forced elements; the finish in particular is abrupt, but there is lots of drama and a sense of mesmerizing tension that sustains the novel through its bumpier parts. Also, secondary characters are well developed, and Janet's interactions with them add interest. This novel has the potential to reach beyond the horse-story crowd to a broader audience.

Publishers Weekly

SOURCE: A review of *Toby the Splendid,* in *Publishers Weekly,* Vol. 231, No. 18, May 8, 1987, p. 71.

Janet knows that if she wants a horse, she will have to buy it herself, pay for its upkeep and work hard not to give her mother any reason to protest the equestrian lifestyle—which her mother considers "snobbish" and

dangerous. Jan buys Toby and boards him in return for work; her riding abilities catch the eye of the stable's owner. Then Jan is hurt by another horse, and her mother insists that Toby be sold. In time Jan and others convince her mother to let her have Toby back. The first-person narration of this is somewhat rambling and disjointed; Jan sounds young and pouting, and then old and wise. Her home life borders on caricature, with a mother who switches from moods of indifference to hysterics in very little time. But the horse scenes give the plot some clarity of purpose and hold the book together.

Pat Pearl

SOURCE: A review of *Toby the Splendid,* in *Voice of Youth Advocates,* Vol. 10, No. 3, August, 1987, p. 120.

Janet, 14, has an elegant and popular older sister, Cynthia, and a mother who is a busy attorney. Although Janet is responsible, intelligent, and becoming attractive, her mother favors Cynthia, whose extracurricular activities (ballet, drama, dating) are far more acceptable than Janet's passion for horses. Defiant and determined, Janet saves enough money to buy dapple grey Toby secretly and install him on a local farm. Her mother is furious. Estranged from her critical and unsupportive family, Janet makes Toby the center of her life. After several unfortunate riding accidents all their relationships reach a crisis stage.

The familiar themes of sibling rivalry, parental conflict, unreasonable prejudice against a cherished activity, and lack of intra-family communication are presented competently and smoothly integrated into a story that moves briskly and resolves into a reasonably happy ending. All is seen through Janet's eyes making her the only real personality. The crisp, easy-to-read style and universal problems presented should appeal to more than just the horse-loving girl readers.

📖 THE CHRISTMAS CAT (1987)

Publishers Weekly

SOURCE: A review of *The Christmas Cat,* in *Publishers Weekly,* Vol. 232, No. 22, November 27, 1987, p. 81.

Peter is a black cat that has had to fend for himself on the streets; he meets Caleb, a dog that has been mistreated. When they scavenge for food together, they link up with a caravan and free a sorrowful, abused donkey, Balaam. The threesome arrives at the stable where the King of Kings is born, and they are filled with love and wonder for him, and for all people, whom they formerly hated and feared. Each of the three kings takes an animal home as a revered gift for his family. Holland's message is a worthy one, if a bit overstated in the constant repetition of the words "important," and "not important," to describe the status of the animals. [Kathy]

Mitchell's opulent pictures—more fluidly depicting the animals than humans—portray both the seamier side of Peter, Caleb and Balaam's pre-Christ state, and their post-visitation glamour.

THIEF (1988)

Publishers Weekly

SOURCE: A review of *Thief,* in *Publishers Weekly,* Vol. 235, No. 6, February 10, 1989, p. 73.

Troubled by her past, Cressida finds it impossible to embrace the future. A decade earlier, she had a terrifying premonition on the very day her parents were killed in a car accident; after their death she was sent to live with her harsh aunt and spiteful cousin. There she was framed for stealing classmates' possessions and expelled from school. When she moves in with her half-brother Alaric and his wife Brenda, Cressida is determined to make a fresh start. However, she is haunted by more premonitions, and once again accused of stealing. Feeling confused and helpless, Cressida turns to her friend Larry who helps her untangle the mystery in which she is unwittingly involved. This is an intriguing, suspenseful novel. Holland creates a solid mystery with credible characters and plot.

Stephanie Zvirin

SOURCE: A review of *Thief,* in *Booklist,* Vol. 85, No. 15, April 1, 1989, p. 1369.

Despite memory blanks and strange premonitions that make her doubt her own sanity, Cressida doesn't think she is a thief. Unfortunately, others do. Further, what is happening now has happened before—shortly after her parents' deaths when missing articles brought classmates' accusations that Cressida never dealt with. At odds with her older half-brother and unable to confide in her preoccupied sister-in-law, Cressida finds a friend and defender in classmate Larry, who, with some advice from a dabbler in the paranormal, helps Cressida prove her innocence once and for all. Farfetched but entertaining.

Susan H. Williamson

SOURCE: A review of *Thief,* in *School Library Journal,* Vol. 35, No. 10, June, 1989, p. 124.

Cressida, an orphan, lives with her half-brother Alaric, a minister, and his wife. Her world seems to be crumbling again: she is once again accused of stealing; she is having premonitions (a premonition had alerted her to—and may have been responsible for—her parents' deaths); and her family life seems to be dissolving. With the help of the one friend who trusts her, Cressida finds her former housekeeper, who explains some of the missing pieces in Cressida's life. She has inherited all of her

father's money, and both Alaric and her aunt have prevented Cressida from living with her former housekeeper despite the fact that her parents left provisions for that arrangement. While the plot is sustained for most of the novel, the ending is too hurried, and those with a real interest in the supernatural will find that some of the subthemes are not fully developed. The idea that a room in the rectory is haunted is not fleshed out, and many readers will be disappointed that it does not figure significantly in the book's ending.

THE UNFRIGHTENED DARK (1990)

Kirkus Reviews

SOURCE: A review of *The Unfrightened Dark,* in *Kirkus Reviews,* Vol. LVIII, No. 2, January 15, 1990, p. 104.

Jocelyn, 16, has been blind since the car accident that killed her parents four years ago. Now she has a guide dog, Brace, who suddenly seems to be the object of attention of people whose voices Joss doesn't recognize—people who intimate that Brace is a slave, about to be liberated. When pet animals around town begin to disappear, she enlists her best friends' aid in discovering the identity of the harassers. Eventually, Brace is dognapped; the aunt in whom Joss was reluctant to confide is drawn into the chase; many of the animals, including Brace, are reunited with their owners; and Joss's friend Pip admits that he's in love with her.

Holland does a fine job of explicating the life of a blind girl; Joss's ability to intuit and process information—as well as her perceptions about people and their attitudes toward her disability—is convincingly drawn. All the major characters and many of the minor ones are interesting enough to draw readers willingly into the action. But, unfortunately, the story is rushed to an unsatisfying conclusion. What *was* this quasi-religious group that stole the animals? Is the pianist at the house where the animals were hidden really a student of Joss's piano teacher? Does the piano teacher recover his dog? The novel begins so well that the overhasty conclusion is a frustrating disappointment.

Elizabeth A. Belden and Judy M. Beckman

SOURCE: A review of *The Unfrightened Dark,* in *English Journal,* Vol. 79, No. 5, September, 1990, p. 93.

Isabelle Holland's treatment of her subject matter—a blinded, orphaned adolescent girl who loves and depends upon her dog—is neither maudlin nor detached. When she was twelve, Jocelyn Hunter was blinded in a car accident that killed her parents. Now sixteen, her life centers around Brace, the guide dog that enables her to feel, at least much of the time, strong and independent.

> It was a huge ache, a certainty that whatever it was I wanted—when it depended on other people . . . I

wouldn't get. It was a feeling related to the knowledge I'd had since the accident: that so much of life would never be for me.

Strong character portrayal and suspense buildup are hallmarks of this novel. Strangers begin harassing Jocelyn about denying Brace his freedom. Then pets begin disappearing. Even a friend of Jocelyn's disappears. Who is responsible? Will Brace be next? Will Jocelyn's greatest fear be realized? Is Jocelyn's Aunt Marion, a priest and "frustrated activist," to be trusted? After all, as a child she did have a traumatic experience with a dog, and she and Jocelyn have never been close.

This one is a quick attention-grabber and keeper.

📖 THE JOURNEY HOME (1990)

Kirkus Reviews

SOURCE: A review of *The Journey Home,* in *Kirkus Reviews,* Vol. LVIII, No. 18, September 15, 1990, pp. 1324-25.

The Children's Aid Society takes a pair of Irish orphans from New York to a new home in rural Kansas.

Heeding their dying mother's wish, responsible Maggie (12) and her feisty little sister Annie (7) accept the chance of going to a more wholesome life despite their apprehensions about being separated or forcibly converted to Protestantism. Both concerns are well-founded, but the girls are lucky: they're adopted by the Russells, a frail but compassionate woman and her stern but ultimately fair husband. Adjustment isn't easy, however. Maggie must look after Mrs. Russell's tyrannical old mother, while the girls face such other challenges as anti-Irish classmates who deride Maggie's scant previous education, a virulently anti-Catholic minister, and learning to milk.

Holland, a prolific author of uneven quality whose 1972 YA novel, *The Man without a Face,* was especially well received, here tells a predictable but satisfying story with authentic historical details and well-developed characters. Though carelessly edited—the early chapters, especially, are burdened by trivial detail, awkward language, and needless repetition—this should serve well enough as enjoyable, undemanding historical fiction.

Leone McDermott

SOURCE: A review of *The Journey Home,* in *Booklist,* Vol. 87, No. 6, November 15, 1990, p. 660.

The West looms as large as ever in the American imagination, judging by the number of fine books it still inspires. In her newest work, Holland freshly approaches two little covered aspects of the Western experience: the orphan trains and religious prejudice. When their mother dies of consumption, Maggie and her younger sister leave their New York Irish tenement aboard a westbound train with dozens of other orphans in search of new homes. After being inspected and passed over many times, the sisters are adopted by James and Priscilla Randall, a Kansas farm couple. Maggie has a rough time in her new life, what with milking, caring for Priscilla's curmudgeonly mother, and facing the anti-Catholicism of strict Protestants. But a spate of illnesses draws the family closer, and Maggie comes to love her spacious Western home. Holland, who has peopled her novel with wonderfully complex and distinct characters, shows a subtle instinct for both the insecurities of orphanhood and the tensions generated by cultural difference. Maggie is hardly perfect but fully engaging, making her a welcome addition to the ranks of prairie heroines.

Zena Sutherland

SOURCE: A review of *The Journey Home,* in *Bulletin of the Center for Children's Books,* Vol. 44, No. 4, December, 1990, p. 86.

Set in the late 1800s, this is a story based on the work of the Children's Aid Society of New York and the "orphan train" they organized, sending homeless children to families in the West. The children here are Maggie (twelve) and her sister Annie (seven) whose only parent has just died. This is a story of adjustment (New York/Kansas) and acceptance (Catholic orphans/ Protestant adoptive parents) and it is adequate in structure and style but slow-paced and rather purposive, reading more like an information-bearing case history that is fictionalized than a narrative with its own momentum.

📖 THE HOUSE IN THE WOODS (1991)

Stephanie Zvirin

SOURCE: A review of *The House in the Woods,* in *Booklist,* Vol. 87, No. 17, May 1, 1991, p. 1707.

Fourteen-year-old Bridget is surly and uncooperative most of the time, but she feels she's got good reasons: she's the only one of the four children who's adopted; she's plump, a fact no one in her family will let her forget; and she hates boating, something her widowed father and the rest of the family are doing more and more of since they came to the lake. She thinks her younger brother, Morgan, who's also "different" (he's unable to speak), is her only family ally. It isn't until she and Morgan discover a tumble-down house in the middle of a nearby wood and meet Elissa Hamilton, a pleasant local woman artist who goes there to paint, that Bridget begins to discover she's wrong. Tantalizing elements— the mystery behind Morgan's troubling silence, Elissa's "scandalous history"—are not developed well enough, and there's a shrill message about alcohol abuse interwoven in an awkward visit Bridget pays to her birth father's home. But Holland is on target when she's depicting Bridget's feelings of frustration about her looks and about her niche in the family, and there are plenty of readers who will identify with those problems, regardless of the lightweight package they're wrapped in.

Kirkus Reviews

SOURCE: A review of *The House in the Woods*, in *Kirkus Reviews*, Vol. LIX, No. 10, May 15, 1991, p. 672.

Uneven but engrossing tale about Bridget, 14, who—suspecting that her father wishes he had never adopted her—suddenly finds her birth parents' old house.

Bridget is furious: Daddy has bundled off the family, including nonspeaking little brother Morgan, to summer in northern New Hampshire instead of on their usual Maine island, largely at the suggestion of new nanny Ingrid, who is maddeningly insistent on reminding Bridget that she's overweight and adopted. There, in a mysterious old house, Bridget finds clues that will eventually lead her to her birth parents' name and the sad reason that she was given up. She also meets Elissa, an understanding artist who offers an acceptance that Bridget and Morgan haven't found at home and who acts as a catalyst for several changes, including a confrontation that finally causes Morgan to speak and Bridget to ask for a chance to meet her natural father.

Beginning with Daddy's choice of the New Hampshire location, there are too many contrivances and unanswered questions here. Elissa's past is unnecessarily mysterious, and it's not clear why Morgan doesn't speak; moreover, his big moment is trampled over by Bridget's argument with her father. Also, Bridget's overwrought sensitivity about her looks and manners becomes tiresome. Still, her concerns are shared by many youngsters, the situation is inherently dramatic, and Holland writes with skill enough that the reader really does care what happens.

Publishers Weekly

SOURCE: A review of *The House in the Woods*, in *Publishers Weekly*, Vol. 238, No. 24, May 31, 1991, p. 76.

Bridget, 14, her mute brother Morgan and their twin sisters spend the summer at a lakeside cottage with their father and new nanny, Ingrid. Morgan and Bridget keep to themselves: Morgan senses that their father cannot accept him as he is, and Bridget, because she is adopted, feels as though she is not part of the family. Her father and Ingrid further alienate Bridget with constant nagging about her weight. Often she fades into a world of her own where she can feel loved and beautiful. When Bridget and Morgan discover an old, weathered house hidden in the forest, the girl is strangely drawn to it and becomes determined to unlock its secrets. When

she does, her entire life begins to change. Holland's enticing narration and pithy dialogue breathe compelling life into her story; readers will empathize with Bridget's struggle to find self-worth and inner peace. However, the story provides no clear sense of time, and the pacing changes dramatically in the final three chapters. Despite these flaws, the unfolding of the mystery is absorbing.

Kathryn Pierson Jennings

SOURCE: A review of *The House in the Woods*, in *Bulletin of the Center for Children's Books*, Vol. 44, No. 10, June, 1991, p. 239.

Five years after her adoptive mother's death, fourteen-year-old Bridget feels that her father is interested only in his biological children. The one member of the family to whom she relates is her younger brother, Morgan, who has never spoken. Bridget's resentment increases when their father indulges his passion for sailing and takes the family to a sparsely populated lake for the summer. As the plot grows denser, it becomes confusing, and the numerous characters are more inconsistent than complex. Is the nanny intentionally, or just stupidly, cruel to Bridget and Morgan? Does Bridget's weight problem stem from her anger at her father? Has Daddy completely forgotten that the lake where they are vacationing is close to the little town where Bridget's birth father once killed a man? And what is the House in the Woods, anyway? Compared to the painful twists and turns of Bridget's adolescence, the neat ending is a disappointment. Holland's competent style holds up the weight of the plot, however, and the pace and natural dialogue keep the story moving.

Mary Helen Smith

SOURCE: A review of *The House in the Woods*, in *Voice of Youth Advocates*, Vol. 14, No. 2, June, 1991, p. 97.

Bridget is faced with more problems than any 14 year old should have. She is overweight; adopted; her adoptive mother died five years ago; her adoptive father is critical of her; her ten year old twin sisters are slim, athletic, and popular; and her seven year old brother, Morgan, does not talk. To make matters even worse, the family is spending the summer in a rented cottage on a lake in New Hampshire with a new nanny, Ingrid, who worries about nutrition and exercise. Bridget prefers the Maine coast where they spent their previous summer vacations in a village where she could eat ice cream and pizza and hang out at the bookstore.

Bridget hates lying on the beach but Ingrid makes everyone spend their first morning there. When they go inside for lunch, Morgan throws his salad on the floor because he wants a peanut butter sandwich, and then he runs into the woods. Bridget goes after him and finds him sitting under a tree. When a cat shows up, Bridget and Morgan chase it and discover a house in the woods. The house is falling apart, but there is a woman inside who comes there regularly for the solitude she needs to paint and draw illustrations for children's books. Morgan takes to her immediately and becomes friendly with the cat and its kittens. Bridget also takes to the woman, Elissa, and seems somehow drawn to the upstairs of the house. The remainder of the novel is crammed with Bridget's discovery of herself. She learns to ride, she discovers that she is attractive to next-door neighbor Steve, and she discovers who her real parents are by responding to the mysterious draw of the house in the woods. When her father discovers that she has been riding at Elissa's farm and criticizes her publicly, she runs off and ends up at the house in the woods where she falls asleep and dreams of the owners, finding herself in the dream.

When her father and Morgan come to the house in the woods to get her, Morgan becomes so upset when his father suggests that Bridget go to camp for the remainder of the summer that he finally talks. Bridget asks her father about the owners of the house and her relationship to them. She finds out that a couple named Bingham were the owners as well as her real parents. Her real mother is dead, but her real father lives on a ranch in Wyoming. This novel is crammed with action and too many adolescent problems, but the mystery of the house in the woods and Bridget's discoveries about herself keep the reader's interest.

📖 THE SEARCH (1991)

Publishers Weekly

SOURCE: A review of The Search, in Publishers Weekly, Vol. 238, No. 24, May 31, 1991, p. 76.

A careless night involving drinking and first-time sex lead to pregnancy for the usually sensible Claudia, 16. At a Vermont home for unwed mothers, a contract she signed releasing the baby for adoption stipulated that the adoptive parents must always remain anonymous to her. But now, a year later, Claudia reads about a spate of child abuse cases in the newspapers and becomes determined to learn of her baby's welfare. A sympathetic teacher, formerly with the home, is the only person likely to help, and Claudia runs off in search of this woman to quell the raging torment within her. Holland's novel keenly dramatizes the burdens of an unwanted teenaged pregnancy and the anguish that follows a baby's release for adoption. Her dialogue could be smoother and more natural, but she has crafted an affecting, unpredictable work that consistently holds interest.

📖 BEHIND THE LINES (1994)

Publishers Weekly

SOURCE: A review of Behind the Lines, in Publishers Weekly, Vol. 241, No. 13, March 28, 1994, p. 98.

Centering on the 1863 New York City draft riots, this historical novel abounds with political, racial and moral conflicts—and protagonist Katie O'Farrell is conveniently at the fore of them all. Just before the 1863 New York City draft riots, Katie works as a kitchen maid for the Laceys, an American family of British heritage with a house on Washington Square Park. While she serves tea and cake to the upper crust, she supports her father and siblings, who live in crowded quarters on the Lower East Side with other recent Irish immigrants. When a draft is instituted for soldiers to fight in the Civil War and Christopher Lacey is obliged to register, his parents offer Katie's brother Brian $300 to take his place. Meanwhile, New York's Irish community, enraged by the draft, angry at the abolitionists and frustrated with their lowly status, begins to riot, looting shops and lynching blacks. Holland's prose is prone to cliche ("Katie stared back at Mr. Lacey, her blue eyes blazing") and the ending somewhat pat (Katie learns to see her black friend Jimmy as an individual who transcends his racial identity; Jimmy learns that not all Irish are the same), but the novel is well-researched and will appeal to those interested in this turbulent time.

Christine Boutross

SOURCE: A review of Behind the Lines, in Children's Book Review Service, Inc., Vol. 22, No. 10, May, 1994, p. 117.

The U.S. finds itself in a civil war in 1863. Katie O'Farrell, a 14-year-old Irish lass, works for the Laceys who live in Washington Square. The more Katie learns about the war, the more she hates it. A new draft ruling allows a rich man to pay $300 to someone who will go in his place and the Laceys want Katie's brother to go for their son. Torn with feelings for her brother, Katie helps an African-American escape from the mobs that are running rampant in the streets. Young readers will get a sense of history through this beautiful, well-written, action-filled story.

Cathi Dunn MacRae

SOURCE: "The Young Adult Perplex," in Wilson Library Bulletin, Vol. 68, No. 9, May, 1994, pp. 100-01, 123.

In Behind the Lines, veteran YA novelist Isabelle Holland focuses on a little-known incident, the New York draft riots of 1863. When wealthy draftees paid Irish immigrants to take their place in the Union forces, the exploited Irish vented their anger on New York blacks, hanging them and looting until troops restored order. The situation appears from the perspective of Katie, a motherless Irish girl working as a maid in the Laceys' affluent home. Katie's prejudices are challenged when she befriends Jimmy, a black groom who helps her care for stray dog Paddy, and her mistress's English mother, whom Katie has been taught to hate. When the riots start, these influences move Katie to courageous action.

Though readers sympathize with Katie, her quick temper and drunken father are Irish stereotypes. Other characters are mouthpieces for causes and classes. Jimmy remains wooden; one cannot see Katie's understanding of him grow. Dependent on one incident, the thin plot is repetitious. Katie saves kitchen scraps for Paddy endlessly, and the same opinions constantly echo when the Laceys pay Katie's brother to take their son's place in the army. Holland ignores an essential element of historical fiction, the setting. Her vague New York has few anchors in time.

Margaret Cole

SOURCE: A review of *Behind the Lines,* in *School Library Journal,* Vol. 40, No. 7, July, 1994, p. 116, 119.

Motherless Katie O'Farrell, 14, works as a live-in maid for the wealthy Lacey family in order to supplement the meager wages of her father and older brother, Brian. Reluctantly, she leaves her younger siblings at home, unsupervised. Ill at ease in this comfortable WASP environment, Katie is treated harshly for being Irish, Catholic, and poor. The year is 1863, and the government begins to conscript young men into the Union army, but allows the wealthy to purchase the services of alternates to fight in their stead for $300. When the Laceys decide to make Katie's brother the target for such an arrangement to save their son, she jeopardizes her job by conspiring to prevent her employers from contacting him; she further endangers herself when she hides a young black friend in the cellar of the Lacey home. Scene after scene of impending disasters and narrow escapes finally end when secrets are revealed and the girl finds allies in the rational Mr. Lacey and his sympathetic mother-in-law. Katie is a vibrant, well-developed character who carries this novel that is mostly populated by minimally drawn representations of the harsh adult world. Holland obviously cares deeply for her heroine and for historical accuracy, but the strain of trying to serve two masters adequately in limited space produces somewhat rushed and cluttered results. Still, the story is skillfully constructed, and the role of the Irish in the Civil War is brought to light. A painless way to fulfill a school assignment.

Elizabeth Bush

SOURCE: A review of *Behind the Lines,* in *Bulletin of the Center for Children's Books,* Vol. 48, No. 1, September, 1994, pp. 14-15.

Katie O'Farrell works as scullery maid for the wealthy Lacey family of Washington Square to help support her siblings. The Civil War rages, and her underage brother Brian is anxious to join the Union Army, despite their father's disapproval. Brian's wish is fueled by the promise of Katie's employers to pay him $300 to enlist in place of their draft-age son. While the New York blue-

bloods buy their way out of the draft and encourage the Irish to do battle for them, the Irish turn against the city's free black population who, they suspect, will usurp their jobs while they are at war. Holland paints a very clear picture of the triangle of social suspicions and jealousies that erupted into the New York Draft Riots of 1863. Mrs. Lacey is thoughtlessly cruel in her comments about the Irish; Katie is indignant over their vulnerability; the black stablehand she befriends is an easy target for rioters. But Katie and her supporting cast deliver their lines as representatives of their respective classes ("The same lack of mercy we English showed toward the Irish," intones a broad-minded matriarch, ". . . they are now showing towards the negroes, who are the only ones who have less power today in New York than the Irish"), setting the tone of a carefully scripted history lesson rather than a richly developed novel. Still, historical fiction buffs will find this topic, which receives little attention in children's literature, to be of interest.

THE PROMISED LAND (1996)

Kay Weisman

SOURCE: A review of *The Promised Land,* in *Booklist,* Vol. 92, No. 16, April 15, 1996, p. 1438.

In this sequel to *The Journey Home* (1990), three years have passed since orphans Maggie and Annie Lavin settled on the Kansas frontier with the Russell family. Although there is no Catholic Church for the girls to attend and Mr. Russell has never filed the necessary adoption paperwork, they have made friends and are treated well. Then Uncle Michael arrives for a visit from New York, intent on taking his nieces back with him so they can practice their faith and live close to other Irish immigrants. Holland offers a realistic portrayal of the personal dilemma the girls face, as well as the intolerance of religions and minorities prevalent at the time. Although a satisfying, happy ending is never in real doubt, well-developed characters and a hint of romance for Maggie add up to an appealing, warm family story.

Gerry Larson

SOURCE: A review of *The Promised Land,* in *School Library Journal,* Vol. 42, No. 8, August, 1996, p. 144.

In this satisfying sequel to *The Journey Home,* orphan-train immigrants Maggie and Annie Lavin have lived for three years on the Kansas prairie with supportive, caring foster parents. Their secure, contented life is disrupted when Uncle Michael Casey appears to reclaim his two nieces and to return them to Catholicism and their Irish heritage in New York City. Torn by loyalty and friendships, Maggie and Annie struggle to accept their uncertain future. Fifteen-year-old Maggie, the focal point of the story, is caught up in the emotional and social turmoil of adolescence and late 19th-century history. She witnesses the lingering animosities of the Civil War; Protestant distrust of Catholics; and stereotypical disdain of "drunk and illiterate" Irish. Through a series of significant events and conversations, she learns that human nature is a constant tension between emotions and rationality. A cast of strong, distinct characters helps shape Maggie's values of commitment, perseverance, honesty, and fairness. With clarity and compassion, Holland portrays the social fabric, geographic isolation, and resourcefulness of 19th-century prairie dwellers. Maggie and Annie are appealing characters whose desire for acceptance, love, and security transcend time and place. The happy ending, in which Uncle Michael realizes that they are content where they are, leaves the door open for another sequel chronicling Maggie and a romantic interest and a return visit from him.

Additional coverage of Holland's life and career is contained in the following source published by The Gale Group: *Authors and Artists for Young Adults,* Vol. 11; *Contemporary Authors New Revision Series,* Vol. 47; *Contemporary Literary Criticism,* Vol. 21; *Junior DISCovering Authors; Major Authors and Illustrators for Children and Young Adults;* and *Something about the Author,* Vols. 8, 70.

Madeleine (Camp Franklin) L'Engle

1918-

American author of fiction, nonfiction, poetry, plays, and retellings.

Major works include *Meet the Austins* (1960), *A Wrinkle in Time* (1962), *A Ring of Endless Light* (1980), *Troubling a Star* (1987), *An Acceptable Time* (1989).

Major works about the author include *Madeleine L'Engle* (by Doreen Gonzales, 1991); *Madeleine L'Engle, Suncatcher: Spiritual Vision of a Storyteller* (by Carole F. Chase, 1995); *Nothing Is Ordinary: The Extraordinary Vision of Madeleine L'Engle* (by J. R. Wytenbroek with Roger C. Schlobin, 1995).

For information on L'Engle's career prior to 1989, see CLR, Vols. 1, 14.

INTRODUCTION

Although L'Engle has tried her hand successfully at many literary genres, she is primarily recognized for her science fiction and fantasy for middle graders and young adults that blend science and spirituality into family epics. Her novels are characterized by their spirit, optimism, and subtle religious overtones, and often fuse action and adventure with philosophical and scientific problems and discoveries. Praised as an especially original storyteller whose works reveal her skillful craftsmanship and personal integrity, L'Engle weaves significant thematic concerns into her tales of home life, international intrigue, and imaginary journeys through time and space. Primary themes underlying many of her lively narratives are personal and spiritual growth and an understanding of the universe and one's place in it. L'Engle also explores the importance of a secure and caring family. This theme is fundamental to *A Wrinkle in Time*, L'Engle's Newbery Award-winning and best-known work, for which she is credited with inventing metaphysical science fiction for young readers. The first novel in her "Time Fantasy" series, *A Wrinkle in Time* introduces a saga of stories about the close-knit Murray family that solves their problems together. The series also includes *A Wind in the Door* (1973), *A Swiftly Tilting Planet* (1978), *Many Waters* (1986), and *An Acceptable Time*. Combining such technical concepts as the tesseract, Einstein's theory of relativity, and Planck's quantum theory with philosophy, literary quotations, and L'Engle's view of spirituality based on a firm Anglo-Christian foundation, these books are all perfect examples of the flavor of L'Engle's fiction.

The solidarity of the Murrays was anticipated by L'Engle's popular books about the Austin family, including *Meet the Austins, The Moon by Night* (1963),

The Twenty-Four Days before Christmas: An Austin Family Story (1964), *A Ring of Endless Light,* and *Troubling a Star*. These works continue to mix compelling story lines with value-clarifying issues like the nature of faith, the complexities of human relationships, and death as an affirmation of life. In addition to her novels, which reflect a variety of time periods and geographical settings, L'Engle has written poetry, drama, allegory, a collection of prayers, and retellings of Scripture. All of L'Engle's books are written in her spell-binding style, which is distinguished by its elegance and control.

Despite her reputation as a Christian writer, however, L'Engle's works have been severely criticized and occasionally banned by some groups. Her use of magic and witches as integral plot devices and characters have elicited charges of Satanism and pornography. L'Engle finds this misreading of her work amusing, and once noted that she is in the very good company of C. S. Lewis, whose Christian-based children's fiction has occasionally received the same label. While L'Engle does not consider herself to be a didactic writer, and claims to be only a storyteller, her abilities as both are unquestionable. Although some reviewers note instances of overwriting, idealized characterizations, and overly complicated structures, the majority agree that L'Engle's absorbing stories and provocative themes have great appeal to young readers and stimulate them to confront life with courage and hope.

Biographical Information

Born Madeleine L'Engle Camp in 1918 in New York City, L'Engle grew up on East 82nd Street, a true New Yorker in love with her city. Her father, a foreign correspondent, insisted on a proper English upbringing for his only child, and so she was raised with, as she explained in *The Summer of the Great-Grandmother*, "nanny, governesses, supper on a tray in the nursery, dancing lessons, music lessons, skating lessons, art lessons." As the daughter of a respected journalist and a gifted pianist, L'Engle was surrounded by creative people from birth, including writers, musicians, and actors. She was an exceptionally sheltered child, however, and was never allowed to go out alone, so she spent her free time reading the books available in her parents' library. When she ran out of books to read, she began writing her own stories. Unpopular and miserable at school because of her shy, introspective ways, L'Engle nurtured herself with her imagination and wrote to keep herself company. She eventually won a school poetry contest; however, there was so much consternation among the staff that her mother had to go into the school—armed with a mass of L'Engle's poems, novels, and stories—to prove that her daughter really could have written the winning entry. Her family later moved to Europe because of her father's failing health, and L'Engle attended a highly regimented boarding school in the Swiss Alps that she found almost unbearable. She drew from these experiences in the autobiographically based novels, *The Small Rain* (1945) and *And Both Were Young* (1949), two of her earliest published works. When L'Engle was fourteen, her family moved back to the United States, where her father died after a long battle with a lung illness. She completed high school and went on to attend Smith College in Northhampton, Massachusetts, graduating cum laude in 1941 with a major in English literature. She returned to New York, where she began submitting her work for publication. She eventually accepted a job as secretary to the well-known actress Eva LeGallienne and soon found herself working as an actress with a steady career in the theater, acting in summer stock productions and traveling around the country. During an engagement as an understudy for *The Cherry Orchard*, she met actor Hugh Franklin, whom she married in 1946, and gave up acting in order to continue writing and raise a family. The couple was married for forty years and had three children. Franklin died of cancer in 1986.

L'Engle wrote *Meet the Austins* between household chores and during nap times. Frustration and disappointment dogged her as the work was rejected by numerous editors. The book was finally published in 1960, with a number of alterations suggested by the publisher. When *A Wrinkle in Time* began having the same problems,

L'Engle steadfastly refused to change it. It was finally published after making the rounds of 26 publishers, and won the Newbery Medal in 1963. L'Engle has since produced book after book, all which reflect her understanding of how spirituality and science combine to explain the universe and the place of human beings in it.

Major Works

Despite its enduring success and status as a modern classic, *A Wrinkle in Time* was rejected by numerous publishers because it was difficult to categorize and did not use an accepted and controlled vocabulary. Publishers also assumed that children would not be able to understand the book's concepts, particularly the science. L'Engle commented in *Booklist*, "[T]he kids laugh when I say the problem is that it's too hard for the grownups." The first of many books about the Murray family, *A Wrinkle in Time* features Meg Murray, an awkward child with a brilliant scientific mind, who becomes involved in a cosmic clash of good and evil. Using a physical phenomenon known as a *tesseract* to travel through space and time, Meg, accompanied by her friend, Calvin O'Keefe, enters an alternative universe to rescue her father and brother from a giant evil brain known as IT. Meg eventually succeeds because of her capacity for love and self sacrifice. Speaking of the multiple levels on which *A Wrinkle in Time* can be read, Charlotte S. Huck said in *Children's Literature in the Elementary School*, "It may be read for its exciting science-fiction plot alone, or it may be read for its themes of love conquering evil and the need to respect individual differences. It is a strange and wonderful combination of science fiction, modern fantasy, and religious symbolism." L'Engle continued the Murray/O'Keefe family saga in her "Time Fantasy" series and the "Canon Tallis Mystery" series. The latter series features as it's protagonist Meg and Calvin's daughter, Polly O'Keefe, and comprises such titles as *The Arm of the Starfish* (1965), *Dragons in the Waters* (1986), and *A House Like a Lotus* (1984).

In *An Acceptable Time*, Polly O'Keefe is visiting her Grandmother and Grandfather Murray in Connecticut when she finds herself transported into the time of the Druids. Mistaken as a goddess, Polly must bring peace between two tribes on the verge of blood sacrifice and war. While lauding L'Engle's storytelling skills and her philosophical attempts to reconcile Christian and pagan beliefs, some critics found this book to be heavy on static conversations that slow the action. A *Publishers Weekly* critic commented, "The story is laced together with L'Engle's now-familiar theme of the transcendent importance of love. This fine fantasy, firmly rooted in reality, is the kind of thoughtful story at which L'Engle excels."

Told from the perspective of young Vicky Austin, *Meet the Austins*, the first in the "Austin Family" series, is an episodic book showing the reactions of various family members to different situations. Initially, many publishers objected to the death, a subject considered taboo in children's literature, that occurs early in the book. The Austins, like the Murrays in the "Time Fantasy" series, explore philosophical and spiritual issues as they negotiate their relationships and the challenges that growing up entails. But the Austins' journeys—unlike Meg and Calvin's voyages—involve more familiar settings and events. In *Meet the Austins,* four Austin children face the prospect of adopting Maggy, a spoiled and unruly foster child who initially turns their household upside down, but slowly adjusts to her new home and becomes a member of the family. May Hill Arbuthnot commented in *Children and Books*, "This is a fine family story, as unusual and provocative throughout as is its first chapter." *A Ring of Endless Light* brings the Austin family to Seven Bay Island to attend to their dying grandfather. The book focuses on sixteen-year-old Vicky's confrontation with death in many forms, not only her beloved grandfather's deterioration, but also the accidental drowning of a family friend, the near death of the suicidal teenager he was trying to save, the death of a baby dolphin at the nearby Marine Biology Station, the near fatal accident of one of the scientists, and the death of a young epileptic child. Through all of these tragedies and through her friendships with three boys involved in them, Vicky's character unfolds and matures. A *Publishers Weekly* reviewer noted, "With customary grace and firm control of an intricate plot, L'Engle has created another irresistible novel about familiar characters. . . ."

Troubling a Star is L'Engle's latest book about Vicky Austin, who makes a seaward voyage to Antarctica. Vicky expects to visit her friend Adam, a marine biology student, but is warned in a mysterious note to stay home. The plot includes political intrigue, mysterious messages, near death experiences, and an exotic cast of characters, with forward flashes of Vicky being trapped on an iceberg. Florence H. Munat praised the book, stating, "Convincing writing, engrossing mystery, exotic settings, environmental message—what more can one ask of a book?"

Awards

During her long career, L'Engle has been the recipient of a host of awards and numerous honorary degrees. Among these were many for *A Wrinkle in Time*, including the Newbery Medal in 1963 and the Lewis Carroll Shelf Award in 1965. She was also runner-up for the Hans Christian Andersen Award in 1964. In 1978, the University of Mississippi presented her with the Silver Medallion for outstanding contribution to the field of children's literature, and she received the Smith Medal in 1980. *A Ring of Endless Light* was named a Newbery Honor Book in 1981. In 1984, she received the Sophie Award, and the Catholic Library Association presented her with the Regina Medal. In 1986, she was bestowed the Adolescent Literature Assembly Award for Outstanding Contribution to Adolescent Literature by the National Council of Teachers of English, as well as the ALAN Award. In 1990, she was presented with the Kerlan

Award for singular attainments in the creation of children's literature, and in 1998 with the Margaret A. Edwards Award for lifetime achievement in young adult literature.

AUTHOR'S COMMENTARY

Madeleine L'Engle with Barbara Leix Braver

SOURCE: "Becoming More Human: An Interview with Madeleine L'Englc," in *The Christian Century,* Vol. 102, No. 36, November 20, 1985, pp. 1067-68.

Madeleine L'Engle was in the fifth grade when, during long afternoons in her parents' New York City apartment, she pecked out her first novel on her father's handed-down typewriter. She was a gawky, "unsuccessful child," she recalls. The lonely daughter of older parents, she tried to make sense of things by writing stories.

Her 75 pages told of three boys who were identical triplets: one was good at sports, the second at school and the third was outgoing and friendly—a social success. Since together they added up to a great fellow, they began to pass themselves off as one person. All went along marvelously until one of the boys was swept off of his feet by just *one* young lady. How could he explain to her that he was but a third of himself? The adult L'Engle is amused at her novel's dramatic close: "And, what more was there to say?"

Ambitious stuff for the fifth grade. The story had taken on a life of its own, as stories do, and it went somewhere.

"The book always knows more than I know," the author said during a recent conversation. "Writing is an act of listening. I just have to get out of the way." . . .

The oft-mentioned difficulty of categorizing L'Engle's work is something that pleases her. She does not like being pigeonholed as a "Christian woman writer." She is all of those things, but the parts don't fit tidily together in an expected fashion. An Episcopalian, and writer-in-residence at the Cathedral of St. John the Divine in New York, she says that the institutional church is "a mess, and always has been—always will be—but is what we've got. If the church is thought of as the 'bride of Christ,' she is somewhat 'a battered bride' and we have done the battering.

"We tend to have a forensic view of God as an angry judge," she explains, "rather than as one who loves us and to whom we respond with our whole being, in love. That response demands creative obedience so we may become more fully human."

That sort of "creative obedience" can lead to new ways of looking at things. As she says, "my religion is subject to change without notice. It is subject to revelation. Most good questions lead to more questions. We must live in hope and be *willing* to change."

This understanding of faithfulness undergirds all that L'Engle writes. "I suppose my hope in writing is to help myself and everybody who reads my books to become more human. As you are willing to become more human, you become more vulnerable. You have to change and to allow change. That is all very scary to us."

L'Engle's rather fluid religious views, though profoundly orthodox, cause her to run afoul of those who take a more fundamentalist position. Some Florida parents want *A Wrinkle in Time* pulled from the school shelves because, they say, it is "anti-Christian" and contrary to biblical teaching. A school in the Midwest removed ten books from its library because of their "pornographic content," and among the books were volumes from C. S. Lewis's *Chronicles of Narnia* and L'Engle's *Wind in the Door*. L'Engle found this action hilarious. "This is the first time C. S. Lewis and I have been listed together as 'writers of pornography'!"

She is not amused, however, about what she sees as a growing tendency for some religious groups to read books looking for "key words." One book which she says is "unfortunately a 'Christian best seller' is nothing more than a list of 'Satan worshipers,' a series of denunciations.

"People can find what they want in a book, witches or pornography, but what an ugly way to read a book," she says.

In spite of her enormous success in the "young-adult" market, L'Engle insists that she does not write for children.

"I have no idea how to write for children. My writing techniques are always the same, though a book for young adults will have a young protagonist. The most difficult and demanding of my books have been those that have been marketed for kids. Kids are far more able to think conceptually than they are given credit for. They are far more willing to say, 'Yes, but what if?' and they are not afraid of new ideas." She also thinks that young people, having been brought up in the age of space exploration, are more open to scientific marvels.

Though L'Engle's scientifically based fantasies for young adults—spawned by her deep interest in relativity, partical physics and cellular biology—are an important part of her work, she has also drawn much of her material from her journals. In the ordinary stuff of life she has found the miraculous, the mysterious, the numinous. A boulder in the woods becomes for her "a star-watching rock" and she reminds us that "disaster" means separation from the stars. A maple tree beside a brook becomes an icon of the holy.

The transcendence of the ordinary is nowhere more evident than in her three Crosswicks Journal Books, which take their name from the old farmhouse in northwest Connecticut that she and her actor husband of nearly 40 years bought a few months after their marriage. After only summering there for a time, they decided to leave New York City "forever" and open a general store. They dealt mainly in products for dairy farmers, such as bag balm and teat dilators. However, after nine years of "forever," Crosswicks became a summer place again, a place where four generations meet under one rambling roof; those who gather include L'Engle's 91-year-old mother and her infant granddaughter.

She speaks with relish of being a wife ("We are still in the risky business of offering ourselves to each other"), a mother and a grandmother in *The Irrational Season*. The book takes its name from a simple verse.

> This is the irrational season
> When love blooms bright and wild.
> Had Mary been filled with reason
> There'd have been no room for the child.

She also speaks with relish about being a woman—and ever more fully so. "I consider myself a feminist," she says, "but I want to be more feminine. I don't want to be a little man. My quarrel with some feminists is that they want to take over the man's world. I don't want that world. I want the woman's world, which is healing, nurturing, creative.

"Throughout the centuries women have been allowed to remain in touch with the intuitive, the numinous, the nurturing, and men have been forced to repress that part of themselves—limit themselves to the rational. Women have had the whole underwater area more available, so mysticism comes naturally to us. Men are just beginning to realize what they have been missing all these years."

At 66, L'Engle says she is still waiting to see what she will be when she grows up. This gives to her work, and to her life, an expectant quality that readers can and *want* to identify with. It also gives her an engagement with the moment that is as apparent in her person as in her work. She remembers what children know and what some adults forget: *it hasn't all happened yet*. We are still in our stories, living our stories. Madeleine L'Engle's readers are delighted that she continues to *tell* her story.

Madeleine L'Engle with Sally Estes

SOURCE: An interview in *Booklist,* Vol. 94, No. 18, May 15, 1998, pp. 1620-21.

BKL: *Let's start with the classic A Wrinkle in Time. I understand that it was turned down by more than 20 publishing houses.*

L'ENGLE: Oh, heavens, many more than 20. It barely got published.

BKL: *Now it has become a children's classic. Would you have thought 35 years ago that all of this would have happened to that little book?*

L'ENGLE: No, I wouldn't. I called it back and said, "Let's just quit."

BKL: *Did you submit the same manuscript each time?*

L'ENGLE: Yes, I submitted the same manuscript. I mean, I thought it was good.

BKL: *There must be quite a few publishers out there today who wish somebody on their staffs could have recognized that, too.*

L'ENGLE: They thought it was too hard for kids. And the kids will laugh when I say the problem is that it's too hard for the grown-ups. Which really is true, I think.

BKL: *Have you had much interaction with kids who read sf and fantasy in general?*

L'ENGLE: Yes, a lot of them say, "I don't like science fiction, but I loved your book." There's a new category now called science fantasy, and I think that's probably a better description than either fantasy or science fiction for my books.

BKL: *I do see more fantasy than sf; however, **A Wrinkle in Time** does have scientific underpinnings.*

L'ENGLE: So does **A Wind in the Door.** I got a wonderful batch of letters from a high-school biology class. The teacher was using the book as her text in a biology class. With what I knew about biology, I was able to get it right about the mitochondria. So there's a lot of science in **Door,** too.

BKL: *What made you depart from the Austin family series, set in "real time," to write **A Wrinkle in Time?** You had a good thing going with the Austins.*

L'ENGLE: The first Austin book [**Meet the Austins,** 1961] also took almost two years to find a publisher. It's a simple little book, but it starts with a death, and at that time, death was taboo, and children weren't supposed to know it existed. With **Wrinkle in Time,** I just became fascinated with the science of it. I felt that the science was very philosophical. I was reading some Einstein, who said that anyone who was not lost in rapture at the power of mind behind the universe is, and I quote, "as good as a burned-out candle." And I thought, "Oh, wow, I've found my predilection." Then I began to read more Einstein and Planck. These scientists are dealing with the nature of being, and I was fascinated by them; of course, I had never read them in school.

BKL: *So you didn't have any science background before you started reading Einstein?*

L'ENGLE: I avoided it as much as possible. We had to take a science in college, so I took psych. That was as far from science as I could get and still fill the requirement.

BKL: *With your interest in science, did you do your own research on the later books? For example, the biological elements in **A Wind in the Door?***

L'ENGLE: Yes, that was the best thing I got out of college, being able to do my own research. I went up to Columbia and got a couple of books on cellular biology. And my eldest daughter helped me go through them. But certainly I had no previous background.

BKL: *Did you plan all along to bring the characters in your different series—the Murrys, the Austins, and the O'Keefes—into contact with each other, or did that just happen somewhere along the way?*

L'ENGLE: It just sort of happened.

BKL: *Are you going to continue with these characters?*

L'ENGLE: Right now, I'm writing a book, and I have no idea what genre it is. It's about Meg, in her fifties, with her kids all leaving the nest, and she's figuring out who she is and where she's supposed to go.

BKL: *Do you use a family tree to keep all your characters straight?*

L'ENGLE: There is one at the beginning of most of the books, which I didn't make. And there are a couple of mistakes in it, but it's pretty good. It appears just in the hardcovers.

BKL: *In all of your books, you have the very good versus the very evil, which is the traditional fantasy mode. But how did you concoct the ecthroi, and where did you get that name?*

L'ENGLE: It's a Greek word, and it means "the enemy." It's an enemy-sounding word, and I didn't want to use any of the words that we had already encrusted with meaning. I wanted something brand new. And I like the sound of the word.

BKL: *How did you develop your concept of evil—that absolute conformity is bad?*

L'ENGLE: I went to a boarding school where I was pushed to conform, and I thought it was terrible.

BKL: *Do you read other authors who write for children and YAs?*

L'ENGLE: I do. The nicest thing is that people send me books that I might not get otherwise, and so I read in as wide an area as possible. Yes, I do read YAs. I think that some of the best literature today is being written in that genre.

BKL: *What do you think of the science-fiction and fantasy genre for children and young adults? How has the genre evolved? What's the state of its health?*

L'ENGLE: I think right now it's in a state of transition—just as the whole planet is, as we head toward another millennium. We're just going to be different; things are changing. Computer chips are changing a lot of things. We're getting more and more used to living in an electronic world, and I think fantasy is probably the best way to reflect what that means to our lives.

BKL: *Do you get lots of letters from kids?*

L'ENGLE: I do. I get about 100 letters a week, but oddly enough, I would say 75 of them are from grown-ups. They're reading both the grown-up books, the non-fiction books, and the fantasies.

BKL: *What do the children who write you ask—what are they most interested in?*

L'ENGLE: One constant question is, Where do you get your ideas? Almost everybody asks that. And then, there are two kinds of letters: those where the writer explains that he or she must do a study of an author, and "I've chosen you." Then there are the kind from kids who want to write; they just love the books and want to talk about them and ask questions. One I loved was from an 11-year-old saying, "How can I stay a child forever and never grow up?" I wrote back and said, "You can't, and it wouldn't be a good idea if you could. But what you can do, and what I hope you will do, is stay a child forever *and* grow up."

BKL: *Very good answer. How do you deal with the inevitable question about where you get your ideas?*

L'ENGLE: I tell a story about Johann Sebastian Bach. When he was an old man, a young student said, "Papa Bach, where did you get the ideas for all these melodies?" And the old man said, "Why, when I get up in the morning, it's all I can do not to trip over them."

BKL: *Religion and science are interconnected in your books. Some would see a conflict there. How do you reconcile the two?*

L'ENGLE: It's never bothered me. Anything we learn about Earth doesn't change God; it doesn't change our concept of God. For instance, when we were forced to accept that Earth is not the center of the universe—everything is not revolving around us—that really shook the religious thinking, and so the concept of God was changed. But God didn't change—just what we think.

BKL: *I have read somewhere that one of your most frequently asked questions is about Charles Wallace. Why haven't you written about him as an adult? Is he coming back?*

L'ENGLE: He is definitely coming back, but I have to wait until he does.

BKL: *So your characters drive you more than you drive them?*

L'ENGLE: Oh, heavens yes. They tell me. I'm not in charge; I don't control; I don't dominate; I don't manipulate; I'm not a dictator. I listen to them.

BKL: *Charles Wallace is certainly a strong character, but your books are especially notable for their strong female characters. I would guess you get lots of letters from girls who identify with the young women in your books.*

L'ENGLE: Oh yes, a lot of them do. Lots of people identify with Meg. Certainly I do myself. I made Meg good at arithmetic and bad at English, and I was good at English and bad at arithmetic. And I was an only child, so I gave her some brothers. But other than that, I'm very much Meg. I have all her problems. One absolutely charming letter I got was from someone, probably around my age saying, "When I die, I really hope to meet some of your characters." I've been lucky in my life in knowing a lot of strong women, and they've been good role models for me, and I come from a family of strong women. My mother was a southerner, and after the Civil War, there were very few men left, and the women had to be strong. So that goes back to tradition as well as my beliefs. I've never seen why women should be weaker than men or stronger, we're all human beings, struggling to be human.

BKL: *You're still writing, and you're still writing for youth.*

L'ENGLE: I think I go back and forth. Actually, when I'm writing a book, I'm not really thinking about where we're going to market it; it's sort of a decision we make after the book is finished. For instance, the book I'm working on now, part of it is from Meg's point of view, but part of it is from the point of view of her kids. So we'll make that decision later.

Madeleine L'Engle with Betsy Hearne

SOURCE: An interview in *School Library Journal*, Vol. 44, No. 6, June, 1998, pp. 29-33.

Hearne: Let me ask you about your perseverance in getting published. Can you tell us what kept you sending out the manuscript for *A Wrinkle in Time* through so many rejections?

L'Engle: My first manuscript was easy. I got letters from several publishers—from stories I had sent out to literary magazines—asking if I had a novel, which of course I did. And I sent it to the first publisher who wrote, it was published, and it did extremely well. So my first half dozen books I had no problem with. Then when I began to grow and change in my writing, nobody wanted it.

[H:] And that was *A Wrinkle in Time?*

L'Engle: Yes, and also *Meet the Austins.* That mild little book took two years to find a publisher. It began with a death and children were not supposed to know about death, but we had more or less the same thing happen in our family. Two of our friends died and we inherited a seven-year-old girl. So again I was writing out of my own experience, and my children were certainly part of that experience.

[H:] Many of your characters, male and female, integrate a passion for work with a dedication to domesticity. Could you talk about the way you balanced family and work when they may have presented conflicts of time and energy?

L'Engle: They presented great conflicts. Jane Austen didn't make the beds, Emily Bronte didn't do the cooking—but I didn't want to give up either writing or children, so doing both was a choice that I made, not an easy one. I know there have been many women who stopped writing during their childbearing years. I would have gone mad. I was slowed down, I didn't write as much, but I did write. I basically wrote *Meet the Austins* as a Valentine's present for my husband. He loved it! I do have several books on the shelf which never got published. I could probably have them published at this point, but that's not where I am now. They were good, but they were further ahead in the YA field than the book world was then.

[H:] As a teenager I read and loved your early realistic novel *Camilla.* Do you have your own favorites, or books that were easier, harder, or more satisfying to write?

L'Engle: Not really. If I don't love them there's no point in my trying to work on them. *Camilla* was first published as an adult novel (*Camilla Dickinson,* 1951). Did you read about her in *Live Coal in the Sea* (1996)? Camilla's probably in her 60s there, a professor of astronomy. That book looks back at how she's gotten to the more or less peaceful place where she now is. I knew I wanted to know more about Camilla, just as when I finished *The Small Rain* (1945) I knew I needed to know more about Katherine. But I had to wait until I was old enough. So I waited lo those many years till I wrote *A Severed Wasp* (1982).

[H:] So it's a lifetime illumination process. And that may be why your characters keep growing.

L'Engle: The amazing thing is that they grow behind my back. When I finished *The Small Rain,* Felix was a second-rate violinist, and a fairly second-rate person. Then in the beginning of *A Severed Wasp* he's a bishop—and he's a good bishop! I never thought he'd turn out that way.

[H:] Let me ask you about the characters in the two series for which you've been cited. There are lots of parallels between the Murry and Austin families. Do these characters reflect your own family, and if so, how did you let the models go and the fiction grow?

L'Engle: I don't see them as being that alike. The Murrys are far more intellectual. The Austins are more like us, just regular people. And of course I used my own family model because it was the only one I knew—I guess my family would come halfway between the two.

[H:] How did you manage to keep sequels and prequels and companion books straight? Was there a master plan to the series or did you take them step by step and trust a subconscious pattern?

L'Engle: There was no master plan. If I plan them they can't grow. If I listen to them, they tell me what they are doing. I never anticipated writing another book about Meg after *Wrinkle,* and in fact I think there are 10 books between *Wrinkle* and *A Wind in the Door* (1973). I don't write the books in chronological order. *Many Waters* (1986) chronologically comes before *A Swiftly Tilting Planet* (1978), but I wrote *A Swiftly Tilting Planet* long before I wrote *Many Waters.*

[H:] The family trees in your fiction connect, through an intergenerational cast of characters, across books and whole series. Did your characters just start to cross paths?

L'Engle: Yes, and they are far more crossed now than when we started! Somebody suggested that we should have a genealogical tree, and I thought it was a good idea. I'm not good at that kind of thing, so I asked if a young writer, Charlotte Weaver Geltzer, would do it. I think she did it for $100.

[H:] A lot of the characters in your books are famous, either as scientists or artists; does that reflect your own circle of contacts, or did you deliberately select world-famous figures because of our culture's obsession with superstars?

L'Engle: None of them are superstars. They are not people you would see on television. They are people doing good solid work. In the book I'm writing now, Meg is explaining to one of her kids that the reason they don't have much money is that Calvin is working alone. He's not with a university getting grants. So I see them as people who are important in their own right, but don't fit the media patterns.

[H:] The parent/grandparent figures in the Murry and Austin families seem almost too good to be true sometimes. Did you perceive of these matriarchs and patriarchs as hero figures? Do you think the ideal strength and security they model is one of the attractions for young readers who are insecure in their own, often fragmented families?

L'Engle: I think grandparents are very, very important. It was important to me to have grandparents and to be a grandmother. And I think the grandparent relation is less stressful than the parent relation. You tell your grandparents what you don't tell your parents. You protect your parents but you don't protect your grandparents.

[H:] What about villains? Is Zachary Gray a kind of perennial trickster/stranger/tempter figure who will always remain dangerously elusive, or do you think he could eventually grow and change in the positive directions he keeps promising to take?

L'Engle: Most of us have had a Zachary in our lives. People keep saying, "you have got to redeem Zachary!" When I started *An Acceptable Time* (1989), I though I was going to redeem him, but instead he hit bottom. Then when I started the one in Antarctica, *Troubling a Star* (1994), I thought he was going to be there. He never got in! I will try to redeem him sooner or later.

[H:] Where did saintly super-sleuth Canon Tallis come from?

L'Engle: My elder daughter and I were playing duets, and we played a canon. I love the hymn the "Tallis Canon." As we played the canon I thought, oh, turn it around, make it Canon Tallis. So it really came from something as silly as that. But I did have a friend here at the Cathedral (of St. John the Divine) who was in a way similar to the character.

[H:] So there was a model?

L'Engle: The character came first and the person who modeled it came later. And he liked being Canon Tallis.

[H:] How do you decide on voice? You wrote *Meet the Austins* as a first-person narrative and *A Wrinkle in Time* in third person. Is one more comfortable for you? Or do you just simply follow your ear?

L'Engle: I think first person has become more comfortable than it used to be. In the book I'm working on now, which is about Meg in her 50s, she's speaking in the first person. All the others are speaking in the third person.

[H:] Do you think kids will continue relating to Meg even though she's 50 and your readers are still 12?

L'Engle: She has seven children. She's in the voices of all those children, too.

[H:] Let me ask you some questions about writing style. Dialogue seems more prominent than narrative in unfolding your plots, and chapters often end in dramatic moments that heighten the reader's attention. Has your interest in theater influenced your writing techniques? And is music and poetry as integral to your life as it is in your literature?

L'Engle: I'm sure that's all true. The fact that I was married to an actor and that I started work in the theater certainly has had its influence. My parents, who were very literate people, read to each other every night. So poetry and music—they adored music—has always been part of my life. I love getting letters saying, "I've just learned this nice music from hearing about it in your book."

[H:] What process or person has been the most important in shaping your style?

L'Engle: I can't think of any one person or process. I've written since I was five. When I was in college I kept trying on styles the way the other girls tried on clothes and finally came to what seemed to me the simplest style, the one that fitted me best. It was trial and error.

[H:] What about themes? Yours reflect two dominant aspects of U.S. history—the religious conviction that led many to found early settlements here, and the scientific technology that some claim has rivaled or even replaced that religious fervor. How and why do you so specifically seek to reconcile these sometimes conflicting beliefs in religion and science?

L'Engle: Well, I have never seen any conflicts. It seems to me that anything science can uncover simply gives us a wider view of the universe and of the Maker. Conflict is where you cling to an idea without allowing it to change or grow.

[H:] There has been some backlash, from both the left and the right, against your fantasy series. Some left-wingers object to your "mysticism," as in love overcoming all problems of the universe in *Wrinkle in Time.* Some right-wingers object to your witch figures or "demonology," as evidenced by the nephilim in *Many Waters.* Have you had direct or indirect interactions with such critics, and if so, what have these interactions been like?

L'Engle: Well, mostly it's been very, very good. Not much protest has come in the mail. It has come when I've spoken at universities. There are people there, usually not the university kids, who've decided ahead of time what they think I think. And I'm trying to explain to them that that's not what I think.

The nephilim are straight out of scripture. *Many Waters* came from lines of Genesis, which a lot of people skipped: there were nephilim (a Hebrew word meaning giants) on the earth in those days. They saw the daughters of men, that they were beautiful. They went into them and married them. My book came from those lines, so I didn't make up nephilim. They're scriptural.

[H:] That reminds me of a radio show I was on where a caller objected to aspects of sex, violence, and obscenity in a children's book and quoted scripture. I had to point out that there was an awful lot of sex, violence, and obscenity in the Bible.

L'Engle: If you had to cut it all out, you'd be left with a very small book. I think there are powers of evil. You can't live in the middle of New York City and not know that. I think the best thing we can do is to give a child light to see them.

[H:] Religion is a neglected subject in children's literature, partly because we have become a secular society and partly out of concern for offending or violating private sensibilities in a multicultural milieu. Yet many children have deep spiritual questions. Can you tell us about your own spiritual quest and how it relates to the worlds you've created in your books?

L'Engle: I am an Episcopalian. Which simply means to me that I have more elbow room, more freedom (than some other Christians) to ask questions. Yet I have a tradition, a literary structure that is beautiful. When things go wrong, a beautiful structure can be very helpful in holding you together.

I think kids are interested in religion. They ask questions about it. Not teaching religion in classrooms simply doesn't work because the children know what the teacher thinks. The teacher doesn't have to say a thing about it. The kids know who the person is. Most kids are concerned about the pattern of the universe and their place in it. Do I matter? Does anybody care? Is there a God? Am I loved?

Briefly, back to the science—to me, particle physics and quantum mechanics are extremely theological because they are dealing with the nature of being, so they are just as theological as a tome on morals. Before I wrote *Wrinkle,* I picked up a book in which Einstein was quoted as saying, "Anyone who is not lost in rapturous awe at the power and glory of the mind behind the universe is as good as a burnt-out candle." And I thought, "oh, I have found my theologian." So I began reading in that area.

[H:] You've woven biblical stories, figures, and passages into your fiction. Even though you solved the problem of Noah's daughter, in *Many Waters,* by having her gathered unto God directly by the seraphim, what do you think of a patriarchal tradition that allows only Noah's sons and their wives to board the ark? I use this as an example of cases in which women such as Eve, weighted down by sin, insure that future generations of institutionalized religions will continue to be patriarchal.

L'Engle: The story of Eve that I like is that God made Adam and looked at him and said, "Hmmm, I can do better."

[H:] You made that up!

L'Engle: No, I didn't. I got it from a friend who grew up in a very fundamentalist church.

[H:] So it's an ongoing dialogue?

L'Engle: Look, the Bible is a very chauvinistic book. Women are not important. Most of them are not named—Potiphar's wife, Jepthah's daughter, Pharaoh's daughter—and when you have a named woman, you have to sit up and take notice. But I've always seen the Bible as a wonderful storybook. One young woman told me she had been taught by her parents never to criticize any of the Biblical characters because they were all good and moral people. And I said, "When did you last open your Bible?"

[H:] In your juvenile fiction, good and evil are almost always clearly delineated. Have you considered developing the kind of situation where there really are no right or wrong choices? Or do you feel that doesn't belong in juvenile fiction?

L'Engle: Oh, I think it does. I think kids, particularly in today's society, are faced with choices, yet they don't have the background they need to think of creative answers.

[H:] Let's talk about the fine line between wisdom and self-righteousness in projecting social and religious ideals through story.

L'Engle: Self-righteousness seldom leads to wisdom. It's an assumption that I know what is right, and if I am right therefore you must be wrong. Wisdom tends to see both right and wrong in almost everything. It's very seldom clearly delineated for us. Some of the people I have admired most of all have done terrible things. And yet that doesn't take away from the great things they did. Some of the people who I've thought were completely awful have awed me by doing something wonderful.

[H:] Universal connectedness is a keynote throughout your fiction. Do you ever feel uneasy about generalizing from a white, middle-class, Christian perspective, as in identifying "Silent Night" as a song universally loved in *House Like a Lotus* (1984)?

L'Engle: In the group I wrote about, it would be. I was writing from something I had experienced.

The idea of interrelatedness comes from particle physics, because in particle physics nothing happens in isolation. Everything is interrelated and everything affects everything else. Scientists have learned that you cannot study anything objectively, because to look at something is to change it and be changed by it.

[H:] That also supports your idea that religion and science reflect each other.

L'Engle: Yes, and certainly as we learn more in science we have to change what we think about God. Once we believed that planet Earth was the center of the universe and the focus of God's attention. Things changed when we discovered we are just an ordinary planet in a nice middle-aged solar system at the edge of an ordinary galaxy, one of many galaxies. So there can't be the same single-minded creator who cares only about Earth.

[H:] What about when science changes its mind? I am thinking of the character Max in *A House Like a Lotus.* We've now seen studies indicating that sexual orientation is inherent, in physiological aspects of brain structure and genetic coding. When you look back on a novel where Max's homosexuality is attributed to an abusive father. . . .

L'Engle: But not Ursula's!

[H:] What about Ursula's?

L'Engle: I think it is encoded in her DNA. I think that is generally the conclusion that most physicians have come to.

[H:] So science, like the Bible, is in constant dialogue with what's going on around us?

L'Engle: Yes. Many years ago, I was autographing in a college town. At the end of the day a young man said, "I rather like what you've been saying to people but I haven't read your books because I hear they're religious." All my little red flags of warning unfurled and flapped in the wind. I said, "What do you mean by religious? Jerry Falwell's religious. Khomeini's religious." Then I heard myself saying, "My religion is subject to change without notice." And I thought, well, I've received my revelation for the year, because if my religion is not subject to change, it's dead.

[H:] It must be satisfying to find answers for yourself when you're answering other people's questions.

L'Engle: That's when the best answers come, when I don't have time to think.

[H:] Based on your fan mail, do your readers express an overwhelming preference for one book or series over another?

L'Engle: I get a lot of mail on the *Crosswicks Journals* [four volumes of autobiography], largely but not entirely from women. I'm getting more and more mail from high school students on the "grown-up" novels. The mail on *Wrinkle,* etc., continues. I get about 100 letters a week, and I write what I call my general epistles about every six weeks. All I have to add is "Thanks for your letter," or I can write a short paragraph rather than have to tell everything in every letter. When people write letters I believe they deserve to have an answer.

[H:] And at the same time you deserve time to write your books.

L'Engle: That's right. I'm at a period now where I've been very frustrated about getting to my books.

[H:] There are too many people calling you for interviews! When fans write to you, do they identify something specific that has appealed to them?

L'Engle: They do that by telling me about their own lives. Quite often somebody will say, "You've said what I've needed to say and wasn't able to say myself," which is a wonderful response. I've had practically no criticism in letters, and the criticism that does come is, alas, always from Christians, usually from Fundamentalists: "You are writing about a medium!" And I'll say, "No, no. She was a happy medium." Meg was always accused of never having a happy medium, so I gave her one. It's a play on words. It's a joke. It's funny. Fundamentalists don't seem to have much of a sense of humor. If you take things lightly you can't get as angry about them.

[H:] That's an interesting diagnosis, doctor. People do sometimes react more intensely to children's books than to those for adults. You've written for both audiences. Could you talk a little about the differences between writing for children and for adults?

L'Engle: The age of the protagonist. There isn't any other difference. I write the best I can possibly write. If I am writing about a 10-year-old, I stay within the framework of what I think a 10-year-old will be thinking. I'm writing about Meg's kids now. Rosie is the youngest and she's 10, one is in college, two in medical school up at the other end, and all those in the middle. I'm writing from seven different points of view.

[H:] All the children you portray seem to go into professions, and yet the mother in the Austin family opts *not* to continue her music professionally.

L'Engle: I think that's a woman's right. When all this first started, women had to have professions. I thought, no, if you're going to be free to choose you can go in either direction. And that's why I gave Meg all those children.

[H:] Would you satisfy the voyeur in us and describe your writing process—both literally, as in when, where, and how—and conceptually, as in translating imagination into story?

L'Engle: Well, literally, I have moved from the pencil to the pen to the typewriter to the electric typewriter to the electronics of the computer. I like to start the day working before things get too heavy. I spend at least part of every day writing and if I don't, I get terribly frustrated. I revise a great deal.

[H:] Can you write on the road when you're traveling?

L'Engle: Oh, it's wonderful—the phone doesn't ring and I don't see the mail. Airplanes are great places because they really aren't anywhere in either time or space.

[H:] What most interests you in your current writing?

L'Engle: Meg is talking with her daughter Peggy—and many years ago I saw about a 10-line squib in the newspaper from Niles, Michigan, which said that the way we fight cancer now is to try cut it out or kill it, whereas we should try to convert it. Meg says we are doing it in a masculine way, by killing and cutting, that the feminine way would be to try to convert these cancer cells back to normal cells. We've been doing things the male way for too long, and it has not proved successful.

[H:] As you mention Meg and Peggy—both nicknames for Margaret—I'm thinking about the way names interweave in your books. Is that a way of talking about how women pass on their knowledge to their children and their children's children, through discussion and role modeling?

L'Engle: Yes, that's another reason grandparents are so important. Sometimes they have more time to talk about what has happened and why it was important or not important.

[H:] Is there anything you'd like to say to your readers?

L'Engle: I would just like to say how grateful I am that—after 10 years of nothing but rejection slips—when *A Wrinkle in Time* was published and did so well, I *stopped* getting the rejection slips. That is a wonderful thing. I would send something out and gear myself for the rejection slip, and I've still not entirely lost that stance. When you have it long enough, it prints itself pretty indelibly on your psyche.

GENERAL COMMENTARY

Katherine Schneebaum

SOURCE: "Finding a Happy Medium: The Design for Womanhood in *A Wrinkle in Time*," in *The Lion and the Unicorn*, Vol. 14, No. 2, December, 1990, pp. 30-6.

When it was first published in 1962, Madeleine L'Engle's *A Wrinkle in Time* presented a view of women which was ahead of its time. The now classic fantasy novel features a female protagonist, Meg, who is a math and science whiz with a sharp and unabashed tongue, and her mother, Mrs. Murry, who is herself a whiz at juggling the roles of mother, faithful wife, and brilliant chemist. In the early 1960s, such success in the male sphere of science was the stuff of fantasy for most young women. L'Engle's portrayal of women was truly progressive for the era, foreshadowing the women's liberation movement, which would not explode with its full force until the later years of that decade.

Today, people talk of "postfeminism," of goals achieved and doors opened. However, even as some cry triumph and close the book on feminism, others, most of them working women, are crying foul. While the Women's Movement has largely succeeded in paving women's path into the "man's world" of business, science, and the like, it has failed to release them from the moral and practical imperatives of "femininity": the roles of primary caregiver, housekeeper, and keeper of the moral flame of the family are expected to be filled by the woman in the family, regardless of and in addition to the less traditional goals and ideas she may cherish and pursue.

The problems facing women in the 1990s are much subtler, and all the more insidious for their subtlety, than were those of the 1960s and 1970s. At this juncture, it is imperative that we scrutinize the "progressive" ideals and icons of feminism's early days with a critical eye, searching for ways of thinking which may serve to perpetuate the dangerous ideals of the so-called "Superwoman" and the archaic, yet incredibly tenacious, moral mother, the sole repository of love and justice in the family. As a children's classic of enduring value, *A Wrinkle in Time* is an important and deserving target for such a critical reexamination. We grew up with this book, and gleaned much from its pages. Today, a rereading of *A Wrinkle in Time* is a lesson in the power of hindsight; trumpeting the breakthrough ideals of feminism in the 1960s, L'Engle could not see the dangers inherent in the realization of the seemingly simple dream.

Meg Murry, the central character in *A Wrinkle in Time,* is constantly being told that she must learn something or change something about herself; this message comes from her mother, her brothers, and herself. The particular way in which she must change seems clear early on, when both Mrs. Murry and Meg's brothers, Sandy and Denys, tell her she needs to seek "a happy medium." In its traditional idiomatic sense, this would imply that Meg must learn to compromise and to be more moderate in her actions and emotions. However, the traditional interpretation of the phrase is not the only possible one, and as the story progresses, its more obvious meanings are belied by the course of events. This gradual refutation of the goals implied by the phrase seems, on the surface, to suggest that those who admonished Meg were wrong, and she need not change. However, a closer examination of the course of events points to another reading of the phrase "happy medium": Meg's real problem has been not a fundamental personality flaw, but a failure to direct her efforts in the manner most suitable to the female role. The "happy medium" she needed to find, and does find, is the "most fortuitous sphere" in which she, as a woman, can function. In keeping with age-old gender-role stereotypes, that sphere is one of morally redemptive love.

"You don't know the meaning of moderation, do you, my darling?" asks Mrs. Murry of Meg after she has fought with a boy at school. "A happy medium is something I wonder if you'll ever learn" (1962). This sentiment is echoed by Sandy when he lectures her: "You don't have to take everything so *personally*. Use a happy *medium,* for heaven's sake". It is in this sense, one of moderation and stability, that the many characters who urge Meg to change advocate a "happy medium" in her behavior. She is repeatedly chided for impatience; Mr. Jenkins, the school principal, suggests that she will do better if she is "less antagonistic" and "more tractable". Sandy and Denys themselves, more "normal" than the other children in the book, epitomize this ideal; they are the level-headed Murrys, self-styled protectors of their strange and seemingly vulnerable family, keepers of the vegetable garden.

The appearance of an actual character who is called "the Happy Medium" puts an interesting twist on the idea of a "happy medium" as something Meg should emulate. The very fact of this pun calls into question the validity of the concept within the story; the Happy Medium is quite literally happy, and a professional medium. Yet the fact that she can in no way be said to practice a "happy medium" herself is important. She is a creature of extremes, and in particular one of very "feminine" extremes. She sits all day in her cave on a barren planet, watching other people's lives. She seeks out only the happy sights in the world, complaining to Mrs. Whatsit, "Oh, *why* must you make me look at unpleasant things when there are so many delightful ones to see?". She "gets fond" of the children, and expresses a maternal desire to feed them. She is a pleasant but ludicrous character, far from an ideal for Meg. When she says, "Where are you going in case I want to tune in?" the reader realizes that she is much like a housewife, sitting in front of her television/crystal ball, living vicariously through others, snoozing and sitting her life away.

This rather contradictory embodiment of the "happy medium" which Meg must seek prompts a skeptical attitude toward the concept of the rest of the story. The broad claim that what Meg needs is moderation is not born out by subsequent events, and is repeatedly contradicted by statements made by the wise women of the book, Mrs. Whatsit, Mrs. Who, and Mrs. Which. When she bestows gifts upon the children to help them on Camazotz, Mrs. Whatsit says to Meg "I give you your faults". Meg identifies these as "Anger, impatience, stubbornness". Indeed, Meg's impatience and stubbornness are driving forces for the quest, keeping the children moving forward when the boys seem inclined to think too much and lose sight of the human center of their quest: the search for Mr. Murry and the battle against the malevolent Dark Thing.

Meg's anger is crucial to her ability to survive the hypnotic evil of It, the grossly oversized brain which controls Camazotz. As she says, "when I'm mad I don't have room to be scared". Before they go to Camazotz, Mrs. Whatsit reminds Meg to "Stay angry," explaining, "You will need all your anger now". Meg's anger and stubbornness, indicative of the very lack of moderation for which she was earlier criticized, help her to maintain her individuality in the face of the soul-engulfing It.

Meg herself does recognize the negative aspects of her supposed faults, for example when she laments her tendency to blow up when she is angry: "Why can't I hide it. . . . Why do I always have to *show* everything?". However, she eloquently expresses the belief that being fully oneself is worth the risks and problems that it may entail, saying "Maybe I don't like being different, but I don't want to be like everybody else, either".

Thus, the first, most obvious interpretation of "happy medium" is not consistent with the meaning shown in the narrative. Perhaps the "medium" implies combining two very different modes of being. Specifically, Meg's mother is presented as a "happy medium" of sorts. Mrs. Murry is a wonderwoman: she is strikingly beautiful, a brilliant scientist, and a loving wife and mother. She can do anything: she cooks stew on the bunsen burner in her lab, so that she can stay with an experiment; she never lets her children see her cry for her lost husband, because they need her to be strong for them. Her dual role, as scientist and as mother/wife, is viewed with admiration and envy by Meg, who seems to see only the successes in her mother's life, ignorant of the strains inherent in such an existence. Calvin, Charles, and the twins also speak worshipfully of Mrs. Murry's beauty, and, to a lesser extent, her intelligence. Yet with all her blessings, Mrs. Murry's situation as temporarily single mother and high-achieving scientist leaves her grieving in solitude for her husband's absence, and cooking dinner on the bunsen burner with little acknowledgement from the children of her sacrifices, aside from the twin's suspicions that she may have gotten chemicals into the stew. She embodies the "supermom" phenomenon of our era, the "liberated" woman who has only been freed to take on more responsibility *in addition to* the traditional female role, rather than being truly liberated to choose for herself what aspects of each gender role she will or will not take on. By day we see her constantly on the move, handling her many roles with seeming aplomb and cheer. Yet by night, we see a darker side of her existence, as she grieves silently in the dark for her missing husband. However, the loneliness and stress in a "superwoman's" life are not touched upon again in the story; the emphasis seems always to be on the admirable, enviable daytime face which Mrs. Murry presents to the world, most notably to her daughter.

"It [is] not an advantage to have a mother who [is] a scientist and a beauty as well," thinks Meg. A "supermom" makes a difficult role-model for an awkward, confused teenage girl, one which sets the child up for constant feelings of inadequacy. In contrast to her mother, Meg could be called an "unhappy medium," since, in Charles Wallace's words, "Meg has it tough. She's not really one thing or the other". Ostensibly, Charles Wallace is referring to the two groups in the Murry family, those who are somehow mentally and/or spiritually exceptional and those who are normal. As applied to Meg, though, this statement can also refer to her androgynous nature, and to the fact that she seems to be teetering between childhood and adulthood. Meg is, in many ways, "like a boy": she gets into fights, excels in math and science, and is vocal and aggressive in her behavior. When we interpret Charles Wallace's statement as a reference to Meg's gender identification, the line between Mrs. Murry and Meg becomes blurred; both combine masculine and feminine roles in their lives. It is curious, then, that the former is portrayed as an ideal woman, while the latter is a flawed female child whom everyone feels has much to learn.

The crucial difference between mother and daughter lies in the fact that Meg is confused by, and in many ways struggling against, her femininity, while her mother is balancing both the male and the female roles in a seemingly harmonious way. In our society, and in this book, Mrs. Murry's way is considered by many to be a triumphant success of the liberated woman, while Meg's tendency to embrace many "masculine" attributes without retaining those of the female gender is looked upon as a confused stage of an adolescent girl's development.

It is this contrast between Meg and her mother which is the clue to a meaning of "happy medium" which is obscured by the more conventional, obvious meanings, a meaning which proves much more satisfactory than any of the others in defining what Meg is supposed to learn. The problem is not that Meg's emotions are too strong and passionate for a woman, or that she is unkempt and good at math; Meg's intelligence, and the power and extremity of her emotions, are largely vindicated by the story. The underlying meaning of the reprimands Meg receives is not that she is too much like a male, but rather that she is neglecting her "happy medium," the setting in which she is most likely to shine: the female role, in particular that of moral savior.

While it is true that Meg's supposed "faults" often seem to be assets, there are numerous instances of her being faulted for traits which are seen as neutral or positive in the book's male characters. When she fights with the boy at school, the twins are "disgusted" and tell her, "Let us do the fighting when it's necessary". There are less obvious instances of the double standard as well. In response to Meg's demand that the three Mrs. take her to her father, Charles Wallace chides "You have to be patient, Meg". Just previous to this, Calvin has been rudely and impatiently firing questions at the old woman, yet he does not receive treatment comparable to Meg's. The most tell-tale incident comes when Meg fails to answer any of Calvin's academic questions besides the mathematical and scientific ones, and Mrs. Murry says to Calvin, "She's a little one-sided, I grant you. . . . She still enjoys playing with her doll's house, though". Calvin is the opposite of Meg: a mathematical moron, but a genius in all other areas; yet his deficiencies are mentioned only in passing, while he "groans" in the face of Meg's. Most interesting here is Mrs. Murry's defense of Meg: "She still enjoys playing with her doll's house, though." It seems the problem is not one of narrow-mindedness on Meg's part, or a simple lack of capability in the humanities; rather, she is "one-sided," and that side is perceived as embarrassingly male. Thus, a continuing interest in dolls is presented as proof of her femininity.

Meg is repeatedly represented as more physically vulnerable than the boys. Each time they "tesser," it is Meg who comes through last, and who is most shaken by the experience. When Mr. Murry takes them through the Dark Thing from Camazotz to Ixchel, Calvin and Mr. Murry emerge seemingly unscathed, while Meg is left literally frozen, with physical and emotional injuries which require much time to heal. It is important to note that Meg's psyche as well as her body are affected by the trip; we are told that the Dark Thing almost got her, and her moral fiber seems noticeably damaged. Another traditional female role is echoed here: the fallen woman, more easily tempted by evil than is man.

The healing of Meg's emotional self as well as her physical self by "Aunt Beast" is a crucial turning point in her growing up into the female role. When Aunt Beast comes to her, Meg is a wounded and bitterly rebellious child. From Aunt Beast she learns the healing power of maternal love. Though the beast is seemingly genderless, its choice of a female name is significant: the lesson Meg learns from Aunt Beast is how to be a woman and a mother.

If Aunt Beast provides the example for Meg's transformation, her realization of her father's fallibility is the catalyst. When she first finds her father again, we are told, "This was the moment that meant that now and forever everything would be alright". That this assumption is idealistic is revealed to Meg through her father's repeated mistakes, most noticeably his leaving Charles Wallace behind on Camazotz. At first, Meg views this as a betrayal. In the end, though, Meg forgives her father, and instead takes his failure as sign that now that the father has failed the children, she must assume the role of mother to save her "baby" brother.

Faced with the silence of Mrs. What, Mrs. Which, and Mrs. Who in response to her questions about the fate of Charles Wallace, Meg comes to the realization that she is expected to save him. At first she refuses, crying "I can't go!" She seeks comfort from Aunt Beast, but "Aunt Beast did not put the protecting tentacles around her," thus enforcing the pressure upon her to volunteer. Then, with baffling suddenness, Meg "understands" that "it has to be me," and loses all of her bad feeling toward her father and the others: "Now the coldness that, under Aunt Beast's ministrations, had left her body had also left her mind". It is like a revelation. The girl, having been morally redeemed by a mother-figure, Aunt Beast, is now transformed into a woman, with the mission of saving her baby brother just as her new "mother" has saved her.

Meg says that she is "the only one" who can save Charles Wallace, yet Calvin has come very close earlier in the book, and only failed due to the interference of It. Mrs. Whatsit says to Calvin: "You will not be permitted to throw yourself in with him, for that, you must realize, is what would happen". It is not clear to the reader as it is to Mrs. Whatsit why this should be the case; in the past, Calvin and Mr. Murry have been extraordinarily good at holding out against It, while Meg was nearly lost. Somehow, then, they all sense that the methods must be different this time; Charles Wallace must be saved not through the mind, but through the heart. Even if love is considered the key, though, it is not as clear as Meg would have it that she is the only one who can do the job; Mr. Murry, despite his prolonged absence, is still Charles's father, and loves him although he may not really know him. The criterion by which Meg and the others choose her as the savior is gender. Meg's strong emotions, misguided until now into masculine behavior, will be most effective in their intended mode: powerful, redeeming love. Love is indeed powerful, and it does save Charles Wallace. It is, however, a passive power; Meg "could stand there . . ." and still save Charles with love.

Meg's deed is highly praised by all, and it is truly a noble one. However, after two hundred pages in which she was criticized much of the time for her lack of femininity, this praise smacks disturbingly of a vindication. Meg is portrayed as in her element, her "happiest medium" as it were, when she is operating in the traditionally feminine sphere of maternal love as redeeming force. The final message is that a girl becomes a woman only when she voluntarily takes on the role of moral leader and keeper of love, subordinating her other interests and capabilities to this one. The seeming inevitability of Meg's transformation and its quality of revelation imply a lack of freedom for a young woman like Meg to choose her own path; it is simply woman's destiny and duty to care for the moral health of others.

Gwyneth Jones

SOURCE: "Writing Science Fiction for the Teenage Reader," in *'Where No Man Has Gone Before': Women and Science Fiction,* edited by Lucie Armitt, Routledge, 1991, pp. 165-77.

The *feminisation* of juvenile SF—a movement towards more thoughtful characterisation, higher literary standards and more female characters—may have done girl readers a positive disservice. This movement, which may be considered as roughly contemporaneous with the same developments in the adult genre, is generally associated with the emergence of certain highly effective women writers. But women writing teenage SF does not necessarily mean a better deal for girls. . . .

Madeleine L'Engle's **A Wrinkle in Time** won the coveted Newbery Medal when it first appeared in 1962 and has remained a favourite, constantly reprinted. Its heroine, Meg Murry, is the 13-year-old daughter of a famous physicist who has disappeared on a mysterious mission. Between the braces on her teeth, her failures in the classroom and her schoolmates' snide gossip about her missing father, Meg is having a miserable time. In the humiliating situation of the (supposedly) abandoned wife, her mother, who is also a scientist but 'a beauty as well', maintains a serene and composed reserve. Meg's most comfortable relationship is with her baby brother, a 6-year-old of prodigious intellect and semi-telepathic powers. . . .

The characterisation of Meg Murry, the sulky and passionate ugly duckling, is vivid and engaging. The science content of the book may be slight, and always subordinate to L'Engle's particular brand of ideological metaphysics, but it does feature a girl who is at home—notionally at least—with maths and physics. And though it is actually quite hard to recall this after the end of the story, it *is* Meg alone who achieves the rescue. The quest and the victory are hers. As the viewpoint character she suffers in comparison with the two boys in that their fears and doubts are not shown. They remain the traditional boy-heroes, smooth and blank as pebbles, so that Meg's *human* weaknesses must appear to be attached to her gender. But at least she is allowed to struggle against the role of eternal weakling.

> She wanted to reach out and grab Calvin's hand, but it seemed that ever since they had begun their journeyings she had been looking for a hand to hold, so she stuffed her fists into her pockets and walked along behind the two boys—I've got to be brave, she said to herself. I will be.

The betrayal of the fictional Meg Murry and her readers is not in the depiction of the character herself, but in her automatic, tacit subordination. We are told that Meg is a genuine ugly duckling. Her awkwardness masks a considerable intellect, her spectacles conceal gorgeous eyes: she will blossom. The two boys, however, are more than considerable. They are *geniuses:* orders of magnitude above poor Meg, as far above her as she is above the miserable O'Keefes. The crude meritocracy of L'Engle's world view masks here a true fable. Every adolescent feels struggling inside herself or himself secret, unrecognised powers—the mysterious promise of adulthood. But Meg is cheated. She has the right stuff, but not enough of it and it is not of the right kind. It is notable that the 'secret power', by means of which she successfully survives her ritual trial, is a conventionally womanly power: her love for the willful baby boy. Indeed her feeling towards her brother seems deliberately calculated to inculcate the bright girl reader's proper nutritive and reverent attitude towards Man: 'the baby who was so much more than she was, and who was yet so utterly vulnerable'.

Like her mother, the beautiful scientist whose lab adjoins the kitchen and whose role is to wait for her husband, she is destined to find fulfilment not in travel through the fifth dimension, but in a serene acceptance of second place. . . .

Lists and bookshop shelves still abound with juvenile SF of the same kind—the story 'about' the superpowered girl warrior who backs Prince Wonderful in his battle against Ultimate Evil, then throws away her sword and falls contentedly into his arms; or 'about' the girl of our world who makes the sandwiches, screams, asks stupid questions and falls madly in love, while her brothers and the dishy alien tackle the machinations of the intergalactic mind-police. The best of these books are not only popular but extremely well written, and though the generic 'romance' formula on which they are built does not challenge the sex roles, it is not crudely derogatory towards girls and women. Perhaps the worst thing that can be said about *feminised* teenage SF is that it reflects all too accurately the state of affairs in the present day.

What would be so different about a specifically feminist teenage SF? Of course it must entertain, or nothing else follows; ideally it should be well written. But along with entertainment and a good prose style it should offer an alternative (whether in a notional future, a formal Utopia, or a new perception of the present) to the misogyny, both covert and open, of everyday reality. It should also provide at least the hope of access to science and technology. It may be taken as self-evident that girls are disadvantaged by their fear of science, and that in our technological age this phobia represents a serious life-long handicap. SF's famous capacity for 'making the strange familiar' has a potentially useful role here. The readers may learn nothing practical (most of the science in any SF is junk, anyway) but they will still have gained if they lose some nervous distaste and acquire perhaps a little disrespectful affection for the mysteries of science and the gadgetry of technology. In the adult genre women writers and critics have been instrumental in liberating SF from the misconception that only engineering, physics and maybe chemistry 'count' as the science in science fiction. But for teenagers science that's instantly recognisable as the school-lab stuff should be preferred. The majority of school girls already know too well that history is their sort of subject, while computers belong to the boys.

I also suggest that it is not appropriate, bearing in mind that all fiction is available to teenage readers if they so choose, to tackle certain standard themes from adult feminist SF. The dystopia in which girls are treated like scum may seem like just more of the same, to those 13 and 14 year olds who habitually, resignedly, surrender the lion's share of teacher's (or visiting writer's) attention to the lords of creation. On the other hand, a girls-only utopia may equally fall flat. Most girls find boys extremely interesting. Pretending that they have vanished is unlikely to appear a desirable alternative to reality, nor does it offer any new ways of dealing with the problems they cause. Moreover, the aim should not be to exclude boy readers: their attitudes too may be shifted by the right kind of fiction.

There remains the question of whether the teenagers themselves will be interested. Is it possible to attract the average 15-year-old girl to a book that's both feminist and scientific—supposing she isn't already deep into Joanna Russ? The young woman who enjoys 'feminised' SF as an exotic extension of the teen-romance genre is not interested in either hard science or uncomfortable politics. The confirmed SF reader and techno-freak who happens to be a girl is placed in a difficult position by

SF that insists on raising questions of gender consciousness. It challenges the bad faith between her and the stories that engage her, and effectively stops up one of her escape routes from the problems of being a girl with inappropriate interests. The advantages of an exciting scientific read that doesn't devalue girls may be obvious—to the writer and the publisher concerned. But is there any way to present feminist SF for teenagers—or indeed any kind of feminist fiction—*without* slipping into the preaching mode?

Donald R. Hettinga

SOURCE: In *Presenting Madeleine L'Engle,* Twayne Publishers, 1993, pp. 1-20, 111-27, 150.

You need not listen long to Madeleine L'Engle to hear her talk about the importance of story. Her vocation is that of storyteller and story itself is part of her story. "Story," she writes, "helped me learn to live." Already as a girl of five or six, she was ordering her life by the stories she heard and wrote. Troubled by the horrific images coming from the trenches of World War I, including that of her father who, though he would live until Madeleine was eighteen, was weakened by mustard gas, she "tried to heal her fear with stories, stories which gave . . . courage, stories which affirmed that ultimately love is stronger than hate". The theme would be one that would inform her life's work, for her fiction and nonfiction alike suggest that for her story was far from the popular notion of escape and entertainment, but was instead a mode of living "creatively" rather than "fearfully". Her fiction, while not rigidly autobiographical as, for example, Ernest Hemingway's, is yet informed and sometimes shaped by the experiences of her life. . . .

As difficult as these experiences were at the time, their value lay in the effect they had in shaping L'Engle as a writer. They forced her to develop a rich interior world, and they provided the material for a significant portion of her fiction. Writing became her means of processing hurt, and this period of pain gave her much to write about. "I built up a body of work," she acknowledges, "that I never would have done if I had been happy and popular with my peers". Such experiences, no doubt, inform the difficulties that Meg and Charles Wallace Murry have with their peers and teachers, but they are more explicitly related to the boarding school experiences of Philippa Hunter and Katherine Forrester.

Those fictional characters are also based, in part, on L'Engle's own ordeal in boarding school, which, she notes, "continued the hell that school had been for me". . . .

Soon after [their] marriage, L'Engle and [Hugh] Franklin bought a two-hundred-year-old farmhouse in northwest Connecticut, a house that was to become a symbol of their marriage and their family life as well as the setting that lies behind many of the scenes and adventures of the Austins and the Murrys. The house, Crosswicks, named after the village in which L'Engle's father spent his youth, is near L'Engle's own starwatching rock. It is where their children, Bion and Josephine, played and began school, just as the Austin and the Murry children would. It is where their adopted daughter, Maria, came to live with them after the death of her parents, just as Maggie came to live with the Austins. Indeed, the surrounding fields and trees and the atmosphere of Crosswicks seem to be very much a part of the novels, from the warm kitchen of *A Wrinkle in Time* to the pastoral scenes of *An Acceptable Time.* Yet if the settings and events of the fiction are sometimes colored by the life of L'Engle's family at Crosswicks and elsewhere, she adamantly asserts that her characters are not based on her family. "I would not presume to write out of my children," she declares. "My protagonists, male and female, are me." . . .

After she wrote [*A Wrinkle in Time*], publishers were not as impressed with the idea as she was. They wanted to know if it was for children or adults, and most did not accept L'Engle's response that it was for *"people"*— that "people read books." When the novel was finally published it was a great success, winning the Newbery Medal in 1963, and as L'Engle looks back on the years in which it was rejected she wonders if the public would have been ready for it when she wrote it, if, indeed, it would have been as popular if it had been immediately accepted by a publisher.

Her difficulties with publishers came, in part, from the fact that L'Engle believes that she has a responsibility as a writer to respond to problems in society and to deal with difficult matters like suffering and death, matters that publishers in the fifties and early sixties were slow to recognize as appropriate for young adults. She says that "A writer who writes a story which has no response to what is going on in the world is not only copping out himself but helping others to be irresponsible, too." Consequently, *A Wrinkle in Time* examines the implications of social conformity whether it be in Middle America or in a totalitarian state, and *The Young Unicorns* not only addresses some of the challenges that the Austins and L'Engle's family met in readjusting to urban life, but it also examines some of the reasons for gang violence and drug use.

Death, moreover, is a frequent topic of her books, because it is a frequent occurrence, and because writing about it is her way of working toward healing in her own life. . . .

Any reading of L'Engle's biography points to the importance she places on story for understanding the world. If, for her, writing is a way of living "creatively" rather than "fearfully," then it is as important to understand her ideas about fiction as it is to understand something of her life. The lesson she had learned from her early reading was that if she "wanted to find out the truth, to find out why people did terrible things to each other, or sometimes wonderful things—why there was war, why

children are abused—I was more likely to find the truth in a story than in the encyclopedia." *Truth* and *story* are terms that are often connected when she discusses her writing because writing has come to be her way of trying to answer those kinds of difficult questions, her way of expressing her optimism and faith in a world in which it is difficult to have either. But for her, story is more than just expression and more than just answering questions, even if they are hard ones; story is our culture's "most sacred possession, just as it is for the "Bushpeople" of the Kalahari, and "it is up to all of us to keep it alive."

This view of story is one reason that L'Engle writes for young adults; they still possess the potential to exercise optimism and faith. She knows that because young people have not moved fully into the adult culture, they have access to a vision of reality that is broader than an adult vision because it is untainted by cynicism. She echoes both Jesus and William Wordsworth in asserting that "only the most mature of us are able to be child-like." Indeed, when she expresses such a faith in youth, she is speaking both as a Romantic and as a Christian. "We all have glimpses of glory" when we are young, she writes. However, "as we grow up we forget them, or are taught to think we made them up; they couldn't possibly have been real, because to most of us who are grown up, reality is like radium, and can be borne only in very small quantities." L'Engle asserts that because of their naive faith and their lack of acculturation, young people are more open to what she terms reality. "Sometimes," she writes, "if I have something I want to say that is too difficult for adults to swallow, then I will write it for" young adults because they "haven't closed themselves off with fear of the unknown, fear of revolution, or the scramble for security. They are still familiar with the inborn vocabulary of myth."

Many of L'Engle's novels are fantasies, and her commitment to that genre comes in part out of her desire to preserve this inborn language of myth in young people. In her view, this commitment runs counter to mainstream educational interests, which in their empirical emphases are equipping young people to function in a limited world using the outdated paradigms of Euclidean geometry, thus "keeping from them the vast open reaches of the imagination that led Einstein to soar out among the galaxies" in his quest for truth. But for her, fantasy is not simply an exercise for the imagination, something "that should be discarded for reality as soon as we come of age." Rather, fantasy serves as "a search for a deeper reality, for the truth that will make us more free." A realistic literary vision is not adequate to the realities of the universe. If, she writes, "our universe is expanding out into space at enormous speeds," then "too our imagination must expand as we search for the knowledge that will in its turn expand into wisdom, and from wisdom to truth". . . .

Here, too, L'Engle's notion of truth is clearly theological. "The fantasies," she says, "are my theology." What she means by this, however, is not conveyed in the ordinary connotations of the word *theological,* but in its literal meaning of *words about God.* Though they are not systematic or rational after the manner of conventional theologies, the fantasies offer her a literary vehicle for apprehending the mysteries of God in the universe. Such an imaginative vision, such "creativity opens us to revelation." Such a vision sees angels and unicorns, the possibility of other worlds and the mysticism of theoretical physics as being as much a part of God's revelation as the birds of the air and the trees of the field. What she seeks to do in her fantasies is what in her view all mythic writers do—"to affirm that the gods are not irrational, that there is structure and meaning in the universe, that God is responsible for his creation." That is what she says she was trying to do in *A Wrinkle in Time,* which, for her, [according to Sharon Donohue] "was a very theological book" because in it she "was writing about a universe created by a God of love". . . .

Although for some writers the dive into the "waters of the subconscious" leads to a theory of narrative that is almost exclusively autobiographical, L'Engle's plunge yields somewhat different results. She draws on the "underwater treasure trove." "I can swim," she writes, for example, of a particular summer of her childhood, "for hours beneath the surface; or I can bring up a shell, a piece of coral, up into the sunlight". Yet instead of focusing the narrative as an exploration of the autobiographical experience, she simply mines it as a tool to develop a character or to advance a plot. This use of the subconscious requires a function of memory that she labels "anamnesis," a function that enables her to write out of her "child self".

> When I am writing in a novel about a fourteen-year-old girl, I must remember what I was like at fourteen, but this anamnesis is not a looking back, from my present chronological age, at Madeleine, aged fourteen. If there is all this distance of years between us, my memory is only from the outside. When I am writing about a fourteen-year-old girl I will not succeed unless I am, during the time of writing, Madeleine: fourteen. The strange wonder of it is that I am also Madeleine: fifty-seven, with all the experience I have gained in the intervening years. But I am not, in the ordinary sense, remembering what it was like to be fourteen; it is not something in the past; it is present; I am fourteen. . . .

To L'Engle's eyes the story of much of theology has been one of reductive miscomprehension; ever since God appeared to humanity, he has been misunderstood and limited by those to whom he has appeared, in part because "we're afraid of the unsheathed lightning; our binding him with ropes of chronology instead of trying to understand his freedom in *kairos.* Not that we've done any of this to the Lord himself, only to our image of the One we worship, and that's bad enough." If this respect for God's ineffable nature sometimes leads L'Engle to make statements that are theologically troubling for some in her audience, such respect is, nonetheless, at the center of her theory of story.

Her stories are her response to this God of mystery; they are her response of obedience and her attempt to understand this God and the wonderful, yet baffling universe that he created. Her stories raise questions: "What is this universe like? What are its possibilities? How deep is space? Why is there so much suffering? What does it mean? What if—." Her questions are not pat ones; they are questions that probe reality, questions that essay her faith—questions of the nature of God and the nature of evil, questions of love and questions of pain. "The questions worth asking," she writes, "are not answerable." But that is exactly her point in asking them. "Could we be fascinated by a maker who was completely explained and understood?" she asks. The pull of story is the pull of the unknowable: "The mystery is tremendous, and the fascination that keeps me returning to the questions affirms that they are worth asking, and that any God worth believing in is the God not only of the immensities of the galaxies . . . but also the God of love who cares about the sufferings of us human beings and is here, with us, for us, in our pain and in our joy." Thus, for L'Engle, the writing of stories is ultimately an exercise of faith, but that exercise inevitably produces friction with some readers because, as she notes, "every new question is going to disturb someone's universe."

Writing fiction, then, for L'Engle, is not merely a way of ordering life, it is a way of living it. The choices before a storyteller as she composes are the same spiritual and moral decisions that any individual confronts daily. The effect that a writer has then also bears moral consequences. "Like it or not," L'Engle asserts, "we either add to the darkness of indifference and out-and-out evil which surrounds us or we light a candle to see by . . ."

One of L'Engle's interests throughout her career has been to retell stories that appear in the Bible. She has done so in a number of genres. She works in poetry in *A Cry Like a Bell;* she works in drama in *Journey with Jonah;* she works in prose in *Ladder of Angels* and *The Glorious Impossible.* But it is in her fiction—in *Many Waters, Dance in the Desert,* and *The Sphinx at Dawn*— that she is most successful in her re-creations. In these works she uses her powers of narrative to flesh out stories that were told in the Bible and to speculate on what might have been. She offers her vision of what life was like for young adults in Noah's day, and she speculates on some of the crises that Jesus must have faced as he grew from infancy through his teen years and into adulthood. But uniting all the stories is the theme that stands at the heart of much of L'Engle's work—that God is a god of love and that such love cannot be quenched. . . .

The importance of L'Engle's fiction for young adults rests in exactly this—in her willingness to address the whole range of human experience in her fiction, to write about pain as well as joy, to essay despair as well as hope. But the real power of her fiction is that in addressing the difficult issues that young adults—that all of us, really—face; she does not, as many contemporary writers do, neglect the spiritual dimension of human experience. The result is a corpus of fiction that ultimately demonstrates what M. Sarah Smedman has called the "triumph of the spirit," a collection of books "which courageously embrace an unwashed world and incarnate its dirtiness, ugliness, and festering sores, yet transmit the conviction that there is some meaning, some justice, some goodness in the face of so much contrary evidence." But justice and goodness do not occur by themselves in a broken world. The novels point to the importance of choosing good over evil, of exercising moral responsibility, of working on the side of love.

Sister Mary Veronica

SOURCE: "Madeleine L'Engle," in *The Book Report*, Vol. 13, No. 3, November-December, 1994, pp. 24-8.

> The story comes and it is pure story. That's all I set out to write. But I don't believe that we can write any kind of story without including, whether we intend to or not, our response to the world around us. . . . [*A Circle of Quiet*]

L'Engle's vision of the writer is both cosmic and simple: "All you have in mind when you are writing is your book. And that is all. You listen to it the same way you listen when you pray, with total focused attention and then you try to serve it."

She believes that the story has an identity all its own. The story uses the writer as a vehicle of communication. L'Engle maintains that the story is created as much with the reader as with the author: "The reader, viewer, listener, usually grossly underestimates his importance. If a reader cannot create the book along with the writer, the book will never come to life. Creative involvement: that's the basic difference . . ." The author must serve the book and then get out of the way enough so that the partnership with the reader may take place.

L'Engle is a versatile writer. Her published works include poetry, drama, theology, literary criticism, and short stories, as well as her well-known novels for children, young adults, and adults. Within each genre, L'Engle is willing to experiment with form and to listen to what each story or work is trying to say to her.

L'Engle thinks that it is important that she not be locked into one particular form of writing. When many people hear her name, they think chiefly of her children's and young adult novels, of *A Wrinkle in Time* or *The Arm of the Starfish*. L'Engle states her position: "When I'm asked why I write for children, I say quite frankly that I don't. I never write for an age group. I write for myself and out of what concerns me. But quite truthfully, when children ask me why, I say that whenever I have something that is too difficult conceptually, or philosophically, or scientifically for the average adult to read, I will put a young protagonist in and mark it a

book for kids, but I do not write for children. That's an insult to children and to art."

L'Engle believes that children are able to hear and to understand truths to which many adults have closed their minds. "In a book for children I am as careful about vocabulary, syntax, style, characterization, structure, as I am in an adult novel, but in a book for children there is one thing that I may not do: I many not despair. I may show a great deal that is wrong in this world. My protagonist may have to hurt a great deal in order to grow and deepen; but there is below all that happens a Yes to the fact of existence."

Love is a motivating factor in L'Engle's life. She writes about this in terms of the creative process: "It is a criterion of love. In moments of decision, we are to try to make what seems to be the most loving, the most creative decision. We are not to play safe, to draw back out of fear. Love may well lead us into danger. It may lead us to die for our friend. In a day when we are taught to look for easy solutions, it is not always easy to hold on to that most difficult one of all, love. . . ."

L'Engle's works convey this message in many ways. Basically, however, the characters in her novels, when faced with the choice between safe mediocrity and dangerous involvement, more often than not choose the involvement. L'Engle's poetry expresses a loving concern for all of creation around her and speaks of everyday situations. Her essays and journals are probing and truthful statements about what she sees happening around her. The journals provide her the source material for many of her other books. Her impressions, faithfully recorded, keep her aware now of how she experienced things then. She does not play safe.

L'Engle emphasizes the responsibility of a writer. She knows from experience that the act of creation is a lonely business. Behind it, however, is the writer's relationship with others and his or her understanding of the world. L'Engle writes: "We write alone, but we do not write in isolation. No matter how fantastic a story line may be, it still comes out of our response to what is happening to us and to the world in which we live."

"If what I have to say is right, or if it is wrong, I'm responsible for it, and I can't pretend that I'm not, just because it's difficult. . . . Like it or not, we either add to the darkness of indifference and out-and-out evil which surround us or we light a candle to see by. . . ."

In an age of anti-heroes and violence in the media and in daily life, L'Engle holds true to the moral choice. Children, young adults, and older people read what she has written and respond to it. L'Engle says that she receives about one hundred letters a week from young people alone. The letters she receives vary from the fan letters of children who read the surface of her books and enjoy them to the letters of the young adults who "write about what is on their hearts, what their own problems are, what they're going to do in their struggle. . . ."

"I have still not got over the image that my fourth, fifth, and sixth grade teachers set up for me: as the non-achiever, the gawky, the unpopular, the not-very-bright-one. I still tend to step aside for the grown-ups.

"I was asked by a group of middle school teachers what my teachers did to shape me as a writer and to help my creativity. Well, the best thing they did for me was to think that I was stupid, to put down my homework, so I did nothing for them whatsoever, there was no point, and I went home and wrote. I don't really suggest that to teachers, but it worked for me. . . .

"I wrote my first story when I was five. It was about a little "grul" because that was how I spelled "girl" when I was five. Of course the events of my childhood enter into my writing. You don't have anyone to write out of except yourself if you want to write true. You can't write out of other people, but you can take what happens to you and change it and extrapolate it and exaggerate. But you have to write out of your own experience.

"The loneliness of my childhood obviously affects my writing. In *A Wrinkle in Time,* which most people know best, I'm Meg. Believe me there are hundreds of Megs, all across not only this country, but the world. A lot of people identify with Meg.

"I think the chief influence my parents had on my writing was that our house was an atmosphere in which reading and music and literature was simply taken for granted. It was a house full of books. My parents were readers. My father was a writer. Writing seemed a perfectly normal thing to do."

When asked why there are so many characters in her books who experience the death of either parents or relatives, L'Engle notes, "Most people have the experience of the death of a parent or a grandparent or a friend or a dog. We tend to shovel it under the carpet instead of dealing with the truth. "I think one of the most moving experiences happened when one of the girls in my eleventh grade writing class died. . . . [The class] came right from chapel to the room where we were having class and I said to them 'We've just heard something terrible, and we're in deep shock and grief. Let's sit down and just write about it. Poems. Just write some poems about how you feel. If you're angry, feel free to be angry. Feel free to write about how you feel about this thing that has caused us so much anguish. . . .'"

After they had shared their poems, "I said, 'Do you realize that this is the best work that you have done all year, all of you, and that it has come out of grief and pain?' And we gathered the poems together, and gave them to [the girl's] parents. But it was an experience for all of us of moving into our experience of that death, not

pushing it aside, which is what grown-ups tend to want kids to do and which is wrong. . . ."

Many people wonder what experiences in L'Engle's life caused her to develop the communication theories of kything and tessering. She comments, "My closest and oldest friend and I were both gawky, inarticulate adolescents. We would borrow the school canoe and go off for the day in black cypress backwaters and we might not say anything for hours. . . . But we communicated, we kythed. I think that kything is something that everybody has. . . . I think that [as] human beings, we have had an ability to communicate with each other nonverbally, which we have lost as we have become involved in the technocratic society. We talk all the time. We don't have any time to listen to each other in silence. And that's a great loss.

"Tessering is not my own idea. It's an actual theory. . . . The word 'tesseract' is found in most large dictionaries or in most science dictionaries, I just took it a little bit further. One of my favorite fan letters for *A Wrinkle in Time* came from the father of a 12-year-old who said 'My son made me read this book. What do you mean? This is not a children's book. This is a book for astrophysicists. I mean, I'm working on tessering.' And I had a letter from a ten-year-old girl who said, 'My father works at the Pentagon, and he's taken the book there.'"

Remembering her own childhood reading, L'Engle recalls, "My very favorite book was *Emily of the New Moon* by Lucy Maud Montgomery because Emily lived on an island and so did I, although Manhattan and Prince Edward Island are not much alike. Emily's father was dying of bad lungs and so was mine; Emily had trouble at school, Emily had some difficult relatives, and Emily wanted to be a writer. Emily also understood that there was more to the world than the thin world of provable fact. So I identified with Emily. I read E. Nesbitt, I read George MacDonald, I read fairy tales and myths. Those are my favorites. I read the English children's annuals which are full of wonderful wild stories."

A long-time teacher of writing, L'Engle comments about her habit of journal writing. "Anyone can write a journal. I don't write everyday. I have people say they can't keep a journal because they can't write everyday. I tell them, don't write everyday, write when you can. I probably average five days a week, and sometimes I will write for ten days straight or go five days without writing.

"But what you write down, you tend not to forget. It gives you an opportunity to write your own story, to write who you are. And possibly because I've been keeping journals since I was eight, I remember a great deal more than the average person. I can pull up conversations that happened around the table four or five years ago if I need them. So writing down is a great memory device."

L'Engle enjoys meeting children in school visits, where she finds that the children of today are "not much different from the children of yesterday. In Beijing, we went to a school of fourth graders in one of the townships. It could have been a fourth grade in Iowa or New Jersey. Fourth graders are fourth graders. I think that probably teaching is better than it was when I was in school, but we've never come across a really good educational theory in spite of all the great educators. What works with one child, doesn't work with another child; what works in one school, doesn't work in another school.

"When I was in Israel, looking at pictures for a contest they had to illustrate Hebrew scripture, if one picture from a school was good, they were all apt to be good. A lot depended on the teacher's ability to excite the creativity of the children. It wasn't that one school was less creative than another, but they had a teacher who was more able to open up the children's creativity.

"Teaching is just as much a talent as painting or playing the piano. And a great teacher is a wonderful thing. A great teacher provides a spark of light for the kids, and an excitement."

"One of the funniest responses I've ever had was when I was speaking at a school, and this must have been a seventh grader, who said 'This book was so imaginative, I didn't realize grownups had that much imagination.' I think they see it is something that tends to drift away as you grow up. And that makes them sad, and the idea that a grownup can still have a wild imagination is a pleasure."

She continues "Readers challenge and stimulate me. First of all, all writers need encouragement. All artists need encouragement. The letters are encouraging. They challenge me to go on sticking my neck out even a little further, not to hold back, but to go on and write what I believe is important.

"I like the letters I get from the students who tell about their librarians who give them books telling them 'I think that you would really love this book,' so I know that the librarian knows the child and has a personal interest and will give the child a challenging book that he or she might not pick up otherwise. I think that's very important."

She sums up her philosophy in her book *Dare to Be Creative!* "The writer whose words are going to be read by children has a heavy responsibility. And yet, despite the undeniable fact that children's minds are tender, they are also far more tough than many people realize, and they have an openness and an ability to grapple with difficult concepts which many adults have lost. Writers of children's literature are set apart by their willingness to confront difficult questions."

"Only as I keep in touch with the child within my very grown-up body can I keep open enough to recognize the God who is Love itself, as that Love is revealed in story."

TITLE COMMENTARY

📖 *AN ACCEPTABLE TIME* (1989)

Publishers Weekly

SOURCE: A review of *An Acceptable Time,* in *Publishers Weekly,* Vol. 236, No. 19, November 10, 1989, pp. 61-2.

For this time-slip novel, L'Engle again reaches into her bag of weird and wonderful knowledge, blending snippets of tantalizing information from a variety of disciplines—history, natural history, physics and Christian metaphysics, to name a few—into a rich and heady brew. Red-haired Polly O'Keefe (last seen in *A House Like a Lotus*) arrives at her grandparents' farm in Connecticut for some private tutoring. There, in a landscape familiar to L'Engle fans (who will be pleased to know that the Nobel Prize-winning Mrs. Murry still cooks over a Bunsen burner), Polly slips back 3000 years into a different time "spiral." She meets Anaral, a Native American girl; Karalys, a druid banished from Britain for his progressive thinking; and Tav, a handsome warrior who accompanied the druid to their new land. Polly travels back and forth between the two worlds, and eventually her purpose becomes clear: with the aid of her new friends she forges peace between two clashing tribes, and helps Zachary Gray (also from *A House Like a Lotus*), a self-centered but very ill young man. The story is laced together with L'Engle's now-familiar theme of the transcendent importance of love. This fine fantasy, firmly rooted in reality, is the kind of thoughtful story at which L'Engle excels.

Kirkus Reviews

SOURCE: A review of *An Acceptable Time,* in *Kirkus Reviews,* Vol. LVII, No. 22, November 15, 1989, pp. 1672-73.

Polly O'Keefe, back for another adventure, is called into the prehistory of the druids.

Polly's first autumn at her grandparents' Connecticut country home is glorious and peaceful. But when she takes daily strolls as breaks from her studies, even open-minded Polly is non-plussed by three people she spots—especially when she learns that they date from 3,000 years ago: exotic Anaral, majestic Karalys, and warrior Tav, who intrigues Polly as no other young man ever has. Soon she crosses the "time gate" into the pagan past, where she eventually takes part in a territorial dispute. Polly's friend Zachary, desperate for a cure for his heart disease, accompanies her and—once again in a L'Engle story—love's redemptive power sets crucial events in motion after Zach surrenders Polly to a blood sacrifice to secure his own healing.

L'Engle is still an able practitioner of time travel, yet even she seems to be wearying of the many explanations and logical twists required for suspension of disbelief—and/or belief—and the "tesseract." Here, the conceptual feats aren't quite so original, invigorating, or accessible. But her storytelling skill (a blend of practiced writing and theological roving) will carry even nonbelievers along while—in her attempt to reconcile pagan with Christian belief—the notion that Christ existed long before the historical Jesus is superbly debated.

Roger Sutton

SOURCE: A review of *An Acceptable Time,* in *Bulletin of the Center for Children's Books,* Vol. 43, No. 4, December, 1989, p. 87.

L'Engle's particular brand of Christianity is skeptical and undogmatic; her challenge has always been to keep her ideas from overwhelming her story. In this sequel to *A House Like a Lotus,* Polly has come to live for a while with her grandparents (Dr. and Dr. Murry from *A Wrinkle in Time*) in a rather remote part of Connecticut. After two mysterious encounters with otherwordly young people, Polly finds herself in another time—a prehistoric time, when the area was populated by Druids. While this is a promising premise, too much of the first half of the book is taken up with provocative—L'Engle is certainly a spirited thinker—but rather abstract conversation having too little to do with the events of the story. When, however, Polly is mistaken for a goddess by two warring tribes—now *there's* a story, somewhat melodramatic ("'Blood!' the people screamed") but very exciting.

Sally Estes

SOURCE: A review of *An Acceptable Time,* in *Booklist,* Vol. 86, No. 9, January 1, 1990, p. 902.

Polly O'Keefe is staying with her grandparents in their rural New England home where her mother grew up. It's the autumn after *A House Like a Lotus,* and to Polly's surprise, Zachary Gray, whom she met in Athens the previous summer, turns up at the farmhouse ready to resume their relationship. But events take a different turn when a time threshold opens and Polly is drawn some 3,000 years into the past, where she becomes involved in the affairs of an early society, the People of the Wind—there's the tall, blue-eyed druid, Karalys; his beautiful disciple, Anaral; and Tav, a fierce and handsome warrior who despite his feelings for Polly is ready to sacrifice her to the goddess if need be. But Polly's real danger comes from Zach and the People

across the Lake, whose lands are withering under a severe drought. Zach's heart is so bad that he has only a short time to live, and in desperation, he turns to the People across the Lake, whose chief promises Zach aid from their healer if Zach will help deliver Polly to them before Samhain (i.e., All Hollows' Eve). There's a great deal of talk about love, responsibility, and human relationships here—more talk than demonstration—and even more discussion of Christian faith and how it parallels pagan beliefs and rites. Characterizations, in general, lack dimension, and the prehistoric people are stereotypical, their life impossibly idyllic despite the threat from across the lake. Neither the mysticism nor the overlapping planes of time ring true in this story: first, the druid can travel to Polly's time almost at will; then, when Polly faces extreme danger, the time gate can't be opened. You can't have it both ways. Still, there are some nice scenes, and readers who have been following the adventures of the Murry family since *A Wrinkle in Time* will want to keep up with the latest episode.

Jennifer M. Langois

SOURCE: A review of *An Acceptable Time,* in *Voice of Youth Advocates,* Vol. 13, No. 1, April, 1990, p. 38.

When Polly O'Keefe visits her grandparents in Connecticut, she finds herself caught up in the lives of three mysterious strangers: Karalys, a tall, blue-eyed man who is a druid; Anaral, a beautiful woman who is Karalys' disciple; and Tav, a brave and fearless warrior. All three live 3,000 years ago, and are able to cross the boundaries of time to be in Polly's world. Polly discovers that she must travel back in time to play a crucial role in an ancient confrontation and finds that love knows no boundaries.

L'Engle has again achieved the award-winning style of *A Wrinkle in Time.* She successfully combines fiction, philosophy, science, and drama in a book that is sure to have a large following.

This book is the fifth in a series following the Murry and O'Keefe families. Young adults who have read the whole series will enjoy the newest adventure of Polly O'Keefe, while new readers will not need to have read the previous books to understand the story. The book does get technical in places regarding scientific and philosophical theories, but they do not overwhelm the story. When these technicalities surface, the author weaves explanations into the story line without appearing to lecture.

I enjoyed reading this book and found the characters to be well developed, especially Mr. and Mrs. Murry in their roles as worried grandparents. Polly is a little too intellectual for her age (late teens), but with her educational background, it could be possible. The cover art is colorful and makes the reader interested in giving the book more than a curious glance. Highly recommended.

THE GLORIOUS IMPOSSIBLE (1990)

Publishers Weekly

SOURCE: A review of *The Glorious Impossible,* in *Publishers Weekly,* Vol. 237, No. 28, July 13, 1990, p. 55.

Illustrated with frescoes by Giotto from the Scrovegni Chapel in Padua, this lavishly produced picture book about the life of Christ is an interesting combination of coffee-table art book and genial sermon. Expanding upon religious views introduced in earlier books by L'Engle, her impassioned narrative is followed by A. Richard Turner's elegant afterword explaining the historical significance of the paintings. Infrequently acknowledging controversy, L'Engle authoritatively decides thorny theological issues: "Even for Jesus, the human being, his understanding of his Godness did not come all at once," she says, but "there was a glimmer when he was a boy of twelve and talked with the elders in the Temple." L'Engle's tale is frequently layered with advice to the young: "Sometimes it is very important to have an older friend who is not a parent," she says of Mary's visit to her cousin Elizabeth. Like a parson interpreting Christ's story to her young flock, L'Engle focuses on those aspects of her faith that require belief in the "Glorious Impossibles [that] . . . bring joy to our hearts, hope to our lives, songs to our lips."

Shirley Wilton

SOURCE: A review of *The Glorious Impossible,* in *School Library Journal,* Vol. 36, No. 11, November, 1990, p. 128.

Inspired Christian belief and high Christian art resonate in this beautiful volume as L'Engle retells 25 of the events of Jesus's life and ministry. Each of the Bible stories is accompanied by a full-page, full-color reproduction of one of Giotto's famed frescoes from the Scrovegni Chapel or, as it is often called, the "Arena Chapel" in Padua. Despite the tragic depiction of the massacre of the innocents, the dark drama of the betrayal and crucifixion, and the solemnity of Giotto's famous lamentation scene, the tone of the retelling is full of joy, the drama explained as the will of Heaven, the death of Jesus as the victory of love, and the miraculous events as the "Glorious Impossible" that faith accepts and knows as truth. The stories are narrated in a poetic, informal style that incorporates familiar Biblical phrasing with modern, conversational comments and explanations. The text flows, and can be read aloud without showing the illustrations. At the same time, Giotto's frescoes are reproduced with such clarity and richness of color that they can be valued as quality reproductions of Renaissance art. The frontispiece photograph of the Scrovegni Chapel (although reversed) and an afterword about Giotto's place in art history add to the potential use of the book for art history. The text and the pictures fit so well together that L'Engle's words enhance the appreciation of Giotto's art, and the magnificence of the frescoes

illuminates the Christian story. The result is a beautiful devotional book that will be a valued addition to the religious shelves of a library or an art-book collection.

Nancy R. Needham

SOURCE: A review of *The Glorious Impossible,* in *NEA Today,* Vol. 9, No. 4, December, 1990, p. 20.

The Glorious Impossible, Madeleine L'Engle's 1990 book, is primarily a religious book, telling the life of Jesus Christ—the "glorious impossible" of the title—in words and paintings. The words are L'Engle's; the paintings are frescoes by the 14th-century Italian painter, Giotto, newly restored on the walls of the Scrovegni Chapel in Padua, Italy. But any book that shows the work of Giotto is a work of art history. For Giotto was a key innovator in European painting—the first painter since classical Roman times to create three-dimensional "physically believable bodies," according to an afterword by art historian A. Richard Turner.

TROUBLING A STAR (1994)

Publishers Weekly

SOURCE: A review of *Troubling a Star,* in *Publishers Weekly,* Vol. 241, No. 27, July 4, 1994, p. 65.

Vicky Austin, the poetry-writing heroine of four of the Newbery Medalist's previous novels, finds herself caught in a web of political intrigue in this exotic, multilayered thriller. The high school junior is overjoyed when given the opportunity to travel to Antarctica to visit good friend Adam Eddington (introduced in *A Ring of Endless Light*), a college student majoring in marine biology. Her enthusiasm wanes only slightly after she receives mysterious notes warning her to stay home. When she embarks on her journey, danger indeed seems to lurk around every corner—in one tense scene atop a pyramid, she is nearly pushed to her death. Her traveling companions, a colorful lot, include Otto, prince of Zlatovica; Esteban, a tour guide; and various eccentrics; as the voyage continues, their odd behavior intensifies Vicky's suspicions. Interspersed with flash-forwards of Vicky stranded on an iceberg, the intricate story line mounts in suspense. L'Engle, writing for a sophisticated audience, contrasts the purity of a frozen paradise with the burning greed of humans, and her stunning descriptions of the Antarctic waters and their inhabitants transmit a strong ecological message. Good overcomes evil in the end, but enough loose threads remain to suggest further adventures for the intrepid Vicky and Adam.

Kirkus Reviews

SOURCE: A review of *Troubling a Star,* in *Kirkus Reviews,* Vol. LXII, No. 14, July 15, 1994, p. 988.

From Madeleine L'Engle, Newbery medalist and author of the beloved classic, *A Wrinkle in Time,* comes this sensitive, well-written story of a young girl who unwittingly becomes involved in high-risk political and ecological intrigue, set against the starkly beautiful background of Antarctica. After a year spent in New York City with her family, Vicky Austin is bored with the quiet Connecticut village where she grew up. School has little savor, especially since her boyfriend, Adam has gone off, first to college and then to Antarctica on a research grant. Vicky whiles away the time writing in her journal and visiting Adam's great aunt Serena, a lively old woman who has taken a shine to her. Then Aunt Serena surprises Vicky by giving her a cruise through Antarctica as a birthday present. Vicky is thrilled. But abruptly Adam's letters—previously warm and affectionate—grow cryptic and cool. Then Vicky begins to receive warnings in the form of anonymous notes and postcards. She's not sure which of her fellow passengers on the *Argosy* to suspect, but soon her growing attraction to a handsome young prince leads her straight into the arms of danger, and she has cause to fear for her life. This is a story that is perfectly seasoned with just the right amount of everything: intrigue, romance, coming-of-age angst. Antarctica is vividly and compellingly rendered; the ecological concerns are timely; the characters fully realized and sensitively drawn. L'Engle is a master.

Roger Sutton

SOURCE: A review of *Troubling a Star,* in *Bulletin of the Center for Children's Books,* Vol. 48, No. 1, September, 1994, pp. 16-17.

Vicky Austin is excited about her upcoming trip to Antarctica, the gift of an elderly friend, especially because she will be visiting the boy she loves, Adam, who is a research assistant at a scientific post on the continent. The book, and each subsequent chapter, opens with a framing scene of Vicky marooned on an iceberg, so we know trouble is afoot from the start, and sure enough, Vicky hasn't even left her Connecticut town when warnings begin, in the form of notes left on her school locker: "THOSE CONSIDERING FOREIGN TRAVEL HAD BETTER WATCH THEIR TONGUES." (Readers will spot the note-leaver easily; the only mystery is why Vicky can't figure it out.) L'Engle is trying to do a lot here; the book is adventure story, international intrigue, love story, travelogue and environmental lesson, all enveloped in the author's characteristic philosophical concerns. The parts, though, never quite come together. The espionage angle relies upon typecasting and formulaic devices; the ecological concerns are often delivered via the shipboard lectures Vicky attends en route; even the philosophy/theology seems layered on via songs and poems Vicky writes rather than being worked into the book as a whole. Still, there's enough suspense engendered by that wandering iceberg to keep readers going, and the romance is passionate in an above-the-neck kind of way. Fans of *A Ring of Endless Light*

and previous books about the Austin family won't hesitate.

Susan L. Rogers

SOURCE: A review of *Troubling a Star,* in *School Library Journal,* Vol. 40, No. 10, October, 1994, p. 145.

In this fourth book about the Austin family, Vicky is almost 16. Adam Eddington, her budding love interest in *A Ring of Endless Light,* is headed for a marine-biology internship in Antarctica. His wealthy great-aunt is so taken with Vicky that she gives the young woman a trip there for her birthday. However, politics and international wheeling and dealing quickly turn the opportunity of a lifetime into a fight for survival as Vicky becomes a pawn in the struggles that surround her. Readers know that trouble is in store from the onset, as each chapter begins with an italicized paragraph of her terrified musings while she waits to be rescued from the iceberg upon which she is stranded. Most of the intrigue is centered on the tiny South American country of Vespugia, which will be familiar to readers of *A Swiftly Tilting Planet.* There is no fantasy here, though—only human foibles such as greed and waste as the environmentalists who want to protect this continent and the various interest groups, who prefer to use it for personal gain, squabble. The narrative is interspersed with the poetry Vicky often uses to express her feelings, and with lively descriptions of the wildlife and habitats of Antarctica. The mystery itself is fairly transparent, even predictable. Those YAs who are accustomed to more contemporary realism in their novels may find the Austins, with their wholesome, intellectual lifestyle and their thoughtful, well-connected friends, as close to fantasy as one can get while remaining on Earth. Hopefully, though, they'll be able to suspend their disbelief long enough to enjoy Vicky's adventure

Florence H. Munat

SOURCE: A review of *Troubling a Star,* in *Voice of Youth Advocates,* Vol. 17, No. 5, December, 1994, pp. 276-77.

What do an eighty-three-year-old retired explorer/lawyer, a young Minnesota divorcee who plays the Celtic lap harp, a handsome prince of a tiny Eastern European principality, a Texas businessman who dresses like a cowboy, a Vespugian rancher whose principal business is forest preservation, a sixty-ish woman who teaches science in Alaska, a scientist with a specialty in penguin behavior, a formerU.S. Army medic who walks with a limp, his gorgeous Caribbean island wife, and a young German girl have in common? They are all passengers on the Argosy, a research ship bound from steamy Vespugia (a fictional South American country) to the Falkland Islands to the icebergs of frigid Antarctica. And at least one of these characters is trying to kill fellow passenger Vicky Austin, the book's sixteen-year-old heroine.

Aunt Serena, an old woman who lives in Vicky's small New England hometown, has planned and financed Vicky's trip to Antarctica. Serena's son Adam disappeared in the Antarctic on a scientific expedition years before. When Vicky reads Adam's journals in Aunt Serena's attic before her own trip, she suspects he was murdered. Adam may have made enemies of certain governments when he publicized their plans to drill for oil beneath the Antarctic ice.

As Vicky plans for her trip, something similar seems afoot. Someone leaves notes in her school locker warning her not to go. And Aunt Serena's great-nephew (also named Adam) who is already in the Antarctic studying marine biology, sends Vicky mysterious letters which also seem to be warning her to stay home. But to whom is she a threat, and why?

The reader knows from page one that Vicky eventually does find herself in dire trouble. The opening paragraphs of each of the eleven long chapters contain Vicky's interior monologue as she floats, alone and freezing and progressively more frightened, on an iceberg in Antarctica. She deteriorates physically and mentally chapter by chapter. What happened to bring her to such a state is related slowly and suspensefully in the chapters' main bodies. Does this plot device work? You bet.

Teenagers now have their own Sue Grafton in Madeleine L'Engle. This novel has mystery galore and memorable (see above) characters. In addition to these assets, the book is laden with facts about the ecology of a little-known and much-endangered continent. Along with Vicky, the reader learns about the political realities and greed that drives nations to exploit pristine areas for their own gain.

Convincing writing, engrossing mystery, exotic settings, environmental message—what more can one ask of a book? Buy it, read it yourself, give it to your good readers, and then wait for some major awards to roll in.

Additional coverage of L'Engle's life and career is contained in the following sources published by The Gale Group: *Authors and Artists for Young Adults,* **Vol. 1;** *Contemporary Authors New Revision Series,* **Vol. 66;** *Contemporary Literary Criticism,* **Vol. 12;** *Dictionary of Literary Biography,* **Vol. 52;** *Junior DISCovering Authors; Major Authors and Illustrators for Children and Young Adults; Something about the Author Autobiography Series,* **Vol. 15; and** *Something about the Author,* **Vols. 1, 27, 75.**

Laurence (Patrick) Pringle

1935-

(Also writes as Sean Edmund) American author of non-fiction, fiction, and picture books; photographer.

Major works include *Throwing Things Away: From Middens to Resource Recovery* (1986), *The Animal Rights Controversy* (1989), *Nuclear Energy: Troubled Past, Uncertain Future* (1989), *Jackal Woman: Exploring the World of Jackals* (1993), *An Extraordinary Life: The Story of a Monarch Butterfly* (1997).

For information on Pringle's career prior to 1981, see *CLR*, Vol. 4.

INTRODUCTION

Noted for his excellence in science reporting, Pringle writes about natural history and environmental issues in books that are often illustrated with his own photographs. He has explored such concerns as forest fires, biological and chemical warfare, oil spills, and acid rain, as well as such subjects as mammals, insects, birds, and fish. In addition, he is also the author of a collection of biographies about prominent naturalists who have worked with such animals as bats, bears, wolves, scorpions, and sharks. His books, which range from picture books for primary graders to more complicated science books for young adults, are commended for presenting detailed scientific information in a comprehensible manner. As a literary stylist, Pringle is recognized for the clarity and fluidity of his texts. Avoiding unnecessary jargon but accurately presenting the facts, his works are praised for their simplification of scientific issues without condescending to young readers. Although some critics have found his works dry and overly fact-oriented, most agree that his books contain enough detail to keep the reader interested and to adequately illustrate the complexity of the topic. However, Pringle also takes pains to ensure that his texts are not bogged down in scientific intricacies that would be difficult for his readers to grasp. He is further credited for the quality of his photographs, which most often represent wildlife and natural settings.

While Pringle openly states his biases, he is commended for his ability to present balanced viewpoints and for discussing even sensitive subjects objectively. Although he writes about issues that are considered dire by some—including global warming and nuclear power—Pringle is not an alarmist. One book, for example, explores the threat of "killer" Africanized bees to North America; in that work, Pringle tones down the media panic to articulate a balanced, if concerned, account. For all his attention to the core science of his topics, and his careful presentation of all sides of an argument, Pringle is able to keep his books interesting and readable. Kathleen Squires noted that Pringle is "an esteemed children's author whose gift is turning natural history and science into page-turning reading." A *Kirkus Reviews* critic further asserted, "Whatever the issue, Pringle can be counted on to draw the lines, identify the parties, make the connections among interest, action, and effect—and demonstrate an approach that young readers can profitably apply to other issues."

Biographical Information

Born in Rochester, New York, Pringle grew up in rural Mendon where he learned to hunt, trap, and fish from his father. His home life was difficult and his parents, distant; thus, he sought solace in the outdoors. In an essay in *Something about the Author Autobiography Series* (*SAAS*), Pringle wrote, "I felt neglected, unappreciated, lonely. I found comfort outdoors, and spent many hours roaming the Hopper Hills, exploring its forests, springs, and ponds." It was this early exposure to nature, and the Kodak Baby Brownie camera he received for Christmas in 1947, that sent Pringle off on his life as a naturalist and photographer. In 1954, Pringle entered Cornell University, majoring in wildlife conservation. While in college, he took two courses on writing nonfiction for magazines and won a campus photography contest with a nature photo he had taken. Shortly after graduation, Pringle had an article published in *The Conservationalist*, the environmental magazine of New York State. He wrote in *SAAS*, "Having a byline with an article and credit lines with photographs felt so good; I began to aim for national outdoor magazines." He received a master's degree from the University of Massachusetts at Amherst in 1960 and, within a year, he entered Syracuse University to earn a doctorate in wildlife biology. However, after having several more of his nonfiction articles and photographs published, Pringle turned to studying journalism—a choice he "never regretted," for it set his career as a writer in motion. Pringle later became an editor at *Nature & Science,* a magazine for young readers published by the American Museum of Natural History in New York City. While at the magazine he wrote many articles on natural history and contributed stories and photographs to other publications.

His first book, *Dinosaurs and Their World*, was published in 1968 and sold more than 70,000 copies. In 1987 he published his first picture book, *Jesse Builds a Road*, inspired by his two young children. Pringle continues to write about science and nature for young people, motivated by his love of the outdoors and concern for the environment. In evaluating his oeuvre, Pringle wrote in *SAAS:* "My approach to writing a book is like that of a teacher planning to present a subject to students—not 'how many facts, dates, and definitions I can jam into their heads' but 'what are the key ideas and how can I spark some enthusiasm about them.' As my knowledge of ecology has grown, so has my appreciation of diversity, complexity, and the interdependence of living things, and a sense of membership in the earth ecosystem."

Major Works

Pringle commented in *Something about the Author* (*SATA*), "I . . . encourage a skeptical attitude toward the fruits of technology and various vested interests that come into play with such issues as nuclear power, environmental health, biocides, or acid rain. . . . My books about controversial issues are not balanced—in the sense of equal space and weight applied to all sides—but are balanced by presenting arguments from the opposing interests. . . ." Pringle is praised for that balance, illustrated in such works as *Throwing Things Away: From Middens to Resource Recovery, Nuclear Energy: Troubled Past, Uncertain Future,* and *The Animal Rights Controversy.* In *Throwing Things Away,* Pringle explores the history of human refuse from prehistoric times to the present, remarking on the social aspects of waste and the ecologies affected by the way humans dispose of their trash. He peppers the text with stories of specific events and situations to keep readers interested. While

he writes in a straightforward, no nonsense fashion about the dangers of continuing current methods of waste disposal, Pringle tempers dire predictions with hopeful accounts of possible solutions.

Nuclear Energy, an update of 1979's *Nuclear Power,* is another work that focuses on a sensitive issue. The book explains the science of nuclear reactors, and includes chapters on the incidents at Chernobyl and Three Mile Island. Alan Newman described the work as "a savvy, well-written book on a subject often confused by hysteria and misinformation." Despite an acknowledged antinuclear slant, Pringle lucidly explains the physics and history of nuclear energy and tracks current trends in nuclear technology in a work that gives voice to arguments on both sides. In addition, *The Animal Rights Controversy* is successful in "explaining and assessing the arguments on all sides of a controversial issue," according to critic Roger Sutton. In this book, Pringle traces the attitudes of humans toward animals and explores the complex topics of vegetarianism, hunting, "factory farming," and animal testing. Without resorting to sensationalism, Pringle makes a case against the abuse of animals, but also gives the opposition its chance to be heard. Other books by Pringle addressing controversial issues include *Chemical and Biological Warfare: The Cruelest Weapons* (1993) and *Smoking: A Risky Business* (1996).

Pringle, with his training as a wildlife biologist and his love of nature, has also written extensively about animals and their environments. His interest in the scientists who study animals in the wild inspired a series of titles about zoologists, including *Wolfman: Exploring the World of Wolves* (1983), *Bearman: Exploring the World of Black Bears* (1989), and *Batman: Exploring the World of Bats* (1991). *Jackal Woman: Exploring the World of Jackals* is a portrait of Patricia Moehlman, a dedicated scientist who studies the scavengers on the Serengeti. Chris Sherman noted that "Pringle captures the zoologist's excitement in her work and the respect and admiration she feels for her subjects." The book is also a portrait of the silver-backed and golden jackals that Moehlman observes. As in the other works in the series, Pringle reveals an animal with a negative reputation to be a misunderstood—and fascinating—creature. *Jackal Woman,* while very much a book about jackals and their habitat, presents the zoologist as a role model and gives young readers a glimpse of possible careers for naturalists. Pringle's unique approach, reviewers have observed, sets this book and the rest in his zoologist series apart from other books about animals.

In a similar vein, the narrative perspective in his *An Extraordinary Life: The Story of a Monarch Butterfly* distinguishes the work from other informational books about wildlife. The story traces the life cycle of the monarch Danaus from her emergence from an egg in Massachusetts, through caterpillar and chrysalis stages, to her extraordinary and dangerous migration to Mexico for the winter. By the time readers return with Danaus north, where she lays her own eggs, they have absorbed many scientific facts about the monarch through Pringle's exciting storytelling. A *Kirkus Reviews* critic remarked, "A superb, well-researched book that finds extraordinary science in the everyday life of a butterfly."

Awards

Natural Fire: Its Ecology in Forests was named a New York Academy of Sciences Younger Honor book in 1980. Three of Pringle's works appeared on the John Burroughs List of Nature Books for Young Readers: *Batman: Exploring the World of Bats* in 1991, *Jackal Woman: Exploring the World of Jackals* in 1993, *An Extraordinary Life: The Story of a Monarch Butterfly* in 1997. Pringle received two honor book citations for the Orbis Pictus Award for Outstanding Nonfiction for Children from the National Council of Teachers of English, for *Dolphin Man: Exploring the World of Dolphins* in 1996, and for *An Extraordinary Life: The Story of a Monarch Butterfly* in 1998. Pringle was the winner of the Eva L. Gordon award in 1983, and the *Washington Post*/Children's Book Council Nonfiction Award in 1999 for his body of work.

AUTHOR'S COMMENTARY

Laurence Pringle

SOURCE: "A Voice for Nature," in *The Voice of the Narrator in Children's Literature: Insights from Writers and Critics,* edited by Charlotte F. Otten and Gary D. Schmidt, Greenwood Press, 1989, pp. 377-82.

First, let's get one thing clear: I don't write informational books, whatever they are. Sounds like something having to do with data, statistics, factoids, and answers to crossword puzzles.

I write nonfiction, which differs from fiction mainly by having no or few invented characters, situations, or dialogue. I do not write in order to jam a lot of jargon and facts into some poor reader's head but to express my feelings, values, my vision of the world—my voice.

My voice is first revealed in my choice to write nonfiction rather than fiction. Some authors write both; most don't. I began to write nonfiction articles for magazines while in college. Maybe fiction seemed too intimate, but more likely the writing assignments in my many science courses—I was a wildlife biology major—simply primed my nonfiction pump. In any event, the publication of a few articles opened a path that became the path of least resistance. My nonfiction voice grew in confidence while my fiction voice remained largely untested and unsure.

Having chosen to write nonfiction, a writer further reveals his or her voice in choice of subjects. For me it is the life sciences, in a broad sense, from cockroaches to the effects of nuclear war. At times I must venture into physics and chemistry, but feel more at home in woods and swamps, and I am happy that we have people like Roy Gallant, a key mentor in my writing career, who feels more at home in astronomy and the earth sciences.

I am a skeptic (*not* a cynic) and tend to challenge authority and accepted truths. This has influenced my choice of subjects, as I have questioned popular but incorrect notions about forest fires, dinosaurs, vampire bats, wolves, coyotes, and killer bees. Part of my goal is to show that the process of science aims for a better understanding of the world. As long as we keep asking questions, that understanding can change.

Skepticism, I feel, should also be directed at new technologies and at the vested interests that come into play with such issues as nuclear power, environmental health, biocides, and acid rain. There are usually extremists on both sides whose motivations bear a close look. My voice is not a bland, neutral one, with equal space and weight given to opposing interests, and I avoid any claims of strict objectivity in jacket blurbs.

I am fascinated by the complex interconnections between living and non-living things, and this aspect of my voice seems to be present in virtually everything I write. It seems especially rich (loud?) in such titles as *Animals and Their Niches* (1977) and *Frost Hollows and Other Microclimates* (1981). It certainly affected the content of *Throwing Things Away: From Middens to Resource Recovery* (1986). This book could have been tightly focused on the contemporary problem of solid waste management: What shall we do with all this stuff we throw away? As the subtitle suggests, however, I roamed further, including ideas about archeology (which is based largely on past trash), on dumps and landfills as cultural institutions, and on the variety of wildlife (including polar bears and wolves) that scavenge at dumps and landfills. I took pleasure in bringing in the voice of Wallace Stegner, with quotations from his essay "The Town Dump," and in writing about how our garbage has caused increases in gull populations, which then led to increasing numbers of costly collisions of gulls and aircraft. Lots of interconnections!

I promote the idea of kinship between humans and other living things—a sort of "we're all in this together" attitude. A few years ago I proposed to an editor a book that I wanted to call, simply, **Home.** As I envisioned it, *Home* would be a picture book of only a few hundred words, about home in its broadest sense. It would include both humans and other animals. It would even include homeless people who live in cardboard boxes and bus stations. It would emphasize the similarities of basic needs among all sorts of creatures.

The editor didn't share my enthusiasm. She wanted a

book focused on animal homes. "Leave the people out." I needed money from a contract advance and couldn't afford the time needed to find a more amenable editor. I am fond of the book that I wrote, *Home: How Animals Find Comfort and Safety* (1987), but feel that my voice was muffled somewhat by an editor (whose judgment was based in part on the marketplace; more about this below).

The book does include a few instances in which I tried to link humans with other living things. An example occurs where I describe worker honeybees "filling in gaps and cracks, especially in early autumn when cold nights reveal where chilly drafts enter the nest. Like many a human family, honeybees caulk and cover the places where precious heat escapes. This reduces their energy cost and provides a more comfortable home in winter."

One of the many reasons I like *Wolfman* (1983) is its title, so I decided to write a similar book about a man who had devoted decades to the study of spiders, and call it *Spiderman*. The editor's initial interest vanished when she talked to the publisher's sales people, who believed they could not sell enough copies of a book about spiders. In essence they said, "Give us a book about something with fur and brown eyes," so I now have a contract for a book about a man who has devoted his life to the study of black bears. The economics of bookselling has at least temporarily stilled my voice on the subject of *Spiderman*.

To return to the idea of fostering kinship with all living things, and an appreciation of nature and its diversity, here is my ending for *Vampire Bats* (1987): "The vampire bat, after all, is not a mythical monster. It is a fascinating real creature that happens to need blood in order to fly, to raise its young, to live."

Sharks are other creatures that so many of us have been taught to fear. In *Sevengill: The Shark and Me* (1986), Don Reed writes: "The shark was a force of nature, like a mountain or a storm. My perception of her had changed, but she herself had not changed, except perhaps in learning to associate me with the availability of food because I fed her. She was neither my friend nor my enemy. She was like the sea itself, a positive part of the natural world, to be respected."

The beginnings and ends of books, as well as those of chapters, are places where nonfiction writers often express their voice most directly. My feelings led me to name *Home*'s last chapter "No Place Like Home," and to conclude:

> The hermit crab's plight shows once more that all of animals' homes can be matters of life and death. It also brings to mind that old saying, "There's no place like home." People say that to express appreciation for the warmth and security of home, but the words can have another meaning. What happens to an animal when it finds "there's no place like

home"—no place remaining that is like the snail shell or nesting site it needs for life?

> Anyone who cares about saving the earth's rich variety of animal life must also care about all of the diverse places that are animal homes.

I didn't know the book would end that way. The facts and my values led me there. In 1987 James Cross Giblin made a similar observation about the ending of his *Walls: Defenses through History* (1984). "Sometimes," he said, "the material leads you to a conclusion you did not expect." Here are most of his last two paragraphs:

> None of the walls was ever entirely successful. If an enemy was determined enough, he usually found some way to get over, around, under, or through the wall. In spite of this, nations and states continued to build defensive walls. . . .

> Today, in the atomic age, some leaders and scientists are still seeking the ultimate defensive wall. But perhaps the time has finally come to admit that no such wall is possible. Confronted by nuclear weapons, any nation that wants to feel secure in the future will have to reach some sort of understanding with its enemies. It can't hope to achieve security by building a wall.

Thus a writer's fascination with the history of walls led him to make a political statement. Individual readers may interpret it differently; my interpretation is "Don't fall for the futile fantasy of Ronald Reagan's so-called Strategic Defense Initiative."

Today, listening to a radio call-in show, I heard a father tell a psychologist of finding a will written by his thirteen-year-old daughter—perhaps a cry for help from someone considering suicide. I recall the wretchedness of my own early teens, when no one told me that for most people life gets better. Today I believe strongly that writers of both fiction and nonfiction must offer hope to young readers.

Most of my books for teenagers deal with tough issues. I don't minimize the difficulties of accomplishing social and political change, but usually conclude with the thought that people have the ability and power to effect change. Thus, the last lines of *Living in a Risky World* (1989) read, "People accept the inevitability of risk. In a democracy they have the right to participate in the dialogue about how hazardous life should be."

In *Nuclear War: From Hiroshima to Nuclear Winter* (1985), I focused on the likely outcomes of nuclear war and did not write about the politics of the arms race and disarmament efforts. I was upset when one reviewer found it lacking in hope. Perhaps he needed a strong dose of hope on the day he read the book, or perhaps he missed parts of the book, including its ending: "What we have learned, together with our unproved assumptions, strongly suggests that the nation that starts nuclear war will be making a murder-suicide pact with its opponent and threatening every living thing on earth. That is knowledge enough, and a powerful incentive for people to work to ensure that all of the rest remains forever a mystery."

The voice of a nonfiction writer can sometimes be detected in specific details, in his or her choice of anecdotes, quotations, and even illustrations. Nonfiction authors usually have a great deal to say about the illustrations of their books. They may provide artists with reference material on key ideas that need illustrating; they locate or take photographs themselves. Within budget constraints I try to illustrate my books with a rich variety of images, including—when appropriate—political cartoons, which can eloquently express wisdom about a controversy.

You can also hear my voice in my selection of words from others. In three of my books for young adults, you will find reference to people "finding wormholes in the fruits of technology." I don't know who coined this phrase—was it Senator Joe Biden?—but I think it wonderfully sums up the risk consciousness and the healthy skepticism toward technology that has grown in the past three decades. My books about land use choices and about restoring environments, among others, include quotations from Aldo Leopold, the ecologist-philosopher whose wisdom about the relationship between humans and nature is part of the foundation on which the environmental movement is based.

Part of the writing process is being alert for those nuggets of wisdom, pithy quotes, and anecdotes about situations and individuals that help convey ideas. The lives of specific people and their words can add greatly to the appeal of nonfiction. Finding these people to write about can be a challenge in scientific fields where many definitions and long explanations are needed to explain what investigators are studying. In my research I am delighted to come upon scientists whose studies can be clearly described, with a minimum of jargon, to young readers, and whose questions—how do vines find objects to climb, why do insects rest overnight within the blossoms of some spring wildflowers—are matters that anyone might observe and wonder about.

One of the unfortunate realities about writing nonfiction is that few readers write to an author to tell of their reaction to a book. Fiction writers are sometimes told how their stories and characters have touched the lives of their readers. Nonfiction authors get much less of this; many letters have a "this week we will write to authors" class assignment taint to them.

Sometimes teachers or librarians tell me how they have used a book of mine, and about how it affected their lives and the lives of specific children. Beyond this extraordinary feedback, and the praise of reviewers, I am left with raw hope—that somewhere out there, young people hear my voice.

TITLE COMMENTARY

WHAT SHALL WE DO WITH THE LAND?: CHOICES FOR AMERICA (1981)

Zena Sutherland

SOURCE: A review of *What Shall We Do with the Land?: Choices for America,* in *Bulletin of the Center for Children's Books,* Vol. 35, No. 6, February, 1982, p. 114.

Broad in coverage, precise in detail, objective and serious in tone, this excellent survey of the intricate problem of land use is written in a straightforward and authoritative style. Whether it is shoreline, forest, or the wilderness, rangeland or farmland, the decisions of today will affect the land and the people for generations to come. The hopes of conservationists, the needs for energy sources, the conflicting demands of individuals, agencies, business interests, and agricultural prerogatives all point to one multifaceted and crucial question: who has the right to decide? . . . a timely and provocative book.

Sallie Hope Erhard

SOURCE: A review of *What Shall We Do with the Land?: Choices for America,* in *Appraisal: Science Books for Young People,* Vol. 15, No. 2, Spring-Summer, 1982, pp. 58-9.

Mr. Pringle has written a very thought provoking essay for all ages on how we as a nation must consider the problems of the conservation of our basic natural resource, the land. He is not primarily concerned with its pollution, but rather its use and/or overuse by conflicting interested parties. Most of the emphasis is on the control of our public lands by different federal and state agencies and their efforts to satisfy environmentalists on one hand and industrial or recreational users on the other. He takes up the subjects of farmland, rangeland, forests, wilderness and deserts, and the coasts in separate chapters. The author has presented a great deal of valuable information about the historical background and laws that have led to the present situation with which readers can try to make their own intelligent decisions.

VAMPIRE BATS (1982)

Terry Lawhead

SOURCE: A review of *Vampire Bats,* in *School Library Journal,* Vol. 28, No. 8, April, 1982, p. 74.

Vampire bats, a subject generally popular with the young, are given as thorough a discussion as possible, considering that not much is known. Many anecdotes and stories amplify the factual text, and the facts are discussed in clear, general terms. The animals are fastidiously clean, easily tamed, cooperative and nurturing creatures that need a high-protein diet (of blood). Overlooking that last fact, to know them is to love them, says the author. Perhaps understanding that they are not bloodsuckers (they lap) will help overcome readers' anxieties, but a photograph of a woman's toe-bitten foot says it all. The black-and-white photographs are clear and helpful; photos of a bat in flight occur in two stunning series, indicating wing positions. The text is easy to read and there is a list of titles for further reading. There is no comparable book available; if you need a vampire bat book, this is the one.

Sarah Gagne

SOURCE: A review of *Vampire Bats,* in *The Horn Book Magazine,* Vol. LVIII, No. 3, June, 1982, pp. 318-19.

Laurence Pringle's latest book is a fascinating exploration of the three types of bats that feed on blood instead of on insects or fruit. They exist in Central and South America, where one species is an especially common pest with cattle and other farm animals. Vampire bats are also responsible for occasional outbreaks of rabies and, as a result, have been studied in some depth. The author gives such information as how the bats are collected with mist nets, how they lick blood from cuts, and which animals in a herd they are likely to bite; he also describes two major methods of killing bats. By the end of the book the reader is completely absorbed and agrees with the author's statement that mass killings which could lead to extinction sadden people who know and appreciate bats; but Pringle is not opposed to less drastic measures of control. A generous number of well-chosen photographs include pictures of Bela Lugosi as Count Dracula as well as of bats in caves, the bat wing in flight, biologists at work, and victims of bat bites.

WATER: THE NEXT GREAT RESOURCE BATTLE (1982)

Denise M. Wilms

SOURCE: A review of *Water: The Next Great Resource Battle,* in *Booklist,* Vol. 78, No. 19, June 1, 1982, p. 1315.

Water shortages are already looming in arid regions of the U.S. and pollution threatens certain eastern water supplies. As Pringle makes clear in a concerned survey of water supplies and management, this vital resource may no longer be taken for granted. Whether problems stem from too great a demand on limited supplies, as in the West, or from poor management and pollution, as in certain eastern areas, resulting water shortages point up the need for revised conservation and allotment policies. Close looks at the water problems of several areas give concrete dimension to the problem and show how polit-

ical and economic clout shape outcomes. Options and strategies for sound conservation measures are outlined in a summary chapter. Timely and to the point, this is a thoughtful, critical look at a problem that will probably get worse before it gets better.

Zena Sutherland

SOURCE: A review of *Water: The Next Great Resource Battle,* in *Bulletin of the Center for Children's Books,* Vol. 36, No. 3, November, 1982, p. 52.

An addition to the publisher's "Science for Survival" series, this is a thoughtful and provocative assessment of the threatened attrition of a valuable resource. Pringle focuses on the United States, in which a combination of pollution, abusive use, or natural events such as drought, has produced shortages in some parts of the country and water that is unusable in others. As he has in other books, the author demonstrates that the problem and the solution are bound into the industrial practices, agricultural patterns, and legislative conflicts of the society, and that there are steps individuals can take in their own use of water and as citizens who may support public policies, irrigation practices, pollution control, and conservation.

RADIATION: WAVES AND PARTICLES/ BENEFITS AND RISKS (1983)

Kirkus Reviews

SOURCE: A review of *Radiation: Waves and Particles/ Benefits and Risks,* in *Kirkus Reviews,* Vol. L, No. 24, December 15, 1982, pp. 1339-40.

Though we soak it up in the form of sunshine, says Pringle, "still for many people radiation is a scary word." Pringle makes it less mysterious, however, with his primer-like explanation of wavelengths and frequencies and their use in such everyday devices as microwave ovens, TVs, and medical X-rays; his definitions of such terms as gamma rays, radioactive isotopes, rems, and rads; and his matter-of-fact survey of the natural background radiation to which we are all exposed. As matter-of-factly, almost blandly discussed are the risks and benefits of medical X-rays, the problem of worker exposure to radiation from uranium tailings, the controversy over underground storage of reactor wastes ("some scientists have confidence in this plan. Others are skeptical and worry that radioactive substances might enter groundwater and reach the surface eventually"), and the recent investigations, with their revelations of government deception, of the fallout effects from nuclear weapons testing in the '50s. On the safety of low-level radiation exposure, Pringle cites official conclusions to the effect that current risks are very small but greater than previously believed, and he notes the possibly more serious risk to certain radiation workers. Rather drab for Pringle, and without the probing direction of his *Nucle-*

ar Power, this is a utilitarian but serviceable orientation to a subject that can benefit from the ABC treatment.

Zena Sutherland

SOURCE: A review of *Radiation: Waves and Particles/ Benefits and Risks,* in *Bulletin of the Center for Children's Books,* Vol. 36, No. 9, May, 1983, p. 176.

Pringle discusses aspects of the subject with his usual thoroughness, beginning with a chapter on the range of radiation, noting that all humans are exposed to some degree of it, and describing the effects of radiation from various sources. When reporting on research, he is both critical of methodology and objective in discussing beneficial versus adverse effects. The writing style is heavier, more packed with facts, than it is in most of his books; the choice of illustrations is often poor, and the captions or labels for illustrations often irrelevant or inadequate.

Margaret J. McFadden

SOURCE: A review of *Radiation: Waves and Particles/ Benefits and Risks,* in *Voice of Youth Advocates,* Vol. 6, No. 2, June, 1983, p. 105.

Humans die if exposed to 800 rads of radiation, but fruit flies can survive up to 80,000 rads and cockroaches up to 100,000 rads. A sobering thought. Many more facts about radiation are found in this deceptively simple-looking book. The first chapter is difficult, but sticking with it rewards the reader with the background and vocabulary necessary to understand the rest of the book. The discussion which follows explains many different kinds of radioactivity and is remarkably detailed in so few pages. Past studies and experiments are recounted and the benefits and risks are carefully described. There are interesting b/w photos and several informative diagrams. There is a bibliography for further up-to-date research and an index.

The most important idea the reader is left with is that scientists still do not know exactly how much radiation is safe, particularly since ten or 20 years may have to pass before serious health problems develop after exposure to varying levels of radiation. Experiments and clinical studies are still underway leading to daily changing theories.

WOLFMAN: EXPLORING THE WORLD OF WOLVES (1983)

Zena Sutherland

SOURCE: A review of *Wolfman: Exploring the World of Wolves,* in *Bulletin of the Center for Children's Books,* Vol. 36, No. 8, April, 1983, p. 157.

Maps and photographs of variable quality illustrate a description of the years of research by David Mech, the wolfman of the title, in the Minnesota wilderness. Mech, a biologist who is an expert in the subject, has spent twenty-five years studying wolves, learning a great deal about how they live and behave, and about how their behavior affects other creatures, particularly deer. The subject is fascinating, and Pringle's account also shows the patience, methodology, and objectivity of the scientist, in a smoothly written text.

Henry A. Mitchell

SOURCE: A review of *Wolfman: Exploring the World of Wolves,* in *Science Books & Films,* Vol. 19, No. 2, November, 1983, pp. 98-9.

Wolfman is a remarkably excellent, easy-to-read adventure story about the life, tribulations, and success of David Mech, Wolfman. Mech is an animal biologist's animal biologist. His love of nature and appreciation of the creatures he studies is evident. His willingness to give of himself, personally and financially, in pursuit of science is frankly moving. Mech's professional story begins in 1954 with his undergraduate days at Cornell, his graduate work at Purdue, his post-doctoral study in Minnesota, his full-time wildlife work as a research biologist in 1970, and finally his research up to today. A keen observer of animal behavior, he embarked on a multi-year study of the wolves on Isle Royale, the largest island in Lake Superior. In 4,400 miles of hiking he was to see only three wolves, yet through aerial observations he described wolf/moose predator relations. An account of two pet wolves follows. Through his observations of their behavior before and after the death of the male, Mech realized that the female wolf must never be penned and domesticated. . . . An adventure story in the strictest sense, this book will excite young readers and encourage them to follow Mech's path. The final chapter, however, closes with sobering reality— "There aren't enough openings for the college graduates who would like to study wolves." We are fortunate that dedicated persons such as David Mech become scientists. We are equally fortunate that persons such as Laurence Pringle bring this story to all of us.

FERAL: TAME ANIMALS GONE WILD (1983)

Zena Sutherland

SOURCE: A review of *Feral: Tame Animals Gone Wild,* in *Bulletin of the Center for Children's Books,* Vol. 36, No. 9, May, 1983, pp. 175-76.

Pringle's text focuses, after an introductory chapter that discusses feral animals, on six animals; in separate chapters, he discusses birds, pigs, dogs, cats, burros, and horses, although the introduction notes that there are other feral creatures: goats and cattle, for example. Each chapter gives some historical background, describes the way they live and the dangers or potential dangers they pose to people, to other creatures and to the environment, and discusses the ways in which the feral animals are studied by scientists and the ways in which they are protected or pursued. Crisp, knowledgeable, and well-organized, the text presents this often-controversial subject with clarity and objectivity.

Charlene J. Lenzen

SOURCE: A review of *Feral: Tame Animals Gone Wild,* in *School Library Journal,* Vol. 30, No. 1, September, 1983, pp. 126-27.

The world of feral birds, pigs, dogs, burros and horses is explored in Pringle's inimitable style. Pringle defines a feral animal as "one that was once domesticated, or which had domesticated ancestors, and does not receive any protection, care, or food as a deliberate act from humans." The controversy over protection of these animals is discussed. Ongoing research is seeking answers to questions concerning food supply, crop damage, social groupings, benefits, both esthetic and practical, and the disadvantages of feral populations for each type of animal. Profusely illustrated with good quality black-and-white photographs, *Feral* is concise and well written. It will appeal to a wide audience, due to the quantity and quality of new information provided.

BEING A PLANT (1983)

Kirkus Reviews

SOURCE: A review of *Being a Plant,* in *Kirkus Reviews,* Vol. LI, No. 21, November 1, 1983, pp. J213-14.

"Plants are, indeed, similar to animals in many ways," says Pringle, after Darwin—partly to counter the separation of organisms into a mere two, contrasting groups ("It is more sensible, some biologists believe, to separate living things into five kingdoms"), partly to emphasize "that plants have abilities and adaptations that are as fascinating as any in nature." But they don't have feelings, he is quick to point out—nor do they move around as animals do. The approach apart, this is a fine exploratory guide to the workings of the higher plants—brightened by the captivating examples Pringle uses to make his points (like the story of the *Calvaria* tree and the dodo). We learn how plants move water and minerals upward from the roots and sugars down from the leaves through a complex plumbing system of specialized cells (scientists use sap-sucking insects, like aphids, to study the process), and how they absorb gases to make sugars (in transpiration) without losing too much precious water. We also learn how and why seeds germinate only under favorable conditions, and how some plants bypass seeding to clone themselves by sending

out runners or tillers. Plants have special sensory cells, moreover, to detect gravity, light, or dark—which leads into a discussion of the role plant homones play in regulating growth and reproduction. Though Pringle avoids mentioning evolution, chromosomes, or genes (like other authors these days), the information is otherwise comprehensive and clearly explained. . . .

Craighton Hippenhammer

SOURCE: A review of *Being a Plant,* in *School Library Journal,* Vol. 30, No. 7, March, 1984, p. 174.

Pringle raises scientific questions about how plants work. How does water move against gravity inside a tree? How do seeds know when to germinate? Why do roots grow down and stems grow up? The answers are fascinating, many of which are explained at the cellular or chemical level. Pringle discusses the evolution of plants, the progression and growth of scientific knowledge about plants and readily admits the areas in which knowledge is still sketchy. His writing style encourages scientific questioning and critical thinking.

Zena Sutherland

SOURCE: A review of *Being a Plant,* in *Bulletin of the Center for Children's Books,* Vol. 37, No. 8, April, 1984, p. 153.

In his usual capable and authoritative fashion, Pringle presents, as succinctly as is consistent with adequate coverage, an introduction to botany. He discusses how plants and animals differ (or are similar), the several divisions of the plant kingdom, how plants feed and grow, and such interesting phenomena as symbiotic relationships, the effects of hormones, killer plants, and chemical messengers.

NUCLEAR WAR: FROM HIROSHIMA TO NUCLEAR WINTER (1985)

Jonathan R. Betz-Zall

SOURCE: A review of *Nuclear War: From Hiroshima to Nuclear Winter,* in *School Library Journal,* Vol. 32, No. 4, December, 1985, p. 105.

A well-known writer on various environmental problems projects the physical and technological effects of nuclear war in an objective, authoritative manner. Beginning with a brief account of nuclear weapons development, the Hiroshima-Nagasaki bombings and the arms race, Pringle describes the effect of a one-megaton explosion on Detroit; reports on studies of "limited" nuclear warfare and large-scale war and reviews the prospect of "nuclear winter." Vocabulary and style are accessible to junior high students. The black-and-white photos and diagrams are well-keyed to the text, and captions are informative. This is excellent material for school reports and debate preparation. However, there is almost no discussion of the political aspects of the arms race and the resistance to it. By concentrating on scientific/military problems, Pringle appears to give little hope to those who would like to end them.

Zena Sutherland

SOURCE: A review of *Nuclear War: From Hiroshima to Nuclear Winter,* in *Bulletin of the Center for Children's Books,* Vol. 39, No. 6, February, 1986, p. 116.

Pringle has built an iron-clad and disturbing case for the physical, social, economic, and ecological devastation that would follow a nuclear war. Beginning with a scientific look at early experiments with fission, he shows how military use of nuclear energy led to the bombing of Hiroshima, the arms race, and ongoing stockpiling of weapons. Statistics of casualties and estimates of destruction get careful consideration here, with frequent quotes from studies by doctors, ecologists, and economists. A final chapter on nuclear winter concludes the report, which, though admittedly anti-nuclear, does air and analyze more optimistic views. Grim but necessary information for discussion and student research. . . .

ANIMALS AT PLAY (1985)

Margaret Bush

SOURCE: A review of *Animals at Play,* in *School Library Journal,* Vol. 32, No. 6, February, 1986, p. 99.

Beginning with cats, dogs and monkeys—animals commonly thought of as playful—Pringle moves on to examining the play behavior of bears, bats, several small mammal species and parrots. He describes patterns of play and discusses many possible purposes of play; finally he draws analogies to human play. The information successfully synthesizes material from many sources (there is a lengthy, diverse bibliography) and the author's extensive personal observations. Many of the well-chosen photographs are also Pringle's own work. The slim, somewhat large size of the book and the large print with a very wide left margin providing generous white space on each page belie the difficult reading level of the book. The text, however, is clear, informative and interesting; it exemplifies Pringle's ability to deduce principles, examine meanings, raise questions and encourage observation—all in a well-woven narrative. The presentation provides children with a substantial, attractive and readable introduction to current scientific theory about animal behavior.

Denise M. Wilms

SOURCE: A review of *Animals at Play,* in *Booklist,* Vol. 82, No. 17, May 1, 1986, p. 1316.

Pringle looks at the role of play in animal development, particularly as it has been observed in canines, felines, and primates. In each of these groups, the author calls attention to studies that have deciphered various play movements common to these animals and speculated on their meaning. He explains that there is disagreement among researchers regarding the reasons why animals play or exactly what play is. Still, the activity is regarded as important, and observers look for clues to human behavior in the play patterns of various species. The text is smooth and straightforward, and there are small but frequent black-and-white photographs; an extensive list of further reading is appended. A useful introduction to a subject where, as Pringle frequently notes, there is still much to be learned.

HERE COME THE KILLER BEES (1986; revised edition as *Killer Bees,* 1990)

Roger Sutton

SOURCE: A review of *Here Come the Killer Bees,* in *Bulletin of the Center for Children's Books,* Vol. 40, No. 3, November, 1986, p. 56.

Despite the sensationalistic title, Pringle's account of the Africanized honeybees is careful, thorough, and sobering. Rather than dwelling on the bee attacks reported so hysterically in the media, Pringle writes of the devastating effects the northern migration of the bees will have on the bee and pollination industries. "Most people in the United States will never encounter Africanized bees, but everyone may be stung by a scarcity of certain foods and with higher prices for some bee-pollinating agricultural products." He discusses the differences between the Africanized and gentler European honeybees, the debated effects on the South American bee industry, and tracks the bees' migration, including their recent inadvertent importation into California. (They were eradicated.) Well reasoned and documented. . . .

Karey Wehner

SOURCE: A review of *Here Come the Killer Bees,* in *School Library Journal,* Vol. 33, No. 3, November, 1986, pp. 92-3.

The accidental release of African queen bees and drones into Brazil in 1957 resulted in an ecological disaster that still haunts scientists in the Western Hemisphere. Pringle presents a lucid, well organized and well researched examination of a subject that captured media attention even before swarms of the ferocious species were discovered in California last year. He describes some of the horrific encounters between humans and the "killer" bees within the last few decades, discusses their aggressive behavioral characteristics, explains their detrimental effect on South American honey production, speculates on what consequences their imminent invasion of the U.S. may have on our agricultural industries, and describes plans scientists are developing to tame them. Twenty-one black-and-white photographs adequately illustrate the text, the best and sharpest being the half dozen or so close-ups of the bees themselves. A list of precautions to take in areas where bees do settle is included. . . . [T]his timely title should help fill a gap in science collections.

Denise M. Wilms

SOURCE: A review of *Here Come the Killer Bees,* in *Booklist,* Vol. 83, No. 6, November 15, 1986, pp. 517-18.

As usual, Pringle does a fine job of scientific reporting, here putting the dangers of killer bees into perspective and pointing out that the real significance of these creatures lies in their potential for causing great agricultural damage. The bees are now in the U.S.; some nests were eradicated in southern California in the summer of 1985. Entomologists foresee the bees' habitat as southern portions of the continent, with summers sending them somewhat farther north. The bees are aggressive and easily excitable but sting only to protect their hive; stinging attacks seem to come in swarming season. Finally, "they kill many fewer people than sensational stories in newspapers, magazines, and other media would have you believe." For example, honeybees kill "at least 40 people a year in the U.S.," while South American bee death statistics sometimes report "only a dozen." More problematic than stinging attacks is the bees' disruption of honey production—they take over hives—and of commercial bee-pollenization projects that are necessary for some 50 agricultural crops. While it doesn't look as if the bees can be stopped, scientists are investigating ways of possibly controlling them through a breeding program aimed at producing the more moderate traits of European bees. Fascinating reading. . . .

📖 THROWING THINGS AWAY: FROM MIDDENS TO RESOURCE RECOVERY (1986)

Kevin Kenny

SOURCE: A review of *Throwing Things Away: From Middens to Resource Recovery,* in *Voice of Youth Advocates,* Vol. 9, No. 5, December, 1986, p. 249.

While states continue to play political hot potato with the issues which revolve around waste disposal and resource recovery, our landfills swell beyond capacity, ground water grows more contaminated, and Americans continue to generate more garbage, per capita, than any other society in the world. Inevitably, a day of reckoning awaits all, and for too many (the residents of New Jersey, for example) that day has come.

Throwing Things Away is a timely and significant over-view of a topic which becomes, with each new day, more critical. Pringle is to be lauded for his careful analysis of the many problems inherent in disposal and recovery methods, the technologies which hold promise for the future, and even the historical practices which have put us in our current situation. Pringle's work is laced with specific ecological horror stories and the tone of the book is rightfully serious without being pedantic. Like his *What Shall We Do with the Land?,* Pringle's *Throwing Things Away* is a must for all libraries. Accessible without being condescending, the work (complete with bibliography) will serve student and teacher well.

Margaret A. Bush

SOURCE: A review of *Throwing Things Away: From Middens to Resource Recovery,* in *The Horn Book Magazine,* Vol. LXIII, No. 1, January-February, 1987, p. 74.

From the refuse pits of the prehistoric peoples to the land fills and the reclamation practices of today, Pringle's readable survey sketches a history of human efforts to deal with the mundane problem of what to do with garbage. Five chapters cover a brief history of practices and problems of major systems of trash disposal, the social aspects of dumping grounds and scavenging, the nourishment provided to animal life by refuse sites, the current practices and emerging problems with the landfill system, and various efforts to recycle waste products. Pringle points out physical problems of handling some types of refuse and of certain recovery techniques, but he does not explore some of the more controversial aspects of disposal now troubling communities and states; this is a more straightforward report than the questioning accounts found in some of his books. The photographs, generally small in size, are uneven in quality but serve their utilitarian purpose adequately. This introduction to a very fundamental set of problems is informative, thought provoking, and very competently stated.

Meryl Silverstein

SOURCE: A review of *Throwing Things Away: From Middens to Resource Recovery,* in *School Library Journal,* Vol. 33, No. 7, March, 1987, p. 175.

Pringle makes a potentially dull topic—the disposal of solid wastes—fascinating in this inviting, well-researched book. He discusses clearly and sometimes humorously the history of waste disposal, the means that have been used to deal with it in the past, recent problems, and some of the proposed solutions. Anecdotes are intermingled with facts for a lively account and fast-paced reading. Plentiful sharp black-and-white photographs illustrate the text, highlighting the written material. . . . Young researchers won't waste their time reading this book.

📖 *RESTORING OUR EARTH* (1987)

Kirkus Reviews

SOURCE: A review of *Restoring Our Earth,* in *Kirkus Reviews,* Vol. LV, No. 11, June 15, 1987, p. 929.

In this timely and readable account of current efforts, scientists and volunteers work to restore areas damaged through deforestation, strip mining, waste disposal, and poorly thought-out crop and waterway management.

The economic, scientific and aesthetic benefits derived from re-creating marshes, prairies, woodlands, rivers and lakes are discussed. According to the author, restorationists "recognize the value of natural places as havens for endangered plants and animals and as storehouses for the earth's genetic diversity." He captures the excitement of restoring the earth; and by recounting the efforts of individuals and organizations who have made contributions, he encourages and challenges others to try. A fine piece of science writing that will have wide appeal for science, nature, and ecology enthusiasts.

Hazel Rochman

SOURCE: A review of *Restoring Our Earth,* in *Booklist,* Vol. 84, No. 1, September 1, 1987, p. 49.

With numerous photographs and a clear text, science writer/environmentalist Pringle discusses the special field of restoration ecology. He emphasizes that while reclamation's aim is to improve and find new uses for damaged areas, restoration's aim is more challenging: to reintroduce *native* plant and animal life to an area and to establish a self-sustaining ecological system as close as possible to the original. From hand-transplanting grass seedlings in a salt marsh in Chesapeake Bay to reintroducing timber wolves in Yellowstone National Park, Pringle uses detailed examples as he discusses the restoration of coastal wetlands, prairies, forests, rivers and lakes, and land devastated by strip mining. He shows the dangers of overprotecting and demonstrates the importance of controlled fires for discouraging nonnative species. Though this is a brief introduction—the discussion of acid rain, for example, is handled in general terms only—it combines fascinating biology with overall environmental concerns.

📖 *HOME: HOW ANIMALS FIND COMFORT AND SAFETY* (1987)

Phillis Wilson

SOURCE: A review of *Home: How Animals Find Comfort and Safety,* in *Booklist,* Vol. 84, No. 8, December 15, 1987, p. 712.

Each home in an animal's life span is vital to its surviv-

al, and human destruction of habitats can threaten the survival of an entire species. This thrust is stated succinctly in the preface—"the need for safety and comfort is so basic that the study of an animal's home leads inevitably to knowledge about its relationships with other things, living and nonliving, in its environment." While Pringle's work is similar to *Animal Architects* . . . his study concentrates on the homes of animals found in North America. Pringle's competent black-and-white photography is no match for National Geographic's, but there is more in-depth thoughtful coverage in his text. His emphasis is on the home's relationship to the animal's way of life rather than on unusual architecture. Information on homes that serve as food-catching devices and the host homes needed by parasites—the human body is home for "an estimated one hundred quadrillion bacterial cells"—is intriguing and will broaden children's understanding of the earth as a fragile habitat.

Betsy Hearne

SOURCE: A review of *Home: How Animals Find Comfort and Safety,* in *Bulletin of the Center for Children's Books,* Vol. 41, No. 5, January, 1988, p. 98.

From a prairie dog's hole in the ground to the aerial architecture of a spider web, Pringle categorizes and describes some of the homes animals build or borrow. He does not spurn the lowly louse, as an example of parasitic dweller; nor the male stickleback, which builds and guards its watery nest; nor the spittlebug, blowing its home of bubbles on a plant stem. What's striking about the style here is the uncompromising commitment to scientific reporting. While young readers may not read the book from cover to cover, the information they search out for reports will be as factually complete as possible in a succinct introduction. The examples are plentiful and diverse enough that one could have wished for more of the generally high-quality black-and-white photographs, and an outline summarizing the principal types of animal shelter would not have been amiss.

Patricia Manning

SOURCE: A review of *Home: How Animals Find Comfort and Safety,* in *School Library Journal,* Vol. 34, No. 7, March, 1988, p. 209.

Pringle shows children that all animals need their "homes," be they snug underground burrows; an airy clump of bubbles; a carefully constructed nest; or merely a small, familiar area or a wide range of space that fulfills the needs for food, courtship, or birth. The accurate text deals with North American species as disparate as caribou and spittlebugs and is divided into such logical sections as "community homes" and "at home on another." Some of the black-and-white photos lack crispness. A list of further readings and an index are included, as are instructions for a bluebird nesting box. . . . Pringle closes with a message for environmental conservation, citing the dismal plight of Bermudian hermit crabs, who depend on ever-larger snail shells (now hunted to extinction by hungry humans) to protect their soft bodies.

RAIN OF TROUBLES: THE SCIENCE AND POLITICS OF ACID RAIN (1988)

Kirkus Reviews

SOURCE: A review of *Rain of Troubles: The Science and Politics of Acid Rain,* in *Kirkus Reviews,* Vol. LVI, No. 4, February 15, 1988, pp. 282-83.

At its rare worst, rain is so acid that it removes paint and can be used to make salad dressing. At their worst, people can also be acid, with shrill environmentalists pitted against petty politicians and do-nothing government agencies. The rest of us are caught in between, watching our lakes and forests die and the noses crumble from our favorite statues, wondering what can be done.

Pringle has written an objective book about this inflamed subject. The chemistry he introduces will tax no one who has had high-school chemistry; those without can skip the equations. He clearly explains and shows the relationships among soil chemistry, forests and trees, the ecology of lakes and ponds, movement of the air, and other wide-ranging topics bearing on acid rain; he outlines the response of governments and industries, touching on many of the factors that make finding an equitable solution such a struggle—loss of jobs, higher cost of power, the panacea or peril of nuclear power, uncertainty concerning short- and long-term effects. The way pollutants are created—most from smelting and power plants burning high-sulfur fuels—and the ways they can be controlled are well-understood; it's who should pay, how, and how fast that remains an international muddle. If Pringle offers no neat solution to the mess, that's real, too.

Stephen L. Gallant

SOURCE: A review of *Rain of Troubles: The Science and Politics of Acid Rain,* in *Voice of Youth Advocates,* Vol. 11, No. 4, October, 1988, p. 205.

In **Rain of Troubles** Pringle discusses a subject that is of great concern today. Beginning with the discovery of acid rain in 1872 by Robert Angus Smith of London, the author traces the growth of our knowledge up to the present day. Pringle describes experiments such as the ones at the Experimental Lakes Area in Ontario that have contributed to our understanding of the problem. Although acid rain is a topic that is still being hotly debated, Pringle is convinced of acid rain's causes and severity and does not take seriously the arguments of skeptics.

NUCLEAR ENERGY: TROUBLED PAST, UNCERTAIN FUTURE (1989)

Alan Newman

SOURCE: A review of *Nuclear Energy: Troubled Past, Uncertain Future,* in *School Library Journal,* Vol. 35, No. 8, April, 1989, pp. 124-25.

With the accidents at the Three Mile Island and Chernobyl nuclear reactors as focal points, Pringle explores the public policy decisions and consequences of nuclear power. Pringle claims to present both sides of this controversial issue; however, the arguments against nuclear power come through loudest. Despite this apparent tilt, Pringle gives an exceptionally knowledgeable and thoughtful treatment of a difficult subject. The book, an update of a 1979 text, starts with the first commercial nuclear power plants in the 1950s and leads up to new reactor designs that could trigger a "second nuclear age." Along the way, Pringle discusses the health risks of radioactivity, the soaring economics of building nuclear reactors, nuclear waste disposal, and the entrenched political opposition to these forms of energy. He also explains how the nuclear industry evolved. Nuclear power proponents will certainly dispute some of Pringle's statements or allusions, especially his emphasis on problem nuclear plants. There are, they would argue, well built, efficiently run, nuclear reactors. Yet, Pringle is correct in subtitling this book troubled past, uncertain future. This is a savvy, well-written book on a subject often confused by hysteria and misinformation.

Denise Wilms

SOURCE: A review of *Nuclear Energy: Troubled Past, Uncertain Future,* in *Booklist,* Vol. 85, No. 17, May 1, 1989, pp. 1552-53.

In a major revision of **Nuclear Power,** Pringle looks at the shifting fortunes of the nuclear power industry, which has fallen on decidedly hard times. What was once touted as clean, safe, and cheap now seems none of these, and worldwide sentiment against nuclear power is growing. Pringle traces the rise of concern stemming from assorted factors, not the least of which are Chernobyl and Three Mile Island. The latter topics receive a chapter each; other areas of discussion include the problem of waste disposal, rising costs, and future prospects that might rest on new designs, such as those for the so-called inherently safe reactors.

Linda Palter

SOURCE: A review of *Nuclear Energy: Troubled Past, Uncertain Future,* in *Voice of Youth Advocates,* Vol. 12, No. 5, December, 1989, p. 305.

Nuclear Energy is one of the best books I have read on nuclear power and the nuclear power industry. The information is current, in depth, and clearly presented. The physics behind nuclear reactors is explained without writing down to readers or losing them in technical jargon. Besides the physics involved, this book looks at the history, politics, economics, and future of nuclear power. It remains interesting reading throughout.

In the preface of his book, Pringle states that he is not neutral about nuclear power, but that he will present views and arguments from both sides of this controversial issue. He does present facts clearly, without editorializing. When opinions are presented they are identified as such. A recommended reading list is included. Highly recommended.

📖 JESSE BUILDS A ROAD (1989)

Kirkus Reviews

SOURCE: A review of *Jesse Builds a Road,* in *Kirkus Reviews,* Vol. LVII, No. 14, August 1, 1989, p. 1165.

Any number of books picture construction equipment for young fans; here, in his first picture book, a noted author of science books for young people adds an imaginative dimension to the standard formula. Jesse brings a big box of toy equipment to the sandpile, where—after donning his hard hat (brought along by his assistant, the family dog)—he gets to work. Then he and the dog are shown driving all their splendid equipment, grown to full size, to shift rocks and build roads and a bridge—until it's time to go home and the machines return to their cardboard box. [Leslie Holt] Morrill's straightforwardly realistic, rather old-fashioned illustrations are just right for children like Jesse who like to pretend and want to know how things work.

Julie Corsaro

SOURCE: A review of *Jesse Builds a Road,* in *Booklist,* Vol. 86, No. 2, September 15, 1989, pp. 188-89.

An unexpected treat from Pringle, an esteemed writer of science books for children. When Jesse determinedly takes his toy trucks out to the sandpile, they are transformed into life-size machines. Accompanied by his one-dog crew, Jesse utilizes these monsters for road and bridge construction. With the task completed, the vehicles, once again toys, are stored for the next day's endeavor. Considering the picture-book format, a surprising amount of information is conveyed about these machines and how they are used. The text is brief, brisk, and simply written, while the realistic line-and-wash illustrations follow the rolling and rugged contours of land and sky. The artwork has appeal despite some awkward facial renderings. The fantasy element and the description of sounds (the bulldozer's steel tracks go "clank, clank, clank") will be enjoyed by young children.

Judith Gloyer

SOURCE: A review of *Jesse Builds a Road,* in *School Library Journal,* Vol. 36, No. 2, February, 1990, p. 78.

A small boy and his dog set out to play with a box full of trucks, bulldozers, and other earth-moving equipment. Morrill's serviceable watercolors and Pringle's straightforward text are not terribly appealing, yet the book does successfully draw readers into the imaginative play of a small child through Morrill's playful use of size and perspective. One page shows child-sized Jesse playing with his toys. In the next, he and his dog are sitting in the driver's seat of various pieces of equipment, hard at work. However, it is unclear if the two have shrunk or if the toys have grown to be full-size, real trucks. In other drawings, with trees for comparison, they appear lifesize; in another, a red bucket provides hints of a smaller scale. This weaving in and out of the imagination and reality is engaging, and it will be with a touch of regret that readers are pulled back to reality as Jesse collects his toys and heads for home.

📖 BEARMAN: EXPLORING THE WORLD OF BLACK BEARS (1989)

Margaret A. Bush

SOURCE: A review of *Bearman: Exploring the World of Black Bears,* in *The Horn Book Magazine,* Vol. LXV, No. 5, September-October, 1989, pp. 641-42.

It would be hard to imagine a more winning photograph than the cover portrait of Lynn Rogers holding two tiny, mournful looking black bear cubs. Rogers, a United States Forest Service biologist, is both the photographer and the subject of this fine science career documentary. Though Laurence Pringle does describe the childhood experiences culminating in long years of academic and research efforts, the book concentrates on Rogers's work tracking and observing black bears in Minnesota. Traveling by small plane or snowmobile or on snowshoes, Rogers has tagged and attached collars to hundreds of bears, often entering winter dens to do so. Since he has been especially interested in hibernation, his photographs focus on female bears and their cubs, and the book tells little about the male bear. The discovery that the black bear, contrary to its supposed fierceness, is quite tolerant of human interaction is certainly the most intriguing aspect of the handsome presentation. Rogers, his wife, and their young children are shown in various situations with young cubs and yearlings, and Rogers appears in several close encounters with adult bears. The fascinating photographs are perhaps misleading in suggesting that these bears are tame or that the black bear is friendly to humans, but the text offers careful explanations of the wildlife biologist's patience and knowledge. Pringle's felicitous collaboration with his subject conveys an immediacy and a vitality that are totally captivating, whether one is caught by the impressive qualities of the bears or the informative view of an unusual type of work with animals. Far from comprehensive with just four chapters, the book leaves the reader wishing for more information about the subject.

Betsy Hearne

SOURCE: A review of *Bearman: Exploring the World of Black Bears,* in *Bulletin of the Center for Children's Books,* Vol. 43, No. 3, November, 1989, p. 70.

With a passion for wildlife since early childhood, Lynn Rogers pursued his dream to study biology and specialize in research on Ursus Americanus, the American black bear. Using Rogers's own superb color photos of bears in the wild, Pringle gives some background on both the man and the animal, following Rogers as Rogers has followed bears for two decades. Starting with radio collars that he attached to bears in their dens, Rogers has now progressed to befriending the animals and typing his notes on a lap-top computer just a few feet away from their activities (his wife and children are shown snuggling with cubs). The book is absorbing not only for its information on a common North American species—Pringle's clear reportage of Rogers' data and anecdotes—but also for its focus on a role model who determined what he wanted to do and then made it happen. *Bearman* will probably be shelved with other books on animals, but it's the best kind of career guide going.

Eva Elisabeth Von Ancken

SOURCE: A review of *Bearman: Exploring the World of Black Bears,* in *School Library Journal,* Vol. 35, No. 15, November, 1989, p. 124.

Pringle traces Rogers's career as a wildlife biologist, intermingling facts, statistics, and observations about the black bears Rogers has spent a lifetime studying. He also discusses the importance of wildlife study in general. Rogers's excellent full-color photographs clearly show his and his family's close relationship with the bears. However, the dry text does not do justice to the subject. Readers are told that Rogers frequently entered the caves of hibernating bears, and they are expected to be amazed at the courage displayed when he follows bears on their treks—but Pringle keeps emphasizing the general docility of these creatures and undermines the drama. Readers are told in detail of Rogers's struggle to complete college and the jobs he held along the way, but there is no mention of the wife and children who share his life and work. A bear shown with Rogers's daughter is later reportedly shot by hunters, but little condemnation or conservationism is shown. The need to preserve the habitat of these and other wildlife is only briefly mentioned. Rogers is an admirable hero, but he is not well served by this bland text.

THE ANIMAL RIGHTS CONTROVERSY (1989)

Roger Sutton

SOURCE: A review of *The Animal Rights Controversy,* in *Bulletin of the Center for Children's Books,* Vol. 43, No. 4, December, 1989, p. 93.

Pringle has done an even better job than usual at explaining and assessing the arguments on all sides of a controversial issue. While animal rights concerns may seem to many to be very much an issue of the 1980s, Pringle traces their history back to the 18th century and the writings of Humphrey Primatt and philosopher Jeremy Bentham: "The question is not, Can they *reason?* nor Can they *talk?* but, *Can they suffer?*" Much of the discussion about contemporary problems is based on the writings of Peter Singer and Tom Regan, whose work Pringle cogently and fairly introduces. Whether describing the procedures of "factory farming" or Draize testing, Pringle is never sensational, making this book both a sensible witness and an effective counterpoint to overheated propaganda. The lack of footnotes is unfortunate, particularly in the face of controversial and or ludicrous quotes ("a spokesperson for the veal industry said that the calves are chained in these small enclosures so they can have 'privacy'"); a reading list and index are appended. Black-and-white photographs illustrate the points without sensationalizing them.

Beth Herbert

SOURCE: A review of *The Animal Rights Controversy,* in *Booklist,* Vol. 86, No. 10, January 15, 1990, p. 1008.

Challenging young people to consider all sides of a troubling moral issue, this engagingly written and ambitiously researched study ponders whether animals have rights. Pringle traces the progress of people's attitudes toward their fellow creatures, and then turns to contemporary writers such as Tom Regan and Peter Singer, who began dealing with a form of prejudice—"speciesism"—in the 1970s. Focusing on how human beings utilize a bias for their own species to ignore the interests of other creatures, Pringle provides a carefully structured comparison of beliefs and philosophies about euthanasia, hunting, consumption of meat and fish, factory farming, experimental research on animals, and zoos. While the balance of evidence tends to weigh heavily against those accused of exploiting or abusing animals, the book gives those accused a place for rebuttal, making this volume thought-provoking and open-ended.

Elizabeth S. Watson

SOURCE: A review of *The Animal Rights Controversy,* in *The Horn Book Magazine,* Vol. LXVI, No. 2, March-April, 1990, p. 222.

The author presents a clear, unemotional discussion of the various elements that make up the seemingly clear, but in fact complicated, issue of animal rights. This title is a basic introduction that gives enough information for the reader to understand both sides of the argument, then follows up with suggested readings and a list of organizations that may be contacted for more information. Pringle examines the issues of vegetarianism, animal welfare, and the use of animals in medical and other types of research. The photographs, while chosen with restraint, leave no doubt about the reality of such practices as animal experimentation, factory farming, and veal production. While the author is clearly in sympathy with those who favor humane treatment of animals, he is able to present arguments from the opposition in an unsensational manner that will encourage readers to develop their own opinions based on fact.

SAVING OUR WILDLIFE (1990)

Kirkus Reviews

SOURCE: A review of *Saving Our Wildlife,* in *Kirkus Reviews,* Vol. LVIII, No. 1, January 1, 1990, p. 50.

An upbeat, positive look at ongoing efforts to preserve endangered North American animals, including the red wolf, California condor, black-footed ferret, and Devil's hole pupfish. The author describes both private and government efforts to protect animals by preventing habitat destruction; developing enlightened hunting and game-management programs; and using zoo breeding programs to reestablish wild populations. He persuasively argues that plants and animals are interconnected, and that even an obscure species may provide a vital contribution to the gene pool of planet earth. The text is occasionally somewhat technical ("There is no specific 'threshold' of population size that protects wildlife from harmful inbreeding or from other threats to survival"), but the details are fascinating and current. An excellent choice for older nature and conservation enthusiasts.

Stephanie Zvirin

SOURCE: A review of *Saving Our Wildlife,* in *Booklist,* Vol. 86, No. 14, March 15, 1990, p. 1457.

Underscoring his discussion with an environmentalist's concern, a prolific science book writer for young people explores endeavors to save North America's vanishing wildlife. With black-and-white photographs (unfortunately of varying quality) adding impact to his discussion, Pringle turns first to some of the factors contributing to species endangerment and extinction. He follows up with a look at how wildlife refuges and captive breeding and relocation programs have operated to preserve a variety of game and non-game species, rounding out the text with a selective overview of the preservation problems faced by five states, and a list of environmentally active organizations. A concise introduction to a complex prob-

lem, but one that will definitely raise awareness among readers.

GLOBAL WARMING: ASSESSING THE GREENHOUSE THREAT (1990)

Denise Wilms

SOURCE: A review of *Global Warming: Assessing the Greenhouse Threat,* in *Booklist,* Vol. 86, No. 17, May 1, 1990, p. 1711.

Global warming is succinctly explained in this slim, handsomely designed account. Pringle states flatly that the earth is warming up; the material he offers concerns the consequences this fact may hold for the planet. The mechanics of global warming (how carbon dioxide and other greenhouse gases raise temperatures) and its conceivable effects on water levels and climate are surveyed; the balance of the book looks at ways to minimize what already seems inevitable. What about the argument that this is speculation and we should "wait and see"? Readers are told that "there is broad agreement among atmospheric scientists that the threat . . . is real" and that "uncertainty about some details . . . should not be used as an excuse for inaction." Indeed, final portions call for cutting harmful emissions now lest the future cost be disastrous. The simple format, which employs many full-color photographs and large type, suggests wide use: older readers unable to handle complex treatments of the subject will find Pringle's approach easy to understand, while sharp younger readers will appreciate the straightforward style and tidy organization.

Roger Sutton

SOURCE: A review of *Global Warming: Assessing the Greenhouse Threat,* in *Bulletin of the Center for Children's Books,* Vol. 43, No. 11, July-August, 1990, p. 273.

Mention of "the greenhouse effect" seems to have become obligatory in any children's book of even tangential relation; here's one that explores the phenomenon logically and thoroughly. Calmly keeping from dire prophecy, Pringle explains why most scientists believe that the earth's temperature is rising, why that increase is occurring, and what effects it could have in the coming century. His explanations of the self-feeding nature of warming are only too lucid: "Most of the sunlight falling on snow and ice is reflected back toward space. As the climate warms, there will be less snow and ice. The sunlight will fall instead on darker soils and plants, which readily absorb sunlight. This will warm the earth further, causing even more snow and ice to melt." Discussion of political considerations is fair-minded and aware of ecological ironies: "Most [trees] are cut by landless people desperate for a place to grow food." The format is as open and clear as the text, with plenty of white space and color photos both informative and atmospheric.

R. Baines

SOURCE: A review of *Global Warming: Assessing the Greenhouse Threat,* in *The Junior Bookshelf,* Vol. 55, No. 2, April, 1991, pp. 67-8.

Despite the honesty with which Laurence Pringle admits "uncertainty about some details of global warming," he will continue to worry. He has produced sound, clearly explained evidence that the combination of ever-increasing burning of fossil fuels, together with the destruction of much plant life, will over-load the atmosphere with carbon dioxide. Beyond this there seems too much uncertainty to regard the warming of the earth as a proven fact: however, it is common sense to agree with this author that increasing the acres of oxygen-producing plants is good, and that efforts should be made to reduce the emission of toxic gases by industry and cars.

BATMAN: EXPLORING THE WORLD OF BATS (1991)

Kirkus Reviews

SOURCE: A review of *Batman: Exploring the World of Bats,* in *Kirkus Reviews,* Vol. LIX, No. 5, March 1, 1991, p. 321.

Merlin Tuttle, the "Batman" subject of this brief biography, dates his enthusiasm for biology to capturing a toad at the age of two. At nine he was keeping a notebook of his wildlife observations and memorizing the scientific names of all the mammals of California. Bat advocate, photographer, researcher, author, and founder of Bat Conservation International, Dr. Tuttle is an excellent example of a contemporary working scientist. Pringle includes fascinating tidbits about bats and their importance to the balance of nature; Tuttle's close-up color photos are stunning.

Roger Sutton

SOURCE: A review of *Batman: Exploring the World of Bats,* in *Bulletin of the Center for Children's Books,* Vol. 44, No. 9, May, 1991, pp. 224-25.

Merlin Tuttle, both subject and photographer for the book, specializes in researching bat behavior, and Pringle fluently blends information about the scientist, the methods of research, and the bats themselves. Refuting many myths about bats ("less than half of one percent of bats contract rabies"), and making a cogent case for their protection, the book discusses bats and their environments worldwide, and Tuttle's color photographs are up close and personal, and in a few instances, even cute.

Stephanie Zvirin

SOURCE: A review of *Batman: Exploring the World of Bats,* in *Booklist,* Vol. 87, No. 17, May 1, 1991, p. 1717.

What Pringle did for David Mech in *Wolfman* he does here for Merlin Tuttle, scientist, photographer, and founder of Bat Conservation International, an organization dedicated to halting wanton destruction of bat populations and to altering the image of the much-maligned creature. Interspersed with Tuttle's own comments, Pringle's text profiles "Batman," as Tuttle has come to be called, beginning with a childhood interest in the natural world fostered by his parents. Including a variety of anecdotes (Tuttle actually trained bats so he could capture them on film), Pringle highlights some of Tuttle's experiences studying and working with bats, giving intriguing information about bat life and behavior as well as a sense of the destructive forces bats face in the modern world. Doing double duty as biography and natural science material, the solid text is never dry, and, of course, one look at the fascinating array of extraordinary full-color photographs, most taken by Tuttle, will immediately entice readers.

LIVING TREASURE: SAVING EARTH'S THREATENED BIODIVERSITY (1991)

Lowell J. Bethel

SOURCE: A review of *Living Treasure: Saving Earth's Threatened Biodiversity,* in *Science Books & Films,* Vol. 27, No. 6, August-September, 1991, p. 172.

With the nation concerned more and more with conservation matters and the imminent danger of the extinction of many plant and animal species, along comes an excellent book that explains the problem and what people around the world must do to halt this destruction of our environment. This little book describes in great detail how humans are destroying the habitats of countless plants and animals worldwide. These acts of destruction will ultimately result in the extinction of many living organisms. Thus, the nation's and even the world's biodiversity will be seriously endangered. The author cites many examples of the earth's environment, including oceans, parks, national lands, the atmosphere, and rain forests in third world countries and vividly describes how these habitats are systematically being destroyed and the impact this destruction has on living things. The text is both well written and informative and is must reading for young people who need to know what is happening and how they can get involved to solve some of the problems that are described.

Margaret Bush

SOURCE: A review of *Living Treasure: Saving Earth's Threatened Biodiversity,* in *School Library Journal,* Vol. 37, No. 11, November, 1991, p. 132.

Pringle's contention is that today many forms of life are being lost—particularly in the ecologically rich rain forests—before they have even been discovered and had their potential benefits to humankind explored. In four thought-provoking chapters, he discusses with clarity how millions of species have diversified, how they are being destroyed, and some of the efforts to halt the damage. He offers intriguing examples of recently discovered, profitable food and medicinal products and of important research and conservation efforts, but he is not very optimistic. Problems of poverty in underdeveloped countries, greed in the industrialized world, and the tendency to put large amounts of money and energy into preserving a few popular species rather than whole habitats are delineated. The book concludes with suggestions for personal involvement, addresses of organizations, and a list for further reading. [Irene] Brady's black-and-white pen-and-wash drawings are precise and even lovely, but some scenes are too gray or suggest a fictionalized work. This volume is attractive, which tends to soften the weight of the discussion, which is sobering and timely.

ANTARCTICA: THE LAST UNSPOILED CONTINENT (1992)

Roger Sutton

SOURCE: A review of *Antarctica: The Last Unspoiled Continent,* in *Bulletin of the Center for Children's Books,* Vol. 46, No. 2, October, 1992, p. 51.

[In *Antarctica*], Laurence Pringle shows—once again—a nose for interesting and telling detail. To convey the immensity of some of the Antarctic's calved icebergs, for example, he uses not an analogy, but a fact. "B-9 contained an estimated 287 cubic miles of fresh water. That is enough to give everyone on earth two glasses of water a day for 1,977 years" (note, too, the precision: 1,977 is more convincing than "almost two thousand"). Pringle's explanations of continental drift, the ozone layer, and the greenhouse effect are clear and aptly placed; along with the discussion of natural and physical phenomena, he describes the research techniques used by scientists to understand the same.

Hazel Rochman

SOURCE: A review of *Antarctica: The Last Unspoiled Continent,* in *Booklist,* Vol. 89, No. 6, November 15, 1992, p. 588.

The beautifully reproduced color photographs will draw browsers into this well-designed photo-essay, but the writing style is flat. The lack of documentation is a serious drawback, especially since controversy exists about some of the issues discussed, including the causes and effects of global warming. There's not even a bibliography of books or articles. However, the subject is fascinating, and Pringle shows how Antarctica's special conditions make the continent an invaluable research site

for the study of evolution, geology, astronomy, botany, zoology, and other subjects of crucial concern to the future of the planet. The section on penguins is the most vivid: the populations have recovered from their widespread slaughter in the nineteenth century, and now Antarctica has at least 100 million penguins. The account of how they survive together in the cold exemplifies how the environment is both rugged and fragile.

David L. Pawson

SOURCE: A review of *Antarctica: The Last Unspoiled Continent,* in *Science Books & Films,* Vol. 29, No. 1, January-February, 1993, p. 22.

In this slim volume, young readers are introduced to the exciting, frigid realities of Antarctic. The author describes briefly the discovery and exploration of the continent, its geological history and natural history, and its great value as a natural laboratory for science. The text is informative, interesting, and accurate, and the author shows how knowledge of this remote area has been gained only at considerable cost in terms of energy, time, discomfort, and the lives of humans, ponies, and dogs. The book concludes with a discussion of the impact of humans on Antarctica and prospects for the future well-being of the continent in light of new treaties. Included are more than 50 good to excellent color photographs, an inadequate glossary, and an adequate index. The increasing evidence of the negative impacts of people on the environment of Antarctica tends to belie the book's hopeful subtitle: "The Last Unspoiled Continent." There is a balanced sketch of the consequences of visits by scientists and tourists to this fragile continent.

CHEMICAL AND BIOLOGICAL WARFARE: THE CRUELEST WEAPONS (1993)

Kirkus Reviews

SOURCE: A review of *Chemical and Biological Warfare: The Cruelest Weapons,* in *Kirkus Reviews,* Vol. LXI, No. 3, February 1, 1993, p. 152.

In a clear and concise overview of major issues of their chemical and biological arms control, Pringle provides background on the dangers present, as well as of the social and political factors that have spread them even more widely than nuclear weapons. Though he cites chemical warfare in ancient Greece, and British smallpox infections of Native Americans, he concentrates on the 20th century: gas attacks by both sides in WW I, Italian attacks on Ethiopians, "Agent Orange" in Vietnam, Iraqi attacks on Kurds. He speculates that the Germans withheld using nerve gases in WW II because of Hitler's experience of being gassed in the previous war, or because of their fear of retaliation. But "bad guys" were not the only experimenters: Americans tried to develop diseases as weapons; later, the CIA experimented on whole sections of the country. One chapter exposes in detail the CIA's attempt to accuse the Vietnamese of using poison gas in the "Yellow Rain" incident. (It turned out to be bee feces.) Pringle doesn't provide much direct documentation but does list his authoritative sources in a bibliography. An excellent summary—so evenhanded that both sides in a debate could find it useful.

Margaret Mary Ptacek

SOURCE: A review of *Chemical and Biological Warfare: The Cruelest Weapons,* in *Voice of Youth Advocates,* Vol. 16, No. 3, August, 1993, p. 182.

Chemical and biological warfare is described as the "poor man's atomic bomb" because it is cheaper and easier to produce than nuclear bombs. Laurence Pringle traces the history of chemical and biological warfare back to 432 BC when soldiers of the Peloponnesian War added chemicals to fires in order to produce fumes that choked or sickened their enemies. Each succeeding chapter introduces a new form of this weaponry and describes its use in military combat. A most interesting weapon used in the 1970s was "yellow rain." It contained three lethal mycotofins—poisons produced by fungi. It turned out that alleged poison was mainly made out of honeybee feces.

This is an excellent book on the subject as well as a historical glimpse of our military past. It is extremely up-to-date, including materials on the recent Gulf War. The concluding chapter covers the efforts to control the cruelest weapons of all. The text includes . . . a list of possible biological weapons, and excerpts from Chemical Weapons Convention held July 23, 1992 and published by the United States Arms Control and Disarmament Agency.

OCTOPUS HUG (1993)

Kirkus Reviews

SOURCE: A review of *Octopus Hug,* in *Kirkus Reviews,* Vol. LXI, No. 17, September 1, 1993, p. 1150.

When Mom goes to dinner with a friend and leaves them with Dad, the gap-toothed narrator and his little sister feel so out of sorts that they begin to squabble—but not for long. These lucky kids have a humongous dad who enjoys roughhousing as much as they do. "You are about to be hugged by an octopus!" he announces, counting to eight as he wraps the boy in his arms. When he sings "Rock-a-bye, Baby," somehow everyone falls, laughing, out of the rocker; before he packs the children into bed, still giggling, he's also been a tree for them to climb, a monster, and a horse. [Kate Salley] Palmer, who's worked as a political cartoonist, represents this ebullient African-American family with appropriately broad humor and enthusiasm.

Publishers Weekly

SOURCE: A review of *Octopus Hug,* in *Publishers Weekly,* Vol. 240, No. 40, October 4, 1993, p. 79.

The imaginative antics that tumble across these pages could constitute a manual for bored baby-sitters. When Jesse and Becky's mother goes out for the evening, it's up to Dad to dissipate their disgruntlement. "Do you know what an octopus hug is?" he asks, then demonstrates his all-encompassing hug. Kicking off an evening filled with his special repertoire of games, the ever-grinning Dad, resembling O. J. Simpson with his massive size and lantern jaw, offers to become a tree for climbing, a mechanical horse for riding, a spirited rocking chair, etc. Palmer interprets the festivities rather literally in her soft colored-pencil illustrations; her characters' happy expressions seem plastered onto their faces. And while the book succeeds in presenting an African-American father in a warm and engaging role, the one-dimensional, all-action story may leave some readers feeling as if they are simply sitting on the sidelines.

Louise L. Sherman

SOURCE: A review of *Octopus Hug,* in *School Library Journal,* Vol. 40, No. 1, January, 1994, p. 97.

A celebration of family roughhousing and imaginative play. Becky and Jesse are left with their father while their mother goes out for the evening. They are out of sorts at first, until Dad demonstrates an octopus hug. This leads to a series of active games, such as "timber," in which the youngsters climb on the man's shoulders and he pretends to be a falling tree (letting them land on soft cushions); "left out toys," in which the siblings pretend to be toys and he carries them into their rooms and drops them on their beds; and "monster," in which he pretends to capture them and they escape. This is the kind of physical fun children delight in, but that might cause cautious adults to shudder. Here, the presentation is positive and young listeners will beg their fathers to play the same games. The illustrations, depicting a burly African-American father and his joyous son and daughter, add to the lively feeling of the text.

OIL SPILLS: DAMAGE, RECOVERY, AND PREVENTION (1993)

Sheilamae O'Hara

SOURCE: A review of *Oil Spills: Damage, Recovery, and Prevention,* in *Booklist,* Vol. 90, No. 2, September 15, 1993, p. 148.

The *Exxon Valdez* disaster awakened the American people to the terrible effects of a major oil spill, but Pringle points out that it was far from being the largest or most destructive such accident. The worldwide demand for petroleum means increased offshore drilling and transportation by supertankers, and spills occur every day. Pringle describes the formation of petroleum, the ways it is naturally or artificially removed from the ground, and its myriad benefits. Then he writes of the damage done by the thousands of major and minor spills that occur each year and the efforts being made to clean them up and prevent their occurrence. Finally, he discusses the responsibility of corporations, governments, and individuals to reduce the demand for oil, which will, in turn, reduce the devastation to the environment. Pringle states his case strongly but without undue alarm and backs his assertions with examples and statistics. Photographs of the areas and animals affected by spills reinforce the written descriptions. This small book contains a wealth of well-organized and clearly stated information.

📖 JACKAL WOMAN: EXPLORING THE WORLD OF JACKALS (1993)

Deborah Stevenson

SOURCE: A review of *Jackal Woman: Exploring the World of Jackals,* in *Bulletin of the Center for Children's Books,* Vol. 47, No. 3, November, 1993, p. 96.

A new entry in Pringle's series on animal scientists, *Jackal Woman* focuses on Patricia Moehlman, who's usually found in the Serengeti plain watching silverbacked or golden jackals, the species she's been observing for nearly twenty years. Jackals, Moehlman explains, aren't shy in the presence of humans, making them easier to study than many wild animals, and her accounts of their lives, as reported by Pringle, are detailed and absorbing. Jackals may not have the same appeal to youngsters as do bats or bears, but this is a compact and readable summary of their habits, and Dr. Moehlman herself is a friendly figure matter-of-factly leading her rustic life. Photographs of the jackals are close and endearing if sometimes shadowy. . . .

Chris Sherman

SOURCE: A review of *Jackal Woman: Exploring the World of Jackals,* in *Booklist,* Vol. 90, No. 5, November 1, 1993, p. 520.

Pringle, whose books *Bearman* and *Batman* showcase zoologists who study animals often frightening to people, now describes the work of Patricia Moehlman, who has made a career of researching the often-maligned scavenger, the jackal. As he did in his previous books, Pringle captures the zoologist's excitement in her work and the respect and admiration she feels for her subjects. He also provides a thorough explanation of how Moehlman became interested in studying jackals and how she conducts her research. Students doing their own

research for reports on African wildlife will find a wealth of information about the habits and characteristics of two species of jackal, the golden and the silver-backed.

Susan Oliver

SOURCE: A review of *Jackal Woman: Exploring the World of Jackals,* in *School Library Journal,* Vol. 39, No. 12, December, 1993, p. 130.

For a third time, Pringle takes readers into the unique world of a behavioral ecologist; for the first time, his subject is a woman. Patricia Moehlman will bring Jane Goodall to mind, and indeed, Moehlman's jackal studies began under the tutelage of that renowned scientist. Her life, including her childhood, is highlighted as it relates to her career. The text and photographs speak in unison of Moehlman's affection and respect for jackals and of her fascination with their behavior. More than another book on animal behavior, this one is about a scientist discussing her field—how animal behavior is affected by environment, and how she conducts her studies and reaches conclusions.

📖 SCORPION MAN: EXPLORING THE WORLD OF SCORPIONS (1994)

Lauren Peterson

SOURCE: A review of *Scorpion Man: Exploring the World of Scorpions,* in *Booklist,* Vol. 91, No. 10, January 15, 1995, p. 922.

This fascinating look at the scorpion is also a revealing profile of the life and research of biologist Gary Polis. Pringle follows Polis's interest in the feared creatures from 1973, when he was a graduate student investigating desert biology at the University of California, to his current status as a worldwide authority. Polis's own vivid, close-up photographs illustrate the book, showing the scorpion in its natural habitat. Among them is a shot of the scorpions' elaborate courtship dance and another of a female eating her mate. Young people with a natural curiosity about animals or who are familiar with Pringle's other, similar books—for example, *Batman*—will be captivated.

Karey Wehner

SOURCE: A review of *Scorpion Man: Exploring the World of Scorpions,* in *School Library Journal,* Vol. 41, No. 3, March, 1995, pp. 217-18.

The work of Gary Polis is the subject of this book. The clearly written and well-organized text succinctly describes the man's childhood and early interest in biology, educational background, career as a science teacher in secondary schools, and research as a scientist specializing in the study of scorpions. As Pringle points out, Polis's project ". . . was the first intensive study of scorpions in their natural habitat, using UV [ultraviolet] light." Another chapter provides brief material on these arachnids' physical and behavioral characteristics. Polis himself supplied over two dozen clear, full-color photographs for the book. Two shots of scorpions taken under ultraviolet light are particularly stunning. There are some minor omissions. Only the sand scorpion is identified by scientific name, and the text states that "Just one deadly species lives in the United States," but neglects to name it. A good companion to Jan Mell's *The Scorpion,* which provides basic information but lacks *Scorpion Man's* fascinating detail on the animals' behavior.

📖 *CORAL REEFS: EARTH'S UNDERSEA TREASURES* (1995)

Frances E. Millhouser

SOURCE: A review of *Coral Reefs: Earth's Undersea Treasures,* in *School Library Journal,* Vol. 41, No. 10, October, 1995, p. 150.

A clear, well-organized introduction to the coral-reef habitats of the world. Short chapters with intriguing titles begin with an overview and go on to describe specific subjects. The pleasing and poisonous aspects of the reefs are described in "A Wealth of Life in a Poor Neighborhood" and "Chemical Warfare." "Fish of the Reef" are grouped according to who eats what (or whom). "Partners" discusses the mutually assistive relationships that exist among the organisms. Good-quality, full-color photographs appear on almost every page. A world map indicates the locations of the reefs. Not all unfamiliar terms are defined in the text or glossary, but most are amply explained and accompanied by a pronunciation guide. . . . Pringle's chapter on "Saving the Undersea Treasures" demonstrates the factors that threaten these beautiful and valuable ecosystems.

Margaret A. Bush

SOURCE: A review of *Coral Reefs: Earth's Undersea Treasures,* in *The Horn Book Magazine,* Vol. LXXI, No. 6, November-December, 1995, p. 757.

Coral, colorful and complex, must be one of the earth's most intriguing creatures. Pringle's lucid and informative text describes the structure and behavior of the coral polyp and the rich habitat and food source that coral colonies provide for a diverse population of ocean plants and animals—"a wealth of life in a poor neighborhood." Photographs depict striking views of coral polyps, colorful fish, and the physical features of the reefs, which protect nearby tropical lands from erosion, supply food and building materials, and are useful for medical purposes. Pringle notes that like the rain forests, reefs are a productive natural resource, vulnerable to the effects

of human activity, and may be in danger. Pringle's presentation, set in a particularly attractive rectangular volume with short chapters, presents the complex nature of coral reef ecology with clarity. This beautiful, thought-provoking book will be widely enjoyed and useful in science teaching.

📖 *FIRE IN THE FOREST: A CYCLE OF GROWTH AND RENEWAL* (1995)

Kirkus Reviews

SOURCE: A review of *Fire in the Forest: A Cycle of Growth and Renewal,* in *Kirkus Reviews,* Vol. LXIII, No. 20, October 15, 1995, p. 1499.

[Bob] Marstall's wondrous landscape paintings are reason enough to own this work, subtitled "A Cycle of Growth and Renewal," about the 1988 fires that burned nearly a third of Yellowstone National Park. Dramatic spreads help readers understand what the forest was like before, during, and after the fire, while thumb-sized drawings show park inhabitants and species up close. Pringle makes his text dense with detail and repeatedly stresses the importance of fires as a natural part of the cycle of growth and renewal in an ecosystem.

Melissa Hudak

SOURCE: A review of *Fire in the Forest: A Cycle of Growth and Renewal,* in *School Library Journal,* Vol. 41, No. 12, December, 1995, p. 123.

Using full-color, double-page spreads of the cycles and stages of life, death, and rebirth of the forest, Pringle presents a positive view of fire as a way for nature to renew itself. The landscape paintings are interposed with whole pages of text. Small paintings of wildlife decorate the textual pages. Pringle's writing is convincing; facts are presented clearly in an informative manner. Unfortunately, the text is at a fairly sophisticated reading level for what is, essentially, a picture-book format. While the illustrations are beautiful, middle grade readers may be reluctant to pick it up.

Carolyn Phelan

SOURCE: A review of *Fire in the Forest: A Cycle of Growth and Renewal,* in *Booklist,* Vol. 92, No. 7, December 1, 1995, p. 629.

Chiding news commentators for painting the 1988 forest fires in Yellowstone National Park as catastrophic, Pringle takes the long view of fire in the Northern Rocky Mountain ecosystem. He discusses the effect of fire on the plants and animals native to the region, showing that the ecosystem is neither destroyed by a fire nor reborn after it, but simply goes through different stages of its natural cycle. Pringle makes his points intelligently, asking readers to look beyond Bambi and Smokey the Bear to see that fire is "as natural as rain." The text, accompanied by small paintings of plants and animals, appears on facing pages that alternate with double-page spread illustrations. Stretching horizontally across the pages, these large, vivid paintings show the same landscape in different stages of growth before, during, and after a fire. The paintings underscore the theme very effectively. A handsome ecology book.

DINOSAURS!: STRANGE AND WONDERFUL (1995)

Sally Erhard and Sharon L. Rizzo

SOURCE: A review of *Dinosaurs!: Strange and Wonderful*, in *Appraisal: Science Books for Young People*, Vol. 28, No. 1, Winter, 1995, pp. 55-6.

LIBRARIAN [Sally Erhard]: *Dinosaurs!: Strange and Wonderful* lives up to its subtitle. Mr. Pringle's text is full of just the right amount of information about dinosaurs for the preschool level. He gives a good balance between what scientists have learned from fossils, and what they do not know. On that note, Pringle offers no suggestion as to why they died out about sixty-five million years ago.

On the other hand, Miss Heyer has painted some very strange creatures that will delight children. Despite the fact that Mr. Pringle states on the fifth to last page that "fossils do not show the color of dinosaurs," she has painted them with bright colored scales in all sorts of wild patterns. Youngsters who cannot read will marvel at the illustrations [by Carol Heyer], but without the accompanying text they may acquire erroneous scientific facts.

Since even tiny tots know about dinosaurs from Barney, it is never too soon to be sure their information is correct. The text for the age level is very good, but the illustrations take the imagination over the border into fiction.

SPECIALIST [Sharon Rizzo]: *Dinosaurs!: Strange and Wonderful* is a simple yet sophisticated book. The information-rich text is succinct and well written. The dynamic illustrations are beautiful and captivating.

This excellent book for young dinosaur enthusiasts is tightly written covering much informational ground without being verbose or obtuse. It is a refreshing change from the many preschool dinosaur books that, in my opinion, tend to wander through the subject material without being direct and simple enough for their young readers.

Dinosaurs! introduces topics ranging from where the dinosaurs lived, what they ate, fossils, paleontologists, to how new discoveries lead to updated theories about dinosaurs' appearance, behavior and evolution.

Publishers Weekly

SOURCE: A review of *Dinosaurs!: Strange and Wonderful*, in *Publishers Weekly*, Vol. 242, No. 1, January 2, 1995, p. 77.

In his addition to the plethora of dinotitles, Pringle presents a picture book introduction to this ever-intriguing subject. He examines the giant creatures' habits and natures, the ways in which paleontologists have gathered the information currently available—including some surprising new discoveries. Clearly written and well-suited to a younger audience, the book is meaty enough for slightly older readers too. Heyer's detailed acrylics, alternately realistic and stylized, offer an up-to-date representation of what the "terrible lizards" may well have looked like.

Kirkus Reviews

SOURCE: A review of *Dinosaurs!: Strange and Wonderful*, in *Kirkus Reviews*, Vol. LXIII, No. 4, February 15, 1995, p. 231.

A book about dinosaurs, from a science writer with a strong track record, who here may have misjudged his audience. The picture book format will turn away grade-schoolers old enough to grasp such complicated concepts as fossils, which are introduced but not fully explained. The writing is skillfully on target, if a bit formal, for younger dinophiles. They will find the full-color, detailed illustrations convincingly scaly and realistically ugly; especially good is Heyer's pachyrhinosaurus with its swirling multi-hued skin. It illustrates Pringle's comment that fossils teach nothing about the colors of dinosaurs, nor about the sounds they made.

DOLPHIN MAN: EXPLORING THE WORLD OF DOLPHINS (1995)

Hazel Rochman

SOURCE: A review of *Dolphin Man: Exploring the World of Dolphins*, in *Booklist*, Vol. 92, Nos. 9 & 10, January 1, 1996, p. 812.

Not just another dolphin book, this focuses on one marine biologist, Randall Wells, and his work with the dolphin community of the Sarasota Bay area in Florida. Wells also took the excellent action color photographs that appear throughout the clearly designed photo-essay. As in a readable magazine article, Pringle integrates facts about dolphin behavior (how they live together, mate, raise their young, fight predators, etc.) with the story of how Wells tracks and observes individual dolphins in the ocean. The scientist talks informally about how he started working with dolphins as early as high school and about his exciting recent work with particular dolphins that "hang out" together. There's a brief bibliography of Wells's own writing in popular and scientific journals.

As in Pringle's *Jackal Woman* and *Scorpion Man,* the personal account will draw readers to the biology.

📖 **TAKING CARE OF THE EARTH: KIDS IN ACTION** (1996)

Susan Dove Lempke

SOURCE: A review of *Taking Care of the Earth: Kids in Action,* in *Booklist,* Vol. 92, No. 12, February 15, 1996, p. 1018.

Noting that "we often hear discouraging news about the environment," Pringle gives children plenty of ideas for concrete things they can do to help protect the earth and its resources. He cites several examples of projects undertaken by school children around the country, such as the penny collection undertaken by Michigan students that yielded enough to buy eight acres of Costa Rican rain forest. Projects involve caring for local sites, composting, and recycling. Pringle is careful to show the complexities of some issues and advises children to do their research. Addresses of environmental organizations are included so that kids can follow through on the enthusiasm the suggestions will inspire.

📖 **SMOKING: A RISKY BUSINESS** (1996)

Susan Dove Lempke

SOURCE: A review of *Smoking: A Risky Business,* in *Booklist,* Vol. 93, No. 7, December 1, 1996, p. 660.

After a brief but intriguing look into the history of tobacco, which was once thought to be a possible cure for asthma, Pringle explores the substances smokers take into their bodies, paying special attention to scientific studies proving the addictive nature of nicotine. He follows with a look at the tactics used by tobacco manufacturers and their organizations to promote smoking and defeat restrictions, concluding with some tips on how to quit. Condemnatory but still restrained and with an excellent array of illustrations, this well-researched volume will satisfy curiosity and be a good source for reports.

Joyce Adams Burner

SOURCE: A review of *Smoking: A Risky Business,* in *School Library Journal,* Vol. 43, No. 1, January, 1997, pp. 132-33.

In a volume packed with information, Pringle clearly lays out the harmful effects of smoking and then takes on the advertising strategies used to discredit such claims. Beginning with a history of tobacco, he jumps into a forthright discussion of nicotine and other ingredients of cigarettes, also considering pipes and smokeless tobacco, the effects of second-hand smoke, and smoking during pregnancy. Much of the book, however, is directed at the claims and advertising put out by the tobacco industry to discount the medical research on the dangers of smoking. The involvement of the federal government in agricultural subsidies, and interest in tobacco as a growth industry are laid out, as well as FDA regulations, congressional bills, and class-action suits.

📖 **AN EXTRAORDINARY LIFE: THE STORY OF A MONARCH BUTTERFLY** (1997)

Kirkus Reviews

SOURCE: A review of *An Extraordinary Life: The Story of a Monarch Butterfly,* in *Kirkus Reviews,* Vol. LXV, No. 4, February 15, 1997, p. 304.

A migration flight from New England to Mexico and back again would be impressive for a large goose; for a monarch butterfly, it's nothing short of miraculous. Pringle and Marstall capture that miracle in this chronicle of the lifetime of a monarch called Danaus (after its Latin name). Readers follow Danaus on her perilous journey from Massachusetts, slipping through cat paws and struggling with bad weather until she and thousands of other monarchs find their winter homes in Mexico and California. Even there, life is dangerous: Cold weather and predators kill off many monarchs before spring arrives, when they mate, fly north, lay their eggs, and die. Pringle writes simply of all the small, fascinating details that make up the monarch's life cycle, while illustrations and captions help readers visualize the information, e.g., that delicate gold dots on a monarch's chrysalis may help disguise the chrysalis from predators by reflecting sunlight like drops of dew, and the caterpillar's markings warn predators that it eats milkweed, making it poisonous to some. [Bob] Marstall provides nearly photorealistic views of biological processes, but never neglects the poetic aspect of the information. A superb, well-researched book that finds extraordinary science in the everyday life of a butterfly.

Carolyn Phelan

SOURCE: A review of *An Extraordinary Life: The Story of a Monarch Butterfly,* in *Booklist,* Vol. 93, No. 14, March 15, 1997, p. 1239.

A map of a monarch butterfly's migratory route from Massachusetts to Mexico sets the stage for this exceptional book. Rather than giving the usual survey of the habits, habitat, life cycle, and predators of butterflies, Pringle brings immediacy to his subject by focusing sharply on one monarch, whom he names Danaus. Beginning as an egg on the leaf of a milkweed plant, Danaus goes from caterpillar to chrysalis to butterfly and makes the long flight to Mexico. There she survives the winter, mates, and flies north to Texas, where she lays her own eggs in a milkweed field. The surprisingly absorbing story of Danaus' life is followed by a discussion of the monarchs' endangered winter refuges in Mexico and an explanation of how to raise monarch butterflies from the caterpillar stage. Throughout the book, Marstall's colorful paintings offer clear, brilliantly colored illustrations of the caterpillars growing, eating, resting, mating, avoiding predators, and flying, flying, flying. An excellent book on a popular species.

NAMING THE CAT (1997)

Kirkus Reviews

SOURCE: A review of *Naming the Cat,* in *Kirkus Reviews,* Vol. LXV, No. 13, July 1, 1997, p. 1035.

From an author best known for nature and science writing a warmly appealing tale based on his family's experiences. While a family attempts to decide on a name for the black-and-white cat they have adopted, several hairbreadth escapes from disaster make it clear that the cat's name should be "Lucky." It's a conclusion most children—to their delight—will have reached before the name is disclosed on the last page. This simple story, with several happy endings and enhanced by lively, intensely colorful illustrations of the rotund feline [by Katherine Potter], lends itself to discussion of such questions as "What happens to feral cats?" and "Do cats always land on their feet?"

Janice M. Del Negro

SOURCE: A review of *Naming the Cat,* in *Bulletin of the Center for Children's Books,* Vol. 51, No. 2, October, 1997, p. 65.

In this light but engaging tale, a family takes in a stray cat and then cannot agree on a name for him. The feline—a black cat with white belly, chin, feet, and tail tip—certainly inspires many monikers (like Panda, Vanilla Fudge, and Nimbus) but none really suits him. It is only after several close calls and near misses that the cat is appropriately named Lucky. Potter's richly hued pastels on colored paper are stylistically naïve and appealing, as the furry little protagonist struts and preens his way through Pringle's simple family story. The narrator, a grade-schooler of indeterminate gender, relates the sequence of events with the grave detachment necessary for such an important family decision. The story goes on a bit too long, and the artwork has a sameness that ultimately tips into the bland. This is, however, certain to have listeners bursting to tell the stories of how they named their own family pets, so get out the library's (stuffed) menagerie and have a naming contest of your own.

Caroline Ward

SOURCE: A review of *Naming the Cat,* in *School Library Journal,* Vol. 43, No. 11, November, 1997, p. 97.

In this harmonious pairing of story and art, a cat, "more curious than afraid," appears at a family's back door and, in typical fashion, adopts them. After ascertaining that the feline does not belong to anyone in the neighborhood, the family set about naming him. None of the monikers—not Bubba, or Fish Breath, or even Macavity—seems to fit. As the mischievous animal cavorts through a series of mishaps, the family find themselves saying over and over again, "You are a lucky cat." And, of course, the name sticks. The art, with its soft, almost furlike texture, nicely complements the mood of this pleasant story. The eye-catching layout varies from action shots of the cat's antics, to full-page spreads, to small portraits of the feline depicting the imagined possible personas. The humorous illustrations and the amusing names make this an enjoyable choice for storyhours.

EVERYBODY HAS A BELLYBUTTON: YOUR LIFE BEFORE YOU WERE BORN (1997)

Kirkus Reviews

SOURCE: A review of *Everybody Has a Bellybutton: Your Life before You Were Born,* in *Kirkus Reviews,* Vol. LXV, No. 15, August 1, 1997, p. 1227.

An excellent book for adults to share with children who are curious about their prenatal lives. Pringle, addressing listeners directly, begins with fertilization (the mechanics of conception are deliberately left beyond the scope of this book), details the various developmental stages of the embryo and fetus, and ends with birth. Soft, discreet drawings on pink, blue, and lavender pastel backgrounds [by Clare Wood] show how a baby grows from a cluster of undifferentiated cells into a newborn being welcomed by happy parents and big sister. There is just enough information, in text and illustrations, for preschoolers; Pringle also offers thoughtful suggestions for personalizing the explanation but cautions against "overtelling." Admirably restrained and formal, but not without warmth.

Susan Dove Lempke

SOURCE: A review of *Everybody Has a Bellybutton: Your Life before You Were Born,* in *Booklist,* Vol. 94, No. 2, September 15, 1997, p. 238.

A bellybutton, or navel, serves as a reminder to all that once they grew inside their mother. Pringle, author of numerous science books for children, offers a gently phrased, solidly scientific look at the growth of a baby from single cell to nine months. Told in the second person ("You could hear"), the narrative gives specific, censorial details that will keep even young children engaged, and the description of childbirth is matter-of-fact and undisturbing. An author's note gives suggestions for adapting the text to meet unusual situations, such as cesarean births. Illustrations are softly realistic pencil drawings on pink and blue backgrounds. This will prove a useful tool for adults needing to explain why Aunt Ruthie has such a fat tummy!

📖 ANIMAL MONSTERS: THE TRUTH ABOUT SCARY CREATURES (1997)

Kathleen Squires

SOURCE: A review of *Animal Monsters: The Truth about Scary Creatures*, in *Booklist*, Vol. 94, No. 1, September 1, 1997, p. 120.

In brief but lively and absorbing entries, Pringle reveals the straight dope on the world's most notorious animals, including alligators, killer bees, vampire bats, tarantulas, and even the Loch Ness monster. With brilliant color photos accompanying the clear, informative text, he presents fascinating facts, the truth being that most of the animals are getting a bad rap. The great white shark, for example, isn't actually a man-eater, and most of these animals avoid human contact whenever possible. Information dispels fear in this accessible, entertaining resource by an esteemed children's author whose gift is turning natural history and science into page-turning reading.

Ruth S. Vose

SOURCE: A review of *Animal Monsters: The Truth about Scary Creatures*, in *School Library Journal*, Vol. 43, No. 10, October, 1997, p. 122.

Profiling 20 creatures, including a couple of imaginary ones that have been considered "monsters," he begins each section with a vivid description of the dangerous aspects of a creature, and then goes into facts that may or may not support the popular view. The author includes the gila monster, the great white shark, killer bees, the Loch Ness monster, the tiger, and the Tasmanian devil. Full-color photos or illustrations of the subjects are included, often with mouths agape showing teeth or fangs. Through this lively presentation, readers will learn that some animals really are dangerous, others just need to be left alone, and still others are completely harmless in spite of terrible reputations. It seems rather disingenuous to promote the "scary monster" aspects of these animals so thoroughly in the illustrations and introductory paragraphs, but the book does present interesting and accurate information. This title will fit well into the role of that much requested "scary book."

Arlyn M. Christopherson

SOURCE: A review of *Animal Monsters: The Truth about Scary Creatures*, in *Science Books & Films*, Vol. 34, No. 7, October, 1998, p. 212.

In this little book, 20 "scary creatures" are discussed, in alphabetical order, from alligator to wolf, with one or two pages of gracefully written text and a dramatic photograph (or drawing, in the case of two imaginary animals). In an excellent introduction, author Laurence Pringle discusses the human need for "a good scare now and then," but goes on to point out the actual risks from these animals to humans, which are usually much less than most people suppose, and how "eyewitnesses" may misinterpret what they see. A number of the animals—tigers, wolves, rattlesnakes, and sharks—have been relentlessly persecuted and now require protection from their slide towards extinction. A few inexplicable errors dot the book. For example, Pringle states that there are no huge octopuses just after he has described one that weighed 600 pounds and measured 31 feet across the tentacles! He also erroneously asserts that an octopus "often . . . stuns its prey by releasing a poison into the water." However, the errors detract very little from this very interesting text, and the book will be relished by middle school youngsters; it should prompt some interesting discussions with younger readers, too. Although "perhaps the human desire to wonder is stronger than the desire to understand," this book will bring considerable understanding to its readers.

📖 ELEPHANT WOMAN: CYNTHIA MOSS EXPLORES THE WORLD OF ELEPHANTS (1997)

Susan Oliver

SOURCE: A review of *Elephant Woman: Cynthia Moss Explores the World of Elephants*, in *School Library Journal*, Vol. 43, No. 12, December, 1997, pp. 145-46.

Cynthia Moss will fascinate young readers. A scientist without formal training, she entered her field through the back door and is now a preeminent researcher of elephant behavior and a compassionate conservationist. Pringle not only writes of Moss's work in Kenya's Amboseli National Park, but also tells the story of a woman who, despite adversity, has reached the heights of her field. Physical and behavioral information about African elephants is seamlessly woven into the narrative. How researchers live and conduct their work—and why it is important—become clear as Pringle describes the subject's observations of elephant family life. Moss's full-color photographs add wonderful detail and atmosphere to the text. . . . Elephants are extraordinary animals, Cynthia Moss is a great role model, and Pringle has brought them together in an exciting presentation.

Margaret A. Bush

SOURCE: A review of *Elephant Woman: Cynthia Moss Explores the World of Elephants*, in *The Horn Book Magazine*, Vol. LXXIV, No. 1, January-February, 1998, p. 95.

As in his other handsome accounts of notable naturalists, Laurence Pringle smoothly melds biographical information with a substantial account of the animal under study. A serendipitous trip to Africa in 1967 led American Cynthia Moss into an unexpected and productive career; she has now spent thirty years studying elephant families in Kenya's Amboseli National Park and working to protect their diminishing numbers. "Becoming Elephant Woman," the first of four chapters, sketches Moss's childhood years and early journalism career that led to an interest in conservation and documentary filmmaking. Subsequent chapters concentrate on the elephants, recounting many of Moss's observations about the temperament of individual animals (she recognizes each of over nine hundred elephants by their individually distinct ears), their social behavior, and their survival strategies in recurring cycles of drought. . . . [Moss's] career as researcher and conservationist has contributed greatly to what is known about elephants, and her story and theirs are well served in this attractive, thoughtfully shaped volume.

📖 *DRINKING: A RISKY BUSINESS* (1997)

Anne O'Malley

SOURCE: A review of *Drinking: A Risky Business,* in *Booklist,* Vol. 94, No. 8, December 15, 1997, p. 690.

An estimated 800 high-school and college students die each year of alcohol poisoning, a condition that results from an excessively heavy bout of drinking. A mid-1990s study indicated that nearly three-quarters of 9- to 11-year-olds recognized television frogs as Budweiser beer promoters. Pringle writes of the toll that alcohol has taken on our society over the years and its pervasiveness in our culture. At the same time, he explores the issue from many angles—the science of alcohol, its history, business and advertising interests, government regulation, and physical and emotional health aspects. A clear, active narrative, well-rendered black-and-white photographs and charts, and a strong anti-alcohol message, which does not become preachy, add up to a fine, informative, well-documented book.

Sheila G. Shellabarger

SOURCE: A review of *Drinking: A Risky Business,* in *School Library Journal,* Vol. 44, No. 1, January, 1998, pp. 128-29.

Seasoned social-issues writer Pringle writes again about risky business. Like his *Smoking,* this book opens with a history of the issue. It identifies alcohol's earliest known use and traces its development and continued used to present day. A discussion follows on alcohol's harmful physical, mental, and emotional effects, including the devastating toll of alcoholism on individuals,

families, and society. . . . Pringle's chapters on the history of the U.S. temperance movement and the economic side of the alcohol industry set his book apart. He stresses that, in addition to being risky business, alcohol is also "big business" in terms of taxation, legislation, employment, and advertising. The book concludes with a discussion of the risks of alcohol use for young people and offers practical advice on getting help with drinking problems. A variety of back-and-white photos, charts, drawings, and reproductions support the text, although some are repetitive of those found in other titles on this subject. Readable and well organized, *Drinking* should be useful to those seeking personal information as well as those writing reports.

📖 *ONE ROOM SCHOOL* (1998)

Kirkus Reviews

SOURCE: A review of *One Room School,* in *Kirkus Reviews,* Vol. LXVI, No. 2, January 15, 1998, p. 116.

An affectionate paean to his one-room schoolhouse turns Pringle into everyone's favorite uncle, telling stories about when he was a child.

They are engaging tales, full of small details that children will love: Helen, who was the only third grader, then the only fourth grader, etc., through most of her school years; the boys' outhouse was farther away than the girls' so boys had more time outdoors; the teacher's floral print dresses and Tabu perfume. [Barbara] Garrison's illustrations are richly textured prints in the soft, blurred colors of memory. She frames them in the white-deckled edges and corners of old photographs, so readers know that it is Pringle's remembrance of school in the last year of WW II that is captured in this evocative "album."

Susan Dove Lempke

SOURCE: A review of *One Room School,* in *Booklist,* Vol. 94, No. 13, March 1, 1998, p. 1138.

A familiar children's author recalls attending School 14, a one-room school where the biggest class had five students, and Helen Hutchinson was always the only child in her grade. The year was 1944, and Pringle's memories of teaching and learning are mixed with World War II recollections of collecting scrap metal and practicing for air raids. Warm, specific memories fill the book and give children a sense of both history and place. The mostly brown-and-white illustrations, in a stiff, childlike style with faces denoted by dots and lines, are set on the page like old photographs in an album. Grandparents will especially enjoy using this book as a springboard for talking about their own childhoods to their grandchildren.

Additional coverage of Pringle's life and career is contained in the following sources published by The Gale Group: *Contemporary Authors New Revision Series*, Vol. 60; *Major Authors and Illustrators for Children and Young Adults, Something about the Author Autobiography Series*, Vol. 6; *Something about the Author*, Vols. 4, 68.

Arthur Rackham

1867-1939

English illustrator of fiction, nonfiction, poetry, and re-tellings.

Major works include *Fairy Tales* (by Jacob and Wilhelm Grimm, 1900), *Rip Van Winkle* (by Washington Irving, 1905), *Peter Pan in Kensington Gardens* (by J. M. Barrie, 1906), *Alice's Adventures in Wonderland* (by Lewis Carroll, 1907), *The Wind in the Willows* (by Kenneth Grahame, 1940).

Major works about the illustrator include *Arthur Rackham: A Bibliography* (by Sarah B. Latimore and Grace Clark Haskell, 1936), *Arthur Rackham: His Life and Work* (by Derek Hudson, 1960), *The Centenary of Arthur Rackham's Birth, September 19, 1867: An Appreciation of His Genius and a Catalogue of His Original Sketches, Drawings, and Paintings in the Berol Collection* (by Roland Baughman, 1967), *Arthur Rackham* (edited by David Larkin, 1975), *Arthur Rackham* (by Fred Gettings, 1976), *Arthur Rackham* (by James Hamilton, 1990).

INTRODUCTION

Considered one of the greatest illustrators in the field of children's literature, Rackham is noted for creating fantastic scenes rooted in carefully observed reality that reflect his highly individualistic vision and recognizable style. Recognized as a particularly gifted and versatile artist, Rackham provided the pictures for more than sixty-five works by such authors as William Shakespeare, John Milton, Jonathan Swift, Oliver Goldsmith, Charles Dickens, Robert Browning, Algernon Charles Swinburne, Nathaniel Hawthorne, Edgar Allan Poe, and Rudyard Kipling. Rackham illustrated books for both children and adults, although the majority of his works are either directed at children or strongly appeal to children. He is perhaps best known for illustrating international folk and fairy tales and for addressing classic books that were thought to have been definitively illustrated, such as *Alice's Adventures in Wonderland* and *The Wind in the Willows*. Fascinated with myths and legends, especially those with Germanic and Norse roots, Rackham provided the pictures for stories based on Richard Wagner's "Ring" operas and Henrik Ibsen's verse drama *Peer Gynt*. He also illustrated Greek legends, the stories of King Arthur, English and Irish fairy tales and ballads, and a volume of international fairy tales. In addition, Rackham illustrated Aesop's fables, Mother Goose rhymes, and the fairy tales of Hans Christian Andersen as well as original fantasies by Christopher Morley and Margery Williams Bianco.

As an illustrator, Rackham characteristically used the mediums of watercolor and black line; he also favored silhouettes. A methodical worker, he drew his subjects in pencil, inked them over, and colored them with a light wash that gave his art an ethereal quality. Rackham's pictures were often inserted in separate sections throughout his books or as independent folios at the end. Considered the master of a variety of styles, Rackham drew on the genres of costume adventure, satire and caricature, and what he called "the fantastic and the imaginative" to create his works. Influenced by such artists as Aubrey Beardsley and Albrecht Durer as well as by Japanese and Persian designs, Art Nouveau, and medieval manuscripts, Rackham is credited with creating a new dimension in illustration. Considered scrupulously faithful to the texts of the books he illustrated, he is further acknowledged for taking these works to imaginative heights that the texts only suggested. Rackham metamorphosed the natural world into forms that were otherworldly. He became well known for creating a variety of fairy folk—elves, dwarfs, gnomes, and other creatures—as well as anthropomorphic trees, root tendrils, mushrooms, ferns, grass, flowers, mice and exotic birds; he also detailed his pictures with humorous versions of himself as well as with fabrics, crockery, dressing gowns, and polka dots. Magical and mysterious, the world that Rackham depicted in his illustrations ranged from lyrical and poetic to macabre and grotesque. By blending the real and the supernatural in a distinctive manner, Rackham created a fantasy land that is often regarded as completely unique.

Biographical Information

Born in London, Rackham always claimed proudly that he was a Cockney. The fourth of twelve children born to a civil servant and his wife, he showed an early talent for drawing, especially sketches of nature and outrageous caricatures. Rackham was educated at the City of London School, where he won prizes for mathematics and was encouraged in his artistic pursuits by both teachers and students. As a teenager, Rackham began to take his talent seriously and became a devoted landscape painter. At the age of sixteen, he traveled to Australia by sea as a cure for ill health. He kept a detailed journal of the six-month trip that included twenty-four watercolors; critics have noted that this voyage cemented Rackham's future. After leaving school, Rackham worked as a clerk in an insurance office during the day and attended the Lambeth School of Art at night. He exhibited his paintings at the Royal Academy, the Royal Institute of Painters in Water Colours, and at several galleries; in addition, his first drawings were published in the magazine, *Scraps.* At the age of twenty-five, Rackham became a full-time illustrator. He began submitting illustrations to various periodicals and was accepted as a staff artist on the *Pall Mall Gazette,* where he drew pictures on a variety of subjects. In 1893, he moved to the *Westminster Budget,* for which he illustrated poems, among other assignments, and created a popular feature, "Sketches from the Life." Rackham later described the early years of his professional career in an article for the *Bookman* titled "The Worst Time in My Life": "Work was hard to get and not well paid, and such efforts I made along the lines I have since followed received little encouragement." However, some observers have noted that Rackham developed his special talents as an illustrator during this period.

Rackham's reputation began to build, especially among other artists. He illustrated his first book, *The Dolly Dialogues* by Anthony Hope, in 1894. Two years later, he provided the pictures for his first book for children, *The Zankiwank and the Bletherwitch* by S. J. Adair-Fitzgerald. Rackham went to Bayreuth, Germany, in 1897; this trip, during which he saw a performance of Richard Wagner's cycle *The Rings of the Nibelungen,* was a turning point for the artist. After publishing well-received editions of *Tales from Shakespeare* by Charles and Mary Lamb and *Gulliver's Travels* by Jonathan Swift, Rackham illustrated *Fairy Tales* by Jacob and Wilhelm Grimm in 1900. This book, which features earthy ogres and hook-nosed witches in eerie, often menacing pictures, is considered the first of his works to demonstrate his signature style; it was both a critical and popular success. In 1902, Rackham exhibited his illustrations for the Grimm tales at the Royal Watercolour Society, where they were greeted with acclaim. The following year, he married Edyth Starkie, an Irish portrait painter; the couple had a daughter, Barbara, who often served as a model for her father. In 1905, Rackham illustrated *Rip Van Winkle* by Washington Irving. Before the book's publication, its illustrations were exhibited at Brown and Phillip's Leicester Galleries, a canny business move that ensured the success of the volume. *Rip Van Winkle* was followed the next year by an even greater success, *Peter Pan in Kensington Gardens* by J. M. Barrie. Once again, Rackham's illustrations were exhibited before the publication of the book, the success of which gave the artist an international reputation. In 1907, the copyright lapsed on Lewis Carroll's *Alice's Adventures in Wonderland.* Rackham now took a major risk: illustrating a book that was associated almost as much with its illustrator, Sir John Tenniel, as it was with its author. Though controversial, *Alice's Adventures in Wonderland* proved to be even more profitable than *Peter Pan* and is still in print.

Rackham became recognized as a wizard-like figure with special ties to fairyland, a reputation that contrasted greatly with the artist's conservative, hard-working nature. He continued to produce successful titles up to the First World War; several of these volumes were marketed as gift books, expensive, sumptuously produced volumes that were often published in limited editions. After the war, the market for gift books declined sharply. Rackham set his sights on a new territory: America. Between 1922 and 1925, he created a series of thirty illustrations for the Colgate Company, which wanted to create an image of English nobility for its campaign for Cashmere Bouquet soap. Rackham's pictures were so successful that the Metropolitan Museum of Art asked to display them. In 1927, Rackham traveled to America for the first and only time. His return to England prompted what some critics consider his second great period of creativity. Asked to illustrate the fairy tales of Hans Christian Andersen, Rackham and his wife went to Denmark to do research. In 1933, he designed the costumes and scenery for Basil Dean's production of *Hansel and Gretel.* He also continued producing books, most of which centered on fantasy and the supernatural. He commented that his pictures for Edgar Allan Poe's *Tales of Mystery and Imagination* (1935) "were so horrible I was beginning to frighten myself." In 1936, American publisher George Macy asked Rackham to illustrate a limited edition of *The Wind in the Willows,* a work that author Kenneth Grahame had asked him to illustrate thirty years before; at the time, the artist had to decline because of other commitments. Although he had been diagnosed with cancer, Rackham worked feverishly on the volume, often drawing and painting in bed. In a letter to Macy, Rackham stated that he thought some of the pictures "are as good as I have ever done." As he finished the last picture, Rackham realized that he had forgotten to draw oars on the boat that carried Rat and Mole. After drawing the oars, he laid back in bed and said, "Thank goodness, that is the last one." Rackham died before the publication of *The Wind in the Willows* in 1940. The book is generally considered a master-work.

Critical Reception

As an artist, Rackham is praised for his originality, ingenuity, and technical skill. Lauded as a draftsman and designer, he is acclaimed for his sensitivity of line and for the delicate yet vigorous quality of his illustrations. Rackham is also commended for the evocative nature of his pictures and for their droll, often sarcastic humor. In addition, he is acknowledged for his commitment to enriching children's imaginations and for the respect that he showed to his audience. Although critics feel that some of his pictures are too disturbing, especially for young people, and that the artist is emotionally detached from his works, most observers agree that Rackham is one of the finest illustrators in literature and that his pictures reveal a beautiful, fascinating world with particular relevance to real life.

Rackham is also considered an influential artist whose style is reflected in the works of Kay Nielsen, Walt Disney, Max Reinhardt, and Maurice Sendak, among others, and even in the title character of Steven Spielberg's film *E. T.* Called "the Goblin Master" and "Court Painter to King Oberon and Queen Titania" during his lifetime, Rackham was dubbed "the official artist of the fairy realm" by Julian Garner and "the greatest living painter of child romance" by Clara T. Mac Chesney. He was also praised by fellow artists: James Daugherty called Rackham "the lyric genius of the English people," as quoted in *Illustrators of Children's Books*, while Robert Lawson stated that Rackham "was in his work a Gentleman. . . . As the temporary fads and madnesses wane and blow away, his high repute will remain clear and unsullied in the hearts of our generation and of many to come"; the critic concluded, "For make no mistake, Arthur Rackham was an *illustrator*." In his biography *Arthur Rackham*, Fred Gettings commented, "It has been said that Rackham invented a new type of child, but the truth is more subtle than this—Rackham invented a new kind of reality. . . . [H]e created a fairy world in the imagination of thousands and perhaps millions of people. . . . Rackham influenced our perception of the world." Writing in *Children's Literature*, Christa Kamenetsky concluded, "As if he were holding up a mirror to the complexity of our souls, Rackham cunningly revealed to us our dreams of beauty as well as the distorted features of our nightmares and secret fears. In that sense, polarity and ambiguity not only mark his poetic vision, but also the special sense of humor that places him, beyond a doubt, in a class of his own."

Awards

Rackham was elected an associate of the Royal Watercolour Society in 1902 and the Societe Nationale des Beaux Arts, Paris, in 1912. He was named Master Chair of the Art Workers Guild in 1919. Rackham also won gold medals at exhibitions in Milan, Italy, in 1906; in Barcelona, Spain, in 1911; and in Paris.

COMMENTARY

Arthur Rackham

SOURCE: "The Worst Time in My Life: Arthur Rackham," in *The Bookman,* Vol. LXIX, No. 409, October, 1925, p. 7.

I think I may say that for a good many years at the beginning of my career I had far from an easy time. I was working mainly as a free-lance for various illustrated journals and magazines. Work was hard to get and not well paid, and such efforts as I made along the lines I have since followed received little encouragement. And then came the Boer War. That really was a very thin time indeed for me, and may be considered the worst time I ever had. The kind of work that was in demand, to the exclusion almost of all else, was such as I had no liking for and very little aptitude. It was also clear that the camera was largely going to supplant the artist in illustrated journalism, and my prospects were not encouraging. But my work was becoming less immature, and before long my special bent began to be recognised—by artists first. I was elected to membership of one or two exhibiting societies, my work was welcomed, dealers and publishers became interested, and the worst was passed.

A. L. Baldry

SOURCE: "Arthur Rackham: A Painter of Fantasies," in *International Studio,* Vol. 25, No. 99, May, 1905, pp. 189-201.

There is most certainly no apology necessary for assigning to Mr. Arthur Rackham a prominent place among the most distinguished of modern water-colourists. We have no one who can quite be compared with him, no one who uses his particular executive method with a tithe of his ability or approaches him in fanciful originality. Nor is there any of his predecessors who can be said to have shown him the way to work the unusual pictorial vein that is providing him with such ample material. Mr. Rackham has found for himself the field in which he is now labouring with conspicuous success, and has developed with delightful ingenuity an absolutely personal style. He owes his position to his special endowment of quaint imagination, and to a rare understanding of the executive devices by which his fancies can be made properly credible. . . .

Mr. Rackham surpasses even that master of fanciful contrivance [(Richard Doyle)] in the richness and strength of his work. He has undeniably an extraordinary imagination, extraordinary in its intricacy, in its unfailing resource, and its endless variety. Mere grotesque extravagance does not by any means satisfy him; there is much more in his art than simple twisting of facts into absurdities, or than the travestying of serious things in a broadly humorous manner. Such an example of it as *The Rescue* is really an intensely dramatic story cast in a definitely comic mould, a drama in which all the actors are playing their parts in deadly earnest, and with the most serious conviction. The humour of it is grim— not so grim, perhaps, as that which distinguishes that other amazing creation, the Langham sketch *Alone*—but in the grimness there is a charming hint of tenderness and of sympathy with the weaker things that suffer under nature's inflexible code of laws. In this drawing Mr. Rackham appears as a moralist, and as a commentator on the tragedies of existence; in *Cupid's Alley,* with its wonderful insight into character, he is quite as convincingly a satirist, and in *Alone* he tells a complete and tragic story in which there is a plain and intelligible symbolical intention. In all these fantasies of his, with their quaint and grotesque presentation, there is an underlying meaning that is well worth seeking out; to treat them simply as clever fooling would be a serious mistake.

But when he ceases to deal with these problems and turns to ideas which are essentially dainty and delicate in sentiment he loses none of his attractiveness as an artist. His illustrations to *Grimm's Fairy Tales, The Old Man, Snowdrop, The Cat,* and *The Young Count;* his exquisite water colours, *Playmates* and *Queen Mab;* even his water colour landscape *The Lake-side,* show a sensitive understanding of artistic refinements which is heartily to be commended. There is in them all an amount of thought, and a degree of ingenuity in design, far beyond what is to be found in the work of the average illustrator, and there is a sympathetic touch which is a clear reflection of his own kindly temperament. Obviously he feels the beauty of nature quite as keenly as her strength, and is as responsive to her charms as to her sternness and inflexibility.

To the executive side of his work, nothing but praise can be given. Whether he is expressing himself in colour, in black-and-white line, in broad masses as in the silhouette, *The Wren and the Bear,* or in that combination of pen-line and tinting in colour-washes which he particularly affects, he is always a complete master of technical method. His practice, indeed, is as intricate and searching as his imagination and as complex as his invention. Everything he does is finished like a miniature and yet is broad, decisive, and confident. The struggle to make himself intelligible, and to keep his mind and hand in proper relation, is never apparent in his drawings; though this struggle is one from which no artist can escape. He has learned with rare completeness how to control the processes of the form of art which he has chosen, and he has acquired that air of spontaneity which more than anything else implies exhaustiveness of preliminary study and long continued effort to acquire a sufficiency of mechanical experience, and in this he has been especial-

ly wise; nothing would have hampered more seriously a man of his peculiarly prolific imagination than technical imperfection. . . .

[Rackham] could not remain a realist, for realism would destroy all the spirit and meaning of his art. He cannot confine himself to the facts that are before him because plain actuality would never satisfy him and would never allow him the scope for expression that he so intensely desires. But he has, all the same, to go through the drilling of the realist or else he would be incapable of expanding in the directions where he can justify his artistic temperament most convincingly. If he had not the basis of sure knowledge he could never construct those delightful perversions of nature which evidently give him such joy and show the rare richness of his imagination. For it must be remembered that his grotesques have to be made credible, and with all their extravagance have to be so dramatically suggestive that they can attract and hold the attention of the people whose first inclination is to laugh at their absurdity. Directly he began to fumble, or to hint at any uncertainty in his own mind, his power to persuade would be gone; he would seem to be attempting something beyond his reach, or to be deliberately poking fun at his admirers. Such a breach of faith would be inexcusable; for if he is not serious in his art, no matter how amusing or fantastic it may be, he stamps himself as a charlatan who is only attitudinising to draw notice which his merits do not entitle him to claim. Only a consummate command over his craft would allow him to show that his amazing departures from strict veracity are deliberate expressions of a very original æsthetic belief and perfectly sincere in their exaggeration.

When he turns from grotesques to purely poetic drawings, the value of his nature study is not less apparent. The course of landscape painting which he began in his boyhood, and has kept up to the present day, has had a most valuable influence upon his art. It has guided him into exquisite suggestion of nature's subtleties, into a true appreciation of her sentiment and tender beauty. The landscape settings of his grotesques are as decoratively appropriate as they are naturally charming, and have the fullest measure of the true poetic spirit. His landscapes with incidental figures, and his pure landscapes of the *Lakeside* type, are sensitive, dainty, and well observed, distinguished by the happiest observation of atmospheric qualities, and by that perfect refinement which comes solely from intimacy of understanding If he had not been so close a student, he could never have grasped so firmly the elusive mysteries with which nature veils herself from the unsympathetic soul, and he could never have ranked himself so high as her faithful and earnest interpreter.

A. L. Baldry

SOURCE: "Arthur Rackham: Painter and Illustrator," in *The Bookman,* Vol. XXXI, No. 183, December, 1906, pp. 128-31.

[Rackham] is no imitator, no follower of a popular leader, no traveller along a beaten track which has been worn smooth by the feet of many patient plodders. He has chosen a way of his own, and with well-founded confidence in his powers he is working out for himself his destiny in the art world. By what he has already achieved he has made quite clear that he has no intention of adopting borrowed plumes to catch the public eye, or of conceding anything to one of the convenient fashions which happen at the moment to be in vogue; and he has proved with equal distinctness that he is strong enough to take an independent course. His admirable originality and exquisite technical skill have, within the last few years, gained him an assured place in the front rank of our water-colourists and draughtsmen; and to this place he has come not by any fortunate accident, nor by the influence of powerful patrons, but solely by his own exertions.

For Mr. Rackham had no special advantages afforded to him at the outset of his career, and was not permitted to enjoy unusual facilities for acquiring a knowledge of art. The associations of his childhood did not tend to develop in him any exceptional preference for artistic pursuits; he was not brought up in surroundings which were in any way abnormal or which were calculated to incline him towards serious speculations on æsthetic questions. Yet he began in very early youth to show the strength of his inclinations, and his tentative essays in drawing and painting were to him, while he was quite a young child, a source of constant pleasure. As he grew older he took himself more seriously, and though he received no regular education in art practice he imposed upon himself a more or less systematic course of training. In childhood he had amused himself with erratic fancies which expressed the imaginative bent of his mind, but later on he perceived the need of a surer and more practical study and of a better understanding of nature. So he gave all the time he could spare in the intervals of his school work to landscape painting, to sketching out-of-door subjects which he felt instinctively were likely to teach him the truths that must underlie all imaginative art and give it the touch of reality required to make it credible. By binding himself down to such a course of study, and by facing, unassisted, the inevitable difficulties which have to be overcome by the worker in the open air, he showed plainly enough his determination to master the fundamental principles of the craft in which he wished to excel; and he showed, too, that he had no fear of the struggle upon which he was entering. . . .

At first it was as an illustrator of books that Mr. Rackham found himself most in request. He executed a large number of drawings for the *Graphic, Black and White,* the *Sketch,* and other periodicals like the *Westminster and Pall Mall Budgets;* he did much work for magazines for children, like *Little Folks;* and he illustrated many books like **Grimm's Fairy Tales** and the **Ingoldsby Legends,** which gave him ample scope for the exercise of his inventive originality and quaint humour. Later on he added to this list a series of illustrations to **Rip Van Winkle** and many designs for *Punch;* and . . . he has been engaged upon pictures for two popular books, Rudyard Kipling's **Puck of Pook's Hill** and J. M. Barrie's **Peter Pan,** as well as further things for *Punch.* [Rackham] has, indeed, done admirable service as an illustrator, responding always in a fashion wholly delightful to the demands made upon him by the subjects he has been called upon to treat, and missing no opportunity of introducing into his interpretations of these subjects a happy touch of personal conviction.

For there is in the whole of his illustrative work a peculiar quality which comes partly from his skilful management of technical devices, but in far larger measure from the mental attitude that he assumes in dealing with the pictorial motives offered to him. The exquisite grace of his draughtsmanship, and the wonderful sensitiveness he shows in his use of line, would make his drawings remarkable even if they were nothing more than examples of executive achievement—if they were simply plain and literal statements of incidents fully set forth in the words of the text before him. As a craftsman he has an extraordinary command over refinements of expression, a perfection of touch and a delicacy of hand which give rare distinction to everything he produces, and which, nevertheless, do not prevent him from attaining, when his subject requires it, the most satisfying vigour and decision.

But in addition to this executive skill he has a faculty for seizing immediately upon the imaginative possibilities of the material he is considering. His mind is as flexible as his hand, as ready to respond to every suggestion which has in it the germ of artistic development. An amazingly prolific imagination, an apparently inexhaustible power of invention which can play with equal power upon notes of tender and dainty beauty, dramatic force, and grotesque exaggeration, are among the most valuable items in his equipment; and he uses them with a readiness of resource which amounts to inspiration. In his **Peter Pan** illustrations, for instance, it is astonishing to see with what a wealth of fancy he has embroidered the threads of the story, and how his inventive capacities have responded to the prompting of the author's imagination. Yet his drawings for this book, like those for the other works with which his pencil has been engaged, are not in any way detached from the text; they enhance its interest and increase its charm by proving how great is its power to stir up thoughts in a receptive and delicately artistic mind.

It is easy to see, both in Mr. Rackham's illustrations and in the paintings which he has exhibited in the gallery of the Royal Water Colour Society, and elsewhere, how seriously directed his earlier studies must have been. If he had not acquired so solid a foundation of knowledge he could hardly have given himself the imaginative license which is now one of the most fascinating characteristics of a great part of his work. To travesty the human form as he does in his quaint gnomes and goblins, to play in a mood of jesting exaggeration upon shades of facial character, and to avoid always by perfectly judicious restraint a descent into the merely ridiculous, is possible only to an artist who has spared no labour to master realistically the facts of the normal world. He can give the fuller meaning to his perversions because they only clothe in a not too impossible disguise something which is actual enough and wanting neither in credibility nor in common-sense. Mr. Rackham in his most erratic moments never rebels against sane discipline; the fault of recklessness, of careless distortion of probabilities can never be alleged against him; whether he is purely a poet or frankly a humorist he remains always an artist, judicious, deliberate, and thoroughly under the control both of his intelligence and his taste.

All that gives distinction to his drawings is to be found quite as evidently in his paintings, with the important addition of colour charmingly felt and sensitively harmonised. As a colourist, indeed, he is particularly deserving of attention. That he often attempts vehement or sumptuous combinations can scarcely be said, but he handles with a singularly happy judgment subtleties and modulations of tints which, with all their complexity, fall together into absolute agreement. His paintings, in consequence, have a freshness of effect, a tenderness of quality, which appeal persuasively for approval; and his landscapes especially, by their reticence and gentle re-

From Rip Van Winkle, *written by Washington Irving. Illustrated by Arthur Rackham.*

pose of manner, acquire a poetic meaning that is not to be found in more obvious transcriptions of nature. In most of his exhibited works there is apparent the same savour of fantasy which so pleasantly distinguishes his illustrations; he chooses subjects that lend themselves to whimsical treatment, and he lavishes upon them endless ingenuities of presentation. And he perfects them, too, by a precision of handling that is quite amazing in its accomplishment. It is an absolute revelation of dainty technique to see how he manages the intricacies of a pattern upon a piece of flowing drapery, how he draws and models some exquisite little figure, or how he elaborates to exactly the right pitch of completion the many small accessories which fill out his pictorial scheme, working always for the highest finish in every part, and yet with true artistic discretion making no parade of his labour.

To such a man a place among the leaders of our modern art can assuredly not be denied. He is decidedly not one in a company of followers at the heels of some master by whose personality he has been enslaved. If he has borrowed from any predecessor it has been simply with the idea of collecting the raw material with which he could construct something new and personal, material which he could so transmute that it could without question be stamped as his own. He has studied not the surface but the spirit of things, and all that he has seen has been viewed through the medium of his peculiar temperament; and it is by the right use of this temperament that he has reached the position in which he stands today.

Punch

SOURCE: A review of *Alice's Adventures in Wonderland,* in *Punch,* Vol. CXXXIII, No. 3465, December 4, 1907, p. 414.

If (as we shall never agree) it was either desirable or necessary to re-draw Sir John Tenniel's unsurpassable and immortal illustrations to **Alice in Wonderland,** Mr. Rackham may be said to have performed the task as well, probably, as any draughtsman could; for he is an artist with a rare sense of grotesque fancy and humour and an extraordinarily delicate and sensitive line. But it were better, we think, for him to employ his imagination upon his own rather than other men's business. Mr. Heinemann, the publisher of the new *Alice,* has secured some exculpatory verses from the pen of Mr. Dobson, which begin

> Tis two-score years since Carroll's art
>   With topsy-turvy magic
> Sent Alice wondering through a part,
>   Half comic and half tragic.

The tragedy is not too apparent; while to be accurate it is two-score years and two, the limit of copyright; for had it been less Mr. Heinemann would not have been in a position to publish this edition at all.

Philip Loring Allen

SOURCE: "The Sketch-Books of Wonderland," in *The Bookman,* Vol. XXVI, No. 6, February, 1908, pp. 648-51.

When new illustrations for **Alice in Wonderland** were first published, one comment was that it would have been quite as sensible and as becoming to issue an edition of Sir John Tenniel's illustrations with a new text, by, say, Richard Le Gallienne or Mrs. Humphry Ward. Now that the expiration of the English copyright—leaving publishers free to reprint the original text but not the original illustrations—has stimulated the production of half a dozen or more new outfits of pictures for this nonsense classic, these are still brought out in a way that is almost sheepish. The artists behave rather as if they had been caught sketching not enchanted domains, where they have a perfect right, but some enemy's fortifications. They want it understood that their work is not intended to supplant the Tenniel pictures, yet even this apology they do not make in person but virtually by literary attorney. "The Tenniel Pictures," says E. S. Martin in his preface to the Peter Newell edition, " . . . are identified beyond fear of separation with Alice and her familiars." "Enchanting Alice!" exclaims Austin Dobson in *his* metrical preface to the Arthur Rackham edition,

> Black and White
>   Has made your deeds perennial;
> And naught save 'Chaos and old Night'
>   Can part you now from Tenniel.

These diffident disclaimers recognise the peculiar relation of text and pictures in the Alice books. . . . If there is one place in the world or out of it where vested rights ought not to be respected, it certainly is Wonderland. If Mr. [Peter] Newell and Mr. Rackham have something to add to our imperfect knowledge of that delectable country, they are benefactors. . . .

Whether anything has been added is not a question for the art critics at all. How do the new creations impress those who look at them as friends and not as samples of technique? . . . Tenniel won his reputation by political cartoons, Newell by illustrations of his own whimsical verses, Rackham by half droll, half uncanny designs for **Rip Van Winkle.** So, as might be expected, Tenniel's Wonderland is in general the most logical, Newell's the most fantastic, Rackham's the most unearthly. This can be seen in their embellishments of the very first paragraphs. Tenniel's White Rabbit is an English country squire. Newell's a half-distracted schoolmaster, Rackham's an apparition in a pearl-coloured frock-coat and ruffles. It is again to be seen in the different choice of subjects. Tenniel alone has drawn Alice at the moment of destiny when, picking up the bottle marked "Drink Me," she, like a prudent little girl, is turning it about to see if it happens to be marked "Poison" on the other side; Newell alone has drawn the three weird sisters, Elsie, Lacie and Tillie, at the bottom of their treacle

well; Rackham alone has drawn Alice at that remarkable crisis when she has nibbled the right-hand bit of mushroom and, shutting up suddenly like a telescope, has received "a violent blow underneath the chin," from her own foot. We see Tenniel at his best in the Duchess, Newell in the Mock Turtle, Rackham in the Caterpillar.

Peter Newell's snub-nosed housewife in a ruff is all very well in her way, but she is not a Duchess. Rackham's lady, with her high beak-nose, her ermine, ostrich plumes and false curls, is every inch a Duchess, probably a Dowager Duchess. As she appears in the Sixth Chapter there is little if any fault to find with her. She is just the woman to sit like a feminine field-marshal under the Cook's galling fire of saucepans, plates and dishes and take "no notice of them even when they hit her." She is just the woman to reply to Alice's confession that she did not know cats *could* grin, "They all can, and most of 'em do." She might, in fact, do all of the things recorded in Chapter Six. But Mr. Rackham must have forgotten Chapter Nine. That is the most charitable explanation. It is simply inconceivable that his Duchess could have said, "You can't think how glad I am to see you again, you dear old thing." His Duchess is austere. She could never have unbent and "tucked her arm affectionately into Alice's." It is the superiority of Tenniel's Duchess that she is no less convincing in her maudlin than in her morose mood. She is not refined or tactful in either. If, like Du Maurier's swell who mistook another duchess for the widow of a cheesemonger in the New Cut, we did not know her rank we might exclaim, "How she goes on to be sure!" As it is, like him, after he was set right, we admire "her aristocratic simplicity of manner." That is because we do know her for a Duchess.

The recipe for mock-turtle soup in the cook-book, and the allusions to "flappers" in the text are—except, of course, the unreported talks between author and illustrator—the only sources of information about the Mock Turtle's appearance. Tenniel made him a helpless, hopeless beast with plated carapace and plastron, scaly flippers or flappers and a mooncalf's head. Rackham's is much the same, only more delicate and anæmic, pensive and sentimental. But Newell had ideas of his own. Zoologically speaking, his Mock Turtle who "went to school in the sea" does belong to a marine species. It is a little hard to believe such a lumbering, blubbering monster capable of passing in "Mystery, ancient and modern, with Seaography; then Drawling—the drawling master was an old Conger-eel, that used to come once a week, *he* taught us Drawling, Stretching and Fainting in Coils." Tenniel's or Rackham's Mock Turtles, though not inspired scholars, can be imagined as obtaining high marks, even from the old Conger-eel. But they lack the one quality which is absolutely essential. Newell's is the only one of the three that would furnish really first-class mock-turtle soup, and this must be the deciding factor.

Mr. Rackham's Caterpillar is similarly the only caterpillar that corresponds strictly to the specifications. The author mentions only two facts about the Caterpillar's exterior: that his colour was blue and that his arms were folded. Even Tenniel ignored the folded arms in his design. This, however, is a minor point. The question is one of delineating a character. This Caterpillar is a perfect incarnation of incisive curiosity. His questions are far more disquieting than the Queen's tantrums. He is a subject worthy of Sargent's brush. It may be that Tenniel sketched him from behind because he felt himself unequal to more exacting portraiture. Newell has drawn a caterpillar with button eyes, a crest like a toothbrush, and an infantile expression. His is a caterpillar that could not possibly impress anybody. But Rackham's snuffy, loose-lipped, spectacled smoker wears the real air of authority. He cannot be imagined as ever turning into a butterfly or moth. If he turns into anything it will be a bookworm. His eyes are dim with study and introspection. He is probably of German extraction and his valedictory observation to Alice, "You'll get used to it in time," sounds like the answer to the Welträtsel.

And Alice herself? Wondering, gentle and considerate, even if she does speak of cats to the Mouse and of "din—" to the friends of the Whiting, she is too dear a child to be treated with anything but tenderness. Tenniel drew her as a little girl of his own time—forty years ago—in starched frock, white stockings and tiny, black strapped slippers. Newell kept the white stockings and much of the old-time quaintness, though his Alice has a thought too much aplomb. The really daring change made by Rackham is in bringing his little heroine down to date. Most of us doubtless will continue to love the old Alice best, but the modern little figure does bear one message of its own. It tells us that the gate of Wonderland has never been closed, that it never will be closed, and that to the children of the twentieth century, old and young, as to their children and their grandchildren, it is still given to eat now and then of the magic fruit of the Amfalula tree in whose boughs the Dinkey bird sings.

International Studio

SOURCE: A review of *Arthur Rackham's Book of Pictures,* in *International Studio,* Vol. LI, No. 204, February, 1914, p. 333.

[*Arthur Rackham's Book of Pictures*] is quite characteristic of the versatility and humour of its gifted maker. It contains between forty and fifty of his most elaborate tinted drawings, and nothing that is not ingenious and skilful to an extraordinary degree. Many of the plates show the most admirable side of the artist's work. It is impossible, indeed, to imagine anything more delightful in illustration than **On the Beach, The Broad Walk, Cupid's Alley, Butterflies**—the style in them is perfect.

Eleanor Farjeon

SOURCE: "Arthur Rackham: The Wizard at Home," in *St. Nicholas,* Vol. XLI, No. 5, March, 1914, pp. 385-91.

There have been three creators of *Rip Van Winkle.* The first, who was Washington Irving, created him with his pen; the second, who was Joseph Jefferson, created him with his personality; and the third, who is Arthur Rackham, created him with his brush. And all three owed much to another, far earlier, and unknown creator—the nameless imagination which, in many lands, through many ages, built up the haunted storehouse of lore and legend to which only the true imaginations of later ages possessed the key. Irving, Jefferson, and Rackham, all true imaginers in their different veins, have all held that key in their possession; and though it is of the third holder, only, that I am writing, it is for a particular reason impossible for me to think of him without thinking of the other two as well. For Joseph Jefferson was my grandfather, and *Rip,* in my family, is regarded as a household god by inheritance.

Rip was the first book to bring Arthur Rackham fame, and I doubt whether it had to pass through so severe a test at the hands of the qualified critics as at our hands, who judged it from a special personal standpoint. But we were captured instantly. There was never doubt that this dear vagabond figure of *Rip* in his tatterdemalion youth—this wild, pathetic figure of *Rip* in his lorn age—was *our* "Rip"; or that the red-roofed village under the haunted mountains was his village, or that the haunted mountains were the "Kaatskills" of Hendrik Hudson.

We knew Arthur Rackham's *Rip* before we knew Arthur Rackham, but it was inevitable that, after knowing the book, we should know the man. . . .

I had always had the impression, from the intimate inside knowledge of Fairy-land which his work betrayed, that Arthur Rackham was a kind of wizard; that he only pretended to call himself Arthur Rackham, and hobgoblins really hailed him by some more mystic name on stormy nights on Hampstead Heath, which is an easy broomstick ride from a certain little house in Chalcot Gardens. Acquaintance has not entirely allayed the suspicion. Arthur Rackham looks rather like a wizard—a wizard of the unmalicious order, who dabbles in sly, freakish, and delightful arts. He watches you from behind the Spectacles of Cunning, and there's a whimsical line in his face that can translate itself into the kindliest of smiles. He is light and spare and alert, so that I imagine his favorite form of transformation to be some kind of a bird. But these are matters I do not inquire into, in case he should turn me into a speckled toad.

If you know Arthur Rackham's fairy-land of books—if you know ancient Æsop and modern *Peter,* and their immortal equals, *Rip, Undine* and *Alice, Puck* and *Mother Goose;* if you know Grimm, who is better than painted gingerbread and striped sugar-sticks, and if you know the gods and giants and dwarfs and nymphs of the legendary Rhine—not only through the wonder-makers who first shaped them for our hearts, but also through the wonder-maker who has reshaped them for our eyes—then you really know as much of Arthur Rackham as can be told. But nowadays we cannot leave our wonder-makers alone; we must know how they live and where they live, and what they do when they are not weaving the spells that have enchained us.

You must not be disappointed to learn that this particular magician does not weave his particular spells underneath a hollow tree, in one of those tiny caverns with pillars and rafters of twisted roots which time and again in his books he has peopled for us with delicate elves. There is nothing disappointing about the little house in Chalcot Gardens. Outwardly it is not unsuited to the pages of fairy tale. It has a mellow red-and-brown charm, and is the kind of house that could very well have been built of gingerbread and candy. Behind the house is the kind of garden that makes me feel six years old again; a place where the grass and trees seem to preserve, in an atmosphere of quiet sunshine, a share of memories that are almost like expectations—it might be memories of a child they expect to come again. Some gardens have this air for me—I never quite know why, unless they resemble a garden I played in when I was six—and I am filled with momentary hope that I am the child they remember and expect. But this garden has its child, blue-eyed and golden-haired, green-frocked and deep in fancy. Her name is Barbara. If you want to find her, do not walk straight down the road, for that is the way to miss the house. It is a house that says "Come and find me" as it steps back a little in the corner of a curbed inclosure, secure from the common traffic of automobiles and motor-bicycles, things which Arthur Rackham has been heard to declare are at the root of most modern evils. With them he classes telephones and type-writers ("I would rather," he told me, "have a page of hand-writing I couldn't read than a type-written manuscript"); and he ought to include the Automatic Piano-Player that lives in his very beautiful unautomatic dining-room. But he must have music at any price, and he has confessed that he is incapable of playing common time with one hand and triple time with the other, so, for once, he has had to fall victim to a machine. I suppose he *has* been seen in a taxi in his day, but I am sure he would prefer to amble across London on a camel; and I know from experience that a magic carpet is kept in the house for personal use. . . .

[Rackham] is willing to talk, and does talk, well and definitely, about a multitude of subjects, with equal keenness and interest; but if you mention *Rip,* he will talk of Irving and Jefferson, rather than of Rackham. And it is interesting to hear *Rip's* last creator on his predecessors. Of my grandfather he has said:

> One feels it was he who made the character for all time the great living entity that it is. At least I, for one, very much doubt whether Irving's playful fiction or morality would have become immovably established—to the degree of a creed, a genuine local legend—if Jefferson hadn't given Rip the living personality that we now recognize him by. I think Rip one of the most remarkable of created characters. Created as the sheerest piece of pleasant moralizing, acknowledging, even, that it was cribbed from old-world sources, here is *Rip* as firmly fixed in the hearts of all good

Americans as any genuine myth. I can think of hardly another modern instance.

Personally, I think that among recent inventions *Peter Pan* might have lived as the same kind of local myth, if his author had not created two entirely different *Peters.* The *Peter* of the play is not the *Peter* of the book, and the play has so outdistanced the book in its power of appeal, that the name of *Peter Pan* now instantly calls to mind, not Kensington Gardens, but the Never-Never Land.

Yet it is impossible to say that the chance of a permanently haunted Kensington Gardens has quite been let slip. Arthur Rackham has many times put a fine imagination to the service of the finest imaginations that have set the earth aglow—he has created kingdoms of humorous goblins and fairies with rainbow-colored wings; of two-headed ogres with knotted clubs; of gnomes, and dragons, and witch-wives, and other shapes minute and mighty, fearsome and fair—but his magic never held so firm as when he took the Kensington *Peter* for his theme.

He had done marvels in the Catskills, and was yet to do marvels in the wood near Athens (which is really a wood in Warwickshire). He was to draw *Robin Goodfellow* (and I do not know who could draw *Robin Goodfellow* that had not really seen him). But when our wizard did marvels with fairy-land in London, he perhaps made *Peter* more inseparably his than any other of his creations.

Under the roots that the trees and plants send down into the earth he has fashioned for us an elfin realm so fantastic, so incomparable, so complete, that we can no longer doubt what we should find if, like the icing off a cake, we should slice the top layer off Kensington Gardens. And the seen has as much enchantment as the unseen, the tree-tops as much fairyhood as the tree-trunks, the colors of the Serpentine as much mystery as the glimmering fairy lights which it reflects.

When the wizard shows us the delicate webs of leafless branches traced against a wintry sky, when he paints evening light for us, or pale marbled clouds, or patterns upon water, or children and flowers as well as fairies in the Gardens—then he reveals a magic which Londoners may encounter day by day. And if, through years of apathy, we have grown numb to it, it is from Arthur Rackham that we may catch the angle of true vision again.

The Outlook

SOURCE: A review of *Arthur Rackham's Book of Pictures,* in *The Outlook,* Vol. 107, May 16, 1914, p. 134.

"In dealing with childish things," says Sir Arthur Quiller-Couch, "as in dealing with love or things divine, there are two stages of initiation." The first is all awe and seriousness, but it has "a knack of being taken for the higher; whereas it is, in truth, rawer and more elementary than the insight which, having taught you to adore, permits you also to smile, as a good husband may (because the understanding is perfect) 'chaff' his wife and at the same time love her more deeply than he ever did in the merely reverential days of courtship." Again he says: "The child himself, set between the mysterious and the absurd, is all the while severely practical. He wants to know how creation was managed; he wants (in the words of that half-forgotten American book 'Helen's Babies') to see the wheels go round. . . . Above all," concludes Sir Arthur, "the child declines the idea of a single Demiurge turning the marvels of the world from one great, lonely laboratory. . . . No, the Demiurge cannot possibly find time for it all. He must employ hosts of small, unseen workmen. . . . Therefore, even if there were no such beings as fairies, the children would have to invent them—pixies, nixies, gnomes, goblins, elves, kobolds, and the rest—to account for the marvels that are happening all the while, but specially while we sleep. How else can we explain toadstools, for instance?"

These sentiments are taken from Sir Arthur's Introduction to Mr. Rackham's book—a book which certainly ministers to this particular need of childhood. Mr. Rackham's delightful pictures are reproductions in color from watercolors, oils, and pastels of children, of scenes from fairy tales and classical mythology, of fantastic scenes and child-folk. Mr. Rackham's draughtsmanship is exquisite and his color schemes charming and restful.

The American Review of Reviews

SOURCE: "Fairy Tales in Picture," in *The American Review of Reviews,* Vol. XLIX, No. 6, June, 1914, p. 760.

Arthur Rackham, the well-known illustrator of fairy tales, shows in his picture, *The Sea-Serpent,* a little girl astride a great, green, frothing sea-monster. In her face are mingled terror and delight; a strand of seaweed has caught her bare foot; beneath, the white waves foam and flying fishes leap. To grown-ups this picture illustrates childhood's love for the unreal and the fantastic—for all the creatures of myth and fable that the mind can invent. Sir Arthur Quiller-Couch writes, in his introduction to Mr. Rackham's *Book of Pictures* for 1914, that the "child's heaven, like the child's earth, is a mixture of the mysterious and the indefinite, the practical and the absurd." And again: "Even if there were no such things as fairies, children would have to invent them—pixies, nixies, gnomes, goblins, elves, kobolds and the rest—to account for the marvels that are happening all the while, but especially while we are asleep. How else can we explain toadstools, for instance?"

The same thing is true in a measure of everyone, young or old, who possesses an imaginative temperament. Pictures carry them through the gates of the imagination to domains of wonder and delight where for the moment the mind is freed from the burden of reality. Arthur Rackham has been making picture-books for a long time. One remembers his exquisite illustrations for *Æsop's Fables, Peter Pan,* and *Alice in Wonderland.* His "book" for 1914 gives reproductions in color of forty-four pictures in oils, pastels, and watercolors. There are little people and fairies, wonderful trees, dryads, plain folks and other "folks" who stepped off the point of the artist's pencil for their first entrance into the world. One might well call their creator a "Barrie" of the brush, who has found Peter Pan's delectable land and remembered it for us.

Clara T. Mac Chesney

SOURCE: "The Value of Fairies: What Arthur Rackham Has Done to Save Them for the Children of the Whole World," in *The Craftsman,* Vol. 27, December, 1914, pp. 248-59.

Can any people afford to sacrifice the fairies? Quite apart from the great use which fairy folk are in making child-life rich with romance, do we not need the fairy spirit to stimulate all progress in the really living arts? . . .

Happily we do not need to plead with our children to make room for the fairies in their day-dreams and twilight hours. For little folks still have the vivid imagination that fills the so-called inanimate world with mysterious life. That is why a perfectly natural little child is never lonely. The woods, the fields, the sands of the sea shore, the winds blown from far countries, even the stars and always the gardens are trembling with life, with infinite romance for really simple normal childhood. . . .

I was told in a recent talk with Arthur Rackham, the greatest living painter of child romance, that, strangely enough, he was a city boy, but being a city boy in London is not the same as being a city boy in New York or Chicago, and one can readily imagine how Arthur Rackham must have been led, when he was a child, through the parks, down the shady streets, into some of the strange old living spots of this wonderful city. Possibly he played along the bank of the Thames or in some mysterious corner of Hyde Park. In some garden place he must surely have found the inspiration that must easily touch the soul of man if it is to be reborn into permanent beauty.

This wonderful, naive imagination which dominates Rackham's art today surely found stimulus in some spiritual flowering spot when he was too young to question and just young enough to believe. In facing Rackham's marvelous, fanciful art you feel always that he is reproducing the quivering, tender beauty that dominates only youth. His is not the mature art save in exquisite technique; it is rather the fine whimsical exuberance of unquenchable youth that is not atrophied because it was never suppressed.

From Peter Pan in Kensington Gardens, *written by J. M. Barrie. Illustrated by Arthur Rackham.*

First of all, he told me that he loved to draw animals. This we can readily understand, for children are really in their sympathies much nearer to animals than to people. There are fewer barriers between childhood and those real friends of childhood known as pets. Later Mr. Rackham went to night school to study drawing and in an amazingly short time he began to exhibit at the Royal Academy, the Royal Institute of Painting and in various other large London exhibitions.

I liked finding Mr. Rackham gay and humorous. All people who know the hearts of little folks should have brightness and rich humor. Life is giving these people so much more than to most mortals that surely a very real and permanent joy is theirs. Real modesty I should have expected from this painter of the fairy world. . . .

The world over, Arthur Rackham really stands alone. His imagination seems to know no bounds. His sense of humor is unique, not only for children but in the animal world, and often he displays a delightful tenderness and a sympathy with the weaker forms of life, as in **"The Rescue,"** where some tiny elves are helping a fly to

escape from the clutches of a fearsome spider. In summing up Mr. Rackham's work you realize that in dealing with human nature, he is a gentle satirist. Ingenuity, great sensitiveness and refinement are inherent in all his work as in all the fairy reaches of his personality. In seeing him in a workshop, he is essentially a man whose work gives one vividly the impression of spontaneity, yet one also with careful attention for detail in work. Here in America we know his illustrations better possibly than those of any other English draughtsman, we know well his **"Undine,"** his *Alice in Wonderland, Rip Van Winkle, Grimm's Fairy Tales, Gulliver's Travels. The Craftsman* readers will recall a presentation of some of Mr. Rackham's illustrations for the Wagner operas, showing a very splendid understanding of the philosophy of this great musician and the symbolism of the great gods of the Valhalla, an extraordinary contrast with the *Midsummer Night's Dream* pictures which are so fantastic, so the product of delicate whimsicality.

The latest work of Mr. Rackham that has come to America is his illustration of **"Mother Goose".** . . . It is hard to imagine any but a child presenting Mother Goose with such sympathy and understanding. It is the Mother Goose of our baby days, dramatic, fearsome, amusing and wonderfully stimulating. Mr. Rackham's art is difficult to compare with any work in America. Howard Pyle possibly has most nearly suggested him, and yet Howard Pyle is really not an American Rackham because first of all we think of him as a colorist. He had the fairy imagination, but lacking the naïve quality which is so essential in Rackham's work. In the French illustrators who rank highest today, Forain, Steinlein, Caran d'ache, Huard, there is not a trace of the fantastic genius of Rackham.

I was greatly interested in Rackham's studio. It was of the ordinary size, with both side and top windows. Its walls were stained a light brown and it contained a few good rugs and pieces of furniture, among them a bookcase filled mostly with illustrations, of which he has an interesting collection, all so exquisitely fresh and in good order. A bar ran across the room from which hung a trapeze. He looked at it smilingly. "I do not use it as much as I used to. It's really for my little daughter now."

There were fine drawings on the walls, one or two of his wife's pictures, but no special studio furniture, such as one finds in the workshop of the unknown. The center of interest in this room is the work-table. Here are being conceived and brought into existence the innumerable fantasies which delight and amuse Mr. Rackham's admirers. The table is adjustable in height and angle, unusually small for a work-table. Over it hung, on a level with the eye, an electric light.

"But you do not work at night?" I said.

"Not much," he answered dubiously. "Altogether too much," his wife answered quickly.

I was interested in his method of work. As one would imagine, he does not work with labored preliminary studies. "I dash off an idea," he said, "which comes to me and often very vaguely. I build as I go on, and the idea develops as I work. I always, however, plan beforehand and always use models."

In talking with Mr. Rackham, I felt him to be a man of the richest interest in life, with a great love of good music and a wide-reaching understanding of the art of his day. "Strangely enough Uccello's 'Battlepiece' and Francesca's 'Baptism' and 'Adoration' are my favorites among old paintings," he told me. "Fra Lippo Lippi, yes, all the Italian School, and the Flemish. I often study Michelangelo's 'Entombment,' and all the Holbeins and Albert Durer's wood engravings." These old friends he spoke of with great enthusiasm, as he did of the big modern men of power—a most charming personality indeed, eager, kind, not unlike some of the humorous gnomes he is so fond of producing—a man whom children must of necessity love as they have loved and thriven by his most valuable and stimulating contribution to the art of his day.

Julian Garner

SOURCE: "The Wizardry of Rackham," in *International Studio,* Vol. LXXVII, No. 314, July, 1923, pp. 338-42.

An artist is not forced to stay in the realm of reality to be convincing. There are those who have made an imaginary world more vivid to us than an actual place. But what is actual and what is real seem to grow more debatable every day, and science encroaches on the prerogatives of the imagination. The existence of fairies is even defended with spirit, and this long discredited little people seems to be in danger of being incorporated into the body politic as a kind of fifth estate. If this is to be, then Arthur Rackham may declare himself to be an explorer rather than a creator, and his pictures of fairies may be filed among state archives as the work of the official artist of the fairy realm. However, whether Rackham believes in fairies is not so important to most of us as the fact that he has breathed into his elves and gnomes, his ogres and witch-wives the breath of life, so that they seem to be more real to us than, say, the inhabitants of Tibet, or even those residing in the street next to our own. . . .

In 1900 he made drawings for Grimm's *Fairy Tales* and his reputation was established. He had created a world of his own, and an assemblage gathered to watch the events that took place there. Whether that assemblage was and is largely composed of children is hard to say. His has always been an art which grown-ups, too, have enjoyed, and yet his pictures, designed for boys and girls, have not suffered the sad fate of being appreciated only by those who are no longer young. Perhaps Rackham's children are most appreciated by older persons, for youth does not know its own charm, while children themselves like his fairies and giants and the whole cosmogony of fairyland which he shows them so vividly.

The richness of Rackham's imagery can be appreciated by only those who have an inborn love of the fanciful. He is not to be classed with imaginative artists because he takes fairy tales for his subjects, as one critic rather naïvely affirmed several years ago. The quality of imagination is not a matter of choice of material, and your faithful realist cannot possess himself of a rich fancy by starting to paint fairies instead of cows. It is in Rackham's treatment of the subject that his invention is displayed. The remarkable thing about him is that he seems to have an inexhaustible supply of inventiveness, which is responsible for the variety of his work, for its spontaneity and for the freshness of its character.

Although Rackham is city born and bred, his spirit seems to be more at home in the country. Trees and hills and sky and flowers are his loves, and also animals. Into this world he introduces children and fairies, but he leaves grown-ups out. His children are different from those of other artists. Some of them look as if they might be distinctly related to Kate Greenaway's, but it is a family resemblance only, for they have a sturdy air of individuality that admits of no mistake as to who portrayed them. They do not seem to be children of today rather than of the past—eternal children, rather; boys and girls whom our grandfathers would have liked and who will certainly be understood by our grandchildren.

Apollo

SOURCE: A review of *The Vicar of Wakefield,* in *Apollo,* Vol. X, No. 59, November, 1929, pp. 293-94.

Mr. Arthur Rackham's hand has lost nothing of its cunning, his mind nothing of its whimsical imaginativeness. In some ways these illustrations of the **Vicar of Wakefield** are better than anything he has done, not excluding his **Peter Pan.** The drawings are not merely decorative in colour and design, and not merely well drawn, but the characters they introduce have also charmingly rendered individualities.

George Macy

SOURCE: "Arthur Rackham and *The Wind in the Willows,*" in *The Horn Book Magazine,* Vol. XVI, No. 3, May-June, 1940, pp. 153-58.

We sat in his studio for hours, in a desultory discussion of other books he might do. I am sure now that it was in a desultory fashion that I said: "What about **The Wind in the Willows?**"

Immediately a wave of emotion crossed his face; he gulped; started to say something, turned his back on me and went to the door for a few minutes. Then he came back and said that he had for many years been trying to persuade an English publisher to let him illustrate **The Wind in the Willows.** He had been asked by Kenneth Grahame, nearly thirty years ago, to illustrate that book; and had for all those years deeply regretted his refusal. . . .

Once these water-colors are given to the world, it will be seen with what affection Mr. Rackham made these pictures. I think them the finest pictures ever made for **The Wind in the Willows** because I think Mr. Rackham has affectionately personalized the little animals, more affectionately and therefore more effectively than did Mr. Shepard. You will find in these water-colors all the soft and glowing tints which are in the best of the Rackham drawings, all the scrupulous attention to detail, all the superb draftsmanship evidenced in each firm strong stroke of the pen.

Robert Lawson

SOURCE: "The Genius of Arthur Rackham," in *The Horn Book Magazine,* Vol. XVI, No. 3, May-June, 1940, pp. 147-51.

The appreciation of Rackham's genius has suffered, I think, by its complete perfection. All his drawings appear so polished, so finished, so graceful, that many fail to realize the great strength and firm knowledge that underlie this seeming ease. This would be especially explainable by the period which we are now enduring and, let us hope, passing through.

I often hear people say, "Oh yes, Rackham. But his work is too *sweet.* His color is not real. His drawings lack strength, they lack guts!"

Poor blind people, brought up in a time when the symbol of strength is the bludgeon and the trenchant skill of the rapier is unknown. Poor dazzled eyes that have never seen a Chinese painting, Nantucket moors in November, a Persian rug, or a world swept into complete harmony by a sunset glow or the cool blue wash of moonlight.

It is understandable, but very sad, that in a time when Strength is indicated by bulging muscles (in the wrong places), distorted figures and a sign-painter's technique, the incisive power of Rackham's pen should be completely missed. That in a time when the ill-matched juxtaposition of all the rawest pigments is hailed as Color, the lovely harmonies of Rackham's tones should go unnoticed.

In an age when the roaring, lumbering efforts of artists to compose strikingly are so blatantly obvious, it is not surprising that Rackham's flowing skill in arrangement is laughed off as Weakness.

Arthur Rackham's guts were where they belonged, in their proper anatomical location. They were not smeared on canvas or the walls of Post Offices.

More important than any technical attributes were his point of view, his understanding, and his unfailing sense of fitness and beauty. It is a dangerous thing to say in these times, and one most easily misinterpreted, but Rackham was in his work a Gentleman.

This may be, in many eyes, a complete condemnation of him and his works. But in the quiet corners of our noisy and complex modern existence there are thousands of minds that cherish the glimpses of quiet beauty and of a clean and color-suffused world which his sensitive genius gave us. As the temporary fads and madnesses wane and blow away, his high repute will remain clear and unsullied in the hearts of our generation and of many to come. . . .

For make no mistake, Arthur Rackham was an *illustrator.*

In spite of the great individuality of his work it was always in its proper place, which is to carry out and make visible the ideas and moods of the author.

Washington Irving's **Rip Van Winkle,** for example. Here, perhaps, the gnomes and gnarled trees might be labelled

"Rackham," but simply because no one has ever done gnomes and gnarled trees as Rackham did. But Rip *is* Rip. The little houses of the Hudson Valley towns *are* Hudson Valley houses of the period, the Kaatskills *are* the Kaatskills and the moods and color and details are Washington Irving's vision enlarged and enriched by the sure touch of a true Master Illustrator.

For many years *The Wind in the Willows* has been a subject of controversy among illustrators I have known. Who could do it? It has never been done as it should be done, with all due respect to Ernest Shepard (and all disrespect to the publishers who gave the United States a cheap and horribly mangled version of his delightful drawings).

In these discussions the name of Rackham seldom entered, I don't know why, except that the perfect solution of any problem is always the last one thought of.

Arthur Rackham has done *The Wind in the Willows* and there is no longer any question. It was, I understand, his last work, and what a fine way that was to wind up things! I have seen only one small reproduction of one of the drawings, but a single glance has assured me that here was the man. The Gilbert of Kenneth Grahame has found his Sullivan, another perfect collaboration has been achieved.

The other day I was re-enjoying Rackham's drawings for Milton's *Comus* which have always puzzled me somewhat. For in this book there are what seem to me to be some of his very finest drawings and some of his worst. Mind you, when I say his worst, I mean *his* worst, which still leaves them very high up.

This day the signature on one of these drawings suddenly caught my eye, "Arthur Rackham, 1914." Perhaps that ominous date explained this strange unevenness. 1914—the year the world that Rackham knew and that knew and loved him burst into flame. The year that the youth of his world was plunged into mud and filth and hate that would always cloud their eyes to the gentle beauty of work like his.

Perhaps an era was dying then and perhaps Arthur Rackham knew it and for once his sure hand faltered.

May Massee

SOURCE: "Developments of the Twentieth Century: Arthur Rackham," in *Illustrators of Children's Books, 1744-1945,* Bertha E. Mahony, Louise Payson Latimer, and Beulah Folmsbee, eds., The Horn Book Inc., 1947, pp. 222-23.

One day Jimmie Daugherty was talking about artists and he said, "Why, Rackham was the lyric genius of the English people." Of course he was. His drawings are lyric poems in line. They range from the grace of a young birch in springtime to the gnarled strength and

eerie root caverns of an age-old beech tree. The earth in its loveliness was his to show, and somehow every drawing was true to the material form of his subject but so imbued with the spirit that his landscapes sing and his people walk the earth in beauty.

A study of the faces he drew proves him both psychologist and philosopher. No drawing is too small to show the character of his model. He knew every line that could be etched on a human face and he drew the lines as carefully and as truly as Nature herself. That is why one can go back to his drawings again and again; every study will reveal more understanding, more kindly and generous humor, and more vivid sense of the things that are unseen. He was equally at home in the best of this world, in the world of faëry and in the world of small animals. He illustrated many books and brought beauty and happy days to thousands of fortunate people who own them.

C. S. Lewis

SOURCE: "Renaissance," in *Surprised by Joy: The Shape of My Early Life,* Geoffrey Bles, 1955, pp. 73-83.

[The] long winter broke up in a single moment. . . . It was as if the Arctic itself, all the deep layers of secular ice, should change not in a week nor in an hour, but instantly, into a landscape of grass and primroses and orchards in bloom, deafened with bird songs and astir with running water. I can lay my hand on the very moment; there is hardly any fact I know so well, though I cannot date it. Someone must have left in the schoolroom a literary periodical: *The Bookman,* perhaps, or the *Times Literary Supplement.* My eye fell upon a headline and a picture, carelessly, expecting nothing. A moment later, as the poet says, "The sky had turned round."

What I had read was the words *Siegfried and the Twilight of the Gods.* What I had seen was one of Arthur Rackham's illustrations to that volume. . . . Pure "Northernness" engulfed me: a vision of huge, clear spaces hanging above the Atlantic in the endless twilight of Northern summer, remoteness, severity . . . and almost at the same moment I knew that I had met this before, long, long ago (it hardly seems longer now) in *Tegner's Drapa,* that Siegfried (whatever it might be) belonged to the same world as Balder and the sunward-sailing cranes. And with that plunge back into my own past there arose at once, almost like heartbreak, the memory of Joy itself, the knowledge that I had once had what I had now lacked for years, that I was returning at last from exile and desert lands to my own country; and the distance of the *Twilight of the Gods* and the distance of my own past Joy, both unattainable flowed together into a single, unendurable sense of desire and loss, which suddenly became one with the loss of the whole experience, which, as I now stared round that dusty schoolroom like a man recovering from unconsciousness, had already vanished, had eluded me at the very moment when I could first say *It is*. And at once I knew (with fatal knowledge) that to "have it again" was the supreme and only important object of desire. . . .

That summer our cousin H. who was now married, asked us to spend some weeks with her on the outskirts of Dublin, in Dundrum. There, on her drawing-room table, I found the very book which had started the whole affair and which I had never dared to hope I should see, *Siegfried and the Twilight of the Gods* illustrated by Arthur Rackham. His pictures, which seemed to me then to be the very music made visible, plunged me a few fathoms deeper into my delight. I have seldom coveted anything as I coveted that book; and when I heard that there was a cheaper edition at fifteen shillings (though the sum was to me almost mythological) I knew I could never rest till it was mine. I got it in the end, largely because my brother went shares with me, purely through kindness, as I now see and then more than half suspected, for he was not enslaved by the Northernness. With a generosity which I was even then half ashamed to accept, he sank in what must have seemed to him a mere picture-book seven and sixpence for which he knew a dozen better uses.

Walter Starkie

SOURCE: "Childhood" and "Dublin and London 1917-1918," in *Scholars and Gypsies: An Autobiography,* University of California Press, 1963, pp. 3-27, 158-94.

One day, when I was with [my] Aunt Edith in her studio, she introduced me to a strange wizened man with goggle spectacles, who, she said, would tell me all about fairies and elves. I thought he was a goblin when I saw him in his shabby blue suit and carpet slippers, hopping about the studio with a palette on one arm, waving a paint-brush in his hand. After presenting me to the painter my aunt said: "It's your turn, Arthur, to take my nephew under your wing. I'm dead beat." I did not know at that time that Arthur Rackham was already engaged to my aunt and that they would get married in the following year, 1903. "You may call him Uncle Arthur already," said my aunt as she handed the painter a shilling which he was to spend on a bun and a glass of milk for me.

My new uncle took me on many exciting journeys through London, but the most enjoyable days were those when Arthur Rackham allowed me to accompany him on a painting expedition. We would sally forth early on a sunny morning and my uncle, loaded with all his paraphernalia of paints, paint-brushes and easel, reminded me of one of the kobolds I had read about in Andrew Lang's *Blue Fairy Book;* but when we were installed in Kensington Gardens and the painter had armed himself with his palette and his paint-brush, he became in my eyes a wizard who with one touch of his magic wand would people my imagination with elves, gnomes and leprechauns. He would make me gaze fixedly at one of the majestic trees with massive trunk and tell me about

Grimm's fairy tales, which he had illustrated, and about the little men who blew their horns in elfland. He would say that under the roots of that tree the little men had their dinner and churned the butter they extracted from the sap of the tree. He would also make me see queer animals and birds in the branches of the tree and a little magic door below the trunk, which was the entrance to Fairyland. He used also to tell me stories of the primitive religion of man which, in his opinion, was the cult of the tree; but he made my blood run cold when he told me of the punishment meted out to those who injured trees. This consisted in impaling the culprit by the navel to the trunk and winding his guts round and round. And he told me to warn any little boy I noticed cutting the bark of a tree of the punishment that would be inflicted upon him for his barbarism. . . .

No two personalities could be in greater antithesis than my Aunt Edith and Arthur Rackham. My aunt quizzical, ironic, imaginative like the Irish; my Uncle Arthur prim, precise and very English in manner, in spite of his bohemianism and his elfish kinks. Aunt Edith always did her best to shock him. He knew that she expected him to react according to pattern, and he would do so, but he would cock his head like a jackdaw, and his eyes would twinkle through his goggles. . . .

During [a] stay in London I spent most of my time with Arthur Rackham, and I used to sit in his studio reading while he went on silently and patiently with his painting. I looked upon him as the only truly happy man I had yet come across because he was absorbed in his work to the exclusion of everything else, and even the grim war news and the air raids left him untroubled. In addition to his detachment he possessed an innate stoicism which made him endure austerity without complaining. Nevertheless, no one could be more thoughtful and good-natured in his concern for the comfort of others. His kindliness and broad-mindedness made him very popular among other artists.

Derek Hudson

SOURCE: "Arthur Rackham: The Gentle Humorist," in *The Connoisseur,* Vol. 166, No. 667, September, 1967, pp. 19-21.

Of all the English illustrators who flourished in the Edwardian hey-day, Arthur Rackham is . . . by far the best known. . . .

Rackham absorbed a wide range of influences, from Beardsley and Keene in England to Dürer and Menzel in Germany; Japanese and Persian designs also affected him, and his work at one time had a passing flavour of Art Nouveau. His genius for the fanciful and grotesque emerged only gradually from a mass of conventional journalism and illustration, but his *Ingoldsby Legends* (1898) and his *Grimm's Fairy Tales* (1900) were both significant portents. He said that he had 'a very thin time' during the Boer War, but in 1903 his marriage to

Edyth Starkie, herself a gifted artist, gave him the encouragement he needed to follow his imaginative bent. *Rip Van Winkle* (1905) established him as the outstanding contemporary illustrator, and the drawings were successfully exhibited at the Leicester Galleries, the first of many such occasions. Henceforth, Rackham had things all his own way.

Peter Pan in Kensington Gardens (1906) was perhaps his greatest triumph, which was exploited in a limited and a trade edition, in American and French editions, and eventually in the twelve enlarged plates of the *Peter Pan Portfolio.* In tackling *Alice in Wonderland* (1907), Rackham was on more controversial ground, but over the years the drawings have established themselves as acceptable alternatives to Tenniel. About *A Midsummer Night's Dream* (1908) and *Undine* (1909) there were no reservations; earlier books like *Ingoldsby* and *Grimm* were profitably revised and re-issued; and Rackham gave deep thought to his Wagner illustrations for *The Rhinegold and the Valkyrie* and *Siegfried and the Twilight of the Gods* (1910-11). Unusual knowledge of the texts was always evident in all that he undertook.

There is no need to attempt a catalogue of the many books that followed, but *A Christmas Carol* (1915) makes one regret that Rackham did not illustrate more Dickens, while *The Vicar of Wakefield* (1929), *The Compleat Angler* (1931) (he had a great aptitude for riverside scenes), Hans Andersen's *Fairy Tales* (1932), and Poe's *Tales of Mystery and Imagination* (1935) all have their discerning admirers. The work of his later years showed a new freshness of colour, evidenced in his sketches for the scenery of a stage production of *Hansel and Gretel* (1933), and most notably in his last commission, *The Wind in the Willows,* posthumously published in 1940, a book which he had always longed to illustrate. Meticulous craftsmanship served him to the end; his last drawing was that of Rat and Mole loading their boat for the picnic; he had forgotten to include the oars, and, though greatly exhausted, he insisted on adding them. Rackham died soon afterwards, on 6 September, 1939.

He influenced Max Reinhardt and Walt Disney. Did his preoccupation with trees and their roots also influence Graham Sutherland, one wonders? What is certain is that this gentle, modest man has inspired the affection of thousands, who have owed their first artistic impressions to his dedicated craftsmanship and poetic integrity.

Selma G. Lanes

SOURCE: "Rackham and Sendak: Childhood through Opposite Ends of the Telescope," in *Down the Rabbit Hole: Adventures & Misadventures in the Realm of Children's Literature,* Atheneum, 1971, pp. 67-78.

One imagines [Rackham] taking the measure of the work he was to illustrate with professional detachment, much as a tailor might size up the idiosyncrasies of figure in a prospective customer. He then applied his considerable skill as an illustrator and fantasist to precisely those places which best suited his own gifts. The author's words stood or fell entirely on their own merits. They were of interest to Rackham only as prods to his pictorial muse. The narrative high points as well were strictly the author's concern. As an illustrator, Rackham felt free to let his fancy carry him where it would. Thus he often chose to illustrate the [unillustratable], or to rescue from oblivion words the reader had most likely never noticed. From Dickens's *A Christmas Carol* he plucked the line "The air was filled with phantoms, wandering hither and thither in restless haste and moaning as they went." And he was one of the few illustrators of that particular tale who avoided the panorama of the Cratchit family's Christmas dinner as a rich opportunity for displaying his graphic invention. He was an illustrator propelled to his drawing board by phrases. The five words "taught them to fly kites," entirely expendable to the narration of Washington Irving's *Rip Van Winkle,* occasioned one of Rackham's most evocative illustrations for a commission that ranks with his best work.

Rackham's charm lay in the very adult matter-of-factness—the emotional detachment, perhaps—with which he went at each task. At their best, his entirely convincing, independent illustrations add considerable weight to the tale in hand. Yet, where the picture-book artist attempts to weave a oneness of spirit between illustration and text—in the process making a new and richer whole—an artist like Rackham cheerfully accepted the independent domains of words and pictures. His illustrations represented a kind of bonus, a gratuitous accompaniment in a separate medium to whatever work they adorned. Often, as in *Peter Pan in Kensington Gardens* or *Rip Van Winkle,* they were inserted as independent folios either at the book's end or in suites during its unfolding.

"Court painter to King Oberon and Queen Titania," as he was called by one admirer of his work for Shakespeare's *Midsummer Night's Dream,* Rackham could render entirely believable the most improbable scenes by pinning them firmly to elements of everyday reality. In his illustration for *Aladdin and His Wonderful Lamp*— a depiction of the vendor's cry "New lamps for old!"— we have no choice but to believe wholeheartedly in the wily lamp-seller's existence at precisely the place and moment depicted. Who could doubt the truth of that marvelous striped turban, the clothes so convincingly rumpled and those inspired Turkish slippers, at once Arabian Nights exotic and realistically well-worn. The conception is so natural, so precise in its mundane details, that we are almost willing to discount imagination as having had a part in its creation. Rackham was simply there and recorded the scene from life. . . .

That Rackham held in deep affection the material things of this world cannot be denied. He had what amounted to an obsession with fabrics—their texture and design— and could render them with a feeling akin to love. . . . Rackham could use ten different, beautifully realized fabrics in a single illustration and still keep us interested in the picture as a whole. Yet that whole, oddly enough, had little substantive content. Like a vision or a dream, it is merely a crystal-clear evocation of a disembodied magical moment.

By richly adorning scenes of fantasy with the furnishings of everyday middle-class English life, he could make them totally believable. He once referred to fairy tales written down as "consigned to cold print." His forte was breathing life into bits and pieces of that cold print as they struck his illustrator's fancy. He had a passion for oddments of crockery (the most memorable part of his depiction of the Mad Hatter's tea party in *Alice in Wonderland* is the Hatter's exquisite tea service); for the dressing gowns and slippers of old men (hardly a book he illustrated escaped having at least one dressing-gown scene—even *Peter Pan in Kensington Gardens*); and for cozy English interiors replete with rugs, quilts and bric-a-brac. Many find in Rackham a broad streak of philistinism, yet his logic worked: clothe a fairy being in a material real enough to touch and she, by extension, can be touched; she exists. At his magical best, he *was* the magical best, as when he uncovered Fairyland be-

neath the English countryside or lent enchantment to Kensington Gardens or Hans Christian Andersen's garret. What did it matter that his fairies were as industrious as the English working class or that they were engaged in the same sort of mundane activities—selling produce, winding yarn, mending clothes? (If he were drawing today, they would probably be found huddled by the "telly"). He makes other, extra-terrestrial worlds exist for us, children and adults alike, and that is what really matters.

George T. McWhorter

SOURCE: "Arthur Rackham: The Search Goes On," in *The Horn Book Magazine,* Vol. XLVIII, No. 1, February, 1972, pp. 82-7.

Modest Arthur Rackham would undoubtedly have blushed had he known the handsome prices his works would fetch in today's book market. For those who delight in the deft imagery of the gifted English illustrator, this inflation is taken as a matter of course. In the last three years the appeal of his art has become even greater. His early works are being avidly sought—a testimony to his solid position among the ranks of the great. In reply to a letter from a collector (July, 1936) Rackham wrote: "I fear collecting my early work can hardly reach the scale of philately, but I trust that when found it will be as innocent—my work I mean."

Bertram Rota, in a fine tribute to Arthur Rackham [in *Antiques International,* 1966], discusses the early collections of George L. Lazarus, Sarah Briggs Latimore, and Grace Clark Haskell, observing: "The well has not yet run dry. . . . Unrecorded printings may yet be found and bring a sense of discovery." Appropriately enough, the eagle eye of Mr. George Lawson of the firm of Bertram Rota, Ltd., noticed an unrecorded publication, which predates by seven years the earliest known book to be published with illustrations by Arthur Rackham. Crona Temple's *The Ferryman's Boy and Other Stories* (1887) contains five full-page illustrations, four of which bear the unmistakable cipher of Arthur Rackham. They are "innocent"—as Mr. Rackham hoped they might be. . . .

Only after Arthur Rackham had become famous was he free to express his individuality. His penchant for polka dots, his personification of natural forces, and his omnipresent humor then became noticeable. To be sure, in the beginning there had been hack work. During his early career he worked for the *Westminster Gazette,* which featured Zoo guides, National Gallery guides, and travel guides. His duties were not unlike those of a roving reporter, who is anxious to succeed but always looks ahead to the time when he might select his own assignments and commissions.

Rackham's earliest published work (of which *The Ferryman's Boy and Other Stories* is a prime example) was conscientious and acceptable—at least for the standards

From Alice's Adventures in Wonderland, *wrtten by Lewis Carroll. Illustrated by Arthur Rackham.*

at which it aimed. But he certainly had no illusions about it and, in later years, tended to dismiss it as unimportant. "Anthony Hope himself [writes Mr. Rackham] hadn't a copy of *The Dolly Dialogues'* first edition, of which probably 99 hundredths went into the wastepaper basket in a few weeks." In the early days, however, Rackham characteristically overcame the drudgery of sketching—for travel guides and family magazines—with humor. Tinged at times with philosophical resignation, his humor was never bitter, and it never left him.

The ever-present sketchbooks were filled with character studies which delineated his search for a mastery of caricature. Those who have attempted to reduce a complex design to its simplest components will appreciate the discipline he underwent to produce convincing caricatures. One need only review the fantastic sketches of Leonardo da Vinci to offer honest rebuttal to those critics who deplored the exaggerated noses and limbs of Rackham's creations. As his individuality grew, his draftsmanship evolved and improved—down to the final stroke in *The Wind in the Willows.*

By 1896, with the illustration of *The Zankiwank & the Bletherwitch,* the Rackham drolleries were an established entity even though they embodied a superficial acknowledgment of the languid aesthetic influence of the previous decades. With the rise of Art Nouveau . . . Rackham assimilated the best qualities of the movement and triumphed. William Morris himself would not have been ashamed of the border designs with which Arthur Rackham decorated the pages of *Irish Fairy Tales* (1920). By 1900, *Fairy Tales of the Brothers Grimm* brought him resounding success and made him a force in the art world. However, his undisputed coming of age dates from the 1905 *Rip Van Winkle,* after which he gained the privilege of selecting his own commissions for the remainder of his eventful life. The rest is legend.

An artist's milieu might include Edgar Guest and lavender sachets or a guru and folk rock. But these influences will always be secondary to the true artist, who separates the topical from the timeless, working subjectively and even impulsively. In retrospect, Arthur Rackham's impulses, tuned to a disciplined pitch through mastery of his tools, have given us an astonishing parade of timeless delights. His works have the curious ability to create nostalgia, even if we view them for the first time.

With respect to Rackham's views on philately, those of us who cherish his illustrations cannot help but approach the collecting field with intensity. The fact remains that the incomparable draftsmanship which gave us *Rip Van Winkle, Peter Pan, A Midsummer Night's Dream,* and *Siegfried and the Twilight of the Gods* had its growing pains in the "innocent" line drawings of such early works as the newly discovered *Ferryman's Boy and Other Stories.* It is to be hoped that other forgotten essays will be discovered and added to the long list of authentic Rackham works.

Kenneth Clark

SOURCE: "An Edwardian Childhood," in *Another Part of the Wood: A Self-Portrait,* Harper & Row, Publishers, 1974, pp. 1-42.

The two most famous collections—those of Hans Andersen and the Brothers Grimm—contain so much that is painful and terrifying. Perhaps the born storyteller (like Dickens) feels impelled to hold his hearer's attention by frightening him, and the teller of children's tales, knowing that his audience is fickle and fidgety, lays on the horrors more abundantly. Or do the majority of people really like being frightened?

Perhaps there are some less alarming stories in Grimm, but I did not dare to open them on account of Arthur Rackham's illustrations. This quiet, gentle man of genius certainly had a vein of *schadenfreude* (what is now misleadingly described as sadism) and took an intense delight in scraggy fingers. I sometimes caught sight of his drawings, before I was on my guard, and they stamped on my imagination images of terror that troubled me for years. Many people have told me that they had the same experience as children. I wonder if anyone ever told Rackham.

Christa Kamenetsky

SOURCE: "Arthur Rackham and the Romantic Tradition: The Question of Polarity and Ambiguity," in *Children's Literature: Annual of the Modern Language Association Seminar on Children's Literature and the Children's Literature Association,* Vol. 6, 1977, pp. 115-29.

The question of identity has puzzled many critics of Arthur Rackham. Judging by the many contradictory essays written about his work, he still appears to be an artist of various styles that escape a definite classification in the history of the English graphic tradition. Was Rackham a Victorian artist or was he a Romantic visionary? [In *Down the Rabbit Hole*] Selma Lanes pointed out Rackham's philistine middle-class tendencies. Although she did not deny his magic in uncovering the fairyland beneath the countryside, she underscored to a greater extent his emotional detachment, his "matter-of-factness," and his affection for detail, texture, and elaborate design in "cozy English interiors replete with rugs, quilts and bric-a-brac." [In *Illustrating Children's Books*] Henry Pitz felt that Rackham's drawings had more "conviction" than those of Caldecott and Greenaway and that he was "English to the very core." This was also Derek Hudson's view [in *Arthur Rackham: His Life and His Work*], who saw him as close to his British "Cockney origins." Eleanor Farjeon [in "Arthur Rackham: The Wizard at Home"], on the other hand, saw in him an artist capable of transporting the commonplace into a sphere of the imagination, a romantic "wizard" bringing to life a world of fairies, elves, and dwarfs.

How do we reconcile such differing opinions, which

emphasize the realistic as well as the imaginative perspectives of Rackham's work? Margery Darrell [in *Once Upon a Time: The Fairy World of Arthur Rackham*] came to the conclusion that in his "strange mix of magic and materialism" lay the very key to the credibility of his work. "Perhaps it was his very worldliness that made his drawings so believable," she suggested.

Without attempting to minimize the British influences upon his work, we will proceed to view Rackham within the broader perspective of European Romanticism, of which English Romanticism was a definite part. A brief exploration of the nature of European Romanticism, in all its complexity, may throw some light upon the complexity of Rackham's subject choice and on the puzzling ambiguities of his style.

Around 1920, Arthur Lovejoy [in "On the Discriminations of Romanticism"] pointed to the diversity of the term "Romanticism," suggesting that one should refer to it only in the plural form. He felt that the confusion of terminology had led not only to the present "muddle" of critical thought, but also to the unfortunate ambiguity now associated with the word. Twenty years later, René Wellek contradicted Lovejoy [in "The Concept of *Romanticism in Literary History*"] by asserting that there were three unifying principles of Romanticism that could be detected throughout the art and literature of Europe. He identified them as: the role of the imagination as the very basis for poetry and art; the organic view of all natural objects; and the creative use of myths and symbols. In more recent times, Morse Peckham tried to reach a synthesis of Lovejoy's and Wellek's views [in "Toward a Theory of Romanticism"]. He felt it was more important to acknowledge the inherent contradictions of Romanticism as an integral part of the movement than to quarrel about "multiplicity" versus "unity." "Since the logic of Romanticism is that contradictions must be included in a single orientation, but without pseudo-reconciliation," he wrote, "romanticism is a remarkably stable and witful orientation."

Keeping in mind Peckham's observation, we will now move on to examine the seemingly contradictory forces in Rackham's work on the basis that they may correspond to those inherent in European Romanticism as a whole. In this connection, we will give particular attention to his subject choice, his use of the imagination, his organic view of nature, and the ambiguous qualities of his style.

In looking at the wide range of Rackham's illustrations, we notice that he gave considerable attention to folklore and imaginative literature. Among the folk literature of the oral tradition which he illustrated—with a natural feeling for the mood and the cultural uniqueness in the heritage of other lands—were such folk tales as *Grimms' Fairy Tales,* Stephens' *Irish Fairy Tales,* and *Aesop's Fables.* Of the illustrations of his native folklore we may mention Steele's *English Fairy Tales* and *Mother Goose.* Among the literary adaptations of traditional folklore we find his unique illustrations of Wagner's *Rhinegold,* and

his *Twilight of the Gods,* Ibsen's *Peer Gynt,* Fouqué's *Undine,* Shakespeare's *Midsummer Night's Dream,* Irving's *Rip Van Winkle,* and Hawthorne's *Wonder Book.*

Rackham's emphasis on universal folklore reflected his romantic interest in the life, language, and literature close to the common folk tradition. As such, it corresponded to the Romantic dream of reviving the folk heritage around the world—a dream echoed also in the so-called color fairy books of Andrew Lang. It was Herder, during the *Sturm und Drang* movement in Germany, who initiated this revival trend by collecting folk songs of many lands. He was followed by von Arnim and Brentano, Tieck, and later the Brothers Grimm. The Grimms' *Household Tales* were still widely read in England at Rackham's time. In 1914, Rackham wrote to one of his friends: "In many ways, I have more affection for the Grimm drawings than for the other sets. . . . It was the first book I did that began to bring success (the little earlier edition, that is)."

Rackham's illustrations of Grimms' fairy tales demonstrate his fine perception and great skill in getting close to another country's folk heritage. The universality of folktale motifs may have helped him in part. Yet it remains a remarkable fact nonetheless that his illustrations of Grimms' *Märchen* made their way back across the channel to give many generations of German children a first glimpse of their own folktales. How well he did capture the spirit of German folklore may be perceived also from his *Mother Goose* illustrations, which were later adapted to an edition of German nursery rhymes. Though some verses in this edition were translated from the English, most of them were of German origin. Yet Rackham's silhouettes seem to fit the text perfectly. Similarly, we may notice that his illustrations of *Rip Van Winkle* capture the very essence of the book, and it would not readily enter an observer's mind that in this case a British artist illustrated an American book. Rackham's illustrations fit Irving as they fit American folklore. We can't well imagine Rip any other way than Rackham has perceived him.

Viewed from the Romantic perspective, Rackham well demonstrated in his work what Coleridge called "the coloring of the imagination." In Wordsworth's "Preface" to the *Lyrical Ballads* we read: "The ordinary things should be presented to the mind in an unusual aspect." Like the Romantic poets, Rackham often chose to illustrate the commonplace, rendering it colorful in the light of his imagination. Whether he illustrated scenes from folklore or fantasy, his drawings always reflected a certain mood or atmosphere. He achieved this partially by using soft pastel colors, in which even the most meticulously drawn details were blended to an antique tone, giving the effect of ancient parchment. In his paintings the soft browns and grey-greens dominate, here and there illuminated by a warm ivory. His colors vary from light, fluffy tones to rich, dark ones of the kind one may find in Flemish or Dutch landscape paintings. The warm hues of Rackham's colors add much to the impression that the imaginary world of fantasy and folk tale is part of the here and now. One is therefore perhaps less surprised than one ought to be at discovering fairy tale creatures amid a world drawn, otherwise, with much attention given to realistic detail.

A second device has helped Rackham in projecting the spirit of imagination into the world of realism, namely, his independent and very peculiar selection of captions for his illustrations. Instead of searching out highlights of plot and action, he would focus upon scenes or lines often overlooked by even the most attentive reader. Selma Lanes observed in this connection: "Thus he often chose to illustrate the [unillustratable], or to rescue from oblivion words the reader had most likely never noticed. From Charles Dicken's *A Christmas Carol* he plucked the line: 'The air was filled with phantoms, wandering hither and thither in restless haste and moaning as they went.'" From *The Wind in the Willows,* we may add, he captured the very atmosphere of a golden afternoon, when "the smell of the dust kicked up was rich and satisfying." Rackham thus created a mood that did not leave the observer untouched. He himself felt that the most fascinating form of illustration for the artist was the one in which he expressed "an individual sense of delight or emotion, aroused by the accompanying passage of literature." Again we are reminded of Wordsworth's theory of poetry, in which he expected the poet to arouse the reader's passions and to give him a certain sense of pleasure and delight.

In regard to Rackham's ambiguity of style, we find another striking correspondence with Romanticism, in the element which Morse Peckham called "the illusion of mutability." Peckham had in mind a certain amphibian quality emerging from Romantic art and literature that belonged neither entirely to the world of reality nor entirely to the world of fantasy. By recognizing its kinship to metamorphosis, he reevaluated imaginative ambiguity as a positive force, suggesting that it represented the Romantic striving for unity between the internal and the external world or toward the "perfect identification of matter and form." By tracing certain correspondences in the art of [John] Constable and the poetry of Wordsworth, Peckham tried to establish their similar views of the concept of "organic nature." In Constable's cloud studies, for example, he noticed an attempt to bring together the appearances of landscape and sky through certain parallel lines, movements, and colors—an attempt which he felt corresponded to Wordsworth's view of nature as a creative soul. In "Tintern Abbey," Wordsworth had spoken of the eye and ear in terms of "what they half create, / And what perceive," whereas Constable had said, "It is the business of a painter not to be content with nature, and put such scene, a valley filled with imagery fifty miles long, on a canvas of a few inches, but to make something out of nothing, in attempting which he must almost of necessity become poetical." Both of these quotes also seem to illustrate Arthur Rackham's view of nature. Miss Farjeon well described his landscapes drawings as "delicate webs of leafless branches traced against a wintry sky; . . . pale marbled clouds . . . and strange patterns upon the wa-

ter." In Rackham's drawings, as much as in Wordsworth's poetry, we sense that "there is a spirit in the woods." His illustrations make trees, grass, flowers, and the very fieldstones come alive. In looking at the strangely twisted, gnarled, and knotty trees in his drawings, we can never be quite sure if nature, man, or a creature from the netherworld is speaking to us. What appears to be a knothole turns out to be an eye or a mouth—and yet, it may be a knothole after all.

In the landscapes of Rackham the very concepts of "manhood," "treehood," and "dwarfhood" often become strangely fused and blurred, leaving the observer with a feeling of ambiguity. We recognize in the ambiguity the Romantic world view, according to which the same spirit flowed through all things. Both macrocosm and microcosm, the animate and the inanimate object, were humanized and alive, revealing at their very source the deepest secrets of God and nature.

In some of Rackham's drawings we may witness the very process of a strange metamorphosis at work, gradually fusing natural objects and imaginative perspectives. At times, his illustrations are gloomy and frightening, suggestive of a dark and evil netherworld, and at other times, they are light and gay—or even grotesque. One can never be sure what mood to anticipate. In *Rip Van Winkle,* for example, we may feel a bit apprehensive while trying to decide whether some of the roots of an old twisted tree might belong as arms or legs to a withered and misshapen dwarf leaning against its trunk. Another illustration in the same book, no less ambiguous in style, makes us smile, as we discover among some hybrid creatures seated high on top of a branch the plumes of birds and the faces of men. Particularly amusing is a female creature among them, who is busily engaged, of all things, in knitting a sock. Her ball of yarn, hanging from her nest in a hopeless tangle, is drawn so realistically that one is tempted to pick it up.

Such opposing moods are very pronounced in Rackham's drawings. Side by side we may observe in them idyllic as well as grotesque elements—moods so contradictory that they do not seem to have been created by the same artist. And yet, it is precisely this sense of contradiction that illustrates the Romantic striving toward unity. Viewed separately, these polarities present such contrasts as those between the contemplative and peaceful mood of Wordsworth, for example, and the grotesque and nightmarish mood of Coleridge. In Germany, the polarities are represented by the "light" bourgeois Romanticism (*bürgerliche Romantik*) of Eichendorff and Brentano on the one hand and the "Dark" or "night side" of horror Romanticism (*Schauerromantik*) of Tieck, Novalis, and E. T. A. Hoffmann on the other. Oscar Walzel commented on these seemingly contradictory forces of European Romanticism [in *German Romanticism*]: "I maintain that two antithetical methods of forming a work of art may be distinguished from each other. . . . The first is rather calm and simple and lays no claim on emotional intensity. The other is more roaring and pathetical and at times grotesque, and even inclined to hyperbolic expression. The current conception of baroque, or as Wörringer terms it, "Gothic," is applicable only to the latter." In some of Rackham's illustrations we find an echo of the idyllic world of the *bürgerliche Romantik,* as seen in the engravings of Ludwig Richter (first German illustrator of the Grimms' *Household Tales*), the paintings of Moritz von Schwindt (well known for his enchanted forest scenes), and later in the works of Karl Spitzweg, master painter of the small town atmosphere. In both Spitzweg and Rackham we discover a similar fondness for crumbling medieval walls bathed in late afternoon sunlight, rooftop scenes, and quaint characters. In some other Rackham drawings we perceive the dark world of the *Schauerromantik* and certain moods reminiscent of E. T. A. Hoffmann. In visual terms, Rackham expressed the dark sphere of Romanticism by means of bizarre line movements and tensions in forms. By using a fairly dark tint of raw umber, he would create the atmosphere of the netherworld, in which the real and the unreal lived together side by side in an ambiguous relationship.

Rackham's dual vision of life comes out well in a work not meant for children. His illustrations for [Izaak] Walton's *The Compleat Angler* show well fascination with both the idyllic and the grotesque. And yet, there are drawings, interspersed with contemplative fishing and village scenes, that seem to have lost their way from the children's bookshelf: insects with spectacles are scribbling something into books; dwarfs are engaged in frog hunts; and fish skeletons, equipped with crutches, are contemplating their future fate in the angler's frying pan. The last drawing, ironically, is accompanied by a delicious fish recipe in the text, which reads: " . . . and pour upon it a quarter of a pound of the best fresh butter, melted and beaten with half-a-dozen spoonfuls of the broth. . . . "

Although we smile at these drawings, we perceive quite a different mood in another one, which is reminiscent of a tale by Edgar Allan Poe or E. T. A. Hoffmann. An odd old couple is bent over what appears to be a huge book of knowledge. Their wrinkled, grinning faces seem out of place in the museum-like surroundings of skeletons and weird-looking stuffed fish and birds. There is a striking incongruity between the rich folds of the neatly arrayed silk and brocade clothing of the couple and the bare spiny bones hanging overhead. The open book may suggest a Romantic symbol of the hieroglyphics of life, yet the facial expressions are far remote from radiating a sense of wonder. Instead, they suggest something resembling more closely the features of the grotesque.

The Romantic grotesque may be translated as ungraceful, out-of-harmony, or incongruous. It was capable of taking on a humorous as well as a horrifying quality, depending upon the emphasis of the writer or artist. [In "Bécquier and the Romantic Grotesque"] Paul Illie characterized it as "a low keyed disquietude." In analyzing the fantasies of Bécquier, Ilie called attention to the hybrid and ambiguous nature of his portrayals of transformation that showed but little resemblance to Ovid's portrayal of metamorphosis. Whereas Ovid had clearly indicated changes from one form to another, the Romantic grotesque remained ambiguous and hybrid in nature, thus transmitting the eerie feeling of metamorphosis still in process. It is just such a feeling which emerges from many of Rackham's drawings. We are never quite sure about his portrayal of nature as nature, of man as man, or of a symbol as a symbol.

It may well have been Beardsley who inspired Rackham with the element of the grotesque. Hudson noted a strong influence, especially with respect to some nightmarish scenes, one of which in fact is entitled: *A nightmare: horrible result of contemplating Aubrey Beardsley after supper.* Further, Hudson noted the influences of Gothic and Italian primitives and also of "Cruikshank, Caldecott, Dickey Doyle, Arthur Boyd Houghton, [and] the artists of Germany and Japan." It is also possible, however, that Rackham received inspiration along these lines from the very writers of the German *Schauerromantik,* not to mention, of course, Edgar Allan Poe, whose works he illustrated. We know that Rackham frequently spent his holidays on the continent, usually in Germany and also that his wife, Edythe, studied art there prior to her marriage. One of Rackham's admirers pointedly commented in 1905 "I have at last been able to get to your exhibition which I enjoyed immensely. Hitherto one had to go to the Continent for so much mingled grace & grotesque as you have given us. . . . "

A study of all of the influences on Rackham will lead us to a complex and varied pattern that easily might distract our attention from his own original contributions to the art of illustration. And yet, a study of some affinities of mind may give us a clue as to the direction of his thoughts—particularly since Rackham himself acknowledged above all other influences his affection for the spirit of the Germanic North. When once asked by a friend how he would explain a peculiar Indian flavor in his drawings, Rackham responded: "I think I myself am more conscious of Teutonic influence." Indeed, Rackham visited Wagner's Bayreuth several times while traveling in Europe, and he was as fond of Wagner's Nordic operas as he was of Norse mythology. It is possibly from here that he drew his inspirations for the thievish, gray, and grotesque dwarfs who appear in his various fairy-tale illustrations. The Nordic *alb* (later Elberich or Oberon) had nothing whatever in common with the dainty dwarfs of Disney. Jacob Grimm in his monumental work *Teutonic Mythology* also commented on the dark or gray complexion of the "dark elves," as he called them. According to the Edda they had emerged originally as maggots from the rotten flesh of the slain frost giant Ymir. It may be noted that Norse or Teutonic mythology represents a common heritage for both the English nation and the German nation alike—a fact which may explain why Rackham's illustrations are so very much at home in the Nordic folk heritage of both countries.

From the perspective of European Romanticism, the double nature of the netherworld of dwarfs and elves held a special interest for writers and artists because it seemed

From Mother Goose Nursery Rhymes, *illustrated by Arthur Rackham.*

to correspond to their own view of the world. Ricarda Huch [in *Die Romantik*] characterized the Romantic movement as one that upheld the contrast between spirit and nature, light and darkness, force and materialism. Swaying back and forth between these opposites, the poets of the time hoped to achieve a synthesis of mind and spirit. Walzel saw in this polarity a reflection of the Romantic dream of harmony. By oscillating between thesis and antithesis, he said, one hoped to recover the "golden age" of the ancient past. This oscillation, in turn, gave birth to Romantic irony, as the inherent contradictions were not resolved but kept alive.

By never committing himself completely either to the one world or the other, Arthur Rackham developed a certain spirit of ironic detachment in his illustrations, which we recognize as his peculiar sense of humor. It was his special gift to create an illusion of reality by giving minute attention to realistic detail. Unnoticeably, he would then introduce, by means of color or ambiguous forms, the spirit of the imagination. It seems that he very much enjoyed the freedom of belonging to both worlds and to neither, thus asserting the very freedom of his creative mind.

There is an odd little drawing among his letters and notes that served as a wedding announcement for his daughter Barbara. It shows an old, twisted, knotty, and leafless willow tree with grotesque branches sticking out like sinewy arms at the sides and like windblown hair on the top. Strangely enough, this tree bears the very features of Arthur Rackham—glasses, long nose, and all. On one of the "branches" sit two little birds ready, it seems, to build their nest. Who was Rackham, we may wonder—a man, a dwarf, or a tree; a "realist" or a "fantasist"?

If we have viewed Rackham's work within the context of European Romanticism, it should be remembered that there is nothing rigid about this attempt. Classifications remain constructs of the mind and, like metaphors, can only be carried so far in bringing out certain affinities of thought. In his work *Beyond the Tragic Vision,* Morse Peckham wrote: "Thus even a single work of art must not be regarded as culturally coherent, as reflecting one and only one aspect of a construct model." Periods or movements were "constructs" or "operational fiction," he warned, and they should be used with caution. In the case of Romanticism however, as both Peckham and Walzel agreed, we have to do not with a single coherent construct but with a multiplicity of patterns characterized by polarity and imaginative ambiguity. For this reason alone, there is little danger that an application of Romantic theories to Rackham's work might lead to a rigid interpretation of his art.

The perspectives of European Romanticism open up new possibilities of viewing the seeming contradictions in Rackham's illustrations as complementary forces arising from a dialectical approach to nature. To Rackham and the Romantics, nature was humanized and alive. By swaying back and forth between the worlds of fantasy and reality, he imparted to both the spirit of his creative imagination.

Like the European Romantics, Rackham felt at home in the folklore and fantasy of many nations. His interpretation of both reflects his capacity to perceive a living creature behind every bush and tree, in the ripples on the water, or in the movement of the clouds. Ambiguity and metamorphosis to him became a way of seeing which corresponded to the Romantic search for a mythopoeic vision of life. As if he were holding up a mirror to the complexity of our souls, Rackham cunningly revealed to us our dreams of beauty as well as the distorted features of our nightmares and secret fears. In that sense, polarity and ambiguity not only mark his poetic vision, but also the special sense of humor that places him, beyond doubt, into a class of his own.

Diana L. Johnson

SOURCE: "Arthur Rackham, 1867-1939," in *Fantastic Illustration and Design in Britain, 1850-1930,* Museum of Art, Rhode Island School of Design, 1979, pp. 82-5.

Rackham's *Alice in Wonderland* was published by William Heinemann in 1907, and has since become one of his most sought-after volumes. Among the more than one hundred artists who tried their hand at illustrating Carroll's classic, Tenniel and Rackham stand out as the most extraordinary and original: it is almost impossible to contemplate *Alice* without picturing the designs of one or the other of the two men. [The] scene of Alice with the rather fatherly-looking caterpillar is one of the best-known and most appealing illustrations in the book. . . .

Rackham's illustrations to Wagner's *The Ring of the Nibelung* appeared in two parts. *The Rhinegold and the Valkyrie* was published by William Heinemann in 1910, *Siegfried and the Twilight of the Gods* in the following year. These two volumes, with their concentration on the heroic drama of the Norse myths, were something of a departure for Rackham, and by no means unsuccessful. In 1912, for example, the Société Nationale des Beaux Arts invited the artist to exhibit the Wagner drawings in Paris and awarded him a gold medal. Despite the appeal of these illustrations, Rackham returned rather quickly to a somewhat lighter vein, issuing an *Aesop's Fables* and a new edition of *Peter Pan in Kensington Gardens* in 1912 and a *Mother Goose* in 1913. . . .

Aesop's Fables was published in 1912 by William Heinemann with an introduction by G. K. Chesterton. In the book, "The Owl and the Birds" appears in black and white without the pictorial border. Since an elaborate color drawing was more marketable, Rackham frequently added color to drawings originally published in black and white or executed watercolor versions of his pen and ink designs. Despite the fact that the cluster of feathered creatures lacks some of the more obvious external trappings of mankind such as clothing, Rackham is in this drawing once again working within that borderland between the human and animal worlds which he portrays so effectively. There is about the gathering a suggestively human purposefulness combined with an array of expressions which the Martin Brothers would envy. Although Rackham quite possibly drew upon Tenniel's illustration of a similar grouping in *Alice in Wonderland,* the final result is his own. The fanciful border which Rackham has added is particularly appealing and forms a link in that long tradition of marginal grotesques which in England reached its height in medieval manuscript illuminations. . . .

Rackham's *Mother Goose* was published by William Heinemann in 1913. The artist's highly successful use of negative space and his fine sense for the overall design of the page are beautifully expressed in this portrayal of "Miss Muffet." The decorative spider web at the top of the sheet effectively balances the figures upon a hillock in the lower half of the composition. Rackham has carefully chosen the moment just before the spider makes himself known to the unsuspecting girl, leaving the actual "surprise" to the imagination of the reader. . . .

The Rackham edition of *The Sleeping Beauty* was published by William Heinemann in 1920. It contained a full-color frontispiece, several three-color illustrations and numerous black and white silhouettes. Although [the] drawing for **"The Thirteenth Fairy"** includes background washes in color, in the book the design appeared as one of the black and white silhouettes. . . .

The literary source for [the] delightful undated illustration [of *Little People*] has not been identified. Within a rather pastoral setting a typical Rackhamesque transformation is taking place as a number of apparently normal toadstools clustered beneath the trees begin to turn themselves into rather devilish-looking gnomes. This change occurs in the presence of two tiny figures who seem quite charmed by the event. The metamorphosis of natural objects into forms exhibiting a varied range of more or less human characteristics is one of the major and recurrent themes in Rackham's illustrations.

Hodder & Stoughton published *A Wonder Book* in 1922. Rackham's illustrations for the [Nathaniel] Hawthorne volume exhibit an impressively broad stylistic range. "The three grey women" recaptures much of the disturbing quality found in the artist's two early books of Wagner illustrations, while his depiction of Pandora opening the box, for example, is quite "twenties" in feeling—the nubile young Pandora displays a bobbed haircut. The published version of the "grey women" is cropped and more subdued in color than this drawing, but these changes do not prevent its being the most dramatic and horrific image in the book. . . .

In April of 1928 Rackham was commissioned to design a version of *A Midsummer Night's Dream* for the Spencer Collection at The New York Public Library. The manuscript, with illustrations by Rackham and calligraphy by Graily Hewitt, was completed in 1929. The frontispiece is among Rackham's most decorative designs and, perhaps because it was a special commission, is far more elaborate than most of his illustrations. . . .

Peter Pan in Kensington Gardens was first published by Hodder & Stoughton in 1906 and later reissued in 1912 with additional and reworked plates. *Peter Pan* firmly established Rackham's reputation as an illustrator of colored books, and it is still considered one of his greatest achievements. The drawing is a reprise of a much more highly finished plate in the book itself. The addition of an original drawing to the half-title page of an already published deluxe volume was not unusual, and Rackham seems to have done these sketches not only for friends but also for commercial advantage as well. . . .

In 1933 Rackham was commissioned by Sydney Carroll to design the costumes and scenery for Basil Dean's production of *Hansel and Gretel,* which opened at the Cambridge Theatre in London on December 26 of that year. The *Hansel and Gretel* designs were Rackham's only attempt at transferring his fantasies from the printed page to the professional theater. Although the artist was apparently not entirely pleased with the results, the reviewers were enthusiastic. His lively representations splendidly capture the essence of "witchliness." . . .

Kenneth Grahame's classic *The Wind in the Willows* was Rackham's last book, published posthumously in a deluxe edition by The Limited Editions Club, New York, in 1940. (It was not published in England until ten years later.) This cosy, intimate scene of Mole and Rat in Mole's abode comes at the end of a long line of anthropomorphized representations which Rackham created with unparalleled sensitivity and charm throughout his career.

Susan E. Meyer

SOURCE: "Arthur Rackham," in *A Treasury of the Great Children's Book Illustrators,* Harry N. Abrams, Inc., Publishers, 1987, pp. 157-76.

Arthur Rackham took possession of whatever he illustrated; his images were the product of a vision so totally and completely his own that they existed almost independently of the words surrounding them. The words were simply suggestions for a visual rendition by the illustrator. "For his illustrations to be worth anything, he must be regarded as a partner [to the author] not as a servant," asserted Arthur Rackham when asked to present his concept of the artist's contribution to the text. ". . . An illustration may legitimately give the artist's view of the author's ideas; or it may give his view, his independent view of the author's subject. But it must be the artist's view; any attempt to coerce him into a mere tool in the author's hands can only result in the most dismal failure."

Arthur Rackham's imagery was every bit as memorable as the prose he illustrated, as clearly discerned as the author's voice he accompanied. Rackham's gift, and his fame, derived from an extraordinary, poetic imagination that produced a world of fantasy never before seen. His world was gossamer, ethereal, and mysterious, populated with gnomes, dwarfs, fairies, goblins, and elves, with sinuous root tendrils, mushrooms, ferns, and massive trees that transformed into humans. The pictures seem other-worldly, magically evoked by a wand passing over the pages. One might imagine that the artist emerged from some distant forest, where sunlight and shadow weave their eternal magic through the web of gnarled branches. Perhaps the artist was even a wizard!

On the contrary. It seems difficult to accept that Arthur Rackham was, in fact, the most *unlikely* wizard or magician. He was British through and through—a cockney, actually—a kindly, mild-mannered gentleman, who enjoyed a game of tennis and the company of good friends. He wasn't even eccentric. The only connection between the man and his pictures seemed to be his face, his "wide and elfish grin," as the writer R. H. Ward described him. But that's not surprising: Rackham frequently used himself as a model for his paintings. It was, after all, more practical, and Rackham was a practical man.

The fantastic nature of Rackham's artistry has attracted a number of romantic biographers who suggest that a distant ancestor may have transmitted magical powers to the illustrator, that a certain John Rackham—a pirate hanged in Jamaica in 1720—might offer the glorious link. Such an explanation is better left to the rapturous zealots who belong to the still-active Rackham cult. It is always painful to acknowledge the discrepancy that exists between the creation and the creator when the contrast is so great. . . .

In 1906, the copyright for the Tenniel edition of ***Alice's Adventures in Wonderland*** expired, and several publishers rushed to issue new editions of the popular book. When Rackham agreed to illustrate ***Alice*** for Heinemann, he fell under attack by critics who felt that the classic Tenniel illustrations were sacrosanct and that any attempt at retelling the Carroll story with new images represented sheer hubris on the part of the illustrator. One critic decried Rackham for taking the assignment, calling it "a piece of exceedingly bad taste, to say nothing of its unfairness." Not defiant by nature, Rackham nevertheless took on the challenge and proceeded with the illustrations for Heinemann.

Unrestricted by the limitations of reproduction that had hampered Tenniel forty years before, Rackham was able to execute subtleties of color and line that resulted in a set of illustrations so remarkably different from the Tenniel work that the controversy grew more intense when the book appeared in 1906. While one group of readers responded with dismay, others applauded the fresh images with enthusiasm. One supporter wrote to Rackham that his "delightful Alice is alive and makes by contrast Tenniel's Alice look like a stiff wooden puppet." Although ***Alice in Wonderland*** was extremely successful (it is still in print), Rackham was too shaken

From A Midsummer Night's Dream, *written by William Shakespeare. Illustrated by Arthur Rackham.*

by the criticism to accept the offer to illustrate *Through the Looking Glass* as a companion volume. . . .

The marvelously fanciful images produced from Rackham's imagination were created very methodically. After all, from the outset his work had improved only because he had been so diligent, and this careful and disciplined approach to illustration never diminished with the years. He had developed a sure sense of line, a quality that dominated even his color work, which explains his fascination with the contours of sinuous tree roots, branches, and wrinkles. With the technical advances that had improved the methods of transferring the artist's line to the printing plate—no intermediaries in between to distort the original intention—Rackham developed a fluid, delicate and sensitive line that reproduced faithfully and he used it to good advantage. . . .

For as much as his images depicted a world of fantasy, the subjects themselves derived from real-world models used over and over again in his pictures: the tree in his garden, portraits of friends and family, and renditions of his own image reflected in the mirror. He kept a collection of costumes and props which he used regularly, and he relied heavily on living models. One model recalled that "a young girl might equally well serve him as the Vicar of Wakefield or an evil old witch. I remember one who even acted as a dismembered corpse." To get the broken plates just right for Alice's tea party in Wonderland, he used as props some dishes he broke himself, and he seated Alice in his own favorite wing chair surrounded by the family china. His model for Alice was a local girl, Doris Dommett, selected from a number of applicants, and her recollections demonstrate his concern for every detail: "I was so pleased he copied my print frock exactly, because it was one my mother had allowed me to design myself. The woolen stockings I wore were knitted by my old French nannie Prudence. They were so thick to keep out the cold, and how they tickled!"

This leap from the real (even mundane) to the fantastic was one Rackham made naturally, a leap he knew children made with him. Like Walter Crane before him, Arthur Rackham maintained that imagination, when stimulated, elevated the child's intelligence, a view clearly expressed in an entry he composed for an American encyclopedia, *The Junior Book of Authors:*

> I can only say that I firmly believe in the greatest stimulating and educative power of imaginative, fantastic, and playful pictures and writings for children in their most impressionable years—a view that most unfortunately, I consider, has its opponents in these matter of fact days. Children will make no mistakes in the way of confusing the imaginative and symbolic with the actual. Nor are they at all blind to decorative or arbitrarily designed treatment in art, any more than they are to poetic or rhythmic form in literature. . . .

His fame was now so widespread that he never wanted for work, but he paid the price celebrated artists frequently must pay; his admirers wanted his work to remain as it was, reacting with skepticism to any attempt on his part to change. During a period in the 1920s, for example, he subdued the linear quality in his illustrations, softening the effect of his images with his color blended and suffused, rather than partitioned by sharply defined lines. His experiments with new forms of expression appeared in *Irish Fairy Tales* (1920) and *The Tempest* (1926), but his public responded less enthusiastically to these new efforts and the artist felt obliged to return to his earlier formulas. His work of the 1930s, while it remained ever popular, revealed signs of the artist's boredom. . . .

After undergoing surgery for cancer, Rackham knew he was fighting for time as he pressed forward on the illustrations [for *The Wind in the Willows.*] Through the summer of 1939, he labored on the drawings until he finally completed the last, a scene in which Mole and Rat are loading the rowboat for a picnic. When presented the drawing for approval, Rackham's daughter pointed out to her father that the oars were missing from the boat. No amount of reassurance could prevent Rackham from returning to the drawing to correct the omission. After rendering the oars with great effort, the ailing illustrator sank back in his bed and sighed, "Thank goodness, that is the last one." He died a few weeks later, and *The Wind in the Willows,* one of his crowning achievements, was published the following year.

Jesse D. Mann

SOURCE: "A Little Known Incident of Plagiarism in the Career of Arthur Rackham," in *The Book Collector,* Vol. 45, No. 2, Summer, 1996, pp. 214-17.

[T]he Chatham Bookseller purchased a large collection of books illustrated by Arthur Rackham. Together with the books came three letters, one from Rackham himself, pertaining to a little known incident of plagiarism in the renowned illustrator's career.

The books and correspondence belonged to the late Julia Smith Berrall of Montclair, New Jersey. Mrs. Berrall, who died in July, was not only an admirer and collector of Arthur Rackham's work, but was also an accomplished author herself. She wrote several books on gardens and flower arrangement and even contributed an article on floral decoration to the *Encyclopedia Britannica.*

In 1933, while employed at the Montclair Art Museum, Mrs. Berrall came across a brief article in the journal *Pencil Points* which prompted her to write to Rackham in care of his English publisher, William Heinemann Ltd. Indeed, together with a cover letter, a draft copy of which still survives, she also sent Rackham a copy of the article she had read 'with interest.' The article deals with the then new murals used to decorate the second and third basements of the North Building of the Metropolitan Life Insurance Company's Manhattan office, which in 1933 had just been completed. Thirty of these murals were the work of Edward Trumbull (d. 1968), who had studied with Sir Frank Brangwyn, and who has been called 'one of America's leading muralists of the day.' In 1933, Trumbull was certainly well-known in New York for his work at the Graybar Building Concourse and especially for his recently finished ceiling of the lobby of the Chrysler Building. For the murals in the lounge and escalator hall of MetLife's second basement, Trumbull took as his subject episodes from Washington Irving's *Rip Van Winkle*. The article in *Pencil Points* includes two illustrations of Trumbull's murals, and these illustrations caught Mrs Berrall's eye. As she put it in her letter to Rackham:

> Being a collector of your illustrated books, I immediately recognized the source of Mr. Trumbull, the mural painter's, inspiration. Since the author of the article mentioned his 'whimsical fertility of imagination', giving no credit to you, I decided that the plagiarism was unknown to her and that there probably had been no arrangements made between you and the artist. Armed with my own copy of *Rip Van Winkle,* I obtained a pass and inspected the murals—all thirty of which are *exact copies* of the figures in your illustrations of *Rip Van Winkle* and the *Legend of Sleepy Hollow*. They are all faithful to the originals, with the single exception that the distant background

of your pictures has been omitted and a general warm buff tone substituted.

Indeed, even a cursory comparison of the two examples given in *Pencil Points* with the corresponding plates in Rackham's **Rip Van Winkle** confirms the accuracy of this judgment.

Mrs Berrall's letter to Rackham seems to have been written on 15 July 1933. Rackham's reply from his home, Stilegate, in Limpsfield, Surrey is dated 28 July. The promptness of his response may indicate just how seriously he viewed the matter. In his brief, but direct, note, Rackham refers to Trumbull's action as a 'theft' and an 'outrage.' He thanks Mrs Berrall, whom he mistakenly addresses as Mrs Lloyd, and states his intention 'to take steps to find out whether there is anything to be done about' the plagiarism. Finally, he expresses understandable surprise 'that a man in such a position as Mr. Trumbull appears to be should so demean himself' by stealing the work of another artist.

Obviously, Rackham's letter adds drama to the whole affair. One is eager to know what steps the artist took and how the matter was finally resolved. The third of the three letters sheds some light on these questions, but, as we will see, a completely satisfactory answer has proven elusive. On 18 April 1934, Frederic G. Melcher, the co-editor of *Publishers Weekly,* wrote to Mrs Berrall about the Trumbull case, apparently in response to an earlier letter from her. Melcher was certainly a logical person for Mrs Berrall to have contacted. As is well-known, he was himself quite interested in graphic arts, children's books (he helped establish both the Newbery and Caldecott medals) and, to use his words, 'the rights of artists and authors.' Moreover, like the Berralls, whom he might perhaps have known socially, Melcher lived in Montclair. His letter deserves to be cited at length:

> When I wrote to the Metropolitan Life Insurance Company, I found that this circumstance had recently been called to their attention and that they had talked with the artist who took the contract and then both had been in correspondence with Mr. Rackham. The artist was all for taking the whole thing off the walls, but the Metropolitan, feeling that the paintings were peculiarly suited to their use, suggested that they get permission to put a proper inscription there with credit to Mr. Rackham. Correspondence on this point seems to be successfully under way, and they are waiting to receive from Mr. Rackham the exact wording he would wish to have in such an inscription.

So it seems that Rackham ultimately received the credit he deserved. However, I am not certain that the happy ending outlined by Melcher actually occurred. Due to on-going and extensive construction at the North Building, it is presently impossible to examine either Trumbull's murals or the inscription Melcher mentions—if it even exists. In addition, my inquiries at MetLife have uncovered only the intriguing but frustrating fact that, while the company has a file on this whole matter, that file is confidential and thus unavailable to the public.

A detailed and comprehensive study of Arthur Rackham's life and work remains to be written. Not surprisingly, no readily available source, not even Derek Hudson's standard biography, mentions this important incident of plagiarism in the illustrator's career. However, the issue and the people involved were clearly significant, and Rackham's response to Trumbull's piracy offers some insight into his character as an artist and as a man. Hence the matter deserves to be more widely known.

It seems likely that many people who knew nothing at all about Arthur Rackham's work might well have admired Edward Trumbull's murals in the MetLife basement. Plagiarism is after all a perverse type of praise and an unwelcome form of publicity. On the other hand, Julia Berrall's true admiration for Rackham's illustrations and her observant eye will perhaps have served to bring this interesting incident in the artist's life to an even larger audience.

John Rowe Townsend

SOURCE: "Pictures That Tell a Story," in *Written for Children: An Outline of English-Language Children's Literature,* sixth edition, The Scarecrow Press, 1996, p. 112.

Arthur Rackham made his reputation before the First World War, though he went on illustrating all through the inter-war years, and the list of books that he illustrated or re-illustrated is a long one. He was not one of my own childhood favourites; I was frightened by his sinister creatures and (above all) by his gnarled, groping trees. While acknowledging him to have been a good artist with strong individual vision, I still do not find his work enjoyable; but this no doubt is a personal reaction caused by too-vivid recollection of the old shudders. Even his **Mother Goose** (1913) has its alarming moments: Jack Sprat casts a menacing shadow on the wall, and the man, wives and cats coming from St. Ives have a disturbing air of witchcraft. And well might Miss Muffet be frightened by the outsize spider that sits down beside her in Rackham's version.

Judith St. George

1931-

American author of fiction and nonfiction.

Major works include *By George, Bloomers!* (1976), *The Halloween Pumpkin Smasher* (1978), *The Brooklyn Bridge: They Said It Couldn't Be Built* (1982), *The Mount Rushmore Story* (1985), *The Panama Canal: Gateway to the World* (1989).

INTRODUCTION

St. George has experimented with genres ranging from historical fiction and biographies to haunting and engaging mysteries for middle graders and young adults. While the fast-paced suspense of her fiction has captured the interest of young readers, St. George is best known for her historical nonfiction, in which she blends closely detailed research with action and adventure to create compelling, exciting, and educational narratives. Lauded by critics for her depth of research and for captivating readers with her amiable and amusing tone, she enthusiastically presents the building of such historic landmarks as the Brooklyn Bridge, the Panama Canal, and Mount Rushmore. In addition, she has explored, in her biographies, the lives of notable Native Americans, including Crazy Horse, Sitting Bull, and Sacagawea. In addition, she draws largely from personal experience in both her fiction and nonfiction, and often writes of young girls confronting challenging situations and of the importance of friendship and family history. While the plots in her fiction are sometimes criticized as weak or forced, her characters are typically regarded as strong and her settings as vivid and realistic. Whether the setting is contemporary or historical, or the genre is fiction or nonfiction, St. George strives for depth and authenticity in all of her writings, and maintains a strong commitment to research all of her subjects. "Since writing my first book more than twenty years ago," St. George told *AAYA*, "I've done a lot of research for my novels, immersing myself in a period, discovering what was happening politically at the time, how people were living, what the economy was like. I hope that all that flavor comes through as an integral part of the story." She continued, "[F]or me, the research is fun, both the library-kind and the physical-kind. It's the writing that's difficult. . . . All I know is that I want my readers to care as much about the outcome of historical events as if they were reading today's headlines. . . . Above all, I want the people in my books to come alive for my readers the way they come alive for me. . . ."

Biographical Information

Born in 1931 in Westfield, New Jersey, St. George was

the second of three children. Although she grew up during the Depression, her childhood on Maple Street was, as she described in *Something about the Author Autobiography Series* (*SAAS*), "idyllic." Raised in a close and loving family, St. George did not greatly feel the effects of the Depression years. Instead, her childhood memories are filled with the escapades of her four best friends in quiet Westfield. Her older brother, Jack, and younger sister, Anne, both influenced these early years and later found their way into her fiction. Her two childhood passions were sports and reading. In *SAAS*, she described her childhood self as a "typical 1930s and '40s tomboy"—being the only girl on the sixth-grade boys' baseball team." Her love of reading drew her to everything from comic books and movie magazines to classics like *The Secret* Garden and *Caddie Woodlawn*. In an interview for *Contemporary Authors* she stated, "As a child I loved reading above all else and remember receiving twenty-two books one Christmas. In grammar school I used to write crazy plays, which my friends and I produced. Looking back, I realize my teachers must have had the patience of Job." She also recalled being afraid of almost everything as a child, and she incorporated her fears into her mysteries. As wonderful as elementary school was for St. George, however, junior high and high school were painful. Separated from her friends and extremely shy, she relied on sports and books for pleasure. During her junior year of high school, she was sent to boarding school for two years, an experience she recalled in *SAAS* as "among my unhappiest." The painful memories of her adolescence also appear in her writings.

In 1949, St. George entered Smith College and received her Bachelor of Arts degree in English in 1952. While in college she took several creative writing courses and, during her senior year, was editor-in-chief of the college humor magazine, *Campus Cat*. In 1954 she married David St. George, an Episcopalian seminary student; the couple had four children. Desiring to do more with herself than parenting, St. George began writing and researching while her children were in school. Her first book was a historical novel, *Turncoat Winter; Rebel Spring*, the story of a fourteen-year-old patriot boy during the winter of 1779-80 who is torn between protecting a friend who saved him and turning him in as a British spy. After nine rejections, the book was finally published in 1970. However, it was five more years before St. George published another book. During that time she joined the Westchester Writers' Workshop, a group of published women writers who met to discuss their works. St. George credits the workshop with motivating her to continue writing. She explained in *AAYA*, "I began *The Girl with Spunk*, a story about a young farm-girl servant in Seneca Falls just before the first woman's rights convention. G. P. Putnam's picked up the book in 1974, and I've been with Putnam's ever since."

Major Works

Set in Seneca Falls, New York, during the mid-nineteenth century, *By George, Bloomers!*, St. George's third published historical novel, features eight-year-old Hannah who wants to wear a pair of the new and daring lady's apparel invented by her next-door neighbor, Mrs. Bloomer. Through a series of events, including the rescue of Hannah's younger brother from the roof, Hannah's mother is finally convinced, and lets her tomboy daughter wear bloomers instead of pantaloons under her dresses. Zena Sutherland commented, "The plot is basically patterned (prove something to parents and win a point) but the story gives historical perspective, it's pleasantly told and illustrated, both text and pictures being lightly humorous, and it doesn't stress its point too obtrusively." Cyrisse Jaffee called the book "an entertaining, subtly thought-provoking novel."

Some of St. George's fiction remains firmly planted in contemporary times and deals with adventure and suspense, including *Haunted*, the story of sixteen-year-old Alex, who is hired to house-sit an estate which was recently the scene of a murder-suicide. Writing in *School Library Journal,* Drew Stevenson found the book to be "St. George's suspense at its best," while M. Hobbs wrote, "The narrative is dramatic, the everyday characters convincing, and the suspense well maintained." The

Halloween Pumpkin Smasher draws many of its events, characters, and places from St. George's childhood memories: The Maple Street Gang, which is named after her brother's gang of friends; the heroine, Mary, who is named after St. George's aunt; and Mary's imaginary friend Nellie, named after another aunt, and who resembles the imaginary friend St. George had as a child. In the story, Mary and Nellie investigate the mystery of who is smashing the neighborhood jack-o'-lanterns. As the young detectives search the neighborhood, they enter an old deserted house, reminiscent of the house in which St. George was raised. Although Nellie inspires Mary to seek out the pumpkin smasher, Mary eventually solves the mystery and discovers that a raccoon is the mischievous culprit.

In an interview with *Contemporary Authors*, St. George stated, "History and mysteries are my two loves. I guess mysteries have to come first, since I find it hard to plot a story without some element of mystery woven into it. On the other hand, historical nonfiction gives me the opportunity to delve into our past and meet fascinating people, as well as do research, which I find as irresistible as eating peanuts." St. George's fiction has given way to nonfiction, and much of her best creative effort has been devoted to that genre since 1982. *The Brooklyn Bridge: They Said It Couldn't Be Built* is her most critically acclaimed book and the winner of several awards. Inspired by a newspaper article about the one hundredth anniversary of the Brooklyn Bridge, the book was published just in time for the centennial celebration of the architectural landmark. St. George's account relates the seemingly impossible job of building a bridge over the East River during the nineteenth century, and focuses on the Roebling family, two of whose members were chief engineers on the project. John Roebling died while surveying the site for the bridge. His son Washington, a former Civil War colonel, continued his father's plans. Emily Roebling, Washington's wife and the heroine of the story, relays messages to the workers when her husband becomes ill. St. George takes readers through adventure and suspense as the builders endured caisson fires, bad weather, and snapping cables. Ilene Cooper noted, "St. George takes what might have been a dry account of a bridge-building (there are lots of facts and figures to wade through) and turns it into an adventure story. It even has a hero and heroine." Richard Shepard concluded, "[St. George] has a knack for narration, so even though you may know a fair amount about the bridge . . . you get caught up in this tale of grit, intelligence and imagination, for it is in the good old Horatio Alger tradition. While she never loses sight of the main characters, she explains with exemplary clarity the engineering problems involved in the building. . . . [St. George] also refers to, but does not become bogged down in, the politics of building the bridge."

St. George once again takes on a familiar landmark in *The Mount Rushmore Story*. This nonfiction work chronicles the efforts of sculptor Gutzon Borglum as he carved out this famous monument in the Black Hills of South Dakota. In her research, St. George climbed atop the monument for her own personal up-close look, and blended stories of Borglum with those of the Sioux Indians for whom the Black Hills of South Dakota was a spiritual home. Ilene Cooper praised the book, noting, "St. George's flawless handling of her main topic is supplemented by her deft and moving descriptions of the Sioux tribe. . . . The smooth narrative and solid research give the book substance. . . ."

Panama Canal: Gateway to the World looks at the history of the canal, the three chief engineers, the political role the canal has played throughout history, and the diseases and harsh weather conditions that builders endured. Praising St. George's in depth research, Margaret A. Bush remarked, "Based on carefully chosen material from newspapers and other writings of the time, the absorbing, balanced narrative incorporates both humorous and sobering ideas as it blends descriptions of social history, technology and the characters of the principal figures." Beth Herbert noted the sheer lure of the book's details, stating, "Grabbing readers' attention with an account of President Teddy Roosevelt's historic visit to the Panama Canal construction site in 1906, this book combines facts and statistics with personal stories to tell the story of the canal's development."

Awards

In 1979, St. George received the Edgar Allan Poe runner-up award from the Mystery Writers of America for *the Halloween Pumpkin Smasher. The Brooklyn Bridge: They Said It Couldn't Be Built* was designated a Golden Kite Honor Book for nonfiction, an American Library Association Notable Book, a *New York Times* Notable Book of the Year, and a Notable Children's Trade Book in the Field of Social Studies from the National Council for the Social Studies and Children's Book Council, all in 1982, and it won the Children's Science Book Award from the New York Academy of Sciences in 1983. For *The Mount Rushmore Story,* St. George won a Golden Kite Nonfiction Honor Book Award in 1985 and the Christopher Award for Young Adults in 1986. The book was also designated an ALA Notable Book and a Notable Children's Trade Book in the Field of Social Studies, both in 1985. In 1989, *The Panama Canal: Gateway to the World* received the Golden Kite Nonfiction Award. *Dear Dr. Bell–Your Friend Helen Keller* received a Young Hoosier Book Award, 1994-95 and a William Allen White Book Award, 1993-94.

AUTHOR'S COMMENTARY

Judith St. George

SOURCE: "On Doing Research; or, How Did Mount Rushmore Get Its Name?" in *Journal of Youth Services in Libraries,* Vol. 1, No. 1, Fall, 1987, pp. 88-92

It is Liz on the phone. "I'm having a terrible time organizing material for a nonfiction book. Can I come over and pick your brain on how you do research?"

Why not? Not only have I written three nonfiction books, but I've also done extensive research for my historical fiction. And because I'm just now finishing *The Mount Rushmore Story,* I'm in fighting shape.

With all due modesty, I show Liz my system of beer cartons: a beer carton for my notes; another beer carton for correspondence; a third beer carton for brochures, pamphlets, and articles; and a fourth for Xeroxed copies of photographs. Research, library, and personal books are stacked separately. The A, B, C, D rewrites of my manuscript are piled on the rug with red, blue, green, and purple reminders pinned to my workroom curtains—a different color for each rewrite.

Liz is horror-struck. "Judy, you've got to be kidding. *I'm* better organized than this."

One writer's organization apparently is another writer's disorganization. For me, writing a nonfiction book is akin to building a house, a project my family and I tackled some years ago. Because we were involved physically, it was a hands-on experience, just as research is a hands-on experience. Are there really writers out there who hire researchers to do what I consider to be the most fun part of nonfiction?

Before I begin, I need my blueprints in hand, a subject that suits me, something I'm enthusiastic about. But drawing up blueprints takes planning. If I'm budgeting $80,000 for a house, there's no point in falling in love with plans that will cost half a million. On the other hand, I'm not interested in building a ticky-tacky house that will be identical to every other house on the block. Which means I talk over my idea with my editor (or agent) to find out if she's interested. *Books in Print* tells me how many books, if any, have already been written on the subject and when.

The idea for my Mount Rushmore book goes back to my childhood. When my father graduated from law school in 1928, he joined Charles E. Rushmore's law firm. Although by then Rushmore was an imposing New York attorney, as a young man in the 1880s he had traveled to South Dakota on business. While riding by stagecoach through the Black Hills, my father relates, Rushmore pointed to an impressive granite mountain in the distance.

"What's the name of that mountain?" he asked the stagecoach driver.

"It ain't got no name. What's your name?"

"Rushmore."

"Then that's the name we'll give it—Mount Rushmore," said the driver.

And that, according to my father, is how Mount Rushmore got its name.

The story stuck with me, as all childhood stories do, and when I was deciding on a nonfiction subject, Mount Rushmore kept nudging at me. Aha! According to *Books in Print,* there were no juvenile books on the subject, and with every other nonfiction writer waxing eloquent about the Statue of Liberty, my editor at Putnam was enthusiastic.

Basic research for a book isn't very romantic—about on a par with sinking the foundation of a house. My basics are right at hand: a 2,000-page dictionary purchased for $5 at a book sale; the *World Book Encyclopedia;* an atlas; an almanac; and pamphlets, brochures, and programs from all the museums, concerts, art exhibitions, and plays I've ever attended. At the risk of the attic floor collapsing, I've also saved thirty years of *National Geographic,* plus maps, filed in (what else?) beer cartons.

From these basics, I now know where Mount Rushmore is located, the name of the sculptor, the time frame of work, and that Mount Rushmore is part of the National Park System. Because government agencies are a wonderful, and usually free, source of literature and information, I write to the superintendent at Mount Rushmore and ask that all available material be sent to me. (P. S. He's sure to be seeing me in the not-too-distant future.)

Now I hightail it to the children's department of my local library to start on the framing; that is, to read all I can about Mount Rushmore, Gutzon Borglum (the sculptor), and the Black Hills. I long ago learned that children's and young adult nonfiction books are clear, concise, accurate, well illustrated, and usually competently written. I also immerse myself in the economic, political, and social climate of the times in which my book is set. As a dividend, the bibliographies in these juvenile books send me on to additional sources, both juvenile and adult, that I might not have known about otherwise.

At this point, my husband has to go to Washington for a week-long conference, an opportunity for me, I decide, to go along and do research at the National Park Service office, the National Archives, and anywhere else I can find information about Mount Rushmore and Borglum. Although I spend the week taking copious notes, I soon realize that I am in a position of selecting my wallpaper before the walls are up. With only the most basic knowledge of Mount Rushmore or Borglum, I have no idea of what is important and what isn't. The week isn't totally wasted, but it would have been a lot more productive at a later date.

My next step is getting a solid roof on, and for that the local library is out and a big-gun library is in. I'm fortunate to be within commuting distance of both the Newark and New York Public libraries. At this point I need contemporary newspaper and magazine articles, and the Newark Public Library has a marvelous periodical collection, as well as open stacks—much pleasanter working conditions than the closed stacks and endless waiting at the New York Public Library.

Up until now, all my research has been from secondary sources, but Borglum was a writer as well as an artist, with opinions on just about every subject under the sun. As I read his articles and books, I am getting down to the lovely nitty-gritty of primary research.

As my quest progresses, I am amazed at how the relationship between the Sioux Indians and the Black Hills begins to take center stage. When I began this project, I hadn't given a thought to the Sioux, and now my book is going in a whole new direction. It is as if a couple building a new house discover they are expecting triplets. All sorts of blueprint changes are needed to expand the house and make the new addition harmonious with the whole.

Now I'm ready to go to Mount Rushmore. I know my material. I know what questions need to be answered, including the question that started me on the book in the first place. How did Mount Rushmore get its name? Obviously, my father's childhood story needs verification, if it can be verified at all. When I mention to a friend that my husband, David, and I are going to the Black Hills for ten days to do research, I mumble under my breath that there probably isn't enough there to keep us a week. How wrong I am. We'd be happy to spend a month.

Tom, the young National Park Service historian at Mount Rushmore with whom I have already corresponded, gives me access to all the park files, tapes, books, articles, photographs, and correspondence. When I'm not working at the park library, David and I are hiking, swimming, picnicking, bird watching, riding horseback (he, not I) and looking at, listening to, smelling, tasting, and experiencing the spectacular Black Hills in every way we can. We also visit friends at their remote cabin site, drive out to the Badlands, and from there go through the Pine Ridge Sioux Reservation.

I tape-record interviews with the director of Indian studies at Black Hills State College, the local National Park Service geologist, the native Americans who run the Sioux Museum, and the experts at the South Dakota School of Mines and Technology. Tapes are a real time-saver, but I learned the hard way always to ask permission. Many years ago a loud buzzer signaled the end of my tape in the middle of an interview, which I had unfortunately neglected to mention I was recording. Embarrassing!

On our next-to-last day, I turn to Tom. "How about it, Tom, are David and I going to get to the top of the heads?" It's a request I've been making on and off ever since we arrived.

To my amazement, Tom's answer is affirmative. With

reservations. "Do either of you have a heart condition, high blood pressure, asthma, diabetes, emphysema, or recent surgery?"

"None of the above," I reply. "Say, how strenuous is this trek anyway?" It doesn't matter. I'm going anyway.

"Pretty strenuous."

Since Tom is approximately the age of my children, my next question is obvious. "Would you take your mother?"

A shrug. "Sure."

The climb turns out to be strenuous, all right. At more than one juncture, David has to heave me over the rocks from behind, and I'm in pretty good shape.

"Hey, Tom," I call ahead. "How old is your mother anyway?"

"She's fifty-two," he shouts back. "but to tell the truth, I'm lost."

Well, how lost can anyone be when the sixty-foot-high heads can be seen from any break in the brush? Needless to say, we make it both up and back, and it is an awe-inspiring experience indeed to stand on the heads and gaze out over the timeless hills.

My only disappointment in the whole trip is that no one seems to know how Mount Rushmore got its name. Although Tom shows me four different National Park Service versions given in tourist lectures, none of them is official.

That is simply a challenge, like having to dig the well a lot deeper than I'd planned to reach water. While at Mount Rushmore, I discover that Charles Rushmore's grandson, C. Rushmore Patterson, graduated from Princeton in 1931. As soon as I get home, I write to Princeton for his address. Although he has died, his widow lives in New York City. I get in touch with her, and a pleasant correspondence ensues. By the way, does she happen to know how Mount Rushmore got its name?

In reply, she sends me a copy of a letter written by Charles Rushmore to the secretary of the South Dakota Historical Society, which describes the exact circumstances of the naming of Mount Rushmore. The letter was written in 1925, when the carvings were only a rumor, which means there was no reason for Charles Rushmore *not* to tell the truth. A sixty-year-old mystery is solved! It is one of those rare moments of ecstacy that only a researcher finding pay dirt can appreciate. (With apologies to my father, the stagecoach driver had no part to play.)

With a National Park Service list of all surviving workers, I write each of them, requesting information as well as any anecdotes they might remember. Like finishing up the plumbing and electrical work, replies are now beginning to come in, not only from the workers but also from the medical authorities I've written to, the Bureau of Indian Affairs, the Census Bureau, and all the other individuals and organizations from whom I have requested information.

Next comes the insulation, the sheet rock, the stairs, and the floors—the organizing of material, the correlating of facts, and the meshing of the technical details with the personal story. At last I begin writing. And rewriting. And rewriting.

Two chapters worry me; the chapter on geology, because science is not my strong suit, and the chapter on the Sioux, because I feel that such an important subject has to be absolutely accurate. I send both chapters off to my experts, the National Park Service geologist and the director of Indian studies at Black Hills State College, with a request for comments and criticism. Both men reply, promptly and with helpful suggestions.

Finding the photographs, like landscaping the property, is the very last job, and it turns out to be more work than I had anticipated. The photographs I want aren't for sale, and, of course, the ones I don't care about are available. Lincoln Borglum, Gutzon's son, who was the official photographer during the carving of Mount Rushmore, is totally uncooperative. It takes almost a whole summer of digging and turning over the soil to find the photographs that I think will best complement the text.

At last, I'm finished. The manuscript and photographs are off to my editor, the word processor disks filed, and the beer cartons full of correspondence, notes, articles, and Xeroxes stashed in the attic. The finished product is a house with the plumb line true and the building materials the highest grade I could find. It's a house, I hope, ready to be lived in.

TITLE COMMENTARY

THE GIRL WITH SPUNK (1975)

Kirkus Reviews

SOURCE: A review of *The Girl with Spunk,* in *Kirkus Reviews,* Vol. XLIII, No. 23, December 1, 1975, p. 1336.

Josie, fourteen in 1848, needs all the spunk she can muster. First, she falls into the water in the process of rescuing little Will Brown from a goat on the wharf as they are about to embark on an excursion boat outing. Josie, having already outraged a solid local citizen by correcting his arithmetic, goes ahead with the trip despite her lost shoes and soaked clothing, and when on top of that she is seen in the company of a strange young man, she's dismissed from her job as the Browns' hired girl and, because of the scandal, is unable to find another. Nor can Josie go home, where her drunken, abusive uncle has inherited her father's farm and married her widowed mother. But Josie keeps hearing references to an upcoming women's meeting at nearby Seneca Falls and at the end she goes to hire her out at the dairy farm of a crazy, independent old woman who's been urging her to attend. There is a sprinkling of ginger in Josie; her trials are realistic (though you can never quite forget the author's feminist intentions), and those who take their adventure on the tame side and their consciousness raising in small stages can share her growing indignation.

Barbara Elleman

SOURCE: A review of *The Girl with Spunk*, in *Booklist*, Vol. 72, No. 12, February 15, 1976, p. 857.

It is 1848, and Josie's struggles are everyday concerns: coping with an often drunk stepfather inclined toward beatings, doing household duties as hired help at the Browns, calming 7-year-old Will's nightmares, and looking forward to a steamboat ride up Seneca Lake on a free day. She is not at all interested in the forthcoming Woman's Rights Convention at Seneca Falls, New York, despite proddings from her friend Charlotte Woodward and other free-thinking radical women in the town. When her boat trip results in a drenching in the lake, a badly ripped dress, and a meeting with an unknown man, stories are whispered about town and twisted completely out of proportion. Without a chance to tell her side, she is dismissed from her job and finds that no other family will hire her. Slowly she becomes aware of the necessity to make her own way. St. George sums it up well in her final sentence—"Now that she knew where she was going, she couldn't get there fast enough." A memorable recreation of a young girl's struggles against the attitudes of the times.

Cyrisse Jaffee

SOURCE: A review of *The Girl with Spunk*, in *School Library Journal*, Vol. 22, No. 7, March, 1976, p. 107.

Not only is the heroine "spunky," so is the writing and characterization in this story set in 1848, a few days before the Women's Rights Convention in Seneca Falls, N.Y. Josie is a likeable and capable young woman, grappling with some very modern predicaments—an alcoholic stepfather, the need to establish economic and personal independence and, ultimately, the problem of living in a society where men set the standards. At first Josie is resistant to the ideas embodied by feminists like Lucretia Mott and Lizzie Stanton, who appear briefly as they meet locally to organize the convention. But, when

she loses her job because of misconstrued public opinion and sees her mother and her employer bullied by their respective husbands, the issues take on new relevance. The romantic interest is played down, and the raising of Josie's consciousness is consistent with the plot and sensitively blended into an entertaining, subtly thought-provoking novel. A good choice in the current wave of historical fiction.

BY GEORGE, BLOOMERS! (1976)

Kirkus Reviews

SOURCE: A review of *By George, Bloomers!*, in *Kirkus Reviews*, Vol. XLIV, No. 3, February 1, 1976, p. 132.

Coltish, tomboyish Hannah wins the right to wear bloomers after she rescues her brother Jamie from the roof while wearing a makeshift pair she fashions from her torn skirt. One may doubt that female derring-do was always so well rewarded, but it's possible to read another motive between the lines—perhaps Mama, who appears in pink flounces, simply got tired of mending all those torn dresses. [Margot] Tomes's winning articulate illustrations demonstrate the difference between bloomers and Hannah's shorter skirts and pantaloons (not all that obvious to the blue jean generation) and the chant the local Seneca Falls boys aim at Mrs. Bloomer and her followers ("Twenty tailors to take the stitches/ Plenty of women to wear the britches") ought to rouse the fighting spirit of readers who might otherwise find Hannah's problem as obsolete as whalebone hoops.

Zena Sutherland

SOURCE: A review of *By George, Bloomers!*, in *Bulletin of the Center for Children's Books*, Vol. 30, No. 1, September, 1976, p. 17.

A story set in the mid-nineteenth century has one real character, Mrs. Amelia Bloomer, originator of the then-shocking innovation of pants (covered by a dress that came below the knees) for women. Mrs. Bloomer is one of Hannah's neighbors, and Hannah's friends Tad and Joel sing a taunting song about her as she goes by. But Hannah thinks bloomers would be wonderful, since she is an active child who likes to climb and run. A young aunt comes to visit, and *she* wears bloomers. A younger brother needs rescue from a roof, and only Hannah can get through the small attic window; wearing bloomers, she can climb easily and also has her hands free to help little Jamie. So Mama relents, despite her previous scathing remarks about such a garment, and Hannah is allowed to wear bloomers. The plot is basically patterned (prove something to parents and win a point) but the story gives historical perspective, it's pleasantly told and illustrated, both text and pictures being lightly humorous, and it doesn't stress its point too obtrusively.

THE CHINESE PUZZLE OF SHAG ISLAND (1976)

Publishers Weekly

SOURCE: A review of *The Chinese Puzzle of Shag Island,* in *Publishers Weekly,* Vol. 209, No. 18, May 3, 1976, p. 64.

Young Kimball Ames Lauder (Kim) and her mother get a call for help from Kim's great-grandfather who lives in an imposing house called the Anchorage on remote Shag Island, off Maine. Arriving at the bleak place, Kim and her mother are surprised to find that the old man doesn't expect them; he denies asking his granddaughter to come and help him close the house and that he plans to sell it. The small heroine is intimidated by the atmosphere on the island, especially when puzzling events convince her that stories of the ghosts of Chinese pirates haunting the Anchorage are true. Everything is satisfactorily explained at the end of a fresh, entertaining mystery for young buffs of the genre.

Andrew K. Stevenson

SOURCE: A review of *The Chinese Puzzle of Shag Island,* in *School Library Journal,* Vol. 23, No. 1, September, 1976, p. 124.

When 13-year-old Kim and her mother come to visit Great-Grandpa Lester on an island in Maine, the old man denies having sent for them. It soon appears that either the family house is haunted by ghostly Chinese music and strange lights in the night or else someone is trying to convince Lester he is insane so he will sell the estate. Before everything is resolved—a mite too easily—the real villain sets Kim and Lester adrift in a leaky boat during a climactic storm. The brisk telling, well drawn characters, and an ideal setting (the rocky island with its old house complete with secret panels and hidden rooms) add up to an enjoyable mystery.

Zena Sutherland

SOURCE: A review of *The Chinese Puzzle of Shag Island,* in *Bulletin of the Center for Children's Books,* Vol. 30, No. 2, October, 1976, pp. 30-1.

When Kim and her mother are asked by Great-Grandpa, age ninety-three, to come help him close his island home, they are surprised, since they've been out of touch—but they go. Kim becomes increasingly suspicious of the housekeeper, who seems to be cheating the old man and trying to make him feel he is senile. While the explanation for a menacing bird, strange Chinese music, hidden relics, and the housekeeper's theft of valuable stamps are explained logically, the mechanics are a bit too intricate. However, the combined appeals of the island setting, the helplessness of Great-Grandpa, and the well-

maintained suspense will probably make the story attractive to mystery fans.

THE SHAD ARE RUNNING (1977)

Kirkus Reviews

SOURCE: A review of *The Shad Are Running,* in *Kirkus Reviews,* Vol. XLV, No. 10, May 15, 1977, p. 539.

More wind-up historical fiction on the order of [Marietta] Moskin's *Adam,* but with a little more substance to the plot and texture to the background. This begins bluntly, with 19th-century Corny Van Loon brooding about the coming fishing season—he has been afraid of going out on the Hudson ever since he fell out of the boat last year and almost drowned. Corny's troubles multiply when his twin cousins sound a midnight shad alarm as an April Fool trick, the men rush to their boats for nothing, and Corny is blamed for the prank. But he has a chance to overcome both his fear and the town's resentment when two steamboats collide. Corny sounds the alarm again and then goes out with the other men in their fishing boats to rescue the crews and passengers from the sinking ships: pat, but St. George's picture of the stern Dutch fishing community gives it an extracurricular edge.

Denise M. Wilms

SOURCE: A review of *The Shad Are Running,* in *Booklist,* Vol. 73, No. 22, July 15, 1977, p. 1730.

Pat in development and resolution, this story of a nineteenth-century boy who overcomes his fear of going out on the Hudson River to help his father with shad fishing will satisfy its young audience by the very ordinariness of its conventions. Facing his father, Corny Van Loon is unable to explain the fear that sprang up after his near-drowning the previous fishing season; he's told to get home and resume his duties looking after his mischievous twin cousins. It's they who steal out one night to sound the shad signal for fun, but it's Corny who catches the duped fisherfolks' wrath when his hat is found nearby. Wrongs begin to right themselves when Corny really does sound the alarm in a frantic effort to rouse the village men for rescue efforts when two racing steamboats have collided. The spectacle of struggling victims pushes Corny to overcome his private fears and help his father in rescuing survivors; their success provides a cathartic release of Corny's fears; his new peace is completed by the twins' belated confession. Light, easily consumed fare . . . there are some novel perspectives and a selective infusion of drama that strengthen the graphic evocation of the text.

Jane Langton

SOURCE: A review of *The Shad Are Running,* in *The New York Times Book Review,* August 7, 1977, p. 24.

Judith St. George is good at showing real American history happening around the edges of the lives of her fictional children. In a previous book, *The Girl with Spunk,* for example, instead of telling a story about a delegate to the first Women's Rights Convention in 1848, she showed why the convention was necessary by describing the unhappy life of a downtrodden hired girl.

In *The Shad Are Running,* we see a Dutch fishing village on the Hudson River in the 1830's. Corny Van Loon, the young hero, gets along as well as he can with a stern, demanding father. When Corny's young cousins pull a prank by ringing the shad alarm in the middle of the night, all the fishermen in the village race for their boats and drop their nets, only to pull them up empty. Corny takes the blame. Later he bravely redeems himself. The austere circumstances of his life and the accurate setting make history real in a workmanlike book that is fun to read and full of pictures. A historical note in the back was a comfort to this grouchy reader.

Patricia S. Butcher

SOURCE: A review of *The Shad Are Running,* in *School Library Journal,* Vol. 24, No. 1, September, 1977, p. 137.

Because he nearly drowned the previous year, 11-year-old Corny Van Loon dreads the advent of the Hudson River shad fishing season. His misery is intensified when the inhabitants of the 19th-Century Dutch fishing village suspect him of sounding a false midnight alarm. While running away from his unsympathetic family and neighbors, Corny witnesses the collision of two steamboats. The accident forces him to overcome his fear of the water, and he and his father save many of the steamboat passengers from drowning. The plot moves along at a good clip, climaxed by a well described rescue scene, but while Corny is sympathetic, the other characters remain flat.

📖 THE HALLOWEEN PUMPKIN SMASHER (1978)

Barbara Elleman

SOURCE: A review of *The Halloween Pumpkin Smasher,* in *Booklist,* Vol. 75, No. 4, October 15, 1978, p. 386.

With Halloween only three days away, Mary Grace Potts, the narrator, and her imaginary friend Nellie are on the trail of the mysterious pumpkin smasher who has been ruining the town's jack-o'-lanterns. With Nellie continually egging on a reluctant Mary Grace, they set a trap for crotchety Mr. Norton, who lives in a spooky house; spy on the Maple Street Gang, who turn out to be secretly smoking corn silk; and hide in Mr. Simpson's new blue and gold Model T Ford Touring Car, hoping to find the true culprit. On Halloween night, an elf-costumed Mary Grace (Nellie is a fairy princess) finally

suspects and determinedly sneaks up on the real prankster—a ravaging raccoon—while a frightened Nellie looks on. Through four lively chapters, the tension continues to build and Mary Grace's ability to finally get one up on Nellie is appealingly portrayed. Soft olive-, salmon- and rust-shaded illustrations combine with black-and-white sketches to give this suspenseful Halloween story an appropriately mysterious air.

Kirkus Reviews

SOURCE: A review of *The Halloween Pumpkin Smasher,* in *Kirkus Reviews,* Vol. XLVI, No. 22, November 15, 1978, p. 1242.

"The Meanest Man on Grove Street," "The Maple Street Gang," and the inept driver of "The Blue and Gold Model T Ford Touring Car": the titles of St. George's first three chapters are also a roster of those whom narrator Mary Grace Potts and her imaginary friend Nellie suspect of smashing several of the neighbors' jack-o'-lanterns. But heart-pounding investigation—in a spooky deserted house, a barn (where the tough Maple St. boys are spied smoking cornsilk), and Mr. Simpson's speeding car—acquits all the suspects; and in chapter four, slyly called "The Pumpkin Smasher," Mary Grace bravely climbs to her own tree house and finds the real culprit, a raccoon. The mystery is never strong or scary enough for a rousing Halloween story hour, and the device of the imaginary playmate adds only a functional utility; but Margot Tomes brings out the best in St. George's agreeable, sprightly style, and together they provide a satisfactory mix of droll humor and old-fashioned Halloween atmosphere.

Mary I. Purucker

SOURCE: A review of *The Halloween Pumpkin Smasher,* in *School Library Journal,* Vol. 25, No. 4, December, 1978, p. 45.

St. George's *The Halloween Pumpkin Smasher* gives promise of being spooky but falls flat when it turns out that a raccoon is the culprit and not a series of suspected neighbors tracked down by Mary Grace and her imaginary playmate, Nelly. The illustrations [by Margot Tomes] in their brown/green tones or shades of black-and-white are imaginative and haunting.

📖 THE HALO WIND (1978)

Gale Eaton

SOURCE: A review of *The Halo Wind,* in *School Library Journal,* Vol. 25, No. 4, December, 1978, p. 56.

Ella Jane Thatcher has always liked Indians, and is more than pleased when her mother agrees to take Yvette, a French-Chinook girl, on the Oregon Trail, but the latter, after a first flash of wordless sympathy, is withdrawn and even hostile. Following an inconsistent course that Ella is reluctant to understand, Yvette sets members of the family against each other and encourages them to take a disastrous cutoff from the regular trail, but at the same time massages Ella's injured leg and cheers her with old Indian tales. Ella's suspicions, temporarily assuaged when Yvette rescues her from a rattlesnake, build in a Gothic manner until at the climax Yvette admits that she has been working for the ruin of the wagon train because the settlers are a threat to her people. The flawed and difficult friendship between the two girls is sensitively conceived, but unfortunately the book, too, is flawed. The main characters are not vivid or focused enough and Yvette's final explanation of her link to the tribe is too cursory. The action is exciting but often mired in detail, and, although neither the narrator nor the characters make consistent use of dialect, there is an occasional jarring grammatical lapse, e.g., "Now if you'll excuse me, I got a supper to prepare."

Betsy Hearne

SOURCE: A review of *The Halo Wind*, in *Booklist*, Vol. 75, No. 7, December 1, 1978, p. 619.

A realistic picture of western expansion emerges through this story of the Thatcher family's covered wagon journey from Fort Boise, Idaho, through Oregon territory to The Dalles in the Willamette Valley. There is nothing glamorous or romantic about the dust, dirt, exhaustion, family tension, illness, accident, and barren discomfort of the trip—nor the loneliness. The friendship that 13-year-old narrator Ella Jane looks for in her Chinook Indian traveling companion Yvette never materializes, for Yvette's mission is to sabotage the wagon train and stanch the whites' greedy acquisition of her people's land. This part of the plot seems contrived and at times confusing: there is no real explanation of the two tribesmen who follow Yvette, the coyote that is her mystical spirit contact, her background in the tribal lore that her Christian mother and French father have purportedly tried to keep from her, nor her knowledge of the area's water holes when the wagons get lost. But her strength speaks clearly, as does the respect that grows between the girls, and family members are well characterized in this vivid history lesson, based on an 1845 incident.

Zena Sutherland

SOURCE: A review of *The Halo Wind*, in *Bulletin of the Center for Children's Books*, Vol. 32, No. 6, February, 1979, p. 105.

Thirteen-year-old Ella Jane is the youngest of the Thatcher family, bound for Oregon in 1845, and she begins her story of the arduous journey by worrying about the fact that her father insists on following a Mr. Meek (a real person) in taking a short cut, leaving other members of the family: a married sister, a grandmother. Their other

passenger is Yvette, a withdrawn French-Chinook girl just Ella Jane's age, and as one misfortune follows another, Ella Jane becomes increasingly suspicious that Yvette is the source of some of their bad luck. Yvette nevertheless saves Ella Jane's life and helps cure her mother, who is ill. Only after Yvette has left to join the Chinooks and they meet again, briefly, does Ella Jane understand her friend's ambivalence: Yvette liked the Thatchers, but her first allegiance was to her tribe. As she tells Ella Jane what the westward trek means to native Americans, the white girl realizes that they are indeed the halo wind, the death wind, to the native tribes and their peaceful way of life. The author gives a clear and convincing picture of the hardships of the trail, the narrative has impetus and adequate writing style, and it is clear that the intent of the book is to show and evoke sympathy for both sides in the cultural conflict—but most of the story is seen from the white viewpoint, and Yvette's explanation comes so late in the story that readers may have already seen her as a malfeasant by the time she discloses her motivation.

Ann A. Flowers

SOURCE: A review of *The Halo Wind*, in *The Horn Book Magazine*, Vol. LV, No. 1, February, 1979, p. 66.

Thirteen-year-old Ella Jane Thatcher was troubled with misgivings when her father decided to join a small group of settlers following an untraveled shortcut in the Oregon Trail. The addition of Yvette, an Indian girl, to their wagon seemed to offer a promise of companionship to the lonely and recently injured Ella Jane, but a series of misfortunes befell the family. Yvette was bafflingly unfriendly, Ella Jane's cherished pet was lost, her mother became very ill, and the normally affectionate family was set at odds. In addition, the hardships of the journey brought tragedy and near disaster to the whole wagon train. Although Ella Jane felt a certain kinship with Yvette and finally established a troubled friendship with her, it became obvious that Yvette was attempting to lead the whole party to catastrophe. In the end, Ella Jane came to realize that Yvette was trying desperately to save her Indian homeland from the overwhelming invasion of white settlers. The strong and sensitive Ella Jane, her steadfast mother, the enigmatic Yvette, and the horrors of the journey are perceptively displayed in a nicely balanced and well-written novel.

MYSTERY AT ST. MARTIN'S (1979)

Barbara Elleman

SOURCE: A review of *Mystery at St. Martin's*, in *Booklist*, Vol. 76, No. 9, January 1, 1980, p. 669.

After Ruth is called in to the school office for making a ski trip payment with a bad ten-dollar bill, she begins to suspect that the counterfeiting operation originates in her father's church. Though she fears that knowing her father is rector of St. Martin's will dim classmate Kenny's interest in her, she can't allow her father to be implicated by the surfacing rumors and decides to act. In the midst of her sister's wedding reception when everyone is occupied, Ruth takes matters into her own hands and goes exploring in the dim, rarely used reaches of the church basement. Not only does she discover a printing press but also finds herself in danger from a man whom she least suspected. The crisp style and brisk pace, accompanied by a rounded characterization of Ruth and a well-developed plot, mix well in this exciting, readable mystery.

Zena Sutherland

SOURCE: A review of *Mystery at St. Martin's,* in *Bulletin of the Center for Children's Books,* Vol. 33, No. 6, February, 1980, p. 118.

Ruth Saunders, twelve, is the narrator of a mystery novel that is well balanced by material about family and peers, but has suspense and (for once) a logical reason for the protagonist's investigating on her own. The mystery: why are counterfeit bills being traced back to St. Martin's, the church of which Ruth's father is rector? The logical reason for Ruth's exposing herself to danger: her father has told her not to meddle in church affairs. Ruth keeps meddling; she suspects almost every adult who is a major character and active in church affairs. St. George tosses in such issues as rehabilitation of criminals (her father hires one), women in the clergy (her father's parishioners object because he wants to hire a woman as his assistant) and how old one should be to have pierced ears. A well-paced story, with good dialogue and a concluding episode in which Ruth is trapped, alone in the church basement, with the counterfeiter.

THE AMAZING VOYAGE OF THE "NEW ORLEANS" (1980)

Publishers Weekly

SOURCE: A review of *The Amazing Voyage of the "New Orleans,"* in *Publishers Weekly,* Vol. 217, No. 10, March 14, 1980, p. 75.

In October 1811, Nicholas Roosevelt and his young wife Lydia embarked on an adventure that was considered sheer folly. Gathering a crew of willing sailors, Roosevelt set out on his personally designed steamboat, the *New Orleans,* from Pittsburgh to Natchez to prove that the boat could navigate the treacherous waters of the Ohio and Mississippi rivers. As St. George mentions in her buoyant history, it would have been an extraordinary trip under optimum conditions. In that year of the country's worst earthquakes, of the Great Comet and of unpredictable weather, the achievement seems more miraculous than amazing. Besides conquering natural disasters, the "stubborn Dutchman" battled attacking Indians,

a fire on board, floods and other hazards—all depicted as only [illustrator Glen] Rounds can.

Kirkus Reviews

SOURCE: A review of *The Amazing Voyage of the "New Orleans,"* in *Kirkus Reviews,* Vol. XLVIII, No. 7, April 1, 1980, pp. 441-42.

St. George takes us on a diverting side trip in history, first rushing down the Ohio River on a flatboat with newlyweds Nicholas and Lydia Roosevelt, and then, two years later in 1811, retracing the route with them, all the way from Pittsburgh to Natchez, in the first steamship seen on the Ohio or the Mississippi. (They eventually reached New Orleans.) To highlight the daring of it all, St. George points to the general skepticism about taking a steamboat through these waters, and to the general amazement of riverbank onlookers along the way. For human interest there is the young wife's new son, born on a Louisville stopover, and for excitement a real humdinger of a day, with the boat rocked by an earthquake (the strongest ever recorded in North America, says the author's introduction), attacked by frightened Indians, and threatened by a cabin fire. There's one shadow on the enterprise—Roosevelt's refusal to pick up earthquake-stranded settlers—which St. George faces as squarely as need be. With Glen Rounds' pot-bellied chorus, a chipper piece of Americana.

Barbara Elleman

SOURCE: A review of *The Amazing Voyage of the "New Orleans,"* in *Booklist,* Vol. 76, No. 17, May 1, 1980, pp. 1298-99.

In 1811 the steamboat *New Orleans,* commandeered by Nicholas Roosevelt, great-granduncle of President Theodore Roosevelt, traveled down the Ohio and Mississippi to prove that such boats could successfully navigate the major rivers. Roosevelt planned the 2,000-mile voyage, built the boat, and took his wife and infant son on an adventure that included dangerous rapids, floods, Indian attacks, and the strongest earthquake ever recorded in North America. To round out the excitement, the Great Comet of 1811 streamed overhead. This extraordinary journey is recounted in an amiable, amusing narrative and is accompanied by humorous sketches that lend a fictional tone, making this most viable for special-interest readers or teachers looking for a classroom read-aloud during a westward movement unit. A map, a short introduction, and an appended author's note fill in historical facts.

Mary M. Burns

SOURCE: A review of *The Amazing Voyage of the "New Orleans,"* in *The Horn Book Magazine,* Vol. LVI, No. 4, August, 1980, p. 430.

In 1811 Nicholas Roosevelt proved that steamboats could navigate the mighty rivers to the west as readily as they plied the calmer waterways of the east. His two-thousand-mile voyage from Pittsburgh to New Orleans lasted more than two months, and for those who lived near the Ohio and the Mississippi Rivers, it ranked— along with an unusual migration of squirrels, an eclipse of the sun, a great comet, and a devastating earthquake— as one of the amazing events of an unforgettable year. A consummate showman, the energetic, persevering man remained undaunted by financial restraints, natural obstacles, and personal danger. His bride Lydia matched him in courage and sailed aboard the *New Orleans* on its initial voyage. Despite the doom-sayers, Nicholas, his wife, and their newborn son survived floods, earthquakes, and Indian attacks and managed to reach their destination, thus changing the course of history. Written in a conversational tone, the book attempts to maintain objectivity toward the venture, reporting its unfortunate as well as its admirable aspects. Progress was not without its price; the coming of the steamboat meant the end of the Chickasaw way of life, and by 1838 the last of the tribe had left for Oklahoma. The pictures suggest on-site sketches, adding a folkloric quality to the book.

HAUNTED (1980)

Sally Estes

SOURCE: A review of *Haunted,* in *Booklist,* Vol. 77, No. 5, November 1, 1980, p. 401.

Hired, along with his older cousin, to house-sit a remote, sinister-appearing mansion where a murder-suicide has occurred, 15-year-old Alex Phillips, who gets there before Bruce, finds the atmosphere oppressive and various strange occurrences terrifying. Bruce's arrival helps, but Alex's fears are renewed when he realizes that something is trying to push him into action having to do with the double death. Although the unexplainable remains unexplained and characterizations are underdeveloped, younger non-demanding readers with a taste for the occult will find enough excitement here to satisfy them.

Zena Sutherland

SOURCE: A review of *Haunted,* in *Bulletin of the Center for Children's Books,* Vol. 34, No. 7, March, 1981, p. 138.

Alex got to Red Roof Farm first; sixteen, he was nervous about taking care of a house in which there had been a murder, and he was relieved when Bruce, three years older, arrived to share their summer job as caretakers. There was something eerie about the house, and strange things happened; it seemed evident that somebody or something else was in the house. It all has to do with a hidden second will, the bequest of the owner's wife, a Nazi who late in life discovered that her real

mother had been in a concentration camp. The investigations, suspicions, and discoveries about the owners is accompanied by the story of a budding romance between Alex and a pleasant, friendly summer visitor to the nearby Pennsylvania town. The writing style is adequate if not polished, the characterization similarly competent but not distinctive; the plot is not convincing nor is it smoothly developed.

Michael P. Healy

SOURCE: A review of *Haunted,* in *Kliatt,* Vol. 16, No. 3, April, 1982, p. 16.

Scary stuff here: Nazi ghosts, vicious guard dogs, a dreary mansion with blood stains on the carpet where a murder-suicide took place only weeks ago. Alex is hired to act as a caretaker for the summer in this setting. He is sixteen years old and eager to prove to himself and his parents that he is able to face responsibilities. The mystery is spooky, the fear acute, and the plot moves very quickly. In short, it's a good choice for junior high readers looking for exciting reading, and a possible choice for less demanding senior high readers.

M. Hobbs

SOURCE: A review of *Haunted,* in *The Junior Bookshelf,* Vol. 51, No. 4, August, 1987, pp. 191-92.

Set in an unbearably hot Pennsylvania summer, which is conveyed beautifully, Judith St. George has written a splendid supernatural suspense story. Alex, who has changed jobs frequently since leaving school, is given by his estate-agent father the summer task of caretaking with a friend a remote luxury mansion where an old man has killed his wife and her cat, and then shot himself. Only after his father has left him, does he learn that the friend will not be turning up straight away, and it becomes plain that the former owners still haunt the gloomy dark house, each concentrating their forces on Alex. A German sheepdog alternates between trying to kill him and being a playful companion on the lonely estate. The insulin in the fridge (the Baroness was a diabetic) decreases in level, and the houseplants are being watered. Gradually, however, the history of the eccentric owners emerges from clues intended to involve Alex in some way: they were Nazis, and the Baroness' money was willed to an American Fascist organisation, but before her death, she had learned something which prompted her to take the action which led to her murder. The Baron's spirit is clearly using every means to prevent the discovery of that action. Alongside the tensions of this plot are those which arise when Alex's friend, older and over-sophisticated, arrives and regards their situation as an opportunity to live it up with a discontented local girl and her buddies. Her sensitive cousin Joanna, however, becomes Alex's friend and ultimately his confidante, though because of her he is strongly tempted to leave the job or at least to ignore the mounting pressure to act for the Baroness. Joanna's knowledge of German finally leads him to the truth, which is nearly destroyed by a fire in which Alex faces the worst danger yet. The narrative is dramatic, the everyday characters convincing, and the suspense well maintained.

THE MYSTERIOUS GIRL IN THE GARDEN (1981)

Michael Cart

SOURCE: A review of *The Mysterious Girl in the Garden,* in *School Library Journal,* Vol. 28, No. 4, December, 1981, p. 68.

Terrie Wright, "'the best domino player in Stilton, Massachusetts,'" is suffering "the most boring, awful summer an almost-eleven-year-old American girl ever had." No, she has not been forced to take in washing. Instead, her parents have insisted she accompany them to England for the summer instead of allowing her to spend it with her grandmother on Cape Cod. Still smarting under this burden, Terrie goes with her mother to Kew Gardens, where she meets a mysterious girl who, improbably, turns out to be Princess Charlotte Augusta, the granddaughter of King George III ("Farmer George" of Revolutionary War fame). It soon develops that Terrie has traveled back in time to the year 1805, where, for the balance of this extremely brief and rather tepid fantasy, each girl helps the other when help is most needed. The author's pleasant, conversational style fails to mask the fact that her well-intentioned book is not terribly successful as either fantasy or history. The Princess might be any bossy ten year old from a broken home, just as the year 1805 might be 1905 or 1705 for all the sense of period or place we are given. Altogether one of St. George's lesser efforts, although the black-and-white illustrations [by Margot Tomes] are pleasantly, vaguely reminiscent of Erik Blegvad.

Barbara Elleman

SOURCE: A review of *The Mysterious Girl in the Garden,* in *Booklist,* Vol. 78, No. 9, January 1, 1982, p. 599.

Bored with being in England, 10-year-old Terrie resents spending her days aimlessly wandering around London's Kew Gardens while her mother takes courses nearby. Then a small white dog leads her back into 1805 where she meets the petulant Princess Charlotte Augusta. A friendship develops and Terrie, realizing that Charlotte's unhappiness stems from a forced separation from her mother, volunteers to change places so that the princess can enjoy a short but forbidden visit. Suspense and touches of humor are nicely woven into a smoothly delivered fantasy that may stimulate readers to seek other titles in the genre. Tomes's black line drawings add an appropriately mysterious tone. An author's note about the real Princess Charlotte is appended.

Kirkus Reviews

SOURCE: A review of *The Mysterious Girl in the Garden,* in *Kirkus Reviews,* Vol. L, No. 1, January 1, 1982, p. 7.

Instead of spending the summer with her grandmother on Cape Cod, ten-year-old Terrie Wright has been hauled off to England: her mother is studying at Kew Botanic Garden—where, somewhat unaccountably, Terrie is supposed to keep herself occupied day after day. As a plight, it's not exactly riveting—and even more out-of-the-way is the parallel fix of the haughty, oddly-garbed girl Terrie comes upon in a thicket: she's Princess Charlotte, granddaughter of George III, and because her parents (history's George IV and Queen Caroline) are estranged, she's virtually a prisoner at "Grandpapa's" Kew Castle. Once that's swallowed and digested, however, the growing rapport between Terrie and Charlotte has the usual time- and milieu-bridging attractions and does lead, eventually, to some outright action. So that Charlotte can have a forbidden visit with her mother, Terrie cuts her long hair; the two exchange clothes; and Terrie, apprehensively playing princess, is almost found out and caught. Though it will be the last time the girls will see each other (Terrie, trying to make contact again, finds herself firmly in the 20th century), "each of them had helped the other when she needed it most." The rest of the summer can be borne. Slight in its presumptions and rather obscure on the historical side, but pleasant in detailing the jeans-vs.-coronets implications.

THE BROOKLYN BRIDGE: THEY SAID IT COULDN'T BE BUILT (1982)

Richard Shepard

SOURCE: A review of *The Brooklyn Bridge: They Said It Couldn't Be Built,* in *The New York Times Book Review,* April 25, 1982, pp. 33, 47.

The Brooklyn Bridge seemed to be a wild dream when it was first proposed, and the subtitle of this small book expresses its theme: "They Said It Couldn't Be Built."

Judith St. George has taken a different tack from that sailed in most Brooklyn Bridge books, such as David McCullough's marvelous and detailed account, "The Great Bridge," written 10 years ago. Here the author has set her sights on the people whose determination brought the bridge to completion. The heroes are the Roeblings, John and—following his death—his son and daughter-in-law, Washington A. and Emily Warren Roebling.

The Roeblings were pioneers in wire making and suspension bridges. The Brooklyn Bridge was the biggest project of its kind ever to be undertaken, and there were times during the late 1800's when people despaired of seeing this colossus, which dwarfed everything on the Manhattan skyline, even Trinity Church spire, completed.

Mrs. St. George has a knack for narration, so even though you may know a fair amount about the bridge (it is better if you don't), you get caught-up in this tale of grit, intelligence and imagination, for it is in the good old Horatio Alger tradition. While she never loses sight of the main characters, she explains with exemplary clarity the engineering problems involved in the building—caisson construction, depth pressures, suspension strains. She also refers to, but does not become bogged down in, the politics of building the bridge.

It was John Roebling's inspiration, and no sooner had it been approved than he died as the result of an accident incurred while he was surveying the site in 1869. The job of bringing the project to fruition was then assigned to Washington Roebling, who was 32 years old. He supervised the entire construction, for which, it seemed, everything was of the largest possible dimensions. Washington was stricken with caisson disease while working on the bridge and was confined to his home from 1872 on. But he continued to oversee everything in detail from his sickroom, his main communication channel being his wife. There were frequent worried queries in the press about who was in charge, if anyone, but the building went on to culminate in a glorious opening in 1883. President Chester A. Arthur and his Cabinet were the first officials to walk across the bridge on opening day.

The book is filled with interesting anecdotes—about what it was like to be a worker on the bridge, about how the public was allowed to totter out on fragile walkways strung between the towers before the construction was completed, about the various deaths and accidents that attended the work. The drawings and photographs are first-rate; they not only convey the period vividly but help explain the technical aspects of construction.

Kirkus Reviews

SOURCE: A review of *The Brooklyn Bridge: They Said It Couldn't Be Built,* in *Kirkus Reviews,* Vol. L, No. 9, May 1, 1982, pp. 557-58.

The story is familiar from other chronicles of bridge-building (such as Corbett's *Bridges,* 1975) or engineering feats (Olney's *They Said It Couldn't Be Done,* 1975); but St. George devotes an entire book, aptly illustrated with old prints, to the personal aspects and easy-to-understand technical wonders of the Roeblings' admired achievement. The project is depicted here as a real family affair: designed in the mid-1800s by engineering genius John Roebling, who died surveying the site, then directed by his capable son Washington Roebling, a Civil War colonel, who drove himself despite several attacks of the bends until he was finally incapacitated, and then coordinated by the Colonel's wife Emily who relayed her sick husband's messages and conferred with engineers, workers, and trustees. Like previous chroniclers, St. George finds the Colonel a monumental hero, and she frequently describes his behavior in terms of military leadership virtues: courage, command, cool head,

quick action, etc. One wishes at times for a Jean Fritz to point up a lovable wart or two. However, the credit St. George gives to Emily will be appreciated. (Mrs. Roebling had "such a good mind," we're told, that she later graduated from law school at age 55.) And the engineering story is an impressive and exciting one, from the lowering of the first caisson, the subsequent frightening fire and other crises, to the jubilant celebration with President Chester Arthur leading a procession across the promenade to a reception at the Roeblings'.

Ilene Cooper

SOURCE: A review of *The Brooklyn Bridge: They Said It Couldn't Be Built,* in *Booklist,* Vol. 78, No. 22, August, 1982, p. 1528.

When, in 1852, engineer John Roebling was delayed aboard a Fulton ferry bound for Brooklyn because of bad weather, he decided there was no reason why the East River should not have a suspension bridge like the one he was building over the Niagara Gorge. Thirty-one years later, at a cost of over 15 million dollars and a number of lives (including Roebling's own), the bridge was opened amidst fireworks and fanfare. St. George takes what might have been a dry account of a bridge-building (there are lots of facts and figures to wade through) and turns it into an adventure story. It even has a hero and heroine: Roebling's son Washington, who completed most of the work after his father's death, and Washington's wife Emily, who carried on for him after his health failed for work-related reasons. The book is illustrated with photographs and reproductions from newspapers of the time. This, in addition to a layout that's crisp and clear, gives an inviting feel to what otherwise might have been formidable. Written in commemoration of the bridge's . . . centennial, this is a fitting memorial.

Karen Jameyson

SOURCE: A review of *The Brooklyn Bridge: They Said It Couldn't Be Built,* in *The Horn Book Magazine,* Vol. LVIII, No. 4, August, 1982, pp. 425-26.

Published in time for the centennial of the Brooklyn Bridge, the book traces the construction process from the moment of the bridge's conception by John Roebling in 1852 until President Chester A. Arthur's triumphant walk across the completed structure thirty-one years later. Although the suspension bridge that links Brooklyn with New York is as sturdy today as it was a century ago, its erection went slowly. Chief engineer Washington Roebling had to contend with one crisis after another: His workers were troubled by outbreaks of caisson disease, and the construction was hindered by caisson fires, snapping cable strands, and bad weather. Having done research on the Roebling letters, notebooks, reports, scrapbooks, and other primary sources, the author presents a clear, detailed text supplemented with numerous illustrations that effectively convey the drama of the dangerous building process. A fascinating history of the "most photographed, painted, written about and perhaps best loved manmade structure in America."

DO YOU SEE WHAT I SEE? (1982)

Judith Geer

SOURCE: A review of *Do You See What I See?*, in *Voice of Youth Advocates*, Vol. 5, No. 5, December, 1982, pp. 35-6.

Matt Runyon is a 17-year-old who has recently moved to Cape Cod with his mother and his younger half-brother. Twice while walking a neighbor's dog, Matt believes he sees violent acts occurring in a cottage at the edge of the salt marsh. Although the police determine that nothing is wrong there, Matt becomes obsessed with proving that Mr. Vossert, the renter of the cottage is a murderer. Matt and his new friend, Julie finally accomplish this mission and Matt is vindicated. This is an excellently written story with firm characterizations and suspense enough to curl your toes. St. George also manages to interject such issues as gun ownership, ecological concerns and the difficulty in controlling a quick temper.

Zena Sutherland

SOURCE: A review of *Do You See What I See?*, in *Bulletin of the Center for Children's Books*, Vol. 36, No. 5, January, 1983, p. 96.

Matt hates Cape Cod, misses his Colorado home, dreams of going hunting again, resists all friendly overtures from his classmates. However, when he becomes suspicious about a man who has just moved into a neighboring house, he does respond to one classmate, Julie, because he needs to tell someone about his detective plans. Matt is sure that the new neighbor has murdered his wife, even though his two attempts to prove his allegations have irritated the police and infuriated the suspect. In a dangerous encounter, Matt and the man are almost killed; Matt's suspicions prove to be valid. The plot seems overextended, although there are moments of drama or suspense; in an unconvincing turnabout at the end of the story, Matt's scorn for conservationists and his longing to have a rifle so that he can hunt are reversed.

Sally Estes

SOURCE: A review of *Do You See What I See?*, in *Booklist*, Vol. 79, No. 10, January 15, 1983, p. 668.

Unhappy on Cape Cod, where his recently divorced mother has moved with him and his younger half-brother, 17-year-old Matt Runyon also feels that his new classmates are cold and unfriendly. Irritated when some ecology-

conscious students, including attractive Julie Chamberlain, chide him for walking an old lady's dog in the salt marsh, he determines to continue his visits there. Then he begins noticing some strange activity on the part of a couple renting an isolated house on its edge. Though no one will believe him, Matt becomes convinced that the man has murdered his wife and enlists Julie's help to gather evidence. The setting is well realized and Matt comes across as a likable if impulsive character in a lightweight mystery with enough suspense (and an exciting climax) to hold the attention of non-demanding readers.

Eugene E. La Faille

SOURCE: A review of *Do You See What I See?*, in *Kliatt*, Vol. 18, No. 1, January, 1984, pp. 18-19.

The main character in this YA mystery is a transplanted Denver teenager, Matt, trying to get used to his new life on Cape Cod—not the Cape Cod of the summer months, but the foggy, cold, sparsely populated Cape of the off-season. As he walks a dog each day through the salt marshes, he starts noticing strange occurrences in one of the isolated beach homes; eventually he believes that he has seen a murder. The complications of why the police don't take him seriously are explained believably, and the reader shares Matt's frustration and understands his determination to find out the truth himself. There is a romantic relationship that is a bit different from most others in YA fiction because the two are so antagonistic toward one another; most of their conversations consist of angry exchanges, insults, and misunderstandings. As the story progresses, they learn to control their irritations and make an effort to communicate clearly with each other to avoid further misunderstandings. The suspense mounts as Matt gets bolder in his efforts to solve the murder and puts himself in an extremely dangerous situation.

Mystery readers will find this a good transition from the mysteries written for the older child to those written for adults.

IN THE SHADOW OF THE BEAR (1983)

Kirkus Reviews

SOURCE: A review of *In the Shadow of the Bear*, in *Kirkus Reviews*, Vol. LI, No. 21, November 1, 1983, p. J207.

St. George, who has tacked timely issues onto the plots of previous suspense novels, gets a little out of hand here: the teenage heroine of this simple, linear thriller is trying to save the new, almost-signed US/Soviet nuclear disarmament treaty—while going through a coming-of-age wilderness trek. Annie Sloane, like her older brother and sister before her, is supposed to spend her 17th summer working at her father's mineral exploration camp in Alaska, 150 miles north of the Arctic Circle. But Annie's no outdoorswoman, and she's disgruntled by the rigors of camp life, terrified of grizzlies, annoyed by handsome field-worker Robert—who calls her "Short Straw." And then, while Annie's father is away from the camp on business, two Soviet defectors suddenly appear at the camp, claiming that they have proof of a serious Soviet violation of the recent, pre-treaty agreement: the USSR military, unbeknownst to the Premier, have nuclear missiles pointed right at Alaska! Furthermore, Russian forces, pursuing the defectors, invade the mining camp—with only two people escaping this takeover: Annie and Robert. So this incompatible duo, becoming ever more compatible (of course), sets out to *somehow* reach civilization with the secret data about the Soviets. They paddle a mud tub downstream towards Niyuk; they set off by foot across the tundra; Robert falls, breaking his ankle. And finally, then, it's up to Annie to go it alone to Niyuk—despite frightening wildlife, rain, and pursuing Russians. (Eventually, however, "in a new and satisfying way, she no longer felt like a stranger in a foreign land.") St. George's handling of the international politics here is the chief drawback: an unacceptable mixture of the simplistic, the alarmist, and the just-plain-confusing. But Annie's initial disappointment is nicely done, and the trek (which begins about halfway through) is brisk, varied, and scenic—making this a passable entertainment for those willing to ignore or laugh off the global pretensions.

Elaine Martindell

SOURCE: A review of *In the Shadow of the Bear,* in *Voice of Youth Advocates,* Vol. 6, No. 6, February, 1984, p. 341.

Seventeen-year-old Annie, following in the footsteps of her older brother and sister, flies to a remote outpost in Alaska with her father for her initiation into living in primitive conditions at one of her father's work camps. Her brother and sister are smart and tough, athletic like mother and father—Annie is the small, fragile one who'd rather be sitting by a swimming pool than airsick in a helicopter coming into camp. She dreads her week here; long, tedious, cold, and she's petrified of grizzly bears. Talk in camp revolves around an upcoming nuclear disarmament agreement with the Russians. With Russia only 60 miles away and one of the workers a Russian who says they can't be trusted, the talk has deeper meaning. When three Russian defectors arrive with the Russians in pursuit the situation becomes extremely dangerous. Annie proves her metal. This is an excellent survival story with a very timely problem.

Sally Estes

SOURCE: A review of *In the Shadow of the Bear,* in *Booklist,* Vol. 80, No. 12, February 15, 1984, p. 853.

The week she has long dreaded is here, and 17-year-old

Annie is at her father's company's exploration camp above the Arctic Circle in Alaska for the traditional "toughening-up summer" that her older brother and sister have already experienced. Near the end of the week, three Russian defectors show up at camp, closely followed by a Soviet military helicopter. Annie and Robert, the young geologist she reluctantly has been assisting, manage to escape downriver and across the tundra in search of help. When an accident puts Robert out of commission, Annie—despite her fear—continues on alone. Annie's changeover from wimp to heroine may seem a bit too rapid to be convincing, but desperation works great things. Though carrying a strong nuclear disarmament message, this will be read by non-demanding teens for the sheer adventure.

THE MOUNT RUSHMORE STORY (1985)

Ilene Cooper

SOURCE: A review of *The Mount Rushmore Story,* in *Booklist,* Vol. 82, No. 2, September 15, 1985, p. 139.

As she did in her book *The Brooklyn Bridge,* St. George examines a familiar landmark, provides fresh insights into the why and how of its making, and introduces the man who made it possible. Sculptor Gutzon Borglum, a child of immigrants, grew up to be a staunch patriot who wanted to show his love of country through large-scale sculpture. When he was invited by a member of the state's historical society, who thought up the idea as a tourist attraction, he did not hesitate to carve a monument in the Black Hills of South Dakota. Borglum conceived of the work as having much more than publicity value however; and even though some disapproved, he pushed on with the job. The sculptor comes alive as an opinionated individualist—choosing his site and his subjects and completing the project in the face of overwhelming odds. St. George's flawless handling of her main topic is supplemented by her deft and moving descriptions of the Sioux tribe, forced to leave the Dakota land they considered sacred. The smooth narrative and solid research give the book substance—the many fascinating black-and-white photographs of the work in progress are the icing on the cake. Map, glossary, and an extensive bibliography are appended.

Luvada Kuhn

SOURCE: A review of *The Mount Rushmore Story,* in *Voice of Youth Advocates,* Vol. 8, No. 5, December, 1985, p. 335.

This history of Mt. Rushmore is more than the story of the famous sculptured heads done by Gutzon Borglum. It is the story of one of the oldest geological formations on Earth; much, much older than the Himalayas, the Alps, or the Andes. It is also the story of the Sioux Indians for whom the Black Hills represented the heart of their religion.

Always a controversial figure, Borglum undertook the vast sculpture project on the heels of the unpleasant experience at Stone Mt., Georgia, where his independent attitude got him fired. A master promoter, Borglum knew how to excite public interest. He staged dramatic ceremonies to call attention to the project and raised funds; but the frustrations and difficulties were so many that a less determined man would surely have viewed the whole idea as impossible. However slowly, the work did progress. A detailed description of the vast operation is made quite clear by the use of photographs taken during the actual construction by Borglum's son, Lincoln, the official photographer for Mt. Rushmore. The reader can picture the thrill of danger as workers drilled the mountain with 65 pound air-powered jackhammers as they were raised and lowered on the mountain face by cables. Of all the statistics involved in the great project, perhaps the most remarkable relates to safety. Although countless dangers existed for every task throughout all the years of carving, only two serious accidents occurred, and no deaths.

WHAT'S HAPPENING TO MY JUNIOR YEAR? (1986)

Publishers Weekly

SOURCE: A review of *What's Happening to My Junior Year?*, in *Publishers Weekly*, Vol. 230, No. 24, December 12, 1986, pp. 55-6.

Steppie Emerson's plans for a perfect junior year in high school begin to go wrong when her mom inherits a pool table. Just as she'd hoped, Steppie gets a boyfriend, Roger Curtis. But how can Steppie impress him when Mrs. Emerson spends every day shooting pool? . . . Steppie feels left out in the cold when Roger avoids her and her best friend Megan finds another confidante. The last straw is when Mrs. Emerson enters a billiards competition in Las Vegas. St. George has created an engaging heroine. There's never a dull moment, as lively characters and realistic situations show how friendship comes in many—sometimes unexpected—guises.

Hazel Rochman

SOURCE: A review of *What's Happening to My Junior Year?*, in *Booklist*, Vol. 83, No. 8, December 15, 1986, p. 642.

Stephanie's carefully organized plans for her junior year go awry when her mother installs a pool table in the basement of their suburban home, competes in national tournaments as "Hot Mamma," and invites the local troubled teenager group home to play pool. Though Steppie's hurt when the domestic mayhem drives away her preppie boyfriend, Roger, she comes to see beyond conventional appearances and class differences. She makes friends playing pool with her punk classmate Wayne, whose streaked hair and fast, tough talk hides a troubled home and a personal fight with alcoholism, and when the affluent parents of her cool, beautiful friend Carolina get publicly drunk at a school hockey game, Steppie realizes that Wayne and Carolina "had both perfected survival acts." The resolution is too jolly, with Steppie's workaholic father learning to relax and the troubled boys becoming much too easily at home, but Steppie's first-person narrative is humane and funny. She doesn't learn to give up the wild boy for a steady life: she becomes his friend and gains the confidence to accept some uncertainty and risk—and when Roger asks to come back, she considers that too.

Zena Sutherland

SOURCE: A review of *What's Happening to My Junior Year?*, in *Bulletin of the Center for Children's Books*, Vol. 40, No. 5, January, 1987, p. 99.

Steppie, who tells the story of part of her junior year, has all her plans made and her priorities set: in order, ". . . finding a boy friend, making the yearbook staff, and keeping up my grades. . . ." With one variation, this is a formulaic teen novel, with a glamorous boy who turns out to be a disappointment, an old classmate who becomes newly interesting, and a third-girl-disruption of a long-standing best friendship. There's a great deal of attention given to the effects of the family's acquiring a pool table. Mom proves to be a pool expert and leaves the family to go to out-of-town competitions; and Mom also uses the basement to set up, working with a clergyman, a pool table rehabilitation program for convicted delinquents, one of whom becomes Steppie's friend. The scenario is turgid with its multiplicity of problems and people; the style is adequate, the characters are believable—but many of them seem more case histories from a file than individuals.

Allison Rogers Hutchison

SOURCE: A review of *What's Happening to My Junior Year?*, in *Voice of Youth Advocates*, Vol. 9, No. 6, February, 1987, p. 287.

Steppie has her plans all lined up for her junior year: she'll find a boyfriend, make the yearbook staff, and keep up her grades. Everything starts out according to plan but, of course, her junior year quickly goes awry. Steppie's mother inherits a family heirloom pool table and proceeds to enter pocket billiards competitions at the national level. Steppie is upset that her Mom isn't doing all the housework she used to, and is mortified lest the right crowd at school finds out about her mother's unusual interest. Not only that, but Mom and the family pastor decide to host meetings for misguided local youths at Steppie's house, so the group can play pool. With all of these teenage boys around, problems pop up between Steppie and Roger, her new boyfriend who just moved into the neighborhood. Although the pool-playing mother plot line is one that most teen readers may not directly identify with, they will sympathize with Steppie's reaction to the upheaval at home and also to discovering Roger's status-conscious nature.

As Steppie gets to know the tough boys in the pool group, she learns to see them as individuals and even becomes close friends with an adolescent alcoholic. Another complication to her junior year is that her long-time best friend finds another close friend, an attractive, mysterious new girl who is reclusive for fear others will learn of her parents' alcoholism. Although a bit weak thematically, St. George's treatment of these plot developments may render **What's Happening to My Junior Year?** useful for counseling purposes.

📖 *THE PANAMA CANAL: GATEWAY TO THE WORLD* (1989)

Kirkus Reviews

SOURCE: A review of *The Panama Canal: Gateway to the World,* in *Kirkus Reviews,* Vol. LVII, No. 2, January 15, 1989, p. 128.

A thoroughly researched, detailed account of the planning and building of the Panama Canal, which the author describes as "a living monument to its builders, to their engineering genius, to their victory over disease, but most of all, to the dedication and courage of their human spirit."

Along with enough technical detail to satisfy budding engineers, St. George's lucid explanations also make the process of construction comprehensible to more general readers. With its unvarnished look at the racist treatment of workers and Panamanians by the US government, the Panama Canal Company, and the Panama Canal Commission, the book also provides insight into the continuing conflicts between the US and Panama—from Roosevelt's "gunboat diplomacy" intervention in 1903 to the present.

A fine piece of technical writing and political analysis—all in the accessible, cheerful, no-nonsense style made popular by Jean Fritz. St. George appends an extensive bibliography of her sources.

Publishers Weekly

SOURCE: A review of *The Panama Canal: Gateway to the World,* in *Publishers Weekly,* Vol. 235, No. 8, February 24, 1989, p. 234.

Like St. George's **The Mount Rushmore Story,** this is a handsome, heavily illustrated history of a major American icon. Celebrating its 75th anniversary this year, the Panama Canal was little more than a "raw and muddy wound" when it was begun; its completion was a polit-

ical and technological feat. St. George makes excellent use of quotations from a veritable mountain of sources. She gives an interesting account of the battle won by Dr. William Gorgas against yellow fever in the region; and she makes revealing distinctions between the three chief engineers who, by turn, impeded or advanced the complex project. She seems reluctant, however, to voice her own views about such central themes as the race problems between the American engineers and the Indians who worked on the project, and the issue of sovereignty of the Canal. She also does not probe the political aftershock of President Roosevelt's "gunboat diplomacy" and other controversial policies. The pale historical photographs, first-rate diagrams and maps add tremendously to the impact of the book.

Beth Herbert

SOURCE: A review of *The Panama Canal: Gateway to the World,* in *Booklist,* Vol. 85, No. 16, April 15, 1989, p. 1472.

Grabbing readers' attention with an account of President Teddy Roosevelt's historic visit to the Panama Canal construction site in 1906, this book combines facts and statistics with personal stories to tell the story of the canal's development. St. George recalls the region's colonization by European nations, the completion of a transcontinental railway, and a French attempt to build a canal in the 1880s. She then turns to TR's efforts to secure financing for a Panama Canal. With moneys authorized in 1902, the canal-building eventually began; attendant social problems, such as disease and segregation, compounded the technical difficulties encountered in the actual digging. These difficulties are clearly analyzed by St. George, whose engaging considerations of the three chief engineers and of the project's head physician help reveal these hurdles. Illustrated by abundant historical photos and artworks, this well-crafted volume adroitly captures the drama of a pivotal historical event.

Margaret A. Bush

SOURCE: A review of *The Panama Canal: Gateway to the World,* in *The Horn Book Magazine,* Vol. 65, No. 4, July-August, 1989, p. 502.

"There are three diseases in Panama. They are yellow fever, malaria, and cold feet; and the greatest of these is cold feet." Attributed to John Frank Stevens, the second American to serve as chief engineer on the Panama Canal project, this pronouncement aptly pinpoints just a portion of the difficulties he encountered. A sense of the monumental nature of the undertaking pervades Judith St. George's well researched and competently narrated account. The challenges of climate and terrain, disease, and the organization of huge numbers of workers were enormous. On the one hand, St. George fully credits the drive and talent of the men who brought this great idea to fruition, particularly Stevens, Dr. William

C. Gorgas, Lt. Col. George W. Goethals, and Presidents Theodore Roosevelt and William Howard Taft. She also details the darker side of the American role in Panama: the power grab of the 1903 treaty, the dictatorial behavior of the Panama Canal Commission, the bureaucratic bungling, and the official discrimination against the thousands of West Indian workers who vastly outnumbered the whites working on the construction. Based on carefully chosen material from newspapers and other writing of the time, the absorbing, balanced narrative incorporates both humorous and sobering ideas as it blends descriptions of social history, technology, and the characters of the principal figures. A fine assortment of photographs, an extensive bibliography, and a statistical table extend thc informative treatment and add to the pleasure of a handsomely designed volume. Only the opening diagram mars the clarity and thoroughness of presentation. This large cross section of the canal places the Atlantic Ocean on the left side of the page and charts the locks and lakes to the Pacific Ocean on the right, counter to our accustomed placement. Later maps suggest reasons for this transposition, but the diagram will seem confusing to many readers. For the most part, an outstanding work of nonfiction.

Civia Tuteur

SOURCE: A review of *The Panama Canal: Gateway to the World,* in *Voice of Youth Advocates,* Vol. 12, No. 3, August, 1989, p. 178.

This well-written, well-documented, concise, and fascinating history of Panama and the Canal is the story of an idea that developed in the early 1500s when Alvaro de Saavedra, a Spanish priest "drew up plans for a canal route across Panama" and came to fruition with the completion of the Canal in 1914. The book also mentions the treaties of Sept. 7, 1977, that will eventually transfer complete control of the Canal from the U.S. to Panama, and will guarantee the complete neutrality of the canal. The sharp black and white photos clearly illustrate the story of a difficult undertaking. St. George has written this volume in commemoration of the 75th anniversary of the completion of the canal. She has captured the spirit of the adventure quite well, the difficulties of the task as well as the clash of personalities. After readers finish the book, they will know what it must have been like trying to transform jungle, swamp, and mountains into a 50-mile long canal.

THE WHITE HOUSE: CORNERSTONE OF A NATION (1990)

Kirkus Reviews

SOURCE: A review of *The White House: Cornerstone of a Nation,* in *Kirkus Reviews,* Vol. LVIII, No. 10, May 15, 1990, p. 734.

Fresh, creatively organized information on the building's architectural history and how it was shaped by events, society, and the personalities of its occupants. St. George uses chronology as a framework for a topical approach: e.g., Lincoln's tenure prompts a chapter on "The White House in Mourning," with a look back at earlier funerals, a survey of Vice Presidents who succeeded deceased Presidents, and an account of Lincoln's ceremonial rites and funeral train to Illinois. Kennedy's death is deferred to the last chapter (". . . on Camera"), which focuses on how TV has familiarized the public with the White House and discusses press coverage throughout its history.

Rich in entertaining as well as instructive particulars, this book is more complete than Fisher's shorter *The White House* (1989) in detailing structural changes and renovation; it also does a better job of making connections and leading readers to consider the larger context. Unfortunately, though, as was *not* the case in this fine author's earlier work, careless editing mars the text: awkward sentences abound, while omitting "that" after "so" repeatedly jars (". . . the old wood was so dry, most of it cracked. . . . "). Meanwhile, the well-captioned photos here serve their purpose, but are less outstanding than those in Fisher's more open, expansive format, which is also pictorially superior in representing the White House itself (St. George includes more people). Both are good sources, then, their strengths complementary.

Zena Sutherland

SOURCE: A review of *The White House: Cornerstone of a Nation,* in *Bulletin of the Center for Children's Books,* Vol. 43, No. 10, June, 1990, p. 253.

Profusely illustrated with black-and-white photographs, **The White House** is a readable account of the history of that famous mansion. St. George qualifies her selection of anecdotal history with a statement in the introduction—"This book is not intended to be a definitive history of the White House or the nation but rather it is a personal selection of those times that have most dramatically influenced the building. . . ." Most interesting are the descriptions of the construction, re-building, and re-modeling of the White House, which is presented in a lively combination of narrative and quotes. The statements of architects, servants, presidents, and their wives create a feeling of immediacy. Dolley Madison, when advised to abandon the White House to the attacking British, stayed to finish a letter to her sister—"Our kind friend, Mr. Carroll, has come to hasten my departure, and is in a very bad humor with me because I insist on waiting until the large picture of George Washington is secured. . . ." Whenever St. George loses track of her topic and attempts to describe presidential administrations, the text jumps from decade to decade; in two pages discussing the effect of the media on the presidency, for instance, nine presidents are mentioned, seemingly at random. However, the author always manages to return to her topic, and her tangents usually add rather than distract. Where else could one learn that Madame Chiang Kai-shek "demanded that her silk sheets and pillowcases be washed and ironed every time she used them"during her White House visit?

Margaret A. Bush

SOURCE: A review of *The White House: Cornerstone of a Nation,* in *The Horn Book Magazine,* Vol. 66, No. 5, September-October, 1990, pp. 624-25.

Americans today know the White House through televised events or perhaps from tourist visits, but Judith St. George reminds us that it wasn't always so. Some of the early presidents, most notably Andrew Jackson, entertained common folk as well as aristocrats with a personal hospitality that would now be unthinkable. This lucid yet intricate account follows the evolution of the White House as a building and as a symbol and focal point in American social history. Ten thematic chapters are set in chronological order, focusing on some periods and skipping over others in exploring the topics. The early years of construction, the destruction by the British in 1814 and the subsequent rebuilding, the major reconstructions under Presidents Theodore Roosevelt and Harry Truman, and some few periods of expansion and refurbishing are all recounted in a richly layered text that incorporates both explanations of historical events and insights into the temperament of various presidents. Other chapters explore the White House in mourning, in isolation, and as host to royalty and other world leaders. The final essay looks at the role of mass media, particularly television, as it has focused national attention on the White House. A handsome format with spacious margins and well-chosen photographs complements the appealing presentation. Not intended as a comprehensive account, the blend of ideas and facts in graceful prose, skillfully threading heritage and ongoing history into an interesting story, makes this a pleasing and memorable book. A chronology of presidents, an extensive bibliography, and an index are included.

Mary Mueller

SOURCE: A review of *The White House: Cornerstone of a Nation,* in *School Library Journal,* Vol. 36, No. 11, November, 1990, p. 145.

St. George describes the White House as a symbol of our nation's government and continuity. She begins with an account of the original construction and then covers the various changes and renovations that have taken place over the years, stressing that as the country has changed, the White House has changed with it. She describes how the building has often reflected the mood of the nation, becoming sober when mourning a dead president, austere in wartime, or glittering during good times. St. George also shows how it has become a prop for modern media coverage of the presidency. The section on the major rebuilding of the mansion during the Truman

administration is outstanding, but she barely mentions Jacqueline Kennedy's extensive interior restorations that gave it much of its modern look. The narrative is clearly written, with plenty of background information and detail. The black-and-white photos and illustrations are well chosen and greatly enhance the text. This book covers much of the same material as Fisher's *The White House,* but it is more detailed and is geared to older audiences. A readable, well-written history.

MASON AND DIXON'S LINE OF FIRE (1991)

Publishers Weekly

SOURCE: A review of *Mason and Dixon's Line of Fire,* in *Publishers Weekly,* Vol. 238, No. 42, September 20, 1991, p. 136.

Familiar history is combined with little-known yet engrossing facts to create an illuminating volume about the Civil War dividing line. St. George lays out in lively prose the events and causes that made the line a symbolic landmark of the nation's growth. Thanks to her sound, extensive research, all points are admirably covered—the colonial border dispute between Pennsylvania and Maryland; George Washington's military stand to enforce federal laws in a new nation; manifest destiny and the extension of the line westward; and the Civil War and the question of slavery. But the book's true strength lies in the obscure information seamlessly blended with textbook material. The account of Mason and Dixon's actual survey, done over the course of many years and at some peril to their lives, makes for intriguing reading all on its own.

Kirkus Reviews

SOURCE: A review of *Mason and Dixon's Line of Fire,* in *Kirkus Reviews,* Vol. LIX, No. 21, November 1, 1991, p. 1408.

By describing the history of a well-known boundary, St. George expertly demonstrates how a narrowly defined subject can illuminate broader historical issues. Beginning with the 1730s, she details the troubled history of the Pennsylvania-Maryland border, which led in 1763 to the employment (by descendants of Lord Baltimore and William Penn) of Charles Mason and Jeremiah Dixon to survey the boundary. Interspersing narrative with excerpts from Mason's diary, St. George depicts the often harrowing circumstances of the survey, which took five years to complete, then discusses the role of the boundary in the Revolution, the Underground Railroad, the Civil War, and even in one of North America's most severe earthquakes.

A well-sourced narrative that ably interweaves personalities and events, most arrestingly in the case of George

Washington, who began and ended his career along the Mason-Dixon line. The result is entertaining history from a fresh perspective.

Anita Silvey

SOURCE: A review of *Mason and Dixon's Line of Fire,* in *The Horn Book Magazine,* Vol. LXVIII, No. 1, January-February, 1992, p. 100.

In an unusual approach, Judith St. George provides a history of a place—the Mason Dixon line—from the 1730s to the 1880s. The French and Indian Wars, the Whiskey Rebellion, and Gettysburg round out the picture she paints, which also includes chapters on Charles Mason and Jeremiah Dixon. Often in danger and great peril, the two surveyed the boundary that divided Maryland, Pennsylvania, Delaware, and West Virginia and that eventually was to divide the slave states from the free. The cast of characters is colorful; the history, fascinating; and the research, as is always true with Judith St. George, superb.

DEAR DR. BELL . . . YOUR FRIEND, HELEN KELLER (1992)

Kirkus Reviews

SOURCE: A review of *Dear Dr. Bell . . . Your Friend, Helen Keller,* in *Kirkus Reviews,* Vol. LX, No. 19, October 1, 1992, p. 1260.

In 1886, six-year-old Helen Keller sat on Alexander Graham Bell's knee and played with his watch. Thus began a friendship that lasted until Bell's death in 1922, with Bell an enthusiastic supporter of all that Keller attempted. She dedicated *The Story of My Life* "To Alexander Graham Bell, WHO has taught the deaf to speak and enabled the listening ear to hear speech from the Atlantic to the Rockies"; in later years, Bell even agreed to appear in a movie of Helen's life, though in the end he wasn't needed. Experienced author St. George has done considerable research into the correspondence and relationship between the two, as well as into their separate lives; in her narrative, Helen comes alive more effectively than Bell, who remains a somewhat distant icon. Helen's astonishing story is still poignant—a bright, impetuous, loving girl finding her way through the walls of blindness and deafness. Bell is portrayed as a somewhat pompous enigma, a compulsive inventor who wasn't particularly impressed with the telephone and who went to Nova Scotia to fly kites. Strange friends? *De gustibus.* . . . An interesting angle on both lives.

Publishers Weekly

SOURCE: A review of *Dear Dr. Bell . . . Your Friend, Helen Keller,* in *Publishers Weekly,* Vol. 239, No. 49, November 9, 1992, p. 88.

In 1886 Alexander Graham Bell, inventor of the telephone and champion of education for deaf people, met an extraordinary six-year-old—a deaf, dumb and blind girl named Helen Keller. Out of that first encounter grew a 36-year friendship and a mutual support system that helped each to pursue the causes of dignity and education for people who are deaf and blind. Quoting generously from Keller's diaries and letters, St. George succeeds in conveying the intimacy shared by this pair. Readers will be fascinated at how two great people could also be such simple and loving friends. But St. George also outlines their lives during the course of the friendship, and this biographical information can't help but leave the impression that one short book cannot begin to cover the breadth of two such vibrant personalities. Still, this is a useful supplementary reference for young biography buffs.

Mary Mueller

SOURCE: A review of *Dear Dr. Bell . . . Your Friend, Helen Keller,* in *School Library Journal,* Vol. 38, No. 12, December, 1992, pp. 129-30.

St. George writes of the affectionate relationship between Alexander Graham Bell and Helen Keller. Despite Bell's fame as inventor of the telephone, his consuming lifelong interest was in helping those who were deaf, including his mother and wife. The author includes plenty of background about the two, covering their lives and many accomplishments in addition to providing the details of their friendship, from their first meeting when Keller was six, through the many encounters and letters until Bell's death. The tone is admiring of both people, but never overly so. A lively style and plenty of quotes from each person's writing and letters show the feelings and thoughts behind the friendship. Black-and-white photographs show scenes from both of their lives as well as of their times together. The author gives young readers added insight to both Keller's and Bell's lives; their story would be a good addition to libraries where books about the two are popular.

Gerrie Human

SOURCE: A review of *Dear Dr. Bell . . . Your Friend, Helen Keller,* in *Kliatt,* Vol. 28, No. 2, March, 1994, p. 32.

This is a highly readable biography that makes two famous people accessible to the ordinary reader. Much of the story of their lifelong friendship is told through parts of Helen's letters. We learn that the great inventor of the telephone, multiple telegraph and phonograph was committed to educating the deaf. Bell's great desire was to bring people closer through his inventions. He and Helen shared many interests, including a love of travel and books, the rights of women and the handicapped. Helen made education history when she proved she could compete at Radcliffe with students who were not handicapped, and graduate with honor. Throughout her struggles at Radcliffe, Bell supported her goals and was her constant encourager. Helen became Bell's most famous pupil and demonstrated through her extraordinary life that the handicapped can lead independent lives and make important contributions to the world around them.

Excellent photos accompany the text, and a helpful bibliography and index are included. I think this biography has multiple uses—in curriculum, for supplementary research and also leisure reading. Highly recommended.

CRAZY HORSE (1994)

Karen Hutt

SOURCE: A review of *Crazy Horse,* in *Booklist,* Vol. 91, No. 3, October 1, 1994, p. 317.

Noting the contradictory accounts of Crazy Horse's life and the mystique associated with him, St. George provides a detailed, if at times stilted, account of the legendary Indian leader whose short life has come to personify the struggles of the Lakota Indians during the last half of the 1800s. The narrative is based on extensive research and on her own travels to western Nebraska and South Dakota, where Crazy Horse grew up and fought to preserve a way of life that was quickly being destroyed by white settlers and soldiers. Though the lack of documentation may frustrate readers who wish to investigate specific incidents or aspects of Crazy Horse's life, the appended lengthy bibliography will be helpful.

Publishers Weekly

SOURCE: A review of *Crazy Horse,* in *Publishers Weekly,* Vol. 241, No. 42, October 17, 1994, p. 83.

The legendary Sioux warrior Crazy Horse is usually remembered for leading the party that killed Custer, but this vivid biography is sure to expand popular perception beyond that single role. St. George's portrait includes not only pertinent historical information about Crazy Horse's dealings with the dishonest U.S. military but fascinating details about his personal life as well. She talks of his disastrous love affair with a married woman, his determination to preserve the Sioux nation, his strong friendship with U.S. lieutenant Caspar Collins and his death, brought about by the jealousy of fellow tribal leaders. Thoroughly researched and filled with passion, the action-packed narrative communicates the author's admiration for her subject. Her attention to detail raises the book above the usual level of biography to forge a lasting image of an American hero and the people he loved.

Susan Knorr

SOURCE: A review of *Crazy Horse,* in *School Library Journal,* Vol. 40, No. 11, November, 1994, p. 117.

St. George's biography is as much a portrait of an era as it is an account of one man's role in history. Using transcripts of interviews conducted in the 1930s with people who knew Crazy Horse as well as other primary sources, the author paints a picture of a taciturn but loyal man who felt it was his destiny to defend his people against the encroachment of white settlers. Woven into the narrative is information about the Sioux culture, alliances, and beliefs (the importance of visions is emphasized). Readers are continually reminded of Crazy Horse's role as a warrior; descriptions of skirmishes and battles (including Little Big Horn) are filled with strategy and tactics, along with comments on failures as well as successes. Although the author states in her introduction that at times she ". . . had to imagine what his emotions and reactions would have been," she avoids speculation and does not fabricate dialogue. She also mentions the conflicting accounts uncovered in her research regarding some of the details of her subject's life and battles, but does not elaborate on them. Although readable, there are times when the book takes on a tone similar to Crazy Horse's quiet nature, leading to some slow-moving, dry sections. Still, the book will be of interest to readers who are studying Plains Indian history and geography.

TO SEE WITH THE HEART: THE LIFE OF SITTING BULL (1996)

Kirkus Reviews

SOURCE: A review of *To See with the Heart: The Life of Sitting Bull,* in *Kirkus Reviews,* Vol. LXIV, No. 7, April 1, 1996, p. 536.

Copious research substantiates this biography of Sitting Bull, but St. George provides no real sense of the man or why he was considered a great leader.

A labored text reads like a cut-and-paste exercise, a grinding out of fact after fact, without insights to behavior or an analysis of Sitting Bull as a real person. Much is made of Sitting Bull the warrior; nearly 100 pages precede the information that he was also a holy man who directed his life and the lives of the people for whom he was responsible through visions. Sitting Bull's joy in fatherhood is presented as dry fact; readers do not see any expression of the depth of his feelings until two-thirds into the book, when he mourns the death of a child. His noted sense of humor is not in evidence until the last pages of the book, when he tells a reporter that white people are "a great people, as numerous as the flies that follow the buffalo." Some incidents beg for explanation, e.g., young Sitting Bull urges his warriors into battle with the cry, "Saddle up; saddle up! We are going to fight the soldiers again." For those still unenlightened as to the bareback-rider stereotype, this is a startling sentence; without attribution in context or in notes, readers have no way of knowing the source of many quotations.

Carolyn Angus

SOURCE: A review of *To See with the Heart: The Life of Sitting Bull,* in *School Library Journal,* Vol. 42, No. 7, July, 1996, pp. 96-7.

Sitting Bull's defeat of Custer is just one episode in the long and eventful life of this courageous and respected leader of the Sioux Indians. St. George treats it as such, giving it only limited space in this biography. The result is a complete portrait of Sitting Bull as son, husband, father, friend, holy man, hunter, and war chief of the Sioux Nation. The author has thoroughly researched her subject. Her use of transcripts of interviews with Sitting Bull's contemporaries available in the Walter S. Campbell Collection, University of Oklahoma, and visits to battlefields and camping grounds in the northern United States and Canada give *To See with the Heart* an attention to detail and a richness that are not found in other accounts of this man's life. Direct quotes from those who knew him contribute to the book's authenticity, but occasionally make the flow of the text awkward and slow paced. St. George's admiration for Sitting Bull comes across throughout this informative, well-documented, and valuable biography.

Elizabeth Bush

SOURCE: A review of *To See with the Heart: The Life of Sitting Bull,* in *Bulletin of the Center for Children's Books,* Vol. 50, No. 1, September, 1996, pp. 31-2.

In this companion piece to **Crazy Horse,** St. George examines the life of the Hunkpapa leader. She explains how Sitting Bull's commitment to preserve traditional hunting grounds against ineluctable white encroachment not only won him honor as a war chief, but led to his temporary emigration, a tenuous rapprochement with U.S. authorities, and finally, violent death at the hands of his former followers. As in her previous work, the author examines the territorial struggles from the Sioux perspective, mindful of the holy visions which guided Sitting Bull's combat strategies and augured his defeat, as well as the simple reality that the Sioux were outgunned and outmanned. The intratribal dissension and personal treacheries which played no small part in Sitting Bull's defeat and death are considered seriously as well. The stilted cover art won't draw readers, but students who pick this up to construct the perennial "American Indian report" should be pleasantly surprised to find it's also an exciting read.

Barbara Flottmeier

SOURCE: A review of *To See with the Heart: The Life of Sitting Bull,* in *Voice of Youth Advocates,* Vol. 19, No. 5, December, 1996, p. 290.

Though extensively researched, this biography of Sitting Bull is ultimately disappointing. It chronicles his life from age fourteen to his death at age fifty-nine. Because the author could use only interviews with his relatives written by other people, the most intense parts of his story come alive toward the end of the book when their memories are fresher. Though the first portion is rather slow going, this is a good historical rendition of Sioux life in the mid- to late-1800s.

The author attempts to use a historical fiction style to keep the subject alive, but fails because the reader has difficulty deciding whether the story is fiction or nonfiction. Phrases like "'Yip, Yip, Yip!' the Crows shrieked," and "'Saddle up, saddle up', [Sitting Bull] cried," remind this reviewer of the biographical style popular in the 50s and 60s. The problem with merging fact with fiction also becomes apparent in that formal saddles were not used by Native Americans at this time in history.

For readers intensely interested in Native American history and Sitting Bull in particular, this would be a marginal addition to a collection. The book is too long and too dry to attract the attention of students wanting an elementary history of Sitting Bull. Cover art was unappealing to this reviewer.

📖 *SACAGAWEA* (1997)

Kirkus Reviews

SOURCE: A review of *Sacagawea,* in *Kirkus Reviews,* Vol. LXV, No. 12, June 15, 1997, p. 956.

So little is known of Sacagawea's life before or after the Lewis and Clark Expedition that its story and hers are virtually the same, but St. George enhances her account of the journey's oft-told incidents and accomplishments with a character portrait based on research and her own intuition.

St. George does not invent dialogue, but recreates scenes, such as Sacagawea's childhood capture by Minnetaree raiders, and suggests thoughts and attitudes: that Sacagawea would have marveled at the oddly regimented habits of the explorers and the way they continued to regard her people as children despite all evidence to the contrary; and that she lost her fear of them by watching them celebrate Christmas. As Sacagawea's pivotal role as translator, provisioner, and peacemaker is clearly laid out, she takes on a heroic cast, as a woman both savvy and wise, cool in emergencies (in sharp contrast to her no-account French-Canadian husband) and, with her newborn son, as much a comfort to the 33 members of the "Corps of Discovery" as she is an employee. It's a credible construct, enlivened by colorful details ("Dinner was spoiled elk, roots and rotten fish") . . . .

Lauren Peterson

SOURCE: A review of *Sacagawea,* in *Booklist,* Vol. 93, No. 22, August, 1997, p. 1896.

In a well-written and well-researched account, St. George humanizes her subject by revealing what she imagines Sacagawea's thoughts and emotions were during Lewis and Clark's 5,000-mile Journey of Discovery. Adventure lovers will find much to like in the book: attacking grizzlies, dangerous rapids, hostile Indians, and mysterious illnesses with unusual cures. But children will also learn details about an important historical event and get a glimpse of Native American life in the early 1800s. Overall, this is an enjoyable read and a pleasant way to incorporate history and social studies into a literature program, or vice versa. The extensive bibliography will be a helpful research aid.

Elizabeth Bush

SOURCE: A review of *Sacagawea,* in *Bulletin of the Center for Children's Books,* Vol. 51, No. 3, November, 1997, p. 103.

St. George follows her recent biographies of Crazy Horse and Sitting Bull with a less successful portrait of Sacagawea, the Shoshone wife of a boorish fur trapper, who served as interpreter for Lewis and Clark's Corps of Discovery. Most information on Sacagawea is gleaned from the journals of her employers, who seem to have regarded her as a useful and agreeable functionary but hardly a major player. As a result, the bulk of this account centers on the adventures of the Corps as a whole, and anecdotes specific to Sacagawea are heavily padded with speculation about her emotional response to the journey. Metaphoric flights of fancy revolving around the literal translation of her Indian name, Bird Woman ("She had stood on the shores of the Great Waters, learned how other tribes lived and had the satisfaction of knowing she had been useful. In other words, she had been given wings") are condescending and pat. Under this fusty sentimentality, though, is an accessible narrative of the adventure which, in casting a resourceful teen mother as protagonist, may lure some history weary girls to reconsider the Lewis and Clark expedition as more than just a "guy thing."

📖 *BETSY ROSS: PATRIOT OF PHILADEL-PHIA* (1997)

Elizabeth Bush

SOURCE: A review of *Betsy Ross: Patriot of Philadelphia,* in *Bulletin of the Center for Children's Books,* Vol. 51, No. 5, January, 1998, p. 178.

In the ongoing debate over whether Betsy Ross actually stitched the first national flag, St. George votes a resounding affirmative, relying on the affidavits of Ross's family and acquaintances that Washington and his committee had met with the now-famed upholstery shop proprietor. Yea or nay, focusing on this bit of trivia deflects attention from the broader significance of Ross as a scrappy survivor in politically troubled times—Quaker outcast, three-time widow, and savvy shop owner who catered to Tory and Patriot as business exigencies dictated. While short chapters bring St. George's offering within easy grasp of younger history buffs, thinly developed episodes and choppy prose somewhat dampen the interest: "George Ross had an idea. His nephew's widow was the perfect person to make the flag. . . . She could be trusted to sew the flag without a word to anyone." Still, readers looking for easy accounts of the Founding Mothers can cut their teeth on this beginner biography.

Carolyn Phelan

SOURCE: A review of *Betsy Ross: Patriot of Philadelphia,* in *Booklist,* Vol. 94, Nos. 9 & 10, January 1 & January 15, 1998, pp. 807-08.

This admiring biography tells the story of Betsy Ross, including details of her childhood as a Quaker in Philadelphia, her apprenticeship to an upholsterer, family life, and the meeting with General Washington that led to her making the nation's first flag. In an appended note, St. George states that although no written records prove that Ross sewed the first American flag, she believes the story to be factual, apparently because Betsy Ross and her female descendants declared it to be true and as "devout Quakers . . . they were women of unquestionable honesty." Whether the flag section is fact or legend, readers will find the book an attractive portrait of a woman living in Philadelphia during the pivotal decades at the end of the eighteenth century. The black-and-white illustrations [by Sasha Meret], which appear to be prints, capture the spirit of folk art in their simplicity, innocence, and good nature.

Starr E. Smith

SOURCE: A review of *Betsy Ross: Patriot of Philadelphia,* in *School Library Journal,* Vol. 44, No. 2, February, 1998, p. 124.

St. George uses historical records to create a well-crafted biography for a slightly older audience than the readers of Alexandra Wallner's *Betsy Ross.* Although the jacket art shows Ross stitching busily on the Stars and Stripes, and the exciting commission from George Washington is a highlight of the narrative, the author's note is careful to explain that there is room for doubt about who was truly responsible for the first American flag. Much more emphasis is placed on Ross within the context of her times: her family history among the Quakers of Philadelphia, her several marriages, her life as a businesswoman, and, most of all, her role as a Patriot during the Revolutionary War. Interesting details of daily life in 18th-century urban America figure into every chapter. Descriptions of Ross's busy upholstery shop are particularly lively and are frequently accompanied by Meret's appealing black-and-white illustrations. A bibliography lists more than 20 primary and secondary sources about the subject and her world.

Additional coverage of St. George's life and career is contained in the following sources published by The Gale Group: *Authors and Artists for Young Adults,* Vol. 7; *Contemporary Authors New Revision Series,* Vol. 14; *Junior DISCovering Authors; Something about the Author,* Vols. 13, 99; and *Something about the Author Autobiography Series,* Vol. 12.

Garth (Montgomery) Williams
1912-1996

American illustrator of picture books and fiction and author/illustrator of picture books.

Major works include *Stuart Little* (written by E. B. White, 1945), *Wait Till the Moon Is Full* (written by Margaret Wise Brown, 1948), *Charlotte's Web* (written by E. B. White, 1952), *Little House on the Prairie* (written by Laura Ingalls Wilder, 1953), *The Rabbits' Wedding* (1958).

INTRODUCTION

Although Williams collaborated with many authors during his forty-year career, his illustrations for such classics as E. B. White's *Stuart Little* and *Charlotte's Web*, as well as for the 1950s editions of Laura Ingalls Wilder's *Little House on the Prairie* series, have landed him an esteemed place in chapter and picture book design for primary graders. His drawings for these titles were as much a part of the storytelling as the accompanying text, as became characteristic of Williams's art. Diana Klemin noted in *The Art of Art for Children's Books*: "*Stuart Little* appears to the child to belong as much to E. B. White as to Garth Williams." Celebrated for his singular ability to endow animals with human-like characteristics, Williams launched his picture-book career with *Stuart Little*, which incorporates his trademark sketches of animal protagonists. A perusal of his titles reveals how much Williams enjoyed animal illustration: *The Chicken Book: A Traditional Rhyme* (1946), *Little Fur Family* (1946), *Baby Animals* (1952), *Baby Farm Animals* (1953), *Animal Friends* (1953), and *Three Little Animals* (1956). Recognized for their warmth and naturalness of form, texture, and expression, Williams's soft, cozy, and engaging creatures are sometimes infused with subtle humor and gentle satire exposing human weaknesses and behaviors. In addition, critics consistently discuss Williams's talent for combining realism and imagination to reproduce details with accuracy and precision and to bring his unique animals to life.

A *Publishers Weekly* reviewer once noted, "Although Williams's illustrations have always been anchored in realistic detail, his narrative drawings of pioneer life . . . marked a notable departure from the more fanciful type of art for which he had become known." Williams's most marked deviation from animal-based drawings is evinced in eight books reissued for Wilder's *Little House* series. His illustrations proved to be such an integral part of the collection that subsequent editions, produced when Williams was in poor health, were illustrated by other artists inspired by his work. Williams incorporated a variety of art techniques in his illustrations, using what seemed to him "the most sympathetic medium to accom-

pany the mood of the text," he once commented in *Illustrators of Children's Books: 1957-1966*. For the *Little House* books, he penciled the illustrations on tracing paper in the size they were to appear in the book. Publishers created a negative for reproduction directly from the drawing. The result was a litho-type image in which "whites remain white, drawing crisp, effect soft and warm," he continued. Williams also used gouache, oil, watercolor, and litho crayon. The decision to use color was left up to the publisher, as it was always a matter of cost. In *Something about the Author* (SATA), Williams described his technique for creating animal illustrations: "I start with the real animal, working over and over until I get the effect of human qualities and expressions and poses. I redesign animals, as it were." Recognizing the timelessness of Williams's art, Zena Sutherland and May Hill Arbuthnot remarked in *Children and Books*, "[W]hether the story he illustrates is realistic or pure fantasy, historical fiction or modern city life, his superb gift for characterization stands out. No pig could look more foolishly smug than Wilbur, no orphan could flee more desperately from the encircling bicyclists than Josine, no pioneers could look more cozy than the Little House dwellers." Whatever the medium,

Williams's work is beloved by readers of all ages. "He so captured the individuality and vitality of characters, created by others," commented Christian Esquevin in *Bookman's Weekly,* "that we can't imagine them not done all of a piece, author and artist working side by side." Esquevin concluded, "Despite his lack of formal recognition, Garth Williams will live on in the minds of growing children whose brains are forever imprinted with the images that he created. For those of us who only came to know him as adults, his work in nonetheless magical."

Biographical Information

Williams was born in New York to parents for whom art was an integral part of their lives: his father was a professional cartoonist, with work published in New York, Paris, and London, and his mother was a landscape painter. "Everybody in my house was always either painting or drawing," Williams told *Publishers Weekly.* His family moved from New York to a farm in New Jersey, where Williams spent his early formative years. He continued, "I remember well most of those early years in New Jersey, especially when I was taken by the farmer, our landlord, on his lap to go harrowing or plowing. Or when we went driving out in his two-wheel buggy to Peterson or the Passaic River, crunching along a gravel road or splashing through puddles. I was a typical Huckleberry Finn, roaming barefoot around the farm, watching the farmer milk the cows by hand, or do his other chores." Williams moved to England with his mother when he was ten years old. Dreams of becoming an architect faded during the Depression, when Williams decided to study art. His studies took him through the Westminster Art School and Royal College of Art. He abandoned a subsequent post as headmaster of an art school near London because he was not spending as much time as he wanted on his artistic endeavors. Fortunately, he had the opportunity to study in Italy for two years, using the winnings from an award-winning sculpture. In 1941, after also studying art in France, Germany, and a host of other countries, and a brief time working with the Red Cross in London during World War II, Williams returned to the United States. He picked up freelance assignments and, in 1943, showed his portfolio to an editor at Harper's who introduced Williams to E. B. White. An illustrator was needed for White's *Stuart Little,* and Williams received the job. The book was quickly established as a children's classic, and its success prompted Williams to commit himself permanently to book illustration. He created dozens of titles since then, including White's *Charlotte's Web.* Williams died in 1996 at the age of eighty-four.

Major Works

Williams's earliest works, *Stuart Little* and *Charlotte's Web,* are also his most widely recognized. Margaret Blount argues that Williams's drawings for *Stuart Little* "show a neat, thoughtful, spare, adult-looking mouse.

This talented artist's animals are all attractive—even the unpleasant ones—and no two look alike." In a review of *Charlotte's Web,* Diana Klemin remarked, "Garth Williams has a lovable, unaffected way of drawing pictures." Famous for illustrating animals with a human-level capacity for emotional expression, Williams has been described by Margaret Blount as "the Rembrandt of animal portrait artists." Some of Williams's most beloved stories are the *Little House on the Prairie* books. In *Children and Books,* Zena Sutherland and May Hill Arbuthnot praised Williams's *Little House* drawings: "Garth Williams spent ten years making the pictures and as a result the pictures and stories are one." Williams's research for the *Little House* series was exhaustive. He first visited Wilder's daughter, Rose Wilder Lane, and then studied cabins in North and South Carolina to make his drawings more accurate. He eventually drove for ten days to reach Laura Ingalls Wilder's home in Mansfield, Missouri, and spoke with the author at length about nineteenth-century frontier life. Later, he traveled to Oklahoma to study the site where the Ingalls family lived in *Little House on the Prairie,* and then to Walnut Grove, Plum Creek, Tracy, and De Smet, Minnesota, the town where Wilder's parents spent the last days of their lives. Williams, however, downplayed research alone in approaching his work. "Illustrating books is not just making pictures of the houses, the people and the articles mentioned by the author; the artist has to see everything with the same eyes. For example, an architect would have described the sod house on the bank of Plum Creek as extremely primitive, unhealthy and undesir-able . . . . But to Laura's fresh young eyes it was a pleasant house, surrounded by flowers and with the music of a running stream and rustling leaves."

Williams's *The Chicken Book: A Traditional Rhyme,* based on an English counting rhyme, is about a mother hen's lessons to her young chicks. The book was praised when it was released in 1946 and when it was reprinted in 1990. Mary Gould Davis noted of the original, "The background of farm and meadow, printed in soft greens and blues, is charming," while Faith McNulty wrote of the reissue, "This funny and trenchant little book . . . is still as fresh as a daisy. It's great to have it back." One of Williams's collaborations with Margaret Wise Brown, *Wait Till the Moon Is Full,* is about a baby raccoon and his mother, who tries to convince her son to limit his exploring to nighttime. "Garth Williams has a gift for humanizing animals," stated K. S. White, "and his raccoons deserve a small niche in the gallery of ingratiating nursery creatures." R. Baines remarked, "The sixteen central illustrations showing the sheltered, humanised home life of the raccoon . . . are pleasant, quite sophisticated and just a little monotonous." In a similar vein, *The Adventures of Benjamin Pink* (1951), Williams's first self-authored work, features a sea-going rabbit who at first becomes ship-wrecked and then makes his way home on the back of a shark. A critic for *The New York Herald Tribune Book Review* noted, "This brings us the best black and white pictures yet from Mr. Williams, in a bolder style than his familiar ones in

Stuart Little." Anne Carroll Moore was as impressed with the tale, stating that Pink carried "too heavy a load of words for a rabbit to bear." Moore concluded, "Is there not a tendency to give [animals] more than they can bear of the human load of problems and speculation?"

Williams's *The Rabbits' Wedding* tells the story of two rabbits—one white and one black—who marry so that the black rabbit can be assured that the two shall always play together. Other forest animals attend their wedding. *The Rabbits' Wedding*, when it was originally published in 1958, generated the greatest controversy in Williams's career. The book was banned in some libraries in the segregationist South, where many argued it promoted miscegenation, with one library director citing "aroused feelings" for the ban. For Williams's part, he was stunned at the reception of his book by pro-segregationists, particularly because the reviewers described it as having "all the soft, defenseless charms of babyhood" and "the warmth and security children love." "The illustrations have the subtle hazy quality often found in Chinese screen paintings," a *Virginia Kirkus' Service* reviewer described. Margaret Libby discussed Williams's art as "[t]he softest of misty gray charcoal sketches, tinted in subtle creamy yellow, dull slate-blue or muted yellow-green. . . ." The story, Libby continued, was "as sweet as you can get without being maudlin."Williams, claiming that the book contained no political significance whatsoever, argued, "I was completely unaware that animals with white fur, such as white polar bears and white dogs and white rabbits, were considered blood relations of white human beings. I was only aware that a white horse next to a black horse looks very picturesque—and my rabbits were inspired by early Chinese paintings of black and white horses in misty landscapes."

Awards

Williams received the British Prix de Rome for sculpture in 1936. *The Rescuers* was selected one of the American Institute of Graphic Arts Children's Books, 1958-60. *Beneath a Blue Umbrella* was chosen as one of the ten best illustrated books of 1990 by *The New York Times*.

AUTHOR'S COMMENTARY

Garth Williams

SOURCE: "Illustrating the Little House Books," in *The Horn Book Magazine,* Vol. XXIX, No. 6, December, 1953, pp. 413-22.

When Ursula Nordstrom asked me to illustrate the new edition of the Laura Ingalls Wilder books I wanted very much to do so. I loved and admired the books myself

and they had meant a great deal to my small daughters when we read them aloud together. But my knowledge of the West at that time was almost zero and I could not see myself undertaking the work happily until I had seen the country that formed the background of the stories. And so I decided to visit Mrs. Wilder in Mansfield, Missouri, where she still lives; and then follow the route which the Ingalls family took in their covered wagon.

I was spending the summer with my family on a very primitive farm in New York State. We had neither telephone nor electricity. The house had five barns and a smokehouse. Our water came down from a crystal-clear spring in the woods, and our only mechanical convenience was a hand-pump in the kitchen, located in a lean-to with a very leaky roof. We were situated on a high hill surrounded by two hundred acres. The house was almost two hundred years old and the main barn was a giant, built when the farmers vied with one another to build the largest. Three years earlier the farm was still being run by the old couple who had lived there for eighty years exactly in the manner of the Wilders in Malone, New York, as described in *Farmer Boy.* It was not surprising then to find as I studied the books that time seemed to slip back seventy or eighty years. I had to clean lamps and trim wicks and I would place little bits of decorative red flannel in the glass bowls of the lamps as Caroline Ingalls had done in the book I had just put down.

Early in September we set out by car, drove through the Smokies and reached Mansfield, Missouri, ten days later. Mrs. Wilder was working in her garden when we arrived and was without any doubt the Laura of her books. She was small and nimble. Her eyes sparkled with good humor and she seemed a good twenty years younger than her age.

She took us into the house and we looked at all her old family photographs. She told us about the people and just where to find Plum Creek and the other places mentioned in the books. Mr. Almanzo Wilder came in and we talked of his youth in Malone, New York. I asked about many things and of course particularly about Pa's fiddle.

Mrs. Wilder told us that it is now kept in a museum in Pierre, South Dakota, and once every year it is taken out of its exhibit case and someone plays on it the songs Pa used to play for Laura and Mary. Some years ago Mrs. Wilder sent it to New York for a book exhibition. In the same package was the calico quilt which Mary made just after she became blind. Everyone was shocked to find that the package had not been insured, especially as the violin proved to be an extremely valuable Amati!

When I said that we were about to go down to the site of *Little House on the Prairie* on the Verdigris River in Oklahoma, and then from there to Plum Creek in Minnesota and on to De Smet, South Dakota, Mr. Wilder was worried because heavy snow was reported to be falling in the Rockies.

"Those blizzards can blow for weeks; I don't think you should risk going to De Smet at that time of year."

But Mrs. Wilder said very characteristically, "Oh, *I* would go!"

Two days later I was in Oklahoma following a dirt wagon road along the Verdigris River. As I rounded a bend I met an elderly man driving a two-horse wagon. I stopped to speak to him and asked if he knew anything of the Ingalls family. He told me that he had arrived in the vicinity when he was a boy and could recall the people that took over the little house on the prairie after the Ingalls family left. The house had now gone but at least I could see where it used to stand.

We drove to Independence, Kansas, following as closely as possible the route taken by Pa. I stood on the banks of the Verdigris River at the place where Mr. Edwards swam across that cold December day in 1873 just so that he could bring Christmas to "two little young girls named Mary and Laura." And I thought of that day in the little house on the prairie when the creek rose so high that "they knew they would have no Christmas, because Santa Claus could not cross that roaring creek." And they were all sad—Pa, Ma and Laura and Mary. And Ma was worried not only about Santa Claus. She also "hated to think of Mr. Edwards eating his bachelor cooking alone on Christmas Day. Mr. Edwards had been asked to eat Christmas dinner with them, but Pa shook his head and said a man would risk his neck, trying to cross that creek now."

And that was just what Mr. Edwards had done. He had risked his neck right here in this river and carried Santa Claus's presents with him so that two little girls could have Christmas.

I went back to the car and we drove on to Walnut Grove, Minnesota, and I could imagine myself as Pa Ingalls in a covered wagon creeping slowly across the vast prairie.

At the offices of *The Walnut Grove Tribune,* Mr. Lantz, the editor, was surprised to learn that *their* Plum Creek was the one Mrs. Wilder was writing about. But in *A Half Century of Progress,* published by the paper in 1916, we found Pa's name:

> The people living within the vicinity of the station petitioned to be set apart as an independent Village, and on March 13, 1879, held their first election resulting in the following officials being elected:

> President, Elias Bedal; Justice, Charles Ingalls. . . .

A Golden Anniversary Edition of *The Walnut Grove Tribune* given me by Mr. Lantz provided me with many early pictures of the town and people.

He directed me to Plum Creek, which I followed on a very muddy cart track until I reached a farmhouse on the bank. The grandparents living in the house remembered many of the characters in the book *On the Banks of Plum Creek* but nothing of a sod house in the bank, although, according to Mrs. Wilder's description, it could not have been more than a quarter of a mile from their place. I left the car in their yard and followed the stream, taking my camera with me. I did not expect to find the house, but I felt certain that it would have left an indentation in the bank. A light rain did not help my search and I was just about to give up when ahead of me I saw exactly what I was looking for, a hollow in the East Bank of Plum Creek. I felt very well rewarded, for the scene fitted Mrs. Wilder's description perfectly. I took my pictures and returned to Walnut Grove and we drove on to Tracy and then to De Smet, the scene of the last four books.

Next morning I went to *The De Smet News* and Mr. Sherwood, the publisher, took me to the shores of Silver Lake and showed me where Pa Ingalls put up their claim shanty. Then he drove me all over town, pointing out the old places and giving me also the history that followed after the last of Mrs. Wilder's books. Pa and Ma remained in De Smet to the end of their lives. Carrie became Mrs. D. N. Swanzey. Grace became Mrs. Nate Dow and lived in a small town nearby, to the west, called Manchester. Mary never married.

Mr. Sherwood gave me the Fiftieth Anniversary Edition of *The De Smet News* of June 6, 1930, and in it I found many references to the characters in the books and to the Hard Winter of 1880. Here are a few:

> Ingalls was first resident of De Smet. He was the first resident, first to have a family with him here, quite possibly first to establish a home on the townsite, first justice of the peace and first town clerk.

> The Ingalls home was a stopping place for the early home-seekers, and they played host as best they could, their house being practically a hotel that first year.

> Another early school was the Bouchie school and the early teacher was Laura Ingalls of De Smet.

> The first religious service in the community was held in the Ingalls home near Silver Lake on February 29, 1880.

> Arriving back here about April 20, 1880, to build his shanty and state residence on his land, Mr. Dow found the beginning of De Smet. He was surprised to see a shanty on his land and at first thought someone had jumped his claim, but found it to be the railroad house, with the Ingalls family living in it. This was moved to De Smet, standing to-day near the entrance to the ball park.

> The first public school of several grades was presided over by Mrs. C. L. Dawley, nee Florence Garland.

Miss Garland received a salary of $20.00 per month for teaching the dozen pupils. She was followed by Miss Wilder [Almanzo's sister]. . . . Miss Wilder taught during the school year of 1881 and 1882.

The square in which the Congregational church stood was used as a pasture for cows, through which the children disliked to pass.

The fall and early winter was fine and Christmas Day people from far and wide gathered at the Ingalls home for a picnic dinner. There were about seventy-five persons present; most of them were strangers, however, they quickly became acquainted and all had a happy time.

That Christmas Day was the beginning of the hard winter described by Mrs. Wilder in *The Long Winter.*

The house, south of Silver Lake, stood empty on the prairie and I wandered around it, peering into the windows where Laura, Pa, Ma, Mary, Carrie and Baby Grace once sat. The air was fresh and clear and the sky a quiet blue. I could imagine the children playing in the buffalo grass out on that vast prairie. I drove south over the muddy roads to where Laura taught school and where Almanzo came courting. Over the same rolling prairie that Almanzo and Cap Garland sledded with the supply of wheat for the starving town in that winter of 1880.

I returned to the town and talked with Mrs. Sterr who had been a playmate of Carrie and Grace and heard her tell many stories of those early days. I talked with Mr. Masters who was a contemporary of Mrs. Wilder. He remembered every change in the town since those first claim shanties. "Those stories," he said, "are more than just stories for us. They are our lives, we lived them."

As the sun set we drove out of De Smet in the direction of Minnesota. The radio reported a heavy snowstorm thirty miles to the west. I thought of Mr. Wilder and drove fast into the dark. When we reached Sherburn, Minnesota, where we were going to stay with friends, a fierce cold wind began to blow and as we sat down to dinner a swirling snow enveloped the house; but I had seen the background of the *Little House* books. Seen the land, the houses and many of the people.

As my own farm was in the same state and territory as the Wilders' of Malone, all I required for *Farmer Boy* were pictures of the town of that day. A letter of mine was thoughtfully sent to a local paper by Mr. Dumas, the acting postmaster, and the people there were most kind and many lent me early photographs and drawings. These included pictures of the church, the Wilder house, the Franklin School, the early streets and the memorial park. This account would be incomplete if I omitted to mention the help given me by Mr. Clarence Dumas, Mr. V. B. Roby, Mrs. M. P. House, Mrs. F. E. Smith, granddaughter of Sarah Wilder, and Mr. Clarence E. Kilburn whose letter from Mrs. Wilder appears elsewhere in this issue.

With costumes and the early pioneer equipment and methods of living I was given great assistance by the Farmer's Museum of Cooperstown, New York. Among the many interesting things I found there was a stoneware jug with the name Ingalls on it.

Yet even with all the data I collected it must not be assumed that every character is a portrait or that every detail is accurate. With the limited space for illustrations I could only dip into the large amount of information available and use what seemed most important.

Illustrating books is not just making pictures of the houses, the people and the articles mentioned by the author; the artist has to see everything with the same eyes. For example, an architect would have described the sod house on the bank of Plum Creek as extremely primitive, unhealthy and undesirable—nothing to seal the walls from dampness, no ventilation, no light. But to Laura's fresh young eyes it was a pleasant house, surrounded by flowers and with the music of a running stream and rustling leaves.

She understood the meaning of hardship and struggle, of joy and work, of shyness and bravery. She was never overcome by drabness or squalor. She never glamorized anything; yet she saw the loveliness in everything. This was the way the illustrator had to follow—no glamorizing for him either; no giving everyone a permanent wave.

It is now ten years since I began to try to recreate in pictures the lives of Laura and Mary. It has been for me a most exciting adventure.

Lee Bennett Hopkins with Garth Williams

SOURCE: "Profile: An Interview with Garth Williams," in *Language Arts,* Vol. 53, No. 7, October, 1976, pp. 806-09.

It would be hard to imagine E. B. White's *Stuart Little* and *Charlotte's Web,* Laura Ingalls Wilder's Little House series, or George Selden's engaging Cricket tales without the accompanying illustrations by Garth Williams. His artwork for these, and the many other books he has brought his talents to, perfectly blend with the texts, and add another dimension to classic writings.

Since his first book, *Stuart Little,* was published in 1945, Garth Williams has moved through the past three decades to become one of America's top illustrators. Not only has his career moved along at a rapid pace, the man, himself, does too!

[Williams] remarks, "My mother says I was born on the fifteenth of April in 1912. The news of the sinking of the Titanic arrived at the same time as I did, and was so sensational that they didn't get around to registering me officially until April 16th!

"I grew up in a variety of places and countries. I was taken to Europe very early in my life to be shown off to my relations. I spoke French first, so my mother told me. But I was soon back in the wilds of Caldwell, New Jersey. Caldwell was farmland then—forest with giant trees being felled for lumber. I would often take a trolley to the subway line which passed under the Hudson River; I loved that. I spent my time in New York looking for fire engines. They would come galloping with six or more white horses, pulling a glorious, smoke-belching machine.

"At the age of six, I recall being taken to Canada. This was during World War I. I remember everyone made cookies and fudge for the soldiers—and me! Everyone went crazy on Armistice Day. We then lived on Lake Simcoe and I still well-remember how planes looped the loop, how boxers fought on the upper wing, and how all the hooters blew. It was a most memorable day.

"When I was ten, I was taken to England to be schooled. There I became the English schoolboy. Tom Brown's school days were very much like my own life. "It was at the time of the Depression that I had to face the point of selecting a college for a profession. I had decided

since the age of ten that I would become an architect. I was practically adopted by one in our town. I worked for him on Saturday mornings as a draftsman—and I got paid! But by the time I was eighteen, the future for an architect was hopeless, so off I went to art school. My parents were both artists. My father, at sixteen, had sold two drawings to *Punch* magazine in England; mother was a painter. I studied painting, sculpture, theatrical design, advertising, was a principal of an out-of-London art school for a year, then won the British Prix de Rome for sculpture and went to Rome. I returned to London just before war was declared in 1939.

"In 1943, I tried to become a *New Yorker* magazine cartoonist. Unfortunately my style was considered too wild and European. I made hundreds of spots while trying to find a style; these kept me alive. Finally, I went to Harper and Row with a portfolio of paintings, photographs of sculpture and architectural projects, my wild cartoons, caricatures, fabric designs, murals, and portrait drawings. Ursula Nordstrom, the editor of children's books, said she had a manuscript coming in shortly which I could perhaps try to illustrate. When the manuscript arrived in her office, E. B. White had pinned a note on it saying, "Try Garth Williams." As it turned out it was a good omen because the manuscript was *Stuart Little*.

"I first met E. B. White a few days after reading the manuscript. We met in the *New Yorker* magazine offices where he worked. He struck me as shy, and after talking for awhile he asked, 'Do you like my story?' This seemed so strange to me as I had thought the story was just wonderful and would have illustrated it for the sheer pleasure. We had been talking about where Stuart lived—Gramercy Park—and E. B. White told me that the book was written during the past eleven or twelve years." Mr. White created the book in the hope of amusing a six-year-old niece but before he finished it, she had grown up.

"E. B. White," continues Mr. Williams, "wanted the old double-decker Fifth Avenue bus of that period. I made the drawings in pencil first. These were sent to him and he scribbled any comments he wished to in the margin. The drawings then came back to me and I inked them in. His comments were always encouraging. Such margin scribbles included:

> I like Stuart's crawl stroke very much, but I agree with you that Harriet isn't right. Her hair should be smoother and neater, also her legs should look more attractive. . . . I am enclosing a clipping from a Sears Roebuck catalogue showing a girl that looks like Harriet.

> I like Stuart's clothes. The shoes in the letter-writing picture are just right for a mouse's feet.

The original sketch I drew of the dentist, Dr. Carey, was wrong he told me. He wanted him to be a perfectly ordinary character, like a President Truman. He sent me photographs of the type of boats for the boat race, as he wanted the rigging to be accurate; he is a great sailor."

From Charlotte's Web, *written by E. B. White and illustrated by Garth Williams.*

Seven years after *Stuart Little* appeared, Mr. Williams and Mr. White teamed up again to produce the now-modern classic, *Charlotte's Web.*

"But," comments Mr. Williams, "I found *Stuart Little* more fun to illustrate than *Charlotte's Web* as there were more moments of fantasy in it. In *Charlotte's Web* I had to keep from disturbing the dull and ordinary background of the family so that the contrast of the animals' lives would be kept as in the text.

"'Stuart' and 'Charlotte', of course, are among my own personal favorites. I feel extremely lucky to be able to share a little of the spotlight of these two books—books I love, admire, envy and emulate as an author."

In addition to the above-mentioned volumes, Mr. Williams has illustrated a host of other popular titles including Natalie Savage Carlson's *A Family under the Bridge* and *A Brother for the Orphelines,* Margery Sharp's *The Rescuers* and the sequel *Miss Bianca,* and Russell Hoban's *Bedtime for Frances.* Among the titles he has written and illustrated are *Big Golden Animal ABC, Baby's First Book, The Rabbits' Wedding,* and *The Chicken Book.*

Commenting on his work habits, Mr. Williams states, "I am allergic to work. I do anything else first. My work habits are very bad. As an old New Yorker I often can't start until 6:00 p.m. and then I work until 3:00 a.m. This I no longer can do as I have to use glasses now and cannot see well in artificial light.

"I have books filled with story ideas that I have thought of at quite odd times. I used to write the first and last pages, but often felt the rest would be boring and never wrote more. When in my teens I was wonderful at writing introductions to a work I was about to do. But I ended with the introduction. Now I have trained myself to begin at the beginning and to go on for at least three chapters.

"To illustrate a book, I read the manuscript with a sheet of paper beside me. As I see the picture suggested by the text, I note down the subject line and page of the manuscript until I have read the entire work. I then use this list to select the illustrations. I use many different techniques. I usually see the finished book in my mind, and from there I begin.

"My adult life has always been an extension of my childhood, it seems. I was born bald, toothless, and impossible. I've always been a horrible perfectionist. I don't like anything I do. I don't like anything anyone else does either. I was five years old only yesterday and have never felt older than twenty. The life of an illustrator is very pleasant, so I have remained one. It has been a wonderful life even with all the disappointments. I am still illustrating and may be doing so until I am ninety—or more—and that's only about thirty years away!"

Be it thirty or fifty or even one-hundred years from now it would indeed be hard to imagine the world of children's literature without the talents of Garth Williams.

GENERAL COMMENTARY

Diana Klemin

SOURCE: "An Introduction To" and "Garth Williams," in *The Art of Art for Children's Books: A Contemporary Survey,* Clarkson N. Potter, Inc., 1966, pp. 15-18, 68-70.

The artist is equally an inspirer with the author in the tradition of children's book illustration. The art and text blend in such perfect harmony that a child remembers the illustrations as an integral part of a story. *Stuart Little* appears to the child to belong as much to E. B. White as to Garth Williams. . . .

With reading books as compared to picture books, Garth Williams has a lovable, unaffected way of drawing pictures. His warm, almost human animals with their amazing facial expressions are inseparable from the story. Charlotte the pig and Stuart Little the mouse join the ranks of memorable artists' characters in children's literature along with Tenniel's Alice, Ernest Shepard's Mr. Mole, and A. B. Frost's Brer Rabbit.

Joanna Foster

SOURCE: "Biographies of Illustrators Active: 1957-1966," and "Williams, Garth Montgomery," in *Illustrators of Children's Books: 1957-1966,* Lee Kingman, Joanna Foster, and Ruth Giles Lontoft, eds., The Horn Book, Inc., 1968, p. 193.

The parents of Garth Williams were both artists. In 1929 he was sent to the Westminster Art School and in 1931 he won a special talent scholarship for oil painting to the Royal College of Art, where he studied mural technique and the craft of painting. At this time he became interested in the theater and made sets for a small theater group. During the first four years at the College he did sculpture in the evenings at the Westminster Art School to improve his drawing, and soon became fully absorbed in sculpture. After finishing his studies at the Royal College of Art, he organized Luton Art School (1935-36), [and] painted murals, including those for the Earl of Dudley's home in Belgrave Square. Garth Williams won the British Prix de Rome for sculpture in 1936. He returned from Rome in 1938, having studied art in Italy, France, Germany, Hungary, Yugoslavia, Albania, Greece, Turkey, Holland, and Czechoslovakia. In November 1941 he returned to the United States and in 1943 he began working for the *New Yorker* and was asked by E. B. White to illustrate his first children's book, *Stuart Little.* This started Mr. Williams on his present career. Since then, he has devoted much of his time to illustrating, his work including *Charlotte's Web* and a new edition of Laura Ingalls Wilder's eight *Little House* books. Illustrating the Wilder books was a task of many years. Before he felt he was ready to begin Mr. Williams visited Mrs. Wilder in Missouri, traveled over all the territory covered in the stories and explored every possible source for background material. In the *Horn Book* for December 1953, he wrote, "Illustrating books is not just making pictures of the houses, the people and the articles mentioned by the author: the artist has to see everything with the same eyes." About his way of working, Garth Williams says, "I have used what seemed to me the most sympathetic medium to accompany the mood of the text." The result is a great variety of techniques, beginning with *Stuart Little,* which was done in pen and ink. The Wilder books were done in pencil on tracing paper in their actual size so that the negative for reproduction could be made by direct contact with the drawing. The result was a litho-type drawing in which "whites remain white, drawing crisp, effect soft and warm." He has used this technique on several other books. He has also used gouache, oil, water color and litho crayon and has often done separations using acetate overlays. "The decision whether to use color, full or only one or two," he writes, "is made by the publisher, as it is a question of cost. We discuss the way the book would look best, then see if we can afford it; if not, I think of a cheaper way to reach the desired effect." Garth Williams designs the books he illustrates and has also written two of them, *The Rabbits' Wedding* and *The Adventures of Benjamin Pink.* He characterizes his work as "highly personalized representation," explaining, "I start with the real animal, working over and over until I can get the effect of human qualities and expressions and poses. I redesign animals as it were." He has four daughters and lives in Marfil, Guanajuato, Mexico. His spare time, when he is not traveling, is spent in continuing with his sculpture and painting.

Margaret Blount

SOURCE: "Lilliputian Life: The Mouse Story" and "The Tables Turned at the Zoo: Mowgli and Stuart Little," in *Animal Land: The Creatures of Children's Fiction,* William Morrow, 1975, pp. 152-169, pp. 226-244.

[In Margery Sharp's *Miss Bianca* books] Garth Williams—the Rembrandt of animal portrait artists—shows very mouse-like mice, quite different from his portrayal of Stuart Little, or Templeton from *Charlotte's Web.* The character of each individual is beautifully evident, from serious, earnest Bernard, to old Caerphilly, the Professor of Geology, who has lectured to an empty hall for several terms. They are amiable and endearing. The humans—apart from poets and children—appear gross by comparison. The cat Mamelouk is a creature of nightmare, not only conceited and greedy but dirty and disheveled. Garth Williams draws it with a flat, Persian face—the type of cat face that is nearest to human. The effect is very evil, with its shortened snout and heavy brows. Garth Williams is good, too, at crowd scenes (all

mouse stories should have at least some crowd action) and at 'borrowing' improvisation; the Ladies' Guild busily at work knitting, with their tea urn made from a Kodak film capsule, the Moot Hall audience, the scene in the Norwegian tavern. He draws no clothes, apart from occasional hats. They are not necessary—neither author nor artist needs them for characterising—not mice like humans, but intelligent mice. . . .

Garth Williams's drawings [for *Stuart Little*] show a neat, thoughtful, spare, adult-looking mouse. This talented artist's animals are all attractive—even the unpleasant ones—and no two look alike. Many of the *Stuart Little* illustrations are drawn from a human point of view, showing, as befits the story, Stuart as a minute dot, or small, desperate and unnoticed as he tries to board a bus, walk down 72nd Street or ask for his petrol and oil to be checked at a filling station.

Zena Sutherland and May Hill Arbuthnot

SOURCE: "The Twentieth Century: Garth Williams," in *Children and Books,* seventh edition, Scott, Foresman and Company, 1986, p. 147.

Garth Williams has won a formidable number of awards and prizes, including the Prix de Rome for sculpture. His first venture into children's book illustration was for E. B. White's *Stuart Little* (1945). He followed this with White's famous *Charlotte's Web* (1952). For a new edition of Laura Ingalls Wilder's *Little House* books (1953), Garth Williams spent ten years making the pictures, and as a result the pictures and stories are one. Equally successful are his illustrations for Natalie Carlson's books about the French Orphelines, Russell Hoban's *Bedtime for Frances* (1960), Margery Sharp's *Miss Bianca* (1962), and George Selden's *Harry Cat's Pet Puppy* (1974). The artist works both in black and white and full color, and his pictures are always characterized by authenticity of detail. The colors are fresh and soft, the composition vigorous. But whether the story he illustrates is realistic or pure fantasy, historical fiction or modern city life, his superb gift for characterization stands out. No pig could look more foolishly smug than Wilbur, no orphan could flee more desperately from the encircling bicyclists than Josine, no pioneers could look more cozy than the Little House dwellers.

Leonard S. Marcus

SOURCE: "Garth Williams," in *Publishers Weekly,* edited by Sybil Steinberg, Vol. 237, No. 8, February 23, 1990, pp. 201-02.

Reminded recently that his eldest daughter is 50 years old, Garth Williams replies with an impish laugh: "How can that be? I'm only 42."

Williams [78], who has also described himself as "really a five-year-old at heart," . . . has long been among the children's book world's preeminent illustrators. He made his auspicious debut in the field in 1945 as the illustrator of E. B. White's *Stuart Little,* contributing full-hearted, bravura comic drawings that have been aptly compared to the work of Sir John Tenniel and Ernest Shepard.

A partial roster of authors he has collaborated with since then indicates the remarkable scope of his career. Along with White (whose second children's fantasy, *Charlotte's Web,* Williams also illustrated), the list includes Margaret Wise Brown (*Little Fur Family, The Sailor Dog,* and several others); Laura Ingalls Wilder (the *Little House* series); Russell Hoban (*Bedtime for Frances*); Randall Jarrell (*The Gingerbread Rabbit*); Margery Sharp (*Miss Bianca* and others); George Selden (*The Cricket in Times Square*). . . .

A restless, private, fiercely independent man, Williams has six children from four marriages and has lived in a great many homes—in New York, Aspen, Santa Fe, central Mexico (where he still owns a sprawling 400-year-old Spanish-built castle that he found in ruins and made over himself), and most recently San Antonio, Texas. The artist, a sporty figure who last met with *PW* during a visit to New York, recently spoke with us again from his new home in Texas.

As a child, Williams recalls, "Everybody in my house was always either painting or drawing, so I thought there was nothing else to do in life but make pictures." Garth Montgomery Williams was born of English parents in New York City in 1912. His mother was a landscape painter and pipe-smoking suffragette. His father was a cartoonist for such popular magazines of the day as *Judge* and *Life.* Drawing came easily to the boy, who remembers his father's tongue-in-cheek comment on a day when young Garth had gotten into his studio and made "lots of additions" to the cartoons he found in progress there: "I'm afraid he's going to become an artist."

By the age of 10, Williams had lived on a New Jersey farm, traveled in Canada and France and, following his parents' divorce, moved to London with his mother. There he dreamed for a time of becoming an architect, in part because "it appeared to be a steady occupation." His youthful designs for houses, however, bore a prescient resemblance to the whimsically far-fetched inventions of Heath Robinson and Rube Goldberg. "I had kitchens where everything was automatic. The plates were washed, came out on a band, went through the kitchen where food was put on them, then went out to the dining room where someone ate the food. Then the dishes went right back into the washing machine." As little actual building was going on in England during the Depression years, Williams realized he "might as well become an artist after all," and enrolled at the Royal Academy of Art where, he recalls, "Portraits were my strong point."

On graduating, he worked briefly as headmaster of an art school outside London. But because ministering to students' needs left little time for art, he resigned the

post despite the financial bind his decision was certain to leave him in. "I had two cars, you see, and couldn't buy any gasoline!" With characteristic brio, he overcame this difficulty by executing a sculpture that won him the 1936 Prix de Rome and two expense-free years in Italy.

Married and back in London when WW II began, Williams joined the Red Cross, working in the city's bomb-torn streets. "I picked up probably 2000 people, most of them dead," he remembers, and was himself injured in a bomb blast. Making his way to New York, he supported himself by freelancing. It was a magazine editor he met in this capacity who first suggested he might do well as an illustrator of juvenile books and showed him a waggish traditional English rhyme that, a few years later, Williams would use as the text of *The Chicken Book.* The mother hen's advice to her hungry chicks must also have seemed wise counsel for freelance artists: "If you want any breakfast," the hen admonishes her little ones, "just come here and SCRATCH!"

Williams sold some drawings to the *New Yorker* but was told his cartooning style was "too wild," "too finished" and "too European" for the magazine. Exposure in the *New Yorker* nonetheless served to attract the notice of Katharine and E. B. White just as the latter was about to deliver the manuscript of *Stuart Little* to Harper & Row. Williams had recently shown his portfolio to the head of Harper's children's department, Ursula Nordstrom, who had spoken of White's much-awaited book and suggested he might like to take his chances in the intense competition she anticipated for the coveted assignment. To their mutual surprise, the matter was settled when the manuscript arrived with a note pinned to it from the author, which read: "Try Garth Williams."

Nordstrom treated White with extreme deference, allowing him to critique Williams's pencil sketches as they emerged from the illustrator's W. 14th St. studio. Of their first meeting in White's midtown office, the artist recalls: "He seemed very regular, on your own level. We had talked about half an hour when he suddenly said to me: 'Well, do you like the story?' To which I replied: 'Oh my goodness, yes!' I was so surprised he would think there was any question."

White proved to be a gracious, perceptive collaborator who was quick to praise Williams's uncanny knack (based on close observation) for knowing, as the author once commented, exactly what sort of shoes a mouse would wear if mice wore shoes. He eventually asked for only two minor changes in the art: that a schoolhouse be made plainer-looking and that a dentist friend of Stuart's also be made to look "more ordinary"—more, that is, White told Williams, "like Harry Truman."

Some people, Williams recalls, objected strenuously to *Stuart Little* when it first appeared, asserting that a story about a "normal American woman giving birth to a mouse" had to be "obscene." Overall, however, the book was very well received—by adult readers as well as by children. "Traveling around New York," he remembers, "I'd get into a bus and see three people reading *Stuart Little*. People everywhere were reading it, which made me feel very good. So I thought, Well, here's my profession."

In 1945, Williams met Margaret Wise Brown, the extraordinarily prolific and innovative picture book author with whom, of his many collaborators, he was to work with the most closely. Book ideas would fly back and forth so freely between them when they got together that they soon adopted the teasing precaution of "copyrighting" their more promising utterances in midconversation. Their whirlwind collaboration yielded 11 books in all.

More often than not, Williams's collaborations have been carried on at a distance, from wherever he happened to be living at the moment. He made the drawings for Laura Ingalls Wilder's *Little House* books while in Rome. He illustrated *Charlotte's Web* while living on an upstate New York farm, much like the one described in White's memorable rural idyll.

Although Williams's illustrations have always been anchored in realistic detail, his narrative drawings of pioneer life for the eight *Little House* books, which appeared as a set in 1953, marked a notable departure from the more fanciful type of art for which he had become known. In a field in which artists are frequently typecast, it was a bold stroke on Ursula Nordstrom's part to choose him for the job.

The artist had at first demurred at the offer: "But it's not about animals . . ." Nordstrom adamantly stood her ground, however, insisting he "must not have read the books properly." She "shooed me out of the office!" Duly impressed by this editorial show of force, Williams accepted the assignment and, before leaving for Italy, set off on a poignant six-month westward journey to meet the Wilders—Laura was then about 80—and see for himself the many places they had called home.

Williams has written a handful of the more than 70 books he has illustrated. In 1959, one of these, *The Rabbits' Wedding,* unexpectedly made international headlines when it was banned in some Southern libraries. In the inflamed atmosphere of the civil rights movement's early days, pro-segregationists were quick to find provocation in the artist's lilting tale about black and white rabbits who marry and "live happily together in the big forest." Williams, who has always denied he intended the book as an allegory, says he was glad for the publicity, but was also saddened to realize that the book-banners "wanted their children to have the same errors they had."

One reason he chose to make *Wedding*'s protagonists black and white, Williams says, was simply to help readers "tell them apart"—this, at a time when full-color printing was often considered prohibitively expensive by publishers. "Fortunately, nowadays you can do color. Publishers don't scream when they see a color

book. So I can try to get a really good effect and leave it at that." Among his illustrations for two books of light verse by Jack Prelutsky, *Ride a Purple Pelican* and . . . year's *Beneath a Blue Umbrella* are some of the artist's most brightly hued and tenderest portraits, along with many touches of vintage Williams tomfoolery.

The art for these books is a mixed media experiment that might set some purists' hair on end. For color, Williams applied "a very thin oil paint, used almost like watercolor." He then added "a variety of pen lines" in certain places for definition. The eclecticism of combining oil and ink is a far cry from what is usually encouraged in art school. "I just say, 'Does it look all right? Does it tell the story?'" Williams explains, though one suspects he also enjoys having tampered a bit with the rules.

Prolific as he has been, Williams has often said he is 'allergic' to work and that he keeps to his drawing table only because his "1950 dollar is today worth 10 cents." Asked if he has spent much time over the years sketching animals, the artist who has given exuberant visual expression to Wilbur the Pig, the Sailor Dog and Chester Cricket among others, suggests: "Only when I had to."

All the same, new illustration possibilities, opened up by the changing state of printing technology, evidently intrigued him. "Nowadays you can do anything," he says. "There's no reason I shouldn't mix a photograph into one of my pictures. I haven't done *that* yet." And, Williams notes, he isn't planning to retire for another 30 years.

William Anderson

SOURCE: "Garth Williams after Eighty," in *The Horn Book Magazine,* Vol. LXIX, No. 2, March-April, 1993, pp. 181-86.

I certainly never started out to become a famous children's book illustrator," admits Garth Williams, whose art has decorated scores of notable books during the past half century. "But, looking back at my life, it appears I don't know there is anything else but drawing. I simply have this defect that I can draw. Others have it in music or mathematics; mine is art," says the man who estimates that he has illustrated ninety-seven books.

Garth Williams turned eighty in April of 1992, and though he can reflect on a laurel-filled career in children's illustration, he says he's far from finished with his work. The urge to draw and to yield to his lifelong creativity is still strong. "I find that as I get older, I remain the same as I was in my twenties and thirties; my tastes and interests haven't changed," he says. "I'm happiest when I'm busy drawing, and I think I should do three more books to make an even hundred that say 'Illustrated by Garth Williams.'"

The Williams family background was well suited to nurture Garth's artistic leanings. When he was born in New

York City on April 16, 1912, both parents, Hamilton and Fiona Williams, were actively involved in the art world. Ham Williams illustrated for the British humor magazine *Punch,* and his wife was a Paris-trained painter. Their British background still colors their son's cultured, BBC-tinted voice, although his earliest memories are of a farm near Caldwell, New Jersey.

Garth Williams's first work of art was a stick-figured pine tree, drawn when he was nine months old. His father told him later that he reached his hand from a highchair to draw with one finger on a steamy kitchen window. "That settles it," his father declared. "He's going to be an artist." The prophecy held true: from that time to this, Garth Williams's life has been one of almost unbroken activity in the creative arts—as a student, a teacher, sculptor, painter, and illustrator.

His first ten years were spent in what he describes as a "Huckleberry Finn boyhood" in the countryside of New Jersey and Canada, experiences which later affected many of his illustrating assignments. For a while he was immersed in music; his sister gave him a ukulele for his eighth birthday. But his tastes later shifted to piano, classical guitar, tenor saxophone, and clarinet. "I learned the first movement of the Moonlight Sonata to impress the eight-year-old girl next door," he remembers today.

In 1922 the Williams family moved to England, where Garth was educated. He discovered that "at ten I could draw as well as any man." His skill landed him a job as an architect's assistant in London. He values that early training and the chances it gave him to crawl around the hidden recesses, domes, and niches of such famous spots as St. Paul's Cathedral.

By the time Williams was ready to enter architecture school, the Depression had slowed all construction in the British Isles and made a career as an architect impractical. Instead, he accepted his mother's offer of what she could afford—three months' tuition at Westminster Art School. Later, he was awarded a four-year scholarship to the Royal College of Art.

In 1936 Garth Williams won the British Prix de Rome for sculpture, an art form he says he still favors. He taught for a while, then lived a bohemian life traveling throughout Europe, painting and visiting galleries. He married the first of his four wives, realized that Hitler's menace would overrun Europe, and returned to London, where illustrators were in scant demand but war workers were greatly needed. He signed on with the Red Cross during the London Blitz and had some hair-raising experiences, including collecting the dead and injured from city streets and surviving a bomb blast which vaporized a friend walking next to him. "I realized," he says, "that I had a fifty-fifty chance of surviving the war." Williams sent his wife and child to Canada and, at Churchill's suggestion, sailed to America, hoping to obtain a commission to do war work for Americans in Europe. The plan fell through; his letter from Churchill was considered a forgery. But this left the Williams family safe in the States for the duration. It also led Garth Williams back to the drawing boards in New York City.

The *New Yorker* started publishing Garth Williams's work, and then he illustrated an old English rhyme which was published as *The Chicken Book.* In 1945, he dropped off his portfolio at the children's department at Harper and Brothers; coincidentally, E. B. White's *Stuart Little* manuscript arrived on Ursula Nordstrom's desk at the same time. When asked about his preference for an illustrator, White had remarked, "Try Garth Williams."

The illustrator tackled *Stuart Little* with gusto. The story of a mouse who became the son of a typical American family sparked for the first time the whimsical, fantasy-oriented Williams style. He says he found his muse in a real-life mouse who moved into the New York studio on the day he started the illustrating job.

Stuart Little established Garth Williams as a children's illustrator. It also showed his special affinity for depicting animals with particular sensitivity. "Some books are so wonderful that I would have illustrated them simply for the pleasure of it," he notes. This includes his second collaboration with E. B. White, *Charlotte's Web.* "It's one of my favorites," Williams says. "I feel lucky to share in any book that I love."

Always eagerly sought by authors as illustrator for their work, Garth Williams cites unusually creative chemistries with many important children's literary figures, including Margaret Wise Brown. He still get misty-eyed when he recalls their teamwork on books like *The Sailor Dog* and her death at an early age. Other notable illustrating jobs have included works by Charlotte Zolotow, Margery Sharp, Randall Jarrell, George Selden, Mary Stolz, and, most recently, Jack Prelutsky.

When approached to re-illustrate Laura Ingalls Wilder's *Little House* books, Williams was at first dubious. He felt comfortable drawing talking animals, but was unsure about portraying realistic historical scenes. Besides, he says, "I had never been west of the Hudson River, and knew nothing of Laura Ingalls Wilder country."

At the insistence of Ursula Nordstrom, he studied the books. The first plan was for Williams to produce eight oil paintings for each book, sixty-four in all. In 1947, he set off on a trip to the American Midwest, to see if he could capture the aura he needed.

The first stop was at Rocky Ridge Farm near Mansfield, Missouri, where Laura and Almanzo Wilder still lived. He visited with them, experiencing awe that "here I stood with the hero and heroine of Mrs. Wilder's books." He found Laura Ingalls Wilder very cheerful, sprightly, very much alive at eighty." He also found her informative and helpful but surprisingly unconcerned as to how he illustrated her books.

"I asked her if she would like to review my work and

criticize it, but she never asked for changes," Williams remembers. He went on to visit all the sites of her books.

Despite the fact that the Wilder books contained "no spiders that talked," Garth Williams became absorbed in creating pictures for the eight-volume series. The original plan, to produce color paintings for the books, was canceled due to costs, so Williams settled on the soft pencil-sketch style that he used for the hundreds of illustrations that grace the books. Much of his work was accomplished in Italy; by the time the *Little House* series was re-published in its new edition in 1953, six years had elapsed since he started the project.

During the 1950s, Garth Williams set up home and studio in Aspen, Colorado, when it was a quaint, quiet town with a single ski lift. With his second wife and four daughters, he immersed himself in family life and his work, which included writing as well as illustrating. His drawing and writing added prestige to the fledgling Golden Book series of high quality, low-cost children's titles pioneered by Simon & Schuster during the 1950s.

In 1958 Williams wrote and illustrated his much-admired but highly controversial book, *The Rabbits' Wedding.* The marriage of a black rabbit and a white rabbit was immediately seen by bigots as a fearfully subtle message during that early era of the civil-rights movement. Ironically, Williams denies any attempt at hidden meanings in the book. He says he simply tinted one rabbit black to distinguish it from the other. He still decries the mentality behind the unexpected hullabaloo his work elicited from book banners.

Of his illustrating craft, Garth Williams admits that his approach to a project is simple. "I won't do a book unless I like the manuscript," he insists. His initial reading of the material may suggest thirty or forty potential pictures. "To compose the pictures is very hard," he admits. "I look for all the action in the story; then I arrange forms and color. I always try to imagine what the author is seeing. Of course, I have to narrow down my ideas to the number of drawings I'm allowed, which might be as few as ten per book. I make a list of illustrations. When I see a picture, I write down the idea and a page number while I read the manuscript. Everyone thinks, 'How nice to illustrate children's books.' But I'm pragmatic. It's a job. My inspiration is my deadline. But when I start, the work usually goes quickly. I never get tired when I'm illustrating!"

Garth Williams's life and work shifted to Guanajuato, Mexico, during the 1960s and 1970s. There he bought, at a small cost, the four-hundred-year-old ruins of a Spanish silver mine. He rebuilt the picturesque structure, transforming it into a huge, fortress-like residence and studio. The compound includes a waterfall, fountains, cathedral arches, and a living room/dining room that seats 150 people. But for the artist-in-residence, the heart of the home is his mammoth studio, with its five work tables, nine skylights, piles of props, and accumulations of art work. His family sees the studio as impos-

sibly messy and in need of organization, but Garth's benign silence on the matter indicates that a non-artist cannot possibly understand the proper ambiance of his working surroundings.

The long sojourns in Mexico gave some publishers and editors the notion that Garth Williams was retired or incommunicado, or both. He cites the series of garbled communications between himself and E. B. White that led to another artist illustrating White's *Trumpet of the Swan* in 1970.

In 1974 Garth Williams married his present wife, Leticia; their courtship began during a portrait sitting. Although several decades separate them in age, the Mexican-born Mrs. Williams and her citizen-of-the-world husband make a successful team. "She's the best business manager I've ever had," Williams declares, obviously pleased to be relieved of some of the mundane requirements of life that interfere with his art. The Williams's only child, Dilys, is now in her early teens. The family currently divides its time between homes in Mexico and San Antonio, Texas.

Letty Williams keeps her husband's publishing deadlines straight, reminds him to be at the right place at the right time, and recently completed collecting and cataloguing the thousands of pieces of original artwork her husband has produced. "There is enough to fill the Metropolitan Museum of Art four times over," she says of the huge collection.

Garth Williams retains a zest that befits his roguish, sometimes irreverent, style. He's a master raconteur who can relate wild and improbable adventures with such diverse characters as Hitler and Picasso. He's a tireless charmer when he makes personal appearances around the country, glib but tender with his admirers. He's patient but incredulous when he autographs his way through mounds of books and always gracious when he accepts the adulation he receives.

When asked how he plans to spend his next ten years, Garth Williams says simply, "I'm going to have a lot of fun!" "And," he mentions humbly, "I hope I can be remembered for illustrating some of the best children's books of my time. Children need good books, and, I'm happy to say, they are getting better all the time. I hope I'm still illustrating them when I'm a hundred!"

Christian Esquevin

SOURCE: "The Art of Garth Williams," in *AB Bookman's Weekly,* Vol. 100, No. 18, November 3, 1997, pp. 1096, 1098.

Of all the artists who created images for the classics of children's literature, none is greater than Garth Williams. His range as an illustrator is unsurpassed, covering the gamut of genres that exploded with the postwar baby boom.

More significantly, such is the force and the "rightness" of his illustrations, for many classics, that we could not imagine them pictured in any other way. He so captured the individuality and vitality of the characters, created by others, that we can't imagine them not done all of a piece, author and artist working side by side.

Try to imagine, for example, the wonderful characters in *Charlotte's Web,* such as Fern or Wilbur, without the images so greatly captured throughout the book. The front cover of the dust jacket says it all.

That this is the job of the illustrator, after all, in no way lessens the towering achievements of Garth Williams. The predicament that is the role of the illustrator in children's literature, however, is made paramount in the case of Williams. He was one of the greats that produced work over the long time span in which awards have been given for children's literature. Yet he remains virtually without any.

He suffers, perhaps, for creating work that is too perfect. His illustrations and images are so much of a piece with the story that they are apparently overlooked as the work of an artist that was not the writer. . . .

In one of those fortuitous quirks of fate, he was pegged by both E. B. White and White's editor Ursula Nordstrom, at Harper & Brothers, to illustrate *Stuart Little.*

The audacity of White in creating a main character, born of a human mother, but who "looked very much like a mouse in every way," and of Garth Williams in bringing him to life, put the potential success of *Stuart Little* in doubt. In fact, renowned librarian and reviewer Anne Carroll Moore went so far as to try to dissuade White from publishing it (she had long since given up trying to influence the trend-setting Ursula Nordstrom). The eventual best-sellerdom of the book, however, launched Williams in his new career.

A little known book, omitted from Williams's bibliographies, came out at the same time. This was *The Door Opens* by Ernest Lothar. It's about the author's two children, growing up in pre-War Austria. Perhaps be-

From Little House on the Prairie, *written by Laura Ingalls Wilder. Illustrated by Garth Williams.*

cause it was published as an adult book, and certainly since Ursula Nordstrom was not its editor, the illustrations in *The Door Opens* did not convey the qualities found in *Stuart Little* and Williams's other works.

In 1946, two books came out that set the tone for much of Williams's later work, and that would account for his work being in such high demand. These were Margaret Wise Brown's *Little Fur Family,* and Williams's own *The Chicken Book.* Both made the most of Williams's ability to illustrate fuzzy and furry animals that simultaneously convey individuality, character, expressiveness, and warmth. In short, the ideal in animal illustration for children, but one so rarely well achieved.

The first edition of the *Little Fur Family* measured no more than 2-1/8 x 3-1/4 inches. It was bound in real rabbit fur and boxed. Williams's early work with Margaret Wise Brown, the "laureate of the nursery," was significant. As Barbara Bader wrote about Williams, "With Clement Hurd, he was to give shape to Margaret Wise Brown's tenderest, most private work for children."

Garth Williams also illustrated some of Brown's works for Simon & Schuster "Little Golden Books," where, along with Feodor Rojankovsky, he would become their top animal illustrator. Their collaboration created such Golden Book classics as *The Golden Sleepy Book* (1948), *Mister Dog* (1952), *The Sailor Dog* (1953), *The Friendly Book* (1954), and *Home for a Bunny* (1956).

Garth Williams also illustrated for Simon & Schuster Dorothy Kunhardt's boxed, miniature sets, *Tiny Animal Stories* (1948) and *Tiny Nonsense Stories* (1949). With their original boxes, the boxes themselves illustrated throughout with tiny animal houses, interiors, and street scenes, they make up what in my vote is the cutest and most clever presentation ever.

His other books for Margaret Wise Brown were also gems. *Wait Till the Moon Is Full* is a precursor to Russell Hoban's classic *Bedtime for Frances,* which Williams also illustrated. Another Brown collaboration, *Three Little Animals* is a sequel of sorts to the *Little Fur Family,* and although in large format, it is equally precious. Long after Brown's death, Williams re-illustrated *Fox Eyes,* a book of hers previously illustrated by the renowned Jean Charlot.

For the Artists & Writer's Guild, Williams did two wonderful anthologies edited by Jane Werner. The first was *The Tall Book of Make-Believe,* published by Harper & Brothers in 1950. It continued their "Tall Books." *The Giant Golden Book of Elves and Fairies* is one of the most beautiful and sought after of the Golden Books. With these books Williams demonstrated that he was as equally talented at illustrating children as he was animals. Indeed, his striking ability to capture the sculptural qualities of the human form, coupled with his abilities

at portraiture, especially of children, make him unequaled, to my mind. In the same year Harper published *The Adventures of Benjamin Pink,* which was both written and illustrated by Williams.

His next collaboration with E. B. White would make both of them immortal. *Charlotte's Web* was published to strong reviews and would become one of five Newbery Award Honor books the following year. That it didn't win over Ann Nolan Clark's *Secrets of the Andes* is one of the classic oversights in children's literature. *Charlotte's Web* has become one of the most well loved children's books ever.

Ursula Nordstrom of Harper had another major commission for Williams—illustrating a multi-volume and eventually best-selling set of Laura Ingalls Wilder's *Little House* books. Several of these books had previously been illustrated by the talented Helen Sewell. For this new edition Garth Williams did extensive research, visiting Rose Wilder Lane and various sites in Missouri and the Carolinas. He ultimately illustrated eight volumes, once again defining the "look" for those classics (the illustrations have also appeared in later repackagings of these books, such as cookbooks, diaries, etc.). Such was the strength of his illustrations that years later, and with Williams in poor health, HarperCollins turned to new illustrators to do work that looked just like Williams's illustrations. As stated on the title page, "Illustrations for the My First Little House Books are inspired by the work of Garth Williams with his permission, which we gratefully acknowledge."

In 1959 Williams found himself at the center of a controversy. The illustrator of little furry animals had just written and illustrated a book about a little white bunny and a little black bunny that were getting married. *The Rabbits' Wedding* was denounced by an Orlando, Florida, editor as "brainwashing . . . open its pages you realize these rabbits are integrated." The book was also banned in parts of Alabama. *Time* magazine and *Life* reported the stories. Many commented on the absurdity of the whole thing. In a letter to this writer Garth Williams stated that his book was already selling very well before the controversy, but that sales of his other books increased. *The Rabbits' Wedding* has never been out of print.

Another indicator of the strength of Garth Williams's stamp on a storybook character is his frequent use in illustrating series books. Following the Laura Ingalls Wilder books, Williams illustrated Natalie Savage Carlson's *The Happy Orpheline* and *A Brother for the Orpheline,* Margery Sharp's *The Rescuers, Miss Bianca, The Turret* and *Miss Bianca in the Salt Mines.* A series for George Selden began with *The Cricket in Times Square,* followed by *Tucker's Countryside, Harry Cat's Pet Puppy, Chester Cricket's Pigeon Ride, Chester Cricket's New Home, Harry Kitten and Tucker Mouse,* and *The Old Meadow.*

Some other notable books that Garth Williams illustrated

are Charlotte Zolotow's *Do You Know What I'll Do,* Randall Jarrell's *The Gingerbread Rabbit,* Jan Wahl's *Push Kitty,* and Jack Prelutsky's *Ride a Purple Pelican.*

It would seem natural that Garth Williams should have won the Laura Ingalls Wilder Award, an award given by the American Library Association, "to give recognition each three years to an author or illustrator whose books published in the U.S. have over a period of years made a substantial and lasting contribution to literature for children." This did not happen before Garth Williams's death on May 8, 1996. One of several ironies was that the Wilder Award was the brainchild of Williams's old editor Ursula Nordstrom, an award, she thought, "for those that hadn't won the big one."

Despite his lack of formal recognition, Garth Williams will live on in the minds of growing children whose brains are forever imprinted with the images that he created. For those of us who only came to know him as adults, his work is nonetheless magical.

TITLE COMMENTARY

📖 THE CHICKEN BOOK: A TRADITIONAL RHYME (1946)

Mary Gould Davis

SOURCE: A review of *The Chicken Book,* in *The Saturday Review of Literature,* Vol. XXIX, No. 50, December 14, 1946, p. 30.

A picture book with its cover and end-papers in the clear, bright yellow of a very young chicken tells the story in verse of five little chickens who each want something different and are rather puzzled about getting it until their mother shows them how to scratch. The chickens are very amusing, and the background of farm and meadow, printed in soft greens and blues, is charming.

Faith McNulty

SOURCE: A review of *The Chicken Book,* in *The New Yorker,* Vol. LXVI, No. 41, November 26, 1990, p. 140.s

Five newborn chicks exploring the world for the first time keep wishing that something tasty would turn up. Finally, Mother Hen, exasperated by their complaints, takes charge and gives them the first lesson in survival: Heaven helps those who help themselves. This funny and trenchant little book was first published in 1946, and is still as fresh as a daisy. It's great to have it back.

📖 WAIT TILL THE MOON IS FULL (written by Margaret Wise Brown, 1948)

The Catholic World

SOURCE: A review of *Wait Till the Moon Is Full,* in *The Catholic World,* Vol. CLXVIII, No. 1005, December, 1948, pp. 221-22.

[A] must is *Wait Till the Moon Is Full,* by Margaret Wise Brown. This is her best story so far, but it is the delectable drawings of Garth Williams that really make the book. The combination is irresistible. The picture of Mother Raccoon at her sewing machine has to be seen to be believed.

R. Baines

SOURCE: A review of *Wait Till the Moon Is Full,* in *The Junior Bookshelf,* Vol. 42, No. 3, June, 1978, pp. 133-34.

Little raccoon wishes to expand his experience beyond the confines of his one-parent family, his home, and the sight of daylight, but his mother is determined that he must wait until the moon is full before he goes out at night. The main text of this book is built up from her injunctions to this effect and two poems, in which she maintains her son's enthusiasm by telling him of the activities of other animals at full moon.

The sixteen central illustrations showing the sheltered, humanised home life of the raccoon are in shades of grey, enlivened by touches of brown. They are pleasant, quite sophisticated and just a little monotonous. The first and last pictures are fully coloured representations of the outer world.

First copyright was in America in 1948, and this story is very much in the old-fashioned, traditional style of picture books.

📖 THE ADVENTURES OF BENJAMIN PINK (1951)

Ellen Lewis Buell

SOURCE: A review of *The Adventures of Benjamin Pink,* in *The New York Times Book Review,* September 9, 1951, p. 30.

As an illustrator, Garth Williams has given a great deal of pleasure to a great many children. *Benjamin Pink* is his first story for children, a highly imaginative, unpredictable yarn about a shipwrecked rabbit and his faithful wife, Emily. The Pinks live cozily in a thatched cottage, surrounded by all the domestic objects which young children can easily imagine are the natural possessions of rabbits. Out fishing one day, Ben's boat smashes up on a desert isle. He finds pirate treasure, is befriended by a turtle, rescued by a shark and becomes, briefly, King of the Monkeys.

All this, of course, is great good fun. There is also a gentle note of satire, especially when Ben comes home full of plans for fame and good works. Fortunately, Ben is saved from complete disillusionment by his loving Emily and his true friends. Whether young children will grasp the underlying philosophy here is debatable, but they will love Ben for himself and have a fine time following him on his seagoing adventures, drawn and described with Mr. Williams's characteristic humor.

Polly Goodwin

SOURCE: A review of *The Adventures of Benjamin Pink,* in *Chicago Sunday Tribune Magazine of Books,* October 7, 1951, p. 18.

One day Benjamin Pink, who lived happily with his wife Emily in a cozy little house and garden, ideally suited to rabbit folk, went fishing. But suddenly a storm came up and swept him onto a desert island—and the discovery of buried treasure. In spite of the cynical warnings of his new friend, wise old Theodore Turtle, Ben yearned to do good with the treasure and so departed on a raft loaded with jewels and gold and a royal crown.

Guided by a porpoise, he reached not home but monkeyland. There his rule as King and would-be reformer was sadly short-lived and it was a happy Ben who, aided by a shark, reached home at last. Snubbed by Tom Cat, the bad mayor, and his council when he failed to produce the treasure, Ben soon realized that Emily and friends like Johnny Skunk and Red, the squirrel, meant more than all the gold in the world.

This is Garth Williams's first written book for small children, who already know his wonderful animal pictures in other books. His gentle satire on city politics and human behavior, resulting here in the disillusionment of the well-meaning Ben, will surely be lost on the littlest ones, but they will love the exciting story and delightful pictures, which make the book well worth the price for all ages.

The New York Herald Tribune Book Review

SOURCE: A review of *The Adventures of Benjamin Pink,* in *The New York Herald Tribune Book Review,* November 11, 1951, p. 14.

A chunky, gay little book, this brings us the best black and white pictures yet from Mr. Williams, in a bolder style than his familiar ones in **Stuart Little,** intended for younger eyes than those which read and reread that favorite by E. B. White. Here again is a matter of dressed-up animals, but, they present their true animal nature, in spite of a certain tenderness proper in a book for

From The Cricket in Times Square, *written by George Selden. Illustrated by Garth Williams.*

those under eight. They all are very alluring, enough so to sell the book on their own merit.

The story is best read aloud to children of about five to seven, and it will take several readings, which the adult will find a great pleasure. This sea-going rabbit is wrecked on a desert isle, finds treasure, is warned against it by a wise old turtle, tries to be king of the monkeys, goes home on the back of a shark. These incidents, with lots of action, will seem very funny to the listeners, while the adult will smile at the philosophy of "treasure" and at Ben's clash with the Tom Cat Mayor and his Town Board. The faint overtones of Benjamin Bunny, the Mock Turtle, and other famous characters, will dissolve before you are through, for this Mr. Pink is quite the nicest dressed-up bunny we have had since Beatrix Potter's.

Anne Carroll Moore

SOURCE: A review of *The Adventures of Benjamin Pink,* in *The Horn Book Magazine,* Vol. XXVII, No. 6, December, 1951, p. 400.

Garth Williams in *The Adventures of Benjamin Pink* has created a peace-loving rabbit whose devotion to his wife Emily and to his ideals may give the much enduring rabbit a fresh claim to the interest of children. I found Benjamin carrying too heavy a load of words for a rabbit to bear. "Rabbits can be very tiresome," Beatrix Potter once confided to me at Hill Top Farm. I think of her comment often in relation to other animals as well. Is there not a tendency to give them more than they can bear of the human load of problems and speculation?

BABY ANIMALS (1952)

Ellen Lewis Buell

SOURCE: A review of *Baby Animals,* in *The New York Times Book Review,* October 12, 1952, p. 26.

This sturdy book, built to resist a good deal of wear and tear, is just the thing for children who have outgrown cloth books and want simple, bright picture books. Garth Williams's portraits of twenty-six baby animals include such domestic creatures as a rabbit, wood-chuck and raccoon and such exotic ones as an orangutan and a giraffe. They are more conventional and less witty and imaginative than most of Mr. Williams's work, obviously designed more for information than esthetics and, as such, appealing. The brief captions are negligible and parents had better be prepared to amplify them with either facts or fiction.

The New York Herald Tribune Book Review

SOURCE: A review of *Baby Animals,* in *The New York Herald Tribune Book Review,* December 14, 1952, p. 12.

By the time this notice appears probably the huge first edition of this little book will have melted away. For here is Garth Williams at his best, and in full color. What a baby bear this is reading his little book so happily, in such a magical little spring meadow, surrounded by other baby creatures! The idea has been carried out over and over again in picture books, but this is fine at its price for the very small child. Its stiff board pages, lovely colors and simple text all are just right. Note the marvelous expressiveness of each little creature; they seem to talk, to say they are feeling merry, careful, wary, mischievous, frightened, smart, or just plain contented. Better get several copies of this, for your own will always be leaving you clutched in happy hands.

BABY FARM ANIMALS (1953)

Virginia Kirkus' Bookshop

SOURCE: A review of *Baby Farm Animals,* in *Virginia Kirkus' Bookshop Service,* Vol. XXI, No. 21, November 1, 1953, p. 709.

Companion piece to the beguiling *Baby Animals* of two years back—and done with the same charm and freshness, the same tricks of humor and imagination. That the competition is keen is obvious: rabbits, guinea pigs, a donkey, ducklings, chickens, a lamb (I'm so glad he made it a black one!), piglets, a calf, and so on, including the house animals like kittens and puppies. Yes, they've been done, but this—in its field—is tops.

Mary Lee Krupka

SOURCE: A review of *Baby Farm Animals,* in *The New York Times Book Review,* November 15, 1953, p. 43.

The highest compliment a very young child can give an artist striving for realism is to reach out and pat the fur of the animals on the page. *Baby Farm Animals,* then, will have some smartly smudged pages, for texture is Garth Williams's forte. With hundreds of quick brush movements he bristles the back of the donkey, the goats, the piglets. With softer, circular dabs he makes silk of the down of the duckings and the fur of the cocker puppy and black lamb. Meticulously he defines the veins on the almost-transparent ear of the white rabbit. And he romanticizes, sketching wistful smiles, large, delicate eyes and writing quaintly personal descriptive notes about the animals. Should this be a child's introduction to these animals, he will be well-primed for meeting the live versions.

THE RABBITS' WEDDING (1958; British edition, (1960)

Virginia Kirkus' Service

SOURCE: A review of *The Rabbits' Wedding,* in *Virginia Kirkus' Service,* Vol. XXVI, No. 5, March 1, 1958, p. 179.

Here is a large, mistily, delicately beautiful fantasy about two frolicking rabbits. They loved to spend all day playing together—Hide and Seek, Find the Acorn, and Race Around the Blackberry Bush. But often the little black rabbit sat down and looked sad. When the little white rabbit asked what was the matter the black rabbit always said he was "just thinking." When the little white rabbit found what he was wishing for, he no longer looked sad. They had a rabbit wedding and all the forest folk attended. The illustrations have the subtle hazy quality often found in Chinese screen paintings. The scale of the pictures makes it ideal to show at a story circle—where the back row can see too.

M. J. T.

SOURCE: A review of *The Rabbits' Wedding,* in *The Christian Science Monitor,* May 8, 1958, p. 15.

A misty, dreamy brush has painted the two little rabbits,

one black and one white, with all the soft, defenseless charm of babyhood. The brief text, kept simple and happy, tells how they met, "were wed and lived together happily in the big forest; eating dandelions, playing Jump the Daisies, Run Through the Clover and Find the Acorn all day long." The heart-stealing water-color illustrations are spread generously over giant pages.

Jennie D. Lindquist

SOURCE: A review of *The Rabbits' Wedding,* in *The Horn Book Magazine,* Vol. XXXIV, No. 3, June, 1958, p. 192.

A lovely big picture book for the youngest children, with really furry-looking rabbits against a background of soft green and gray-blue. The story has the warmth and security small children love with a happy ending in which the little black rabbit and the little white rabbit, decked with dandelions, celebrate their wedding while their rabbit friends dance in a ring around them. "The other animals of the forest came to watch the wedding dance"—the picture Mr. Williams has made of this scene has the magic quality of something one might be allowed to see if one were very young indeed and out alone on Midsummer Eve.

Margaret Sherwood Libby

SOURCE: A review of *The Rabbits' Wedding,* in *The New York Herald Tribune Book Review,* June 8, 1958, p. 9.

In the softest of misty gray charcoal sketches, tinted in subtle creamy yellow, dull slate blue or muted yellow-green, Garth Williams's two little rabbits, one black, one white, cavort happily on the pages of a huge flat picture book. Sometimes they seem tiny against the sweep of the forest or meadow, sometimes almost as big as live bunnies. The little black one is occasionally sad until he is reassured that they can be together forever, "and so the two little rabbits were wed and lived happily together in the forest." It is all as you can get without being maudlin, a sentimental variation on the theme of *Home for a Bunny,* by Margaret Wise Brown which Mr. Williams illustrated in brilliant colors with beguiling spring flowers festooning the pages.

Inger Boye

SOURCE: A review of *The Rabbits' Wedding,* in *Library Journal,* Vol. 83, No. 12, June 15, 1958, p. 1940.

A large picture book of unusual beauty. The watercolor illustrations are lavishly spread across the big pages. A misty, diffused tone gives them a mysterious, enchanting appearance. Simple brief story tells how the little black rabbit and the little white rabbit play together in forest and meadow, among the dandelions and clover, and how the little black rabbit's wish comes true. A book which will delight the youngest ones.

The New York Times

SOURCE: "Children's Book Stirs Alabama: White Rabbit Weds Black Rabbit," in *The New York Times,* May 22, 1959, p. 29.

A children's book about a fuzzy white rabbit marrying a fuzzy black rabbit has been withdrawn from the open shelves of the state agency that serves Alabama's public libraries because of segregationist protests. The book has been placed on reserve shelves, to be taken out only by specific request.

The Harpers book, *The Rabbits' Wedding,* was published last year for children between the ages of 3 and 7 years. It has stirred racial feelings in the deep South state because it describes the two rabbits at a moonlight wedding attended by all the other animals of the forest.

The book, written and illustrated in color by Garth Williams, has been attacked by *The Montgomery Home News,* a publication of the Montgomery, Ala., chapter of the White Citizens Council on the ground that it promotes racial integration.

The weekly publication criticized the story of the wedding between a black and a white rabbit in a front-page article entitled: "What's Good Enough for Rabbits Should Do for Mere Humans."

After the article appeared, a few weeks ago, Emily Wheelock Reed, director of the Alabama Public Library Service Division, which lends books to local libraries throughout the state, issued orders to place the book on the agency's reserve shelves.

Librarians who go to Montgomery to borrow books for their local centers cannot select *The Rabbits' Wedding* at random, but are still permitted to take out copies for local circulation if they specifically request them of the state agency.

Harpers issued a statement from Mr. Williams, who is in California, emphasizing that his book had "no political significance."

"I was completely unaware that animals with white fur, such as white polar bears and white dogs and white rabbits, were considered blood relations of white human beings," he declared. "I was only aware that a white horse next to a black horse looks very picturesque—and my rabbits were inspired by early Chinese paintings of black and white horses in misty landscapes."

Mr. Williams said his story about the rabbits "was not written for adults who will not understand it, because it is only about a soft, furry love and has no hidden messages of hate."

Reached at her home in Montgomery last night, Miss Reed said that the book had not been "banned" but that the agency had had some "difficulty" about it. She said that some local libraries in the state still carried the book on their open shelves, but that because of aroused feelings it was felt best to pull the book off the state agency's open shelves.

Margo Alexandre Long

SOURCE: "The Interracial Family in Children's Literature," in *Interracial Books for Children Bulletin,* Vol. 15, No. 6, 1984, pp. 13-15.

The Rabbits' Wedding by Garth Williams was the first picture book to suggest an interracial theme in both story and illustrations. This is a charming tale of two rabbits, one white and the other black, who frolic happily together in the forest. The black rabbit often pauses during his play to wish that he and the white rabbit could be together forever. A wedding between the rabbits takes place and they live "together happily in the big forest, eating dandelions, and playing Jump the Daisies."

As might be expected, *The Rabbits' Wedding* caused much rage when it appeared in the late 1950s, especially among staunch segregationists. In Montgomery, Alabama, a weekly paper attacked the "bunny book" as integrationist propaganda, "obviously aimed at children in the formative years of three to seven." The book was quietly removed from the open shelves of Montgomery's state library to reserve shelves—out of harm's way. In Florida, a similarly vigilant editor denounced the book as brainwashing, declaring, "As soon as you pick up the book and open its pages you realize that these rabbits are integrated."

In response, author Garth Williams replied: "I am unaware that animals with white fur were considered blood relations of white beings." The debate threatened to multiply, rabbit-like, until one astute Florida politician put things in perspective. "This book will have to go," he told fellow legislators. "I won't have my daughter grow up and marry a rabbit."

My only criticism of *The Rabbits' Wedding* is that the black rabbit wanting to marry the white rabbit hints at the stereotypic notion that black men prefer white women. Still, this is a pleasant story that would certainly captivate many young readers. The delightful illustrations, alone, give an important message that black and white (albeit rabbits) can play happily with one another.

THE FAMILY UNDER THE BRIDGE (written by Natalie Savage Carlson, 1958; British edition, 1969)

Gertrude B. Herman

SOURCE: A review of *The Family under the Bridge,* in *Junior Libraries,* Vol. 5, No. 4, December, 1958, p. 34.

Old Armand, a Parisian vagrant, has managed to keep free of possessions and obligations, until a mother and her three children invade his nook under one of the Seine bridges. Armand becomes involved in spite of himself—ultimately to the point of respectability. Garth Williams's illustrations are perfect for this thoroughly delightful story of humor and sentiment which includes a Christmas Eve party given by the ladies of Notre Dame for the homeless of Paris and an inside view of a gypsy encampment.

CHESTER CRICKET'S PIGEON RIDE (written by George Selden, 1981)

Zena Sutherland

SOURCE: A review of *Chester Cricket's Pigeon Ride,* in *Bulletin of the Center for Children's Books,* Vol. 35, No. 1, September, 1981, p. 16.

Unlike the earlier books about Chester, this is in picture book format, with a continuous text. Despite the format and the brevity of the book, there is little difference in level of vocabulary difficulty and probably little difference in the age of the audience to which this will appeal. It is set in time between *The Cricket in Times Square* and *Tucker's Countryside;* the cricket is still in Manhattan and is, in fact, taken on a tour of the city by a friendly pigeon. It's a nice story, but it has a shade less spontaneity than the earlier books, and the drawings are a shade less consistently deft, although many of them have that particular combination of softness and humor that distinguishes the work of Garth Williams.

Mary M. Burns

SOURCE: A review of *Chester Cricket's Pigeon Ride,* in *The Horn Book Magazine,* Vol. LVII, No. 5, October, 1981, pp. 539-40.

An unrecorded episode in the adventures of the musical hero of *The Cricket in Times Square* is developed in picture-book format. Longing for the bucolic pleasures of his country home after two weeks in New York City, Chester ventures forth into the hurly-burly atmosphere of Times Square at night. The chance scent of sycamore on the breeze compels him to explore until he finds a small park and a curious pigeon. The two strike up an acquaintanceship, for, as Chester ruminates, "If a cat and a mouse can live in a drain pipe, maybe me and a pigeon can also be friends." Determined to share the city with her country companion, Lulu takes Chester on an aerial tour of Manhattan. The illustrations present such familiar scenes as the Statue of Liberty, the city skyline, and Fifth Avenue from a pigeon's perspective, affording young readers a kind of New-York-by-night tour with a talkative guide. References to Chester's earlier arrival in Times Square are integrated into the text in the first few pages; there are also tantalizing glimpses of Tucker Mouse and Harry Cat. The pen-and-ink illustrations, perhaps because of the larger size, are more robust and less delicate than those for the earlier stories; but the added dimension is necessary for the realization of the panoramic cityscapes. Like Robert Lawson, the artist is at his best depicting animals; the human figures have less personality and appeal, or—as in the case of the rushing Times Square pedestrian—are exaggerated to the point of grotesqueness. A fine introduction to the previous works about Chester and friends.

CHESTER CRICKET'S NEW HOME (written by George Selden, 1983)

E. Colwell

SOURCE: A review of *Chester Cricket's New Home,* in *The Junior Bookshelf,* Vol. 48, No. 1, February, 1984, p. 29.

A fifth saga about the people of Tucker's Countryside. Chester-Cricket, at one time of New York, is now living contentedly in the country. Unfortunately his home in an old tree stump is *sat* upon by two portly ladies and disintegrates. Chester's friends offer him shelter, but after spending a night with each, he returns to Simon Turtle in despair, for their ways are not his. Eventually he finds not only a home but a friend, the zany, irrepressible but compassionate Walt Snake.

By means of gentle satire the author laughs at the foibles, mannerisms and weaknesses of human beings, disguised here as animals and birds. The unlucky hero, insect though he may be, has, like most human beings, a longing for affection and the comfort and security of a home of his own. The story is a shrewd appraisal of human conduct and is very funny at times. The author's habit of giving incongruous names to the animals and birds—Dorothy Robin, Lady Beatrice Pheasant, Henry and Emily Chipmunk—will irritate some readers.

Garth Williams's illustrations are as delightful as always. Look at the nestful of birds who attend Chester's 'House-warming'. They are obviously exchanging gossip, birds as they are, while the owner of the house sits unnoticed in a corner! The artist's sensitive feeling for the text extends what the author has to say—as illustrations should.

Margery Fisher

SOURCE: A review of *Chester Cricket's New Home,* in *Growing Point,* Vol. 22, No. 6, March, 1984, p. 4213.

George Selden's buoyant humour carries him through the difficulties which are bound to occur when the home life of a cricket, water-snake, chipmunk and pheasant are represented in part natural and part human terms and when these animals are shown in closer relations than they would naturally enjoy in a real American land-scape. This new look at lively Chester lacks the firm structure of that inimitable first tale *The Cricket in Times Square,* but there is much to enjoy in the account of how Chester's friends, when his log home is wrecked (by two stout ladies landing on it to rest their feet), set to work to find him another. No doubt Simon Turtle could have gnawed out a suitable hole in a log, with the help of Walter Water-snake: we believe in the enterprise because of the engaging chat of these improbable allies. Meanwhile Chester tries to accommodate to several unsuitable temporary homes—tossed by wind on the dragonfly's perch, uneasy in the grass clumps offered by the snobbish pheasants and miserable in the home of the obsessively tidy chipmunks. In each case the comparison with human types is as neat as it is entertaining. Part of the attraction of the book, as well as its inner logic, must be attributed to Garth Williams's superb drawings, in which natural animal shapes are modified by a subtle exaggeration of posture or of facial features. Though we may regret the absence of Harry Cat and Tucker Mouse, we must allow that Chester plays admirably in this new frolic.

RIDE A PURPLE PELICAN (written by Jack Prelutsky, 1986)

Publishers Weekly

SOURCE: A review of *Ride a Purple Pelican,* in *Publishers Weekly,* Vol. 230, No. 4, July 25, 1986, p. 183.

A rollicking, rambunctious collection of rhymes by the author of the popular and acclaimed *The New Kid on the Block.* Prelutsky's nonsense verse is simple and tongue-twisting by turns as he carries his readers along on fantastic flights of fancy "from Seattle/ to the city of New York." Kids will enjoy the stops along the way to visit "Timble Tamble Turkey," "Jilliky, Jolliky, Jelliky, Jee" and "Hannah Banana," or pronounce such locales as Saskatoon, Albuquerque or Cincinnati. The verse is made all the more engaging by the flowing full-color pictures by Williams. The book vibrates with these paintings that can create a mood, communicate a feeling or expand on the zaniness of Prelutsky's characters and situations. This is a fine and funny introduction to poetry for the very young. Kids will want to climb on board for another trip, and soon.

Ethel L. Heins

SOURCE: A review of *Ride a Purple Pelican,* in *The Horn Book Magazine,* Vol. LXIII, No. 1, January-February, 1987, pp. 66-7.

A new collection of bouncy nonsense rhymes is aurally inviting with rhythm, onomatopoeia, and alliteration: "Jilliky Jolliky Jelliky Jee,/ three little cooks in a coconut tree,/ one cooked a peanut and one cooked a pea,/ one brewed a thimble of cinnamon tea" or "Rumpitty Tumpitty Rumpitty Tum,/ Buntington Bunny is beating the drum." Children might almost make a participatory game of the playful incorporation of North American place names. One finds lines like "Rudy rode a unicorn, / its mane was silver spun,/ and west from Nova Scotia/ they raced before the sun"—not to mention "Justin Austin/ skipped to Boston/ dressed in dusty jeans,/ he sipped a drop/ of ginger pop/ and ate a pot of beans." Since his debut as a children's book illustrator in 1948, Garth Williams has produced a distinguished body of work usually associated with subdued color and soft-edged drawing and with animals that—like those of Beatrix Potter—retain their natural appearances. Now, adapting his style to Prelutsky's racy verses, the artist has made forthright full-page pictures chiefly characterized by absurd humor and flamboyant color. Occasionally, when a rhyme assumes a lyrical tone, the illustration takes on a more poetic feeling, while a gentle, impressionistic painting is inspired by "A white cloud floated like a swan,/ high above Saskatchewan,/ the cloud turned gray at ten past noon,/ it rained all day in Saskatoon."

Donnarae MacCann and Olga Richard

SOURCE: A review of *Ride a Purple Pelican,* in *Wilson Library Bulletin,* Vol. 61, Vol. 9, May, 1987, p. 48

Ride a Purple Pelican is almost like a Garth Williams retrospective. He uses some bold, unusual concepts to produce a range of styles, while always responding intuitively to the poems (that is, "Minnie and Moe" really do spin and blow in their visual interpretation, and "Cincinnati Patty" is regal and snobbish on her mouse-horse). Williams's most familiar style is the use of traditional line with color added, but he extends his approach with a painterly, visionary style on some pages, a dramatic bird's-eye perspective for another scene, a rhythmic, off-center arrangement for "Bullfrogs, bullfrogs on parade," and some multiple style combination on other pages. He reserves an innocent, childlike facial expression for the animal figures and makes his child characters somewhat calculating and adultlike—a treatment that corresponds with [Jack] Prelutsky's wily sense of humor.

📖 *HARRY KITTEN AND TUCKER MOUSE* (written by George Selden, 1986)

Publishers Weekly

SOURCE: A review of *Harry Kitten and Tucker Mouse,* in *Publishers Weekly,* Vol. 230, No. 26, December 26, 1986, p. 56.

Everyone should enjoy this charming prequel to the duo's beloved *The Cricket in Times Square.* From the wryly humorous opening, in which the infant Tucker Mouse—already so definitely Tucker Mouse—chooses his name, to the satisfying warmth of Tucker and Harry's defense of their drainpipe home in Times Square, the characters of these quintessential New Yorkers are as vibrant and joyful as they ever were. Added to Tucker and Harry's comic escapades, as they search for a home, are Williams's wonderfully expressive black-and-white illustrations.

Betsy Hearne

SOURCE: A review of *Harry Kitten and Tucker Mouse,* in *Bulletin of the Center for Children's Books,* Vol. 40, No. 6, February, 1987, p. 119.

A warm but meandering story spiced with occasionally sentimental aphorisms ("And friendship, like a frail tree, grew between them") recounts the meeting of young mouse Tucker and kittenish Harry, close companions in *The Cricket in Times Square.* Here, Tucker chooses a name for himself, inspired by a bakery sign, and stumbles into Harry, who, much to Tucker's surprise, offers him something to eat instead of offering to eat him. The two then explore the basement of the Empire State Building and spend a miserable night on a decaying pier before finding the shelter of a subway hole in Times Square. Even this, they must protect from invading rats before establishing it as their permanent home. Although the story itself lacks the cohesive momentum of Selden's other work, there's humor in the characters and flavor in the New York setting. Fans will be glad to catch up on the backgrounds of these two fabled friends. Garth Williams's pen-and-ink drawings have the dual appeals of familiar style and vigorous line work.

Carolyn Phelan

SOURCE: A review of *Harry Kitten and Tucker Mouse,* in *Booklist,* Vol. 83, No. 12, February 15, 1987, p. 905.

In a brief, oversize prequel to *The Cricket in Times Square,* Selden tells how Harry Kitten and Tucker Mouse met. Together the two ramble through New York City from the bowels of the Empire State Building to the decrepit abandoned docks and genteel Gramercy Park, finally setting up housekeeping in the Times Square subway station where they learn to defend their turf from a gang of invading rats. Williams's large line drawings on every double-page spread bring situations and characters to life, but the fight scenes might better have been avoided. After watching Tucker sink his teeth into a rat's tail in two successive illustrations, it is hard to keep your sympathies entirely on our hero's side, where the author obviously feels they belong. Actually the verbal depiction of the villains is overdrawn too, ultimately weakening the story. A reader who starts the series chronologically with this volume may never progress to Selden's best work. However, given the strong following for *A Cricket in Times Square,* there will certainly be an audience for Selden's latest creation.

J. B.'S HARMONICA (written by John Sebastian, 1993)

Linda Wicher

SOURCE: A review of *J. B.'s Harmonica,* in *School Library Journal,* Vol. 39, No. 4, April, 1993, p. 102.

A bit of understated bibliotherapy couched in an appealing story about a family of talented bears. J. B. likes to play the harmonica, but he feels insecure about being compared to his famous harmonica-playing father, who has appeared in Bearnegie Hall. Faced with this first identity crisis, he stops playing for a while until he's coaxed out of his silence by his mother. The story bogs down during page-long heart-to-heart talks with his parents about being himself. The resolution, in which J. B. accepts his father's words, "All of us have our very own song inside," waivers somewhere between the heartfelt and the saccharine. However, the sincere and loving looks on these furry musicians make the ending work. Williams's charcoal drawings enhance the story's warmth and quiet humor; the most effective are those in which backgrounds are almost eliminated so that attention is focused on the round bodies and expressive faces of animals, silhouetted against a white background. A book best for one-to-one sharing or for a primary-grade story session in which discussion is encouraged.

Additional coverage of Williams's life and career is contained in the following sources published by The Gale Group: *Contemporary Authors*, Vol. 134; *Dictionary of Literary Biography*, Vol. 22; *Major Authors and Illustrators for Children and Young Adults; Something about the Author*, Vols. 18, 66; *and Something about the Author Autobiography Series*, Vol. 7.

CUMULATIVE INDEXES

How to Use This Index

The main reference

> Baum, L(yman) Frank 1856–
> 1919 .... **15**

list all author entries in this and previous volumes of *Children's Literature Review:*

The cross-references

> See also CA 103; 108; DLB 22; JRDA
> MAICYA; MTCW; SATA 18; TCLC 7

list all author entries in the following Gale biographical and literary sources:

AAYA = *Authors & Artists for Young Adults*
AITN = *Authors in the News*
BLC = *Black Literature Criticism*
BLCS = *Black Literature Criticism Supplement*
BW = *Black Writers*
CA = *Contemporary Authors*
CAAS = *Contemporary Authors Autobiography Series*
CABS = *Contemporary Authors Bibliographical Series*
CANR = *Contemporary Authors New Revision Series*
CAP = *Contemporary Authors Permanent Series*
CDALB = *Concise Dictionary of American Literary Biography*
CDBLB = *Concise Dictionary of British Literary Biography*
CLC = *Contemporary Literary Criticism*
CMLC = *Classical and Medieval Literature Criticism*
DAB = *DISCovering Authors: British*
DAC = *DISCovering Authors: Canadian*
DAM = *DISCovering Authors: Modules*
    DRAM: Dramatists Module; *MST: Most-Studied Authors Module;*
    MULT: Multicultural Authors Module; *NOV: Novelists Module;*
    POET: Poets Module; *POP: Popular Fiction and Genre Authors Module*
DC = *Drama Criticism*
DLB = *Dictionary of Literary Biography*
DLBD = *Dictionary of Literary Biography Documentary Series*
DLBY = *Dictionary of Literary Biography Yearbook*
HLC = *Hispanic Literature Criticism*
HW = *Hispanic Writers*
JRDA = *Junior DISCovering Authors*
LC = *Literature Criticism from 1400 to 1800*
MAICYA = *Major Authors and Illustrators for Children and Young Adults*
MTCW = *Major 20th-Century Writers*
NCLC = *Nineteenth-Century Literature Criticism*
NNAL = *Native North American Literature*
PC = *Poetry Criticism*
SAAS = *Something about the Author Autobiography Series*
SATA = *Something about the Author*
SSC = *Short Story Criticism*
TCLC = *Twentieth-Century Literary Criticism*
WLC = *World Literature Criticism, 1500 to the Present*
WLCS = *World Literature Criticism Supplement*
YABC = *Yesterday's Authors of Books for Children*

CUMULATIVE INDEX TO AUTHORS

Author Index

Author Index

Author Index

Author Index

CUMULATIVE INDEX TO NATIONALITIES

Sachs, Marilyn (Stickle) 2
Salinger, J(erome) D(avid) 18
Sanchez, Sonia 18
San Souci, Robert D. 43
Sattler, Helen Roney 24
Sawyer, Ruth 36
Say, Allen 22
Scarry, Richard (McClure) 3, 41
Schlein, Miriam 41
Schwartz, Alvin 3
Schwartz, Amy 25
Scieszka, Jon 27
Scott, Jack Denton 20
Sebestyen, Ouida 17
Selden, George 8
Selsam, Millicent Ellis 1
Sendak, Maurice (Bernard) 1, 17
Seredy, Kate 10
Shearer, John 34
Shippen, Katherine B(inney) 36
Showers, Paul C. 6
Silverstein, Alvin 25
Silverstein, Shel(by) 5
Silverstein, Virginia B(arbara Opshelor) 25
Simon, Hilda Rita 39
Simon, Seymour 9
Singer, Isaac Bashevis 1
Singer, Marilyn 48
Sleator, William (Warner III) 29
Slote, Alfred 4
Small, David 53
Smith, Lane 47
Smucker, Barbara (Claassen) 10
Sneve, Virginia Driving Hawk 2
Snyder, Zilpha Keatley 31
Sobol, Donald J. 4
Soto, Gary 38
Speare, Elizabeth George 8
Spier, Peter (Edward) 5
Spinelli, Jerry 26
Spykman, E(lizabeth) C(hoate) 35
Stanley, Diane 46
Steig, William (H.) 2, 15
Steptoe, John (Lewis) 2, 12
Sterling, Dorothy 1
Stevenson, James 17
St. George, Judith 57
Stine, R(obert) L(awrence) 37
St. John, Nicole 46
Strasser, Todd 11
Suhl, Yuri (Menachem) 2
Tarry, Ellen 26
Tate, Eleanora E(laine) 37
Taylor, Mildred D. 9
Taylor, Theodore 30
Thomas, Ianthe 8
Thomas, Joyce Carol 19
Thompson, Julian F(rancis) 24
Thompson, Kay 22
Tobias, Tobi 4
Tresselt, Alvin 30
Tudor, Tasha 13
Tunis, Edwin (Burdett) 2
Uchida, Yoshiko 6, 56
Van Allsburg, Chris 5, 13
Viorst, Judith 3
Voigt, Cynthia 13, 48
Waber, Bernard 55
Walter, Mildred Pitts 15
Watson, Clyde 3
Weiss, Harvey 4
Wells, Rosemary 16
Wersba, Barbara 3

White, E(lwyn) B(rooks) 1, 21
White, Robb 3
Wibberley, Leonard (Patrick O'Connor) 3
Wiesner, David 43
Wiggin, Kate Douglas (Smith) 52
Wiggin (Riggs), Kate Douglas (Smith) 52
Wilder, Laura (Elizabeth) Ingalls 2
Wilkinson, Brenda 20
Willard, Nancy 5
Williams, Barbara 48
Williams, Garth (Montgomery) 57
Williams, Jay 8
Williams, Vera B. 9
Williams-Garcia, Rita 36
Wisniewski, David 51
Wojciechowska, Maia (Teresa) 1
Wood, Audrey 26
Wood, Don 26
Woodson, Jacqueline 49
Worth, Valerie 21
Yarbrough, Camille 29
Yashima, Taro 4
Yep, Laurence Michael 3, 17, 54
Yolen, Jane (Hyatt) 4, 44
Yorinks, Arthur 20
Young, Ed (Tse-chun) 27
Zelinsky, Paul O. 55
Zim, Herbert S(pencer) 2
Zindel, Paul 3, 45
Zolotow, Charlotte S(hapiro) 2

AUSTRALIAN

Baillie, Allan (Stuart) 49
Baker, Jeannie 28
Base, Graeme (Rowland) 22
Brinsmead, H(esba) F(ay) 47
Chauncy, Nan(cen Beryl Masterman) 6
Clark, Mavis Thorpe 30
Crew, Gary 42
Fox, Mem 23
Graham, Bob 31
Hilton, Nette 25
Jennings, Paul 40
Kelleher, Victor (Michael Kitchener) 36
Klein, Robin 21
Lindsay, Norman Alfred William 8
Marsden, John 34
Mattingley, Christobel (Rosemary) 24
Ormerod, Jan(ette Louise) 20
Ottley, Reginald Leslie 16
Phipson, Joan 5
Rodda, Emily 32
Roughsey, Dick 41
Rubinstein, Gillian (Margaret) 35
Southall, Ivan (Francis) 2
Spence, Eleanor (Rachel) 26
Thiele, Colin (Milton) 27
Travers, P(amela) L(yndon) 2
Trezise, Percy (James) 41
Wrightson, (Alice) Patricia 4, 14

AUSTRIAN

Bemelmans, Ludwig 6
Noestlinger, Christine 12
Orgel, Doris 48
Zwerger, Lisbeth 46

BELGIAN

Herge 6
Vincent, Gabrielle (a pseudonym) 13

CANADIAN

Bedard, Michael 35

Blades, Ann (Sager) 15
Buffie, Margaret 39
Burnford, Sheila (Philip Cochrane Every) 2
Cameron, Eleanor (Frances) 1
Cleaver, Elizabeth (Mrazik) 13
Cox, Palmer 24
Doyle, Brian 22
Ellis, Sarah 42
Gay, Marie-Louise 27
Godfrey, Martyn N. 57
Grey Owl 32
Haig-Brown, Roderick (Langmere) 31
Harris, Christie (Lucy) Irwin 47
Houston, James A(rchibald) 3
Hudson, Jan 40
Hughes, Monica (Ince) 9
Johnston, Julie 41
Katz, Welwyn Wilton 45
Khalsa, Dayal Kaur 30
Korman, Gordon (Richard) 25
Kovalski, Maryann 34
Kurelek, William 2
Kushner, Donn (J.) 55
Lee, Dennis (Beynon) 3
Little, (Flora) Jean 4
Lunn, Janet (Louise Swoboda) 18
Mackay, Claire 43
Major, Kevin (Gerald) 11
Markoosie 23
Matas, Carol 52
Milne, Lorus J. 22
Montgomery, L(ucy) M(aud) 8
Mowat, Farley (McGill) 20
Munsch, Robert (Norman) 19
Oberman, Sheldon 54
Pearson, Kit 26
Poulin, Stephane 28
Richler, Mordecai 17
Roberts, Charles G(eorge) D(ouglas) 33
Smucker, Barbara (Claassen) 10
Stren, Patti 5
Wallace, Ian 37
Wynne-Jones, Tim(othy) 21
Yee, Paul (R.) 44

CHILEAN

Krahn, Fernando 3

CHINESE

Namioka, Lensey 48
Young, Ed (Tse-chun) 27

CZECH

Sasek, Miroslav 4
Sis, Peter 45

DANISH

Andersen, Hans Christian 6
Bodker, Cecil 23
Drescher, Henrik 20
Haugaard, Erik Christian 11
Minarik, Else Holmelund 33
Nielsen, Kay (Rasmus) 16

DUTCH

Biegel, Paul 27
Bruna, Dick 7
DeJong, Meindert 1
Haar, Jaap ter 15
Lionni, Leo(nard) 7
Reiss, Johanna (de Leeuw) 19
Schmidt, Annie M. G. 22
Spier, Peter (Edward) 5

Nationality Index

CUMULATIVE INDEX TO TITLES

Title Index

Title Index

Title Index

Title Index

Title Index

Title Index

Title Index

Title Index

Title Index

Title Index

Title Index

Title Index

ISBN 0-7876-3222-8